Moab in the Iron Age

ARCHAEOLOGY, CULTURE, AND SOCIETY
Ian Hodder and Robert Preucel, Series Editors

A complete list of books in the series is available from the publisher.

Moab in the Iron Age

Hegemony, Polity, Archaeology

BRUCE ROUTLEDGE

PENN

University of Pennsylvania Press

Philadelphia

10   9   8   7   6   5   4   3   2   1

Published by
University of Pennsylvania Press
Philadelphia, Pennsylvania 19104–4011

Library of Congress Cataloging-in-Publication Data

Routledge, Bruce Edward.
    Moab in the Iron Age : hegemony, polity, archaeology / Bruce Routledge.
        p.   cm.   (Archaeology, culture, and society)
    ISBN: 0-8122-3801-X (cloth : alk. paper)
    Includes bibliographical references and index.
    1. Moabites—Politics and government. 2. State, The—Origin. 3. Iron Age—
Jordan—Moab (Kingdom). 4. Excavations (Archaeology)—Jordan—Moab (Kingdom).
5. Social change—Middle East. 6. Moab (Kingdom)—Antiquities. I. Title. II. Series
DS154.9.M6 R68   2004
939'.46—dc22   2004049482

Epigraph selection from William Blake, *Jerusalem* copyright (c) 2003
the William Blake Archive. Used with permission

In Memory of Harland Routledge (1931–2001)
Primus inter pares

Contents

Figures and Tables

Figures

Tables

The Amalekite, the Canaanite, the Moabite, the Egyptian,
And all that has existed in the space of six thousand years,
Permanent & not lost, not lost nor vanish'd, & every little act,
Word, work & wish that has existed, all remaining still
In those Churches ever consuming & ever building by the Spectres
Of all the inhabitants of the Earth wailing to be Created,
Shadowy to those who dwell not in them, meer possibilities,
But to those who enter into them they seem the only substances;
For every thing exists & not one sigh nor smile nor tear,
One hair nor particle of dust, not one can pass away.

—William Blake, *Jerusalem*

Preface

In my more optimistic moments, I imagine at least two audiences for this book. One will be drawn by disciplinary compulsion to key phrases like "Moab" and "Iron Age." The other, perhaps for similar reasons, will be drawn by words like "hegemony" or "polity." One audience, I imagine, will be concerned with data, sequence, and regional synthesis, the other with theory, comparison and conceptual themes. In some circumstances, members of my two audiences will even occupy one and the same body (mumbling "Çatal Höyük, Çatal Höyük" in their Jekyl-to-Hyde transformation). Such imaginings are common in a world where most of us occupy multiple intersecting communities and hold a diverse set of intellectual allegiances. Indeed, in these days of web-based search engines and on-line booksellers, beyond even the audiences that we can imagine lies a potential reading community of the most serendipitous variety (though one defined by English language proficiency and computer access, the apparent price of admission to the global ecumene).

Typically, in archaeological publications, the strategy for addressing audience diversity is to offer one or more lengthy theoretical chapters to be read by the many, followed by a test case or two to be read (in truth) by the few. Certainly, I must admit that I have often sided with the many when reading (by way of example) books on the Maya, the British Neolithic, or the empire of Vijayanagara. The programmatic statements that constitute theory in this literature are undeniably valuable. I have often used them in my own work as bibliographic strip mines—raking them over for interesting references—or as conveniently quotable "type fossils" of particular theoretical positions. To the extent that the best of this work forms common points of reference, whether to build on or to rebut, such programmatic statements are the foundations for whatever coherence may now exist within archaeology on a global scale.

In writing the book that follows, I set out to do something within this well-established genre of archaeological writing. Truth be told, I had hoped I might appease both my empirically and my theoretically minded colleagues by making the book easy to read in a selective manner. In the end, I was only partially successful. Constantly, and despite my intent, theory and evidence refused to be separated. Not surprisingly, evidence proved itself theory laden, but it is also true that theory only become evident in relation to the particular contexts and localized questions through which my data were defined.

I did, of course, begin with a theme. In a phrase, this book is about state formation. If one turns to the first two chapters one will find developed, in a general and hence theoretical manner, an approach to the study of state formation informed in particular by the political and social theory of Antonio Gramsci. Reconsidering the state is, I think, rather timely (see Hansen and Stepputat 2001; Steinmetz 1999). Both classic and neoevolutionary approaches to the state flounder under the present paradox of a state that is simultaneously strong and weak, an author of destiny and a victim of global economic change. Whatever postprocessual archaeology is or was, it has shown a marked fear of universals and increasingly of structure in even a local sense. Hence, despite an early interest in power, hegemony, and ideology, there is no postprocessual theory of the state, nor, for that matter, even a serious deconstruction of the term. Given that the legitimacy of the state as an analytical category in "premodern" contexts is an open question, this is a notable absence. A wise and ambitious person might conclude that a manifesto was in order, one that would pave the way to a renewed critical engagement by archaeologists with this most influential and troublesome construct. Unfortunately, wisdom and ambition have never been my forte.

My generalized account of the state, or, better, of state formation, is in the end entirely dependent on the particular case of Iron Age Moab, and indeed I argue that it must be so. While I do believe that it is both possible and useful to discuss general processes and structural conditions under the rubric of state formation, all such schemata are necessarily incomplete. States are neither singular "social facts" nor virtual structures recursively produced by agents as the ends and means of action. They consist, rather importantly, of people objectifying, naming, and codifying specific structures (e.g., laws, symbols, institutions, myths), creating terrain that orders, excludes and enables action differentially by subject position and historical moment. Abstract schemata provide us with hints as to where we should look for such state-forming activity, but the state itself is content and history specific.

At the same time, for my more empirically minded colleagues, it is important to stress yet again that empirical arguments are theory laden. Hence, when scholars in Biblical/Syro-Palestinian archaeology debate the historicity of Solomon's kingdom or work against the backdrop of the current Israeli-Palestinian conflict, abstract images of the state lurk everywhere unacknowledged. Because we know and say very little about these images, our work is continually marked, indeed marred, by absences. For this reason, I have not left my own abstract image of the state to be read between the lines. In short, I would ask the reader to take this book as a whole, linking theory and evidence by both pressing on and looking back.

In the end, however, I cannot tell you how to read this book, or even to read it at all—this is the beauty of the book as an object, and why the "pdf file" is a pale competitor. All I can do is entice you to go on. So, with this in mind, I give you a preview of the book that follows.

The Structure of This Book

As noted, Chapters 1 and 2 each review different aspects of state theory, taking off from the critique of neoevolutionism of the past twenty years. Here I bring forward the deep paradox of the state, namely, its existence as an agency that literally does not exist. This implies the necessity of a theory of the state but requires this theory to begin, not from the state as a thing in itself (taxonomy), but from the processes that create this "thingness" as a historical effect. In Chapter 2 I argue that these processes are effectively understood with reference to Gramsci's concept of hegemony and its subsequent development in so-called neo-Gramscian political theory.

The remainder of the book does the truly important work of showing how Chapters 1 and 2 illuminate the specific process of state formation in Moab—an Iron Age (1200–525 B.C.E.) polity that occupied the south central portion of what is now the Hashemite Kingdom of Jordan. Chapter 3 shows the problem of fixing Moab in time and space, considering its highly interested incorporation into the Tanak ("Old Testament") and its ambiguous and contested physical boundaries.

Chapters 4 and 5 analyze survey and excavation data from the Late Bronze Age through to the emergence of a bounded polity named Moab in the ninth century B.C.E. Here, fragmentation, mobility, and house-centered dwelling are emphasized as a prelude to analyzing the state form in which Moab was constituted.

Chapter 6 considers "local" models of state formation that have been devised to account for the decidedly nonclassic patterns that characterize Iron Age states like Moab. In particular, these are (1) theories of "tribal states" that emphasize flexible genealogical reckoning as an adaptation to Jordan's agricultural marginality and (2) Weberian theories of "patrimonial states" that take the household as a cognitive model for all social relations. While recognizing the advancement such local models represent over the universal models of neoevolutionist thought, I show in detail how their underlying essentialism fails to account for the local contexts they were designed to explain. In turn, I suggest how the particular cultural practices central to these local models (genealogy, segmentation, and domestic autonomy) might be effectively articulated in a historically contingent manner through the concept of hegemony.

Chapter 7 examines the syntactical and semantic structure of the Mesha Inscription, a mid-ninth-century Moabite royal inscription discovered at Dhiban, Jordan, in 1868. Drawing on my discussion of hegemony, I show how the Mesha Inscription uses the cultural resources of local segmentary identities to constitute a newly incorporative Moabite state identity.

Chapter 8 extends the insights of Chapters 6 and 7 by looking at the segmentary use of material culture in the Iron Age Levant as a language of replicative kingship. Repetition, contrast, and comparison are brought out as features of "memorial" inscriptions, royal statuary, royal architecture, administrative structures, and luxury items across the Levant. I argue that kingship in the Iron Age Levant is formed by this outward-looking gaze of competitive contrast. Included in this chapter is largely unpublished Iron Age material from William Morton's excavations (1955, 1956, and 1965) of what he labeled "Mesha's palace" at the site of Dhiban.

Chapter 9 turns from these local concerns to the "global" context of the Neo-Assyrian Empire. Here I examine the dynamics of Neo-Assyrian patron-client relations, which seem to have played a significant role in solidifying the centralization of administrative authority throughout the southern Levant. Ironically, the result was the subsumption of local segmentary identities into a "national" polity constituted in part from these same local cultural resources. Here I point to dramatic changes in settlement patterns and to an increase in the administrative use of writing (e.g., lists, tax records, and official titles) as possible evidence for the emergence of new subject positions in the form of state-dependent elites. I then link these newly emergent identities with the end of Moab as a state identity and the widespread reorganization of ethnic, political and religious identities that comes with the end of the Iron Age.

In my concluding chapter I reflect back on the theoretical concerns of Chapters 1 and 2 with the benefit of the intervening substantive analysis. Here an effort is made to speak directly to the tragedies and possibilities of human communities that live locally and globally as both the means and the ends of collective violence.

Readers will well note that, for all my concern with "evidence," certain obvious avenues of research are at best poorly represented in the pages that follow. Most particularly, although I say a good deal about the construction and form of Moab's hegemonic projects, I say very little of substance about how these projects were received, resisted, incorporated, or subverted in the daily lives of those who were denied authorship on the macro scale. Similarly, although I speak frequently of the articulation of state hegemony and prevailing systems of production, I provide little or no analysis of actual circuits of production, distribution, and consumption. Such criticisms are wholly justified, but they stand as critiques of the current state of Iron Age archaeology in Jordan, where such studies, indeed even the excavations necessary to support them, have yet to be done. This book, therefore, is from one perspective premature. Yet, presumptive moves are not always such a bad thing. Above all else, in painting a big picture, I hope that others, whether from admiration or from dissatisfaction, will be inspired to succeed where they see this study fail.

Chapter 1

The "Thingness" of the State

Truth is the Unity of the universal and subjective Will; and the Universal is to be found in the State, in its laws, its universal and rational arrangements. The State is the divine Idea as it exists on earth.

—*Georg Hegel,* The Philosophy of History

[T]he state lies in all tongues of good and evil; and whatever it says it lies; and whatever it has it has stolen.

—*Friedrich Nietzsche,* Thus Spoke Zarathustra

The state is a problem that subtly persists at the interstices of the words and concepts we use to invoke it. It is at once a collective fiction that acts as an agency in the world and a universal claim realized only in historically specific social formations. Despite persistent predictions that it is "withering away," the state remains modernity's central solution to collective existence. Indeed, even the ostensibly postmodern phenomena of transnationalism and "global flows" occur across the (policed) borders of thoroughly modern states. Certainly, the state is not the whole story, nor even most of the story. However, with apologies to Hegel and Nietzsche, it remains the site of many of the most important truths and lies that inform our lives, at times with our consent and in spite of it at others.

For archaeologists, the problem of the state is particularly acute. Embedded in particular modern states, looking back to past polities arguably to be named to the same category, our position is rather precarious. We forever risk the danger of which Pierre Bourdieu (1999: 53) warns when he writes:

To endeavor to think the state is to take the risk of taking over (or being taken over by) a thought of the state, that is, of applying to the state categories of thought produced and guaranteed by the state and hence to misrecognize its most profound truth.

For the most part, archaeologists have engaged the problem of the state only partially and in a rather constrained manner. There is a large and well-developed body of archaeological literature that continues the neoevolutionary concerns of mid-twentieth-century anthropology, viewing the state as a meaningful category within an evolutionary sequence of increasingly differentiated and centralized forms of political organization. There is an equally well-developed body of literature that challenges the coherence, explanatory value, and universality of such neoevolutionary sequences and categories. Yet in struggling for and against the formalism of "what" and "why" while diligently pursuing cultural historical questions of "when," archaeologists have seldom asked the question of "how." That is to say, we have seldom inquired as to the practices, institutions, and discourses that give agency to a name with no body.

The question of how the state exists is fundamental, indeed unavoidable, due to the historical position of archaeology as a practice of modernity. The state is a historically specific concept that may, or may not, name a universal phenomenon, but which has most certainly played an important role in the historical formation that constitutes the modern world. Hence, the very act of studying the state, of naming and defining it, forms a metalanguage of structure and abstraction that is part of the modern state system's own existence and reproduction (see Asad 1992; Bourdieu 1999; Meyer 1999). Work on the state, be it oriented to the past or present, is always implicated in this ongoing process of state formation. In particular, this involves the great magic trick of the state, namely the concretization of itself as a "thing" with agency; a veritable rabbit drawn from an invisible hat. An earlier political philosophy, coming as it did at an important transition point from divine right to secularized rule, was much more acutely aware of this illusion than most of us are today. Hence social contracts, juristic individuals, and universal wills emerged between the seventeenth and early nineteenth centuries as rational explanations for the apparent "thingness" of the state. While these paradoxes remain clear to those of us living under the curse of "interesting times" (Afghanistan, Somalia, Palestine, Iraq, the Congo, etc.), many of the rest of us (myself included) must struggle simply to remember that the state is really a rather odd "thing."

To recognize that the state is a problematic category is not to embrace a debilitating double bind or to jettison the state for a common-sense version of methodological individualism (*pace* Radcliffe-Brown 1940: xxiii). States do act as an agency in the world, and named collectives in the past seem to have been linked to similar effects. Hence, questions of how the state exists that critically engage the role that the category of the state plays in that existence, promise general theoretical insights by bringing together past and present. Indeed, I will argue that while the state in one sense is not a universal category, it does address a general, perhaps even universal, problem relating to political domination in human collectives. Critical state-theory, although focused primarily on the modern era, highlights this problem in many helpful ways. At the same time, engaging the "premodern" world in these same terms not only illustrates the historically specific nature of current social formations, it also reminds us that human collective life can indeed take many alternative forms.

Historical Answers to General Questions

While the question of how the state exists is an astonishingly general one, the approach taken in this book is historically specific. That is to say, although I initially develop the central problem of how the state exists in general terms, I am primarily concerned with the specific case of Iron Age Moab. Historical specificity is fundamentally important in engaging "a state which still thinks itself through those who attempt to think it" (Bourdieu 1999: 55). Indeed, there are few other options in the case of Iron Age Moab, situated as it is, both geographically and chronologically, in the midst of the continuous flow of ancient Near Eastern history. While one might pretend to isolate holistic systems (or authentic cultural forms) and singular trajectories in "core cultures" like Egypt or Mesopotamia, Moab highlights the confusion between power and its representation that such bracketing entails. Across the ancient Near East one finds common objects, images, institutions, even specific phrases and patterns of speech, dispersed with different concentrations and temporalities but without rigid borders or vectors of dispersal. In such a context, the idea of origins and fixed forms is unworkable. Rather, there are many thousands of origins of the discordant elements being woven together at particular times and under particular conditions to constitute Moab. Less poetically, our recurrent theme is that Moab is not a thing, a unit, or an entity, yet it existed as a historical effect. Therefore, it seems reasonable to expect that something produced in and through history is best understood in those same terms. Conceptually, historical specificity makes it easier to break free of the abstract form of the state and recognize that it is open to contest, refutation, or modification. Indeed, put baldly, the argument I will develop asserts that the state can really only be said to exist in this historically specific sense.

Beyond these methodological concerns, with the hubris only a Near Eastern archaeologist can possess, I believe that Iron Age Moab provides an excellent focal point for raising questions about the meaning of the state in the premodern world. This last claim, made for a polity obscure to all but the most thoroughly Sunday or Hebrew schooled, requires some initial justification, which in turn will set the stage for the substantive arguments that constitute the remainder of this book.

What Is Moab?

Moab is a Northwest Semitic term that refers to a geographic region in the south central part of what is now the Hashemite Kingdom of Jordan (Figure 1.1).[1] It also refers to the polity and people that occupied this region during the Iron Age (ca. 1200–525 B.C.E.). In what might be termed a lull between empires, Moab emerged as one of a number of small-scale Iron Age states situated between southern Turkey and the Sinai desert (see Kuhrt 1995: 385–472 for a convenient introduction to the regional history of this period).

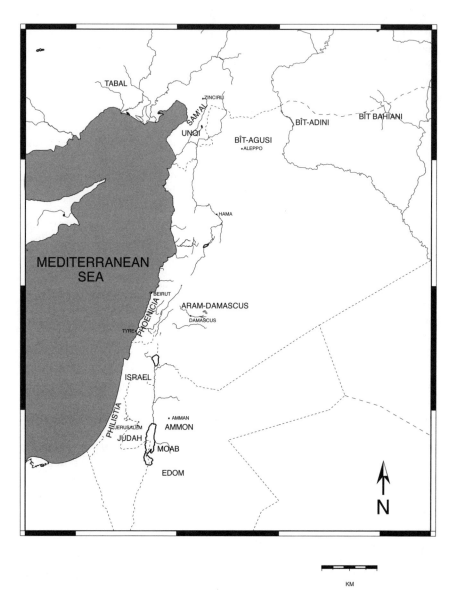

Figure 1.1. The Iron Age Levant.

During the Late Bronze Age (ca. 1540–1200 B.C.E.), the territory border-ing the eastern shores of the Mediterranean Sea (French "Levant," Arabic *Bilad ash-Sham*/"Land of Damascus") was incorporated into the empires of Hatti (the Hittites of central Anatolia) in the north and New Kingdom Egypt in the south.[2] These two empires collapsed rather dramatically circa 1200 and 1140 B.C.E. respectively, as part of the widespread disruption char-acterizing social and political life in the eastern Mediterranean Basin at the transition from the Bronze Age to the Iron Age (see Chapter 4). Begin-ning in 934 B.C.E. and reaching full fruition after the campaign of Tiglath-Pileser III in 734 B.C.E., the Neo-Assyrian Empire expanded from its core in the vicinity of the city of Aššur in what is now northern Iraq to eventually claim dominion over all of the Levant (see Kuhrt 1995: 473–546).

Between these two episodes of subjugation, specifically during the late tenth and ninth centuries B.C.E., the Levant underwent significant political and cultural transformations. While the city-states typical of the Bronze Age continued to be found, especially on the Mediterranean coast, limited territorial states like Moab emerged, invoking a variety of novel ideological formulations that involved politicized concepts of genealogy and/or land.

Culturally and linguistically the Iron Age states of the Levant were divided into Neo-Hittite (Luwian-speaking)[3] and Aramaic-speaking states in north Syria, Phoenician and Philistine city-states on the Mediterranean coast, and states speaking Hebrew and related south Canaanite dialects (Israel, Judah, Ammon, Moab, and Edom) in the south. With the exception of Luwian (an Anatolian Indo-European language), all these languages/dialects were close cognates that shared a common alphabetic writing sys-tem (with regional differences and distinct lines of development). Between the eighth and mid-sixth centuries B.C.E. the Neo-Assyrian Empire and its successor, the Neo-Babylonian Empire systematically decimated all these states. Quite a few were violently disassembled by means of mass deporta-tions (Oded 1979), and few survived as independent polities under the Achaemenid Persian Empire (539–333 B.C.E.). Hence, Iron Age Moab emerged in a mosaic of small-scale polities whose political boundaries were drawn across similar histories and fluid cultural and linguistic borders.

In comparative terms, all of these Iron Age states are quite distant from anything a neoevolutionist might term pristine. Complex polities with apparent class divisions and distinct temple and palace architecture appear in the Levant by the end of the fourth millennium B.C.E.[4] In the southern Levant the emergence of these Early Bronze Age polities is immediately preceded by direct evidence for the presence of Egyptian trade colonies connected with the founding Dynasty "0" (van den Brink and Levy 2003). Indeed, the fourth through second millennia B.C.E. in the southern Levant are best described in terms of discontinuous episodes of small-scale com-plex polity formation and fluctuating episodes of economic and/or politi-cal incorporation as a periphery of Egypt (Falconer 1994; Redford 1992).

Moab not only inherits these Bronze Age political forms, it also develops secondarily, even tertiarily, in local terms. Textual evidence suggests that Moab emerges in the context of an "uprising" against the occupying forces of the neighboring Iron Age state of Israel, which formed slightly earlier and expanded relatively rapidly (Finkelstein 1999; 2000). In turn, it is hard not to see militarization and state formation occurring across the Levant in the late tenth and ninth centuries B.C.E. as a chain reaction to the beginning of regular military expeditions into Syria by the emergent Neo-Assyrian Empire.

Clearly Moab, like virtually every state beyond the chosen few (and conveniently obscure) pristine examples, requires one to invoke the ancillary evolutionist category of the "secondary state," as well as some more global frame of reference (e.g., "world system," "interaction sphere," "core-periphery") in order to account for the exogenous forces that "move" the state from its primary to its secondary locations. The "secondary state" designation is also a convenient means of explaining the decidedly nonclassic features of Iron Age Levantine state forms and state formation. Like many of its neighbors, kingship (including palace architecture) and the core historical identity of Moab seem to emerge at least a century before the appearance of anything resembling a centralized administrative apparatus or a multitiered settlement hierarchy (see Chapters 5 to 9). Furthermore, in contrast to the venerable theoretical divide between kinship and state, many of these Iron Age states make explicit use of domestic ("House of X") or genealogical ("Sons of X") metaphors in constituting a hegemonic identity (see Chapter 6). Surviving evidence suggests that in Moab metaphors of land were employed; yet, even these were conceived in a segmentary, rather than centralized, manner (see Chapters 6–8). Labeling such polities as something other than a state (e.g., "complex chiefdom") would be pointless, as they maintain consistent historical identities and core royal institutions before and after the emergence of specialized administrative apparatuses, and both the most and the least "developed" of these states seem to interact as taxonomically equivalent entities in local historical terms.

A Critical Doubt

Already, in relaying this abbreviated historical narrative and providing some brief analytical comments, I have performed the state's great magic trick with little thought or fanfare. In the easy flow of a narrative, I have invoked Moab as an entity, providing it with solidity and unity by the simple act of naming it as a thing. In fact, it is surprisingly difficult to narrate political history in any other way, and so we regularly and "naturally" experience states as things and agencies. Yet, if we step back from this narrative and turn a radically empirical eye upon this "thing" called Moab, we can begin to see some of the problems central to the question of how states exist.

Moab is attested for the first time as a geographic designation in topographic and campaign lists of the Egyptian pharaoh Ramses II (ca. 1279–1213 B.C.E.).[5] Moab appears as a polity in the Exodus narratives of Numbers 21–24, although both the composition and the chronological placement of these biblical stories are extremely problematic (Miller 1989a; Timm 1989: 62–157; Van Seters 1972). More certainly, Moab is used as a polity designation in the Mesha Inscription (ca. 850 B.C.E.—see Chap. 7), where we find both a king of Moab (Mesha) and a national deity (Kemosh). Finally, Moab returns to being a geographic designation by the fifth century B.C.E., eventually limited to the role of geographic specifier in hyphenated place names (Rabatha-Moba; Charac-Moba) by the beginning of the common era (Weippert 1994–95).

These fragments of a semantic "life history" highlight the topography of our problem, raising questions but pointing to no direct answers. At different points in time, and under different circumstances, Moab became, and then ceased to be, a way to identify people, personify a political order, and perhaps (though much less certainly) to identify oneself. Already one can begin to see the problem, since these three referents of Moab, place, polity, and people, are not in any sense the same thing. Once we recognize the fact that the term Moab represents a familiar, but complex, elision of these three (conveniently alliterative) categories, we are faced with a problem. Can we accept this package (labeled "Moab") as a historical category and begin to fill it with various facts (sequential history, political organization, settlement patterns, religion, economy etc.) by means of which it becomes possible to classify Moab as an individual example of some more universal type such as "the state?" Should we assume that Moab is simply the superstructural projection of an underlying unity formed in the realm of production, energetic flows, or the structures of information processing? Is it in any sense possible to extract the state as an abstract structure from Moab as a historical identity?

The concept of a secondary state brings this problem sharply into focus. Secondary states are said to be distinguished by the fact that exogenous forces, generated by the territorial or economic expansion of preexistent states, push or pull societies on the periphery of such states toward statehood (Price 1978). This occurs even though conditions internal to such peripheral societies may not have initially favored such a transformation. Hence, secondary states are reorganized on the *Bauplan* of the state as an adaptive response to a competitive environment defined by the encroachment of a preexisting state.

This scenario is seemingly logical, so long as we accept the unity and coherence of both the societies and the state forms in question. If we doubt this unity, that is to say if we view neither societies nor states as things but as the emergent effects of specific human practices, then the logic of the secondary state begins to unravel. In short, we are led to ask, what is secondary about secondary state formation? If societies are not bounded wholes that can reorganize themselves into the new form of the state, then the problem of state formation is quite different from that of the prime movers and sufficient conditions so typical of the neoevolutionist literature. Instead, the problem is now one of explaining how divergent practices come to be channeled along complementary pathways so as to give the state its paradoxical existence as a named agency with no body. How is it, for example, that people come to accept, and even identify themselves, with the "thingness" of a particular historical state, when in the simplest sense no "thing" actually exists? How is it that a set of administrative practices, applications of force, public rituals, and historical narratives comes to be seen as a unified polity with a name and spatial presence? It is this concretization of practices into polity that must be at the heart of any viable theory of the state.

The concept of a secondary state takes such concretization for granted, as it treats society and state as hypostatized entities that form or transform under given conditions that are sometimes endogenously pristine and sometimes exogenously secondary. Under such an approach, theories of the state become lists of necessary and/or sufficient conditions that facilitate the emergence of a holistically defined entity. Not surprisingly, it is these two components of neoevolutionary state theory, its focus on sufficient conditions and its holistic definition of the state, that have been the focus of a large body of critical literature since the early 1980s. Hence, it is worth turning to the archaeological literature on the state to see how the critique of neoevolutionist approaches might connect with the focus on the "concretization" of a state identity that seems essential for understanding the semantic shifts associated with the term Moab.

The Archaeology and Genealogy of the State

The Vicissitudes of Neoevolution

By the beginning of the 1990s, even the most robust archaeological expressions of neoevolutionism's stepwise paradigm (e.g., Flannery 1972) had been subjected to withering critique on both conceptual and substantive grounds (e.g., Bawden 1989; Dunnell 1980; Gailey and Patterson 1987; Gledhill 1989; Kohl 1984; McGuire 1992: 150–57; Paynter 1989; Shanks and Tilley 1988; Yoffee 1979,1993). To some extent, these critiques reflected a general rejection of social evolutionism in the human sciences (e.g., Giddens 1984: 227–80; Mann 1986: 34–72; Thomas 1989), as well as the growing awareness of the role of colonialism in forming "the primitive Other" as the subject of anthropology (e.g., Diamond 1974; Fabian 1983; Kuper 1988; Wolf 1982). However, the critiques of the 1980s also addressed themselves directly both to logical inconsistencies and to explanatory and empirical inadequacies found in dominant archaeological formulations of neoevolutionism.

The main foci of the critiques of neoevolutionism remain important touchstones in a diverse range of current research programs (e.g., Diehl 2000; Pauketat 2001; Stein 1998). This is especially true with regard to so-called complex societies, hence it is worth reflecting on the substance and effect of these critiques in framing our consideration of the state. The most important criticisms of neoevolutionism addressed its teleological sub-sumption of historical change to universal processes and its holistic view of society. This holistic view promoted a model of homogeneous, or homeo-statically integrated, bounded units of individuals whose agency was sub-sumed in the structural properties of a social system. These structural properties, in turn, were said to evolve as qualitative changes of state along the band-tribe-chiefdom-state continuum characterized by increasingly differentiated and hierarchically centralized forms of political organiza-tion (Flannery's "promotion" and "linearization"). Such changes were ex-plained principally as a means of solving problems generated by a limited set of objective conditions ontologically external to the system itself (e.g., population growth, environmental change, resource competition, etc.).[6] In short, the critique of neoevolutionism moved historical contingency, diver-sity, conflict/contradiction, context, agency, and structuration to center stage in archaeological research.

In many ways, the use of the state and its fellow stages in neoevolutionist literature perfectly embodied all of these shortcomings. Its status as a cate-gory implied the bounded existence (the "thingness") of that which it classified (human societies). Its definition by trait correlation suggested universal (hence transhistorical) relationships between sets of political/institutional attributes. Its embeddedness in a single set of hierarchically related categories (band-tribe-chiefdom-state) implied a teleology of uni-versal directionality that haunted all claims for multilinear, or specific evo-lution. Finally, with no viable theory of transmission/inheritance between historically disconnected social formations labeled as states, the very status of the state as a taxonomic category inevitably resolved itself in a meta-physic of necessity in social change.

For these reasons, several critics of neoevolutionism suggested dissolving the category of the state altogether (Bawden 1989; Kohl 1987; cf. McGuire 1992: 161–67), recommending in its place the study of general processes of change in specific cultural and historical contexts, unfettered by universal typologies. Such concerns have been most notably carried through in cri-tiques of the residual holistic assumption that tight and unitary correla-tions exist between hierarchy, centralization, and complexity (Crumley 1987; Ehrenreich, Crumley, and Levy 1995; McIntosh 1999). More com-monly, scholars have continued to employ the state (and chiefdom) as an analytical category but have shifted their research focus from definitions and general explanatory models of origins to documenting the diversity, internal workings, and historical trajectories of specific polities so labeled (see Stein 1998).

Neoevolutionist scholars have explicitly addressed these criticisms in only a partial manner. Primarily, this response has focused on demonstrating the ability of their research program to incorporate issues of historical contingency and human agency (e.g., Flannery 1999; Marcus and Flannery 1996; Spencer 1990, 1993, 1997). Some scholars continue to work within the stepwise paradigm, arguing for its heuristic value for cross-cultural comparison (Flannery 2002) and seeking further identifying correlations between material traits and specific evolutionary stages (e.g., Earle 2000; Flannery 1998). Furthermore, one finds a continued appeal to biological metaphors to justify the theoretical unity of these stages, particularly the idea of evolutionary stages as so-called *Baupläne*, apparently reoccurring due to their adaptive fitness (Spencer 1997: 235–37; Flannery 1998).

Without problematizing the holistic model of society (Mann 1986: 1–2; Laclau and Mouffe 2001) and without a theory of transmission/inheritance that links category members, these new analogies constitute little more than a cosmetic makeover. Yet, taken broadly, neoevolutionist scholars have made some rather significant changes in reaction to their critics. Accompanying the newfound focus on historical contingency and agency, many scholars have diversified, or largely abandoned, holistic typologies to attempt generalized accounts of specific factors and processes of social evolution, such as hierarchy, leadership, and scale (Blanton et al. 1996; Blanton 1998; Drennan 1996, 2000; Feinman 1998, 2000). A distinct, but similarly "unfettered," concern with technological evolution in complex societies has also emerged (Adams 2001; Trigger 1998: 186–263). On the whole, the state as a category seems rather unloved even among those for whom it was once indispensably important. This act of disownment is close to explicit in several recent publications (Flannery 1998: 15–16; Stanish 2001: 44), where one reads the interestingly odd assertion that the task of the archaeologist is not to define the state (a job for social anthropology and political science) but simply to find examples of it in the archaeological record.

Agents, Structures, and Panaceas?

In contrast to the somewhat tattered remains of neoevolutionism's stepwise paradigm, Timothy Pauketat has suggested that a new paradigm may be emerging to unify archaeology under the banner of practice theory and history. Pauketat (2001: 75–78) notes striking convergences between seemingly disparate neo-Darwinian, cognitive-processual, and agency theory archaeological approaches in the privileging of structured human action realized contingently in and through real historical sequences. It is certainly true that almost everyone writing archaeological theory these days cites Giddens (1979, 1984) and Bourdieu (1977), uses the word "agency" and quotes Marx's famous line from the *Eighteenth Brumaire* ("Men make their own history, but they do not make it just as they please"). Yet these commonalties mask deep and abiding differences (many of which Pauketat notes) that divide current scholarly positions, as well as conceptual problems that seem to be looming, if not fully articulated, within the current "agent-o-rama" world of archaeological theory.

The major differences are familiar ones, namely between those seeking cross-cultural regularities within practices, decision making, and historical sequences; and those for whom practice and history by definition imply local, nontotalizing approaches. Similarly, the meaning of agent varies widely (Dobres and Robb 2000: 8–9), from a universal atomized subject (hence definable in terms of operational conditions) to a Foucauldian subject position, constituted discursively in and through specific "technologies of the self" (Foucault 1988). Less clearly articulated—and more interesting, as it may well divide so-called postprocessual approaches—is the question of what it means to transcend the opposition between structure and agency.

The adoption of a relatively uniform language of agency and structuration (Giddens 1979, 1984) has until recently disguised the inadequacy of this language for conceptualizing the issues at hand. For example, does transcending structure-agency dualism mean abandoning all structural determination, even structuration itself? Few archaeologists would answer "yes" when the question is posed in this manner. However, the current focus on self-fashioning, and the fluidity of being as a reaction to the fixity of identity categories used in past research (e.g., Hodder 2000; Meskell 1999, 2001), seems deeply suspicious of structure, even as a specific historical experience. Yet, rather than basking in the light of post-Cartesian thought, perhaps we should interrogate our newfound emancipation from structure and ask what historical conditions (i.e., structures) make this revelation possible. Michael Hardt, for example, has argued that the final subsumption of labor to the process of capitalist production has resulted in dramatic changes in the structure and meaning of power, rendering Foucault's emphasis on discipline and the fixing of identities insufficient for understanding the present.[7] Instead, Hardt (1995: 36–37) suggests that now:

The diagram of control . . . is not oriented toward position and identity, but rather mobility and anonymity. It functions on the basis of "the whatever," the flexible and mobile performance of contingent identities. . . . Fordist and Taylorist production schema elaborated long ago a model of interchangeability, but that interchangeability was based on common roles, fixed positions, and defined parts. The postfordist productive model of "the whatever" and contingent performativity proposes a broader mobility and flexibility that fixes no identities, giving repetition free rein. . . . Elaborate controls over information flow, extensive use of polling and monitoring techniques, and innovative social use of the media thus gain prominent positions in the exertion of power. Control functions on the plane of the simulacra of society. The anonymity and whateverness of the societies of control is precisely what gives them their smooth surfaces.

My point is that even the recognition that identity is performed and not pregiven is made from within a specific historical position, one that is structured by regimes of knowledge and material conditions that serve to limit the possible in specific contexts and in relation to specific people.

Let us, for the moment, accept a relatively orthodox version of structuration theory and recognize the recursive embedding of structure in practice by means of "virtual rules and resources" (Giddens 1984: 17–28). Can one then argue for emergent effects in cumulative practices? Is there a "big picture" that is not simply the laissez faire of so-called self-organizing systems (e.g., van der Leeuw and McGlade 1997)? The journal *Sociology*, for example, has become a focal point for debates over efforts to reinscribe both the methodological and the ontological independence of structure as a counterpoint to Giddens' theory of structuration (Archer 1996; Domingues 2000; Healy 1998; McLennan 1995; Mouzelis 1997, 2000; Perkmann 1998; Shilling 1997). This literature has returned to and reassessed David Lockwood's (1964) distinction between "social integration" (actors) and "system integration" (structural parts/positions), which had previously served as a jumping-off point for both Habermas (1987: 117) and Giddens (1984: 39 n.31). There is no united paradigm here, but one can illustrate the issues at hand with reference to the influential work of Margaret Archer. Archer (1996) argues that Giddens' focus on the co-presence of structure and agency ignores the temporality of practice that allows structures to have historically emergent properties. For Archer, this grants structures ontological independence because these emergent properties cannot be reduced to the practice of agents.

I do not find "analytical dualism" entirely satisfactory, as it tends to conflate structure and system into a totality, a single coherent level located above and before practice. This ignores what Bob Jessop (1996: 124) calls the "strategically selective" nature of structural constraints, which are always temporally, spatially, agency and strategy specific in their impact.[8] At the same time, this concerted reexamination of structure as something other than Giddens' (1979: 65–69) virtual constraints of "rules and resources," does articulate a tension that remains latent in recent archaeological theorizing. For example, Kristian Kristiansen and Michael Rowlands have wondered at the demise of structure in archaeological explanations. In particular, they ask if viewing structure simply as practice in aggregate captures the realities of practices sedimentized in history. Furthermore, they ask if institutions and structures experienced as external to agents and available as the terrain for strategic action (exploitation, resistance, revelation, change) are best analyzed simply as reifications of practice or as autonomous historical forces that result from practice (Kristiansen and Rowlands 1998: 16–24).

The problem of accounting for historically systematic qualities in given contexts without reifying totalities like society or mode of production is acute, particularly in the case of political domination in large-scale hierarchical polities. John Barrett (2001: 154–61) makes a brave attempt to tackle this problem, employing Bourdieu's concept of "fields" as domains of specific social practice (e.g., kinship, religion, food production) constituted by interrelated sites, embodied skills, and culturally transmitted information. The regular distribution of such fields in time and space is what constitutes what might be termed the "society effect," that is to say the fuzzy-edged sense of coherence that pervades most lived human contexts (see Barrett 2001: 161). At the same time, the linking of the same agents across numerous fields presents opportunities for conflicts of interest (Kristiansen and Rowlands 1998: 19), the accumulation and transfer of cultural capital (e.g., reputation, wealth, authority), the hierarchical linking of fields (e.g., religion and food production in the form of offerings or "tithes"), and the possibility of discursively objectifying the fields themselves in crafting strategies of domination (or resistance) that reshape the conditions under which other agencies can act (Barrett 2001: 161).

Unfortunately, here the language of structuration begins to fail us. As Barrett moves from individual fields as domains of social practices to ensembles of fields arrayed in a hierarchical manner, the language of practice and structuration begins to resemble that of analytical dualism. For example, Barrett (2001: 158) suggests that we must explore "fundamental issues that operated at different levels of analysis," including most importantly, in the case of hierarchical political systems, "mechanisms of systemic integration" (Barrett 2001: 161). Given his references to the work of the analytical dualist Nicos Mouzelis (1991, 1995), Barrett's use of terms drawn directly from Lockwood (1964) cannot be accidental. The thrust of this work argues that one should treat agents and structures as independent, both ontologically and methodologically. Hence, Barrett is trapped into the employment of conflicting interpretive paradigms out of his need to develop a nontrivial account of the apparent coherence of large-scale hierarchical polities in terms of Giddens' theory of structuration.[9]

The agency-structuration paradigm provides a limited array of conceptual tools by which to understand, for example, the relationship between the existence and reproduction of objectified cultural forms (texts, images, rituals, institutions, buildings, etc.), the unequal distribution of "know-how" by structural position, and the ability of some to form partial global strategies that are experienced by others as a form of agency distinct from their own (e.g., cosmological, power immanent, abstract, collective). Without developing such concepts, our attempts to discuss the macroscale of hierarchical polities (e.g., states) will veer between old and new (self-organizing) versions of systems theory, either reifying the whole on one hand or denying the differential abilities of agents to form partial global strategies on the other.

I raise these issues not as the prelude to some new formulation of social theory for archaeology. Rather, I do so out of the necessity of addressing Moab as a state. Certainly, neoevolutionism's view of the state as a holistically defined, structural *Bauplan* said to be found in the form of bounded political societies is deeply problematic. However, despite their evident nature as a discordant ensemble of discourses and sedimentized practices, historical polities do understand themselves holistically in the sense of possessing a name. That is to say, if nothing else, polities are recognizable as named entities with an overt symbolic identity that constitutes the "thing-like" existence of any particular state. Being named, they present the possibility of a narrative presence, one that is generated by and for people, but which also presents itself as external to people. It is also a presence that is transmittable through time and across space in the form, for example, of texts, symbols, and specific acts.

It would appear, therefore, that we cannot wholly dissolve the category of the state in the unfettered pursuit of specific processes or historical pathways. We need to postulate some kind of bounding effect in order to grasp the "thingness" of specific historical polities. To do this in a manner that moves us beyond stepwise typologies, we should perhaps go back before neoevolutionism and see what can be learned from a genealogy of the category of the state itself.

"Only something that has no history is definable"

Nietzsche's aphorism (Nietzsche 1969: 80) highlights a central problem in state theory, namely that the terms of reference in question are themselves historically specific, rather than universal or timeless categories. For example, neoevolutionist approaches to the state are grounded in classic concerns of political philosophy that draw a fundamental distinction between state and stateless societies. Such discourse emerged as a distinct aspect of European thought in the seventeenth century (e.g., Hobbes and Locke), seemingly in relation to the immediate experience of early colonial encounters and the not disconnected social impact of merchantile capitalism on the political consciousness of an emergent middle class (Trigger 1998: 26–41). From the beginning, this discourse included divergent perspectives on the moral status of the state as either a solution (Hobbes and Locke) or a problem (Rousseau and Marx), a division that long continued to be expressed, for example in the opposition between Elman Service (solution) and Morton Fried (problem).

Quentin Skinner has presented a thorough review of the changing semantic field of the word "state" (and its cognates) leading up to its embodiment of a "doubly impersonal character" as an entity distinct from both rulers and ruled (Skinner 1989: 112). While there are a large number of studies that cover this same terrain, Skinner's contribution is both thorough and particularly insightful on the relation between changes in semantics, concepts, and practice.

As Skinner (1989: 91–92) notes, already by the fourteenth century the Latin term *status* and its vernacular cognates were widely used in political contexts to refer to the state or standing of rulers themselves. From this usage, it was regularly transferred to the state or condition of the ruler's realm. In this same context, the state of the realm became the mirror of the ruler, with moral and ethical treaties focused on how ideal rulers should behave to best manage the state or condition of the realm (Skinner 1989: 97). Both dynastic/institutional continuity and territorial integrity become tied to the concept of the state or condition of realm and ruler, leading to an association between spatialized regimes and the term "state" (Skinner 1989: 98–102). These concepts were further developed in the writings of early modern Italian Republicanists, who regularly addressed the relationship between a citizen body and its rulers and hence provided the foundations for a state/civil society divide (Skinner 1989: 104–12).

The modern sense of the state as an abstract structure of power and governance is hinted to some extent in Machiavelli's *Il principe* (1532), where at certain times, under the term *lo stato*, he allows institutions of power to exist independent of power holders. However, the "doubly impersonal character" of the state does not emerge fully until the seventeenth century in the work of absolutists, like Thomas Hobbes and Jean Bodin. In particular, absolutists were concerned to write against the idea that the power of the sovereign is simply that invested in him or her by the community (i.e., a commonwealth) and against the idea of divine right embodied in the physical person of the ruler (Skinner 1989: 116–21). Hobbes, in particular, evokes the state in dramatically new ways as an "artificaill person," or "mortal God," as well as "Leviathan," the unfathomably powerful creature by whose example Yahweh demonstrates to Job the limits of human understanding (Job 41). Skinner (1989: 123–26) points out that the triumph in Europe of this absolutist concept of the state led to the conceptual reorganization of a wide range of other terms, including allegiance, treason, and majesty.

From this perspective it is relatively easy to see the ways in which the neoevolutionist definition of the state as a centralized and internally specialized structure of governance (Wright 1977, 1978; Spencer 1990) continued this tradition of political philosophy (see Haas 1982: 19–33). One might argue that, although interesting, this semantic genealogy is irrelevant to current usage, simply marking as it does the history of the discovery of the real world referent of the term "state." Not much is gained, for example, by arguing that matter was not constituted by subatomic particles before Gell-Mann coined the term "quarks."[10] However, these transformations in the semantic meaning of "state" are not simply a question of word use or isolated political ideas.

Governmentality

In Europe, the sixteenth through eighteenth centuries in particular saw notable changes in the theory and practices of both government and civil life. Michel Foucault (1991), for example, has noted the mania for (male) governance found in post-Machiavellian political writers. These writers explicitly move outward from the governance of the self and the household through care, discipline, and efficient organization to that of a population encompassed by a state to be cared for, disciplined, and efficiently organized as an aggregate. Importantly, according to Foucault, this new "governmentality" (*gouvern* + *mentalité*) is distinguished from the sovereignty of a ruler because it seeks not simply the obedience of laws for a common good (meaning in fact the perpetuation of sovereignty itself) but rather the planned disposition of people and things for effective results (see Scott 1998). From this arises the modern arts of government that deal with the ordering of people and things in time and space (statistical monitoring, fiscal policy, penal codes, sanitation and public health, state education, etc.). For Foucault, governmentality is an effect of discursive formations that inform the daily lives of citizens. This discourse may be densely concentrated and continually elaborated within the state apparatus, but the state is not its exclusive author. On the same historical terrain, Norbert Elias' (1978, 1982) studies of the self-disciplining role of public etiquette in the context of an emerging middle-class public culture point to the fashioning of self-governed citizens suited to a governmental state (cf. Stallybrass and White 1986: 80–124).

For Foucault it is this governmentality, rather than the newly emerged meanings of "the state," that defines modernity. In contrasting the unity and importance assigned to the state in most analyses, regardless of their goals or politics, Foucault writes:

> the state, no more probably today than at any other time in its history, does not have this unity, this individuality, this rigorous functionality, nor, to speak frankly, this importance; maybe after all the state is no more than a composite reality, a mythicized abstraction, whose importance is a lot more limited than many of us think. Maybe what is really important for our modernity—that is, for our present—is not so much the *étatisation* of society, as the "governmentalization" of the state. (Foucault 1991: 103)

Foucault's rejection of the unitary state in favor of his "composite reality, mythicized abstraction" is very much in keeping with the vision followed in this book. Yet, in disconnecting governmentality from newly emerged understandings of "the state," Foucault seems to treat the idea of the state as superstructural, that is as mere ideology. If this were the case, then governmentality would be reduced to a series of decentered material techniques. However, some of these same "arts of government" can be found in the more highly centralized, surveillance-oriented regimes of antiquity, such as the Third Dynasty of Ur or New Kingdom Egypt. Furthermore, the Confucian linking of personal morality (by social position) and a moral government order has many points in common with Foucault's image of governmentality. The differences between ancient and modern examples here seem quantitative, rather than qualitative, hence governmentality alone appears as a unique development only within the context of European history (and even this might be questioned if one introduces the case of Rome).

What is missing in Foucault's discussion of governmentality is the relationship between these arts of government and state discourse. In a widely cited article, Philip Abrams has drawn a rather sharp distinction between these two aspects of the state, which he refers to as the state system and the state idea. Unlike Foucault, Abrams is particularly concerned with the question of how the latter masks the former, such that he writes: "The state is at most a message of domination—an ideological artefact attributing unity, morality and independence to the disunited, amoral and dependent workings of the practice of government" (Abrams 1988: 82).

Abrams' account provides a significant challenge to so-called instrumental theories of the state, including the most frequently employed forms of Marxist state theory in Anglo-American archaeological literature (e.g., Gailey and Patterson 1987; Gailey 1987; for alternative Marxist approaches, see Jessop 1982, 1990: 24–47). In such approaches, the state serves as an instrument, either positively as a managerial tool for processing information or negatively as a means of securing and perpetuating dominant class positions, or of reproducing a class system in toto. Yet, as Abrams argues, the illusory nature of the state idea means that it cannot be wielded, seized or smashed as a unitary thing.

At the same time, Abrams invokes an instrumentality of his own in arguing that the state is a mask that covers the workings of power. For this reason, the minor points that Abrams makes are often more interesting than his primary argument that the state idea is a kind of false consciousness. In particular, Abrams notes that the state idea attributes unity, morality and independence to what is otherwise disunited, amoral, and dependent (i.e., socially embedded). Abrams also recognizes that the state idea arises as a "structuration within political practices" (Abrams 1988: 82), which he claims is then reified as an overt symbolic identity divorced from practice as an illusory account of that practice. Abrams' use of "structuration" here is not entirely clear, as this essay was written in 1977 and published posthumously, and hence predates the fixing of this term in academic vocabularies through the widespread impact of Anthony Giddens' work (Giddens 1979; 1984). To my reading, Abrams implies a recursive relationship between changing political practices and a changing political vocabulary that comes to include the state. Such a suggestion is very much in keeping with Skinner's etymological history of the word "state," outlined above.

Timothy Mitchell (1999: 76–77) notes that attending to the ways in which the state does not exist, as Abrams (1988: 82) would have us do, is problematic if we fully appreciate the thrust of Foucault's arguments. If the state idea provides a legitimizing autonomy, unity and coherence to a state system that is otherwise embedded in general systems of political and economic subjugation, then one cannot suppose an exterior to such a state system that would allow its definition or analysis without reference to the state idea. For Foucault, of course, power was not a thing that could be located or concentrated, it was the name for historically and culturally specific discourses of domination distributed in a capillary fashion through all human relations (Foucault 1980: 96–99). Governmentality is one such form of power, referring not merely to the arts of government as techniques of a governmental apparatus but also to the relation between those techniques and the formation of distinctly governmentalized subjects (cf. Lemke 2001). Hence, one cannot understand state power strictly in terms of the workings of a state system that is somehow definable within its social context without reference to the idea of the state as an entity. As Mitchell (1999: 77) points out, "the phenomena we name "the state" arise from the techniques that enable mundane practices to take on the appearance of an abstract, nonmaterial form." Consequently, the state is a structuration that arises in political practice, but it is not merely an illusory account of that practice. The idea of the state as a unitary, moral, and independent entity is a precondition for the strategic imaginings by which political practice is reproduced and/or channeled in particular ways. The state emerged as a name for a form of political subjugation that had already begun to exist, but in being named, it provided the terrain on which those practices of subjugation could be imagined forward toward otherwise inconceivable ends.

We might illustrate this by returning briefly to Thomas Hobbes. In a recent article, Quentin Skinner (1999) has looked closely at Hobbes's construction of the state as an "artificaill person," especially in chapter 16 of *Leviathan*, titled "Of Persons, Authors and Things Personated." For Hobbes, persons are those who can represent themselves in action (as natural persons) and possess the capacity to authorize others to represent them (as artificial persons). Hence, Hobbes argues, women, children, servants, and "Fooles and Mad-men" are generally artificial, rather than natural, persons in this sense; the first three because they are fully represented in the person of the adult male "master" of their household and the last two because they cannot take responsibility for their actions and hence represent themselves.

Hobbes notes that there also exist entities that are purely artificial, like churches, hospitals, and bridges, which are represented in the person of a rector, master, or overseer. It is in this sense that Hobbes refers to the state as an artificial person. As Hobbes develops the idea of state sovereignty in chapter 17 of *Leviathan* he argues that the state is a single artificial person formed as a unity of the community represented by its sovereign.

Importantly, the personhood of the state does not exist in the diversity of the multitude but only in the unity that is formed when it is represented singularly in the person of the sovereign. Hence, we have Hobbes's absolutist argument. Sovereigns rule as representatives of the state, not in themselves (contra divine right). However, that state is not reducible to the collective consent of the community (contra monarchomachs and social contract theorists). The state as a single artificial person exists by being represented in the sovereign, and indeed Hobbes goes so far as to argue that the very fact of the state's existence precludes the withdrawal of communal consent, which exists only in the unity of the state.

By invoking a specific concept of "persons natural and artificaill," Hobbes's theory of the state embedded itself in particular sets of gender- and class-determined social relations. One need not be particularly astute to see how such arguments naturalized his polemical defense of absolutist state power while reproducing these domestic relations through their transferal to the national stage. At the same time, the "doubly impersonal" state that emerges from Hobbes's arguments was not without implications and effects; it was in short more than a mask for the workings of power. Hobbes moved from the concrete and the personal to the abstract and the national in a manner that made it viable for others to imagine the state legitimized by the community but not reducible to the will of that community. As Andrew Vincent (1992: 51) notes regarding absolutist state theory: "It was in practice an absurdity. . . . However, it provided a lasting vocabulary for the discussion of the state." Such a vocabulary would seem to be a necessary presupposition of governmentality, where state agents engage populations rather than community members. Hence, the idea of the state as a thing (i.e., an artificial person) played (and continues to play) an essential role in the local coherence and general trajectory of what Foucault termed governmentality.

Civil Society

In the relationship between state discourse and governmentality we find that the overt, coherent, and relatively formal discourse of the state idea is complemented by the more dispersed, decentered, and inarticulate discourse of governing oneself and others as a way of life. To this pairing we must add the concept of civil society, a phrase that also comes into its own after the seventeenth century (cf. Chatterjee 1990; Gordon 1991; Taylor 1990). Civil society is commonly understood as the collective institutions (voluntary associations, religious institutions, communities, families, etc.) standing between the individual and the state. Governmentality moves across this state-civil society divide, pointing out the ways in which the private and the public domains are boundaries drawn over a continuous (though importantly not complete) ordering of everyday life (Gordon 1991).

Yet, exposing the rhetorical nature of this divide does not remove its political effects. Indeed, it was only by distinguishing between the state and civil society that the doubly impersonal character of the modern state could emerge. The modern state presents itself as a "thing" precisely because, on one hand, it confronts its citizens as a distanced abstraction (a purely artificial person) embodied in the apparatuses of government, while on the other hand, it is experienced as a force pervading daily life in the orders and arrangements of a civil society that is not itself the state. Modern state power removes itself from the reciprocal domain of sociability, but not from the oversight of that domain.

Of course, the intersection of governmentality, with state and civil-society discourse lies not in abstraction but in the formation of specific polities. Here, the form of each modern state has been shaped by specific historical and cultural content, by the polity's articulation with the global forces of capitalist production, and by variable configurations of the practices and discourses we have been discussing. This has resulted in a very wide range of state forms (e.g., Keynesian welfare state, military dictatorship, neoliberal "night watchman," postcolonial patronage state, etc.) that participate under tension in a global arena that constrains this diversity (Meyer 1999).

Premodern States?

Thus far, we have been discussing the state in a limited and historically specific sense. While much more could be said, it is sufficient for our purposes to note that the form of the modern state took shape under specific historical conditions and in relation to culturally and politically specific practices and discourses. Modern taxonomic approaches to the state are embedded in these same historically specific conditions and thereby face a fundamental problem. Put simply, we cannot offer a universal definition of the state that is not implicated in the specific history of this term and its (changing) referents since the seventeenth century. This is because, as Jessop (1990: 339–40) notes, "the concept of the state has a central role in political life itself."

All this would seem to suggest that there is little sense in treating the category of the state as anything but a modern phenomenon, a problem for analysis, rather than an analytical tool. One could argue that premodern hierarchical polities, never embedded in self-referential state discourse, should be studied in entirely different terms. The strength of this argument is implicitly recognized in the tendency for scholars to employ modifying adjectives, like "early," "inchoate" (Claessen and Skalnik 1978), "archaic" (Feinman and Marcus 1998), and "traditional" (Giddens 1985) when categorizing premodern states. Yet, to reach this "obvious" conclusion is to sell short the insights we might gain from a genealogical study of the state.

To say that the form of the modern state (including the idea of the state) is historically and culturally dependent is not to follow neo-Weberian historical sociologists (e.g., Giddens 1985; Hall 1985; Mann 1986) in claiming that it is dichotomously unique. The distinctiveness of the modern state is not one side of a binary relationship (i.e., modern : premodern). It arose, after all, through the transformation of already existing polity forms and was marked by significant continuity between individual moments of change (cf. Anderson 1974; Bourdieu 1999; Corrigan and Sayer 1985). Hence, the modern state is only one of the many forms in which large-scale hierarchical human polities have existed, or indeed could exist. To put this in perspective, we might ask what meaning a "universal" modern/traditional division would have for a Confucian scholar in Han China. The absurdity of this question lies not in its asking but in the parochial modernism it reveals.

To give a concrete example of what I mean, let us consider Mogens Herman Hansen's (1998) comparative study of the ancient Greek polis. Hansen has looked closely at the meaning and use of the term "polis" in a variety of rhetorical, judiciary, and philosophical texts from classical Athens. In comparing these directly with what we have termed modern state discourse, Hansen concludes that polis and state have intersecting, rather than identical, semantic fields. Like state, polis is used as a collective abstraction, with an apparent will and agency that can be distinguished from officeholders. However, polis is never distinguishable from the body politic (free adult male citizens) and hence is not doubly impersonal in the sense of the modern state. The case of the *polis* illustrates the point that what is not modern is not therefore of necessity the opposite of modern. We need to theorize the diversity of complex hierarchical polities, such that we can account in specific cases for both abstract and personalized representations of collectivized power.

To see how this might be done, let us return for a moment to a definition of the state still commonly found in archaeological literature. Henry Wright (1977: 383) influentially defined the state as a society with a decision-making subsystem that is both internally and externally specialized. Both managerial and conflict-based approaches have made use of this definition (Haas 1982), with scholars varying primarily in the instrumentality they ascribe to this decision-making subsystem. Built into this definition one can see quite clearly the "doubly impersonal character" of the modern state. Yet, as we have seen, this abstract form of the modern state is an effect of specific discourse about the state and the object of its governance (civil society), as well as of social practices and discourses not limited to, or strictly emanating from, the state apparatus itself (governmentality). Hence, for clarity if nothing else, it would seem that we need to unpack this definition.

Certainly, the emergence of perpetual social inequalities and of decision-making structures with the sanction of force are fundamentally important problems for investigation (e.g., Clastres 1977; Feinman and Price 1995; Gledhill 2000: 23–66; McGuire and Paynter 1991). However, we need to look at what is glossed over when we move from these phenomena to the above definition of the state. A society with an externally and internally specialized decision-making subsystem assumes several paradoxical processes that are unarticulated in the definition itself. First, it assumes a bounding effect, whereby a society is defined as the object of decision making. Second, it assumes a differentiating effect whereby a subsystem is distinguished from within that which has been bounded. Third, it presumes a further bounding effect, whereby the diverse ensemble of people/roles/ institutions that constitutes the decision-making subsystem (its internal specialization) is somehow tied together. None of these is a straightforward, natural, or obvious process. Rather, as we saw in the case of the modern state, these processes are cultural, discursive, historical, and contingent. Furthermore, because these effects are directly assumed in the definition of the state, they cannot be set aside as issues relevant only to specific instantiations of the state. To put it differently, and more precisely, by not considering bounding and differentiating effects as realized in specific instantiations of the state, the universal definition of the state is rendered trivial.

If we move from the minimal definition of the state to its ascribed instrumental function, we again see that the actual processes of state formation are assumed rather than defined. In order to manage "information flows" or to secure class interests, one first must presume bounding and differentiating effects that define those "parts" of the "whole," such as economic production, that the state apparatus is said to manage or secure. Furthermore, this definition also presumes articulating effects, whereby these various "parts" are brought into alignment such that both internal autonomy and system-wide unity are maintained.

These problems are not merely critiques of Wright's definition of the state, which in many ways remains quite useful when shorn of its systems-theory presumptions. For example, Weber (1978: 54) defines the state as a political organization whose administrative staff successfully upholds the claim to a monopoly on the legitimate use of physical force over a given territory. This definition is widely favored in political science and sociology (e.g., Geuss 2001: 14–68; Hoffman 1995: 33–61) because it distinguishes a central feature of state societies (legitimate physical force) without specifying the particular structures and forms of these monopolistic organizations. Yet, even here the definition implicitly presumes both bounding (territoriality, political organization) and differentiating (administrative staff) effects. Furthermore, Weber directly raises the vexing question of legitimacy, which remains latent in Wright's definition (i.e., his definition implies a *legitimate* decision-making subsystem). One can measure the problematic nature of this concept by the hundreds of pages Weber dedicates in *Economy and Society* to specifying and developing ideal-types of legitimacy and their political-historical implications. Interestingly, in Weber's specific discussions of traditional, charismatic and rational forms of legitimacy and their instantiation in patrimonial, hierocratic, and bureaucratic regimes, the question of a monopoly on physical force largely falls by the wayside. This is perhaps understandable in that such a monopoly implies a contradiction between the right and the need to use violence as a form of political practice (Beetham 1991; Hoffman 1995: 62–93). Every application of physical force implicitly divides the legitimacy of the state between those on the giving and receiving ends. Indeed, since the underlying threat of physical force is held to be the defining feature of the state, the state is latently illegitimate for every citizen (i.e., force could be directed against her or him). If one adds to this the fact that Weber only requires a monopoly on violence to be successfully claimed, not actually achieved, then the question of the unity, form, and discursive practices of the state becomes very complicated indeed.

Bourdieu (1999: 56) proposes transcending this problem by extending Weber's definition of the state to include the claim to a monopoly over the means of both physical and symbolic violence. By symbolic violence he seems to mean the ability to constrain people's actions by means of the embodied structures through which people orient action. According to Bourdieu,

If the state is able to exert symbolic violence, it is because it incarnates itself simultaneously in objectivity, in the form of specific organizational structures and mechanisms, and in subjectivity, in the form of mental structures and categories of perception and thought. By realizing itself in social structures and in mental structures adapted to them, the instituted institution makes us forget that it issues out of a long series of acts of *institution* (in the active sense). (1999: 56–57)

For Bourdieu, the state is able to do this (be legitimately illegitimate) by ordering the timing, spacing, and rhythm of daily life (e.g., workplace regulation, statutory holidays, family law), as well as the content and categories of public discourse (e.g., by means of standardized education). The result is a correspondence between embodied cognitive structures and objective structures, such that people forget both the role of the latter in generating the former and the historical, contingent, and contested process by which these objective structures of government took shape (Bourdieu 1999: 70–71). This "doxic submission" is what Bourdieu means when he speaks of legitimacy.[11]

In this closed relationship between objective and mental structures (embodied or otherwise), over which the state looms as a master intelligence, we see what is now a standard problem in Bourdieu's thought (see Calhoun et al. 1993). How, under this hermetic seal, does one account for radical change,[12] the diversity of state forms, or even Bourdieu's own critical analysis? As we shall see in Chapter 2, more insight can be gained from viewing the state as selective and strategic in bringing forward, coopting, or containing certain "mental structures," rather than acting as a puppet master. Moreover, such strategies are possible because they occur in the context of specific projects, executed by specific agents, carried out on the terrain of specific structural constraints (see Jessop 1990: 260–71). Hence, we need not imagine the state metaphysically as the "mind of a mindless world" (Abrams 1988: 82). For ancient states such as Moab this position is more workable than Bourdieu's, since the articulation and cooptation of largely autonomous social forces (e.g., kinship, temple ritual, patron-client relations) seem to have been more prominent than the space-time restructuring of the modern state.

Despite these criticisms, Bourdieu does introduce two very important insights. First, he characterizes the state as "the culmination of a process of concentration of different species of capital" (Bourdieu 1999: 57). By this he means the concentration of creative, or generative, power across a variety of fields described as physical force, economic, informational, symbolic and juridical capital. He illustrates this process with reference to the long development of the French state and its progressive acquisition of powers from the twelfth century on. Here Bourdieu makes his second important point, namely that this process of concentration, although carried out piecemeal and often under intense opposition in specific cases (e.g., the first imposition of federal taxation), led with each success to newly structured circumstances. These newly instituted structures, although in a sense arbitrary (other results could have obtained), are experienced subsequently as natural and hence further entrench the state. Moreover, although often beginning independent of one another, the various species of capital become coupled through this cumulative process of state formation,[13] hence leading to an interdependence from which the state derives its own unique powers to direct, disperse, and control various fields of practice, what Bourdieu (1999: 58) terms "statist capital" (*capital étatique*). This approach can be productively compared to Philip Corrigan and Derek Sayer's (1985) more detailed study of English state formation as a long-term and continuous process of cultural revolution. Here again we see a process of struggle and restructuring that continually extends the state's ability to intercede in cultural production and social reproduction.

Bourdieu's work marks an improvement over the taxonomic approaches of Wright and Weber, in that it focuses on state formation rather than on the state. Though seemingly subtle, the difference is in fact quite profound. In taxonomic approaches, state formation is a prelude to the state, a trajectory that results in a thing. Centering state formation, on the other hand, suggests a process, rather than a form. Furthermore, as Bourdieu suggests, it is a process whereby contingent events and specific struggles have restructuring implications and within which the cumulative effect of such structuring is to couple together institutions, practices, and resources in a complementary manner under a centralizing dynamic.

Toward an Outline of State Formation

We are now in a position to say something more positive about premodern states, particularly in relation to the study of Iron Age Moab. First, it seems clear that we cannot begin with the abstract form of the state as something to be identified archaeologically (e.g., Flannery 1998: 15–16; Stanish 2001: 44). As we have seen, this social form is inseparable from both a historically specific mode of political discourse (the "state idea") and a particular set of practices oriented to the ordering and monitoring of populations ("governmentality"). Furthermore, we suggested that the "thingness" of the state, its agency, unity and coherence, is an effect of these discourses and practices rather than a prior, underlying condition. Hence, one might argue that there are no states, only the process of state formation itself. Indeed, I would argue that it is precisely this realization that opens the door to the study of premodern state formation. Studying the state as a singular *Bauplan* already takes for granted both the content and the effect of the practices that concretize the state as a "thing." Yet, comparative study remains possible, indeed necessary, when we focus not on the predetermined form of the state but on the practices that give form to what is intrinsically formless.

Bourdieu provides us with a starting point in reworking Weber to focus on the process of capital accumulation without an endpoint or teleology. In other words, in certain human collectives, but importantly not in all, overarching claims to legitimate domination have been asserted that seek as their logic the status of ultimate arbiter within a given territory. As Bourdieu's image of accumulation implies, this monopolistic logic need not be fully realized but only effectively and continually asserted.

Our consideration of the modern state has already given us three specific effects by which we might identify this process of state formation, namely bounding, differentiation and articulation. Bounding and differentiation are tied up in the demarcation of the social space of the state, most practically and visibly in the assertion of an identity, a bounded territory, and an authoritative center. Hence, incorporation and internal differentiation work together in constituting the "thingness" of any particular state, making political domination possible by limiting its extent and naturalizing its hierarchical arrangements. Articulation refers to the specific configurations of power in which selected cultural resources and social forces are aligned so as to give material substance and symbolic coherence to the ideological claims of the state.

All this is potentially interesting, but it remains both abstract and imprecise. We need to develop these catchwords in two specific directions. First we need to fill out their theoretical and operational descriptions, and second we need to ground their realization thoroughly in the historically specific empirical context of Iron Age Moab. The first task will be addressed in

Chapter 2, where we will look in detail at Antonio Gramsci's distinct contribution to state theory. Here we will develop a number of Gramsci's key concepts (hegemony, historical bloc, etc.) in order to make specific and pragmatic links between the state formation process and the actual historical context of Moab. The second task will be addressed in the remainder of the book and will involve the detailed demonstration of how a neo-Gramscian approach to state formation illuminates and helps explain the specific empirical evidence currently available from Iron Age Moab.

Chapter 2
Hegemony, Polity, Identity

> *Dans dessins d'un roi, comme dans ceux des cieux*
> *De fidels sujets doivent fermer les yeux*
> *Et soumettant leur sens au pouvoir des couronnes*
> *Quelles que soient les lois, croire qu'elles sont bonnes*
>
> —*Jean de Rotrou*, Vencelas

Gramsci and the State

The abstract notion of state formation introduced in the preceding chapter remains quite distant from any specific lived reality such as Iron Age Moab. Insofar as we fail to bridge this gap by theorizing the historical specificity of Moab (or any other social formation), these abstractions remain empty exercises. The task of theorizing the historical specificity of the state was one that occupied Antonio Gramsci and to which he turned considerable attention in his writings. It is therefore not surprising that both in Gramsci's work and in the vast body of literature these writings have inspired we should find considerable help in addressing the paradoxical problem of state formation as outlined above.

Gramsci was general secretary of the Communist Party of Italy (PCd'I) at the time of his arrest in 1926 by the Fascist government of Mussolini. For most of the remaining eleven years of his life he was imprisoned, during which time he wrote some 2,848 pages of notes on a variety of topics, from the state to colloquial language to the culture of mass production. These have been published posthumously as *Quaderni del carcere* (*Prison Notebooks*) and since the 1960s, more than his preprison writings, have formed the basis for Gramsci's widespread and highly variable influence outside Italy. While the break between his prison and preprison writings is often exaggerated (Buci-Glucksmann 1980: 112–13), the ideas that interest us are developed most extensively in the prison notebooks.

Gramsci's primary objective in his prison writings was to think through the establishment of a proletarian state in Italy. In doing so, Gramsci felt it was necessary to understand the general failure of working-class revolutionary movements in the industrialized West and the general resilience of the "bourgeois" state in the face of numerous political and economic crises in the decades following World War I. This process caused him to give particular attention to the relationship between the state, culture, leadership, and power.

Gramsci's notes, it should be stated, are wideranging, incomplete, and aphoristic, lending themselves to exegesis. Hence, it is often possible to use Gramsci's writings to reach theoretical positions that diverge considerably from those of Gramsci himself (Bellamy and Schecter 1993; Kurtz 1996). Gramsci, for example, never abandoned mainstream Marxist thought and, in particular, privileged the realm of production in assuming the fundamental nature and natural unity of economic classes. Yet already in his preprison writings ("The Revolt Against *Capital*"; "Our Marx") Gramsci resisted economic determinism in favor of a historicism that made both determinate economic classes and the base/superstructure division of secondary importance to his work (even though he continued to employ these categories). In what follows, I pursue a number of Gramsci's key concepts ("the integral state," "hegemony," 'organic intellectuals," "common sense," and "historical bloc") as a means of working through the problem of defining state formation, recognizing that the conclusions reached are not necessarily continuous with those of Gramsci himself.

Gramsci's understanding of the state begins with the division between the state and civil society discussed above in Chapter 1. Gramsci maintains this as a methodological distinction but argues for a necessary unity between these two components, especially in the industrialized nations of the West. Most famously, in contrasting czarist Russia to western Europe, Gramsci states:

In the East the state was everything, civil society was primordial and gelatinous; in the West, there was a proper relationship between state and civil society, and when the state trembled a sturdy structure of civil society was at once revealed. The state was only an outer ditch, behind which stood a powerful system of fortresses and earthworks. (Gramsci 2000: 229)

While never unambiguously developed (Anderson 1976–77: 10–14), it seems that over time Gramsci expanded his concept of the state so that it referred not only to the administrative apparatus of a polity but also to a social totality that supported and reproduced that polity (Buci-Glucksman 1980; Sassoon 1980). As Gramsci writes: "state = political society + civil society, in other words hegemony protected by the armour of coercion" (2000: 235). This "integral state" encompasses civil society in the recognition that the state is culturally constituted and dependent for its reproduction on specific cultural practices, orientations, and ideologies—while at the same time making possible particular social orders and ways of life.

Force, Consent, Hegemony

Gramsci's own definition of the state builds into it another of his key concepts, namely that of hegemony.[1] Using Machiavelli's image of the Prince as a centaur mixing human reason and animal force (Fontana 1993: 140–63), Gramsci argues that state rule is based on both moral/ethical leadership (hence consent) and domination (as in Weber's definition of the state as an administered territorial monopoly on violence). Again, Gramsci fluctuates in his writings (Anderson 1976–77: 20–32), usually implying that hegemony is equivalent to consent (Femia 1981: 24–26), but at times implying that hegemony is the total effect of domination and consent operating together.

It is the former understanding of hegemony as consent that is often rejected by scholars who distance themselves from Gramsci despite working in a broadly similar mode, with common concerns and goals (e.g., Corrigan and Sayer 1985: 2). James Scott (1985, 1990), for example, has influentially argued that subordinate groups are fully aware of being dominated, fully capable of resisting in a thousand subtle foot-dragging ways, and fully engaged in imagining alternative social orders. However, Scott argues, simple inequities in access to the means of both physical violence and production require public acquiescence to dominant social orders, relegating resistance to what he terms "hidden transcripts." This latter point is echoed by Derek Sayer, who writes: "it is the exercise of power pure and simple that itself authorizes and legitimates, and it does this less by the manipulation of beliefs than by defining the boundaries of the possible" (Sayer 1994: 375).

For Sayer, accommodation to domination, rather than consent, characterizes the nature of state rule. Yet Sayer's formulation is incomplete; force cannot work alone and is bound to consent in a necessary manner. As David Kertzer notes, "these sorts of power to constrain are not simply, or even essentially, a physical power, for they presuppose a symbolic power. The power of the government to compel people to act in certain ways is based on its ability to mobilize people to do its bidding" (Kertzer 1996: 3).

Both Scott (1990: 90–107) and Sayer (1994) recognize this fact in that they do not argue that the state exists simply as a wielder of force. Scott (1990: 95) suggests that hegemonic ideologies provide political resources and frames of reference within which subordinate groups strategically, and perhaps even cynically, pursue their own interests in a limited manner. Hence, these "public transcripts" are perpetuated despite the absence of consent. However, Scott seems to presume that differences between dominant and subordinate groups are already constituted outside of these public encounters (in the realm of production?). Hence, hegemonic ideologies are portrayed as principally made by and for dominant groups, leaving only force as the guarantor of the content of public transcripts. Corrigan and

Sayer (1985: 199–200) are more subtle, suggesting that the state uses its monopoly on physical force to suppress certain forms of existence and to encourage others, regulating cultural forms and through this constituting specific kinds of subjects. As they express rather colorfully: "The ordinary procedures of the state inflate to become taken-for-granted boundaries of the possible, occupying—in the way an army does a territory—the field of social vision" (199).

This in fact is not far off Gramsci's own view in emphasizing the contradictory consciousness of the "man-in the-masses," where the verbal means available for conceiving of the world does not match ones (economically determined) practical existence (Gramsci 2000: 333). Similarly, Joseph Femia (1981: 46–48) has identified three different levels or types of consent on the part of subordinate groups in Gramsci's notes. These range from moral and intellectual unity with dominant groups ("integral hegemony") through a fragmented and fragile resignation to the system ("decadent hegemony) to a virtual exclusion facilitated by the incorporation of subordinate group leaders into the elite network ("minimal hegemony"). Hence, Gramsci's concept of hegemony cannot be reduced to a uniform false consciousness or a simple theory of a dominant ideology.

On the issue of force versus consent, a convergence between Gramsci and his sympathetic critics can perhaps be found around the image of hegemony as a frame of reference. This, indeed, is what William Roseberry argues in portraying hegemony as the process of constituting a common discursive framework between groups distributed and constituted within a "field of force" (i.e., asymmetrical relations of power). As he writes (Roseberry 1994: 361): "What hegemony constructs, then, is not a shared ideology but a common material and meaningful framework for living through, talking about, and acting upon social orders characterized by domination."

This position clearly accommodates what Scott (1990: 105) terms "critiques within hegemony," namely the critique of domination in its own terms ("the anointed king has been rejected by god(s)"; "the just judge is corrupt"; etc.). However, it also opens up a more complex and realistic view of the world. Neither dominant nor subordinate actors are presumed to be singular and unreflective in their conceptual orientation, nor wholly disingenuous in their engagement with the values and priorities of a specific state system. Rather, as a common frame of reference, undergirded by relations of force, hegemony provides shared symbols of power that can be appropriated and used to different ends (Herzfeld 1997: 25, citing Mbembe 1992: 8). It is this consent through use of a common frame of reference that is central to hegemony and allows its reproduction over time.

Hegemony, therefore, is a more powerful concept when it is seen as being constituted by both the coercive (law, discipline, punishment, and retribution backed by the use or threat of force) and the consensual (e.g., religious sanction, systems of values, emotional dispositions) elements of state power. Hegemony, however, is not the sum total of these coercive and consensual elements of state power; rather, it is a process of rule made possible by these elements. Hegemony is the moral order that allows polities such as the state to exist. This existence is an effect of repeated practices carried out by historically situated agents. Hence, it is participation (including nonresistance), rather than cognitive consent, that is most important to the reproduction of the state.

Intellectuals

Having raised the issue of hegemony, Gramsci's historicism required a specification of how such hegemonic orders were constituted. Of primary importance for Gramsci was the role of intellectuals. For Gramsci, intellectuals were not defined by the nature of their activities, so much as by their position in a system of social relations. Indeed, he states that "All men are intellectuals . . . but not all men have in society the function of intellectuals . . . Thus there are historically formed specialized categories for the exercise of the intellectual function" (Gramsci 2000: 304).

This "intellectual function" is the leading, educating, and articulating of group hegemony. In the case of the state, for example, intellectuals become all who act as functionaries in the sense of reproducing or developing the consensual and coercive elements of state hegemony (Gramsci 2000: 307). According to Gramsci, intellectuals are not simply generated by and for the state but arise organically within fundamental social groups, a phrase he seemed to use in place of class when avoiding censorship in prison. Furthermore, according to Gramsci, the intellectual function is not exercised exclusively by individuals but can be carried out collectively, as in the case of political parties (309–11). However, while Gramsci is correct to identify the existence of historically and culturally defined roles where these intellectual functions are concentrated (e.g., priest, general, scribe, scientist, politician), limiting the intellectual function to these roles misses much of the important hegemonic work done on a day-to-day basis by virtually everyone. Indeed, it seems more productive to speak of intellectual products (e.g., texts, buildings, art, material symbols, administrative systems), than of intellectuals as the locus of an "intellectual function," an approach that has the added benefit of being well suited to archaeological evidence.

Gramsci's views on how this "intellectual function" might actually operate were best expressed in his writings on "common sense," by which he means the unsystematized practical consciousness of the masses. For Gramsci, hegemonic orders could not simply be invented as a kind of facile false consciousness. As he states: "It is evident that this kind of mass construction cannot just happen 'arbitrarily,' around any ideology, simply because of the formally constructive will of a personality or a group" (2000: 341). Hegemony is realized in continuous collective action, in the ability to mobilize consistently for mass activity or passivity (i.e., nonresistance). For Gramsci, this occurs when intellectuals are able to draw out and make coherent problems and orientations of practical experiences found in an inchoate form in the realm of common sense.

Here we encounter an interesting problem in Gramsci's work. Throughout his writings one can trace an orthodox Marxist strand that begins from determinate economic classes. Hence hegemony is leadership by a class, articulated by organic (i.e., internal to the class) intellectuals and aimed at gaining or maintaining control of the state as the vehicle of class domination. Yet Gramsci's historicism, that is to say his need to document a lived reality and his resistance to determinism, causes him to vary from this orthodoxy in several interesting ways. In his writings on common sense Gramsci recognized that (1) individual conceptions of the world often are highly variable, such that without systematic criticism "one belongs simultaneously to a multiplicity of mass human groups" (2000: 325–326); (2) the "man-in-the mass" often possesses a contradictory consciousness, namely, her verbal or theoretical conception of the world does not match her (economically determined) practical existence; (3) this contradiction is not simply self-deception but rather part of a social historical order (333); (4) states do not have a "unitary, coherent and homogeneous conception" (342), and hence are not pure class vehicles. As a result, hegemony is historically contingent—it must be constituted and reproduced through intellectual mediation, rather than emerging as an inevitable by-product of economically determined classes. In Gramsci's words, "Critical understanding of self takes place therefore through a struggle of political 'hegemonies,' from opposing direction" (333).

Historical Bloc

By recognizing the constructed and contested nature of hegemony, by recognizing, in his own words ,the importance of "a cultural front as necessary alongside the merely economic and political ones," (Gramsci 2000: 194) Gramsci opened the door for a cultural theory of the state. As Laclau and Mouffe (2001) have shown, because Gramsci presumes that hegemony must be formed rather than unfolded, one can push farther to conclude that the economy itself is not an a priori, independent, domain generating group identity and consciousness. Rather, economy, politics, and culture are distinctions drawn within a single domain (cf. Mitchell 1999), one that is formed in the hegemonic process itself. While this definitely moves us away from Gramsci's own privileging of determinate classes, he still provides us with a vocabulary by which to define this unity in his conception of the "historical bloc."

For Gramsci, a historical bloc represents "the unity of the process of the real" (Sassoon 1980: 120). Here Gramsci is emphasizing the unity of structures and events as manifest in concrete historical contexts, such that their division in deterministic or dualistic terms (e.g., cause and effect, base and superstructure) misrepresents the reality of their complex unity and reciprocal interdependence. As Gramsci states:

> The analysis of these propositions tends, I think, to reinforce the conception of 'historical bloc' in which precisely material forces are the content and ideologies are the form, though this distinction between form and content has purely indicative value, since the material forces would be inconceivable historically without form and the ideologies would be individual fancies without the material forces. (Gramsci 2000: 200)

Gramsci's concept is more than just theoretical, since a historical bloc is the point in time and space where form and content are realized in practice, that is to say, where hegemony is exercised. For Gramsci this hegemony is the cement of a unified class, hence his comparison of a historical bloc to human anatomy, where surface elements such as skin and structural elements such as the skeleton are of equal importance to the living being as a whole (2000: 197). Once again, we would do well to go further than Gramsci by means of Gramsci. In particular, he writes that in a historical bloc "the complex, contradictory and discordant ensemble of the superstructures is the reflection of the ensemble of the social relations of production" (192). This image of an ensemble is more helpful than the unitary metaphor of a human body. A historical bloc is a moment in time given shape by hegemony, or competing hegemonies, but such hegemonies (e.g., state rule) are not monolithic. A historical bloc includes that which is excluded or only marginally included in any particular hegemonic formation, (e.g., slaves in classical Athens, the *'apiru* in the Late Bronze Age Levant—see Chapter 4). These subaltern elements are sites for both generalized resistance and the formation of new counterhegemonies.

System or Strategy?

By emphasizing intellectual products over intellectuals and the ensemble of social positions in a historical bloc over class unity, we move Gramsci in a particular direction and raise the specter of hegemony depersonalized as a systemic quality, rather than activated as a means of leadership. Donald Kurtz (1996) has criticized just such a trend in the application of the concept of hegemony within anthropology. As Kurtz points out, much of the anthropological application of the concept of hegemony has been filtered through Raymond Williams's (1977) characterization of hegemony as power embedded in the taken-for-granted order of tradition; that is, as an unrecognized generative force lying behind cultural practices.

Kurtz is quite correct in pointing out the misunderstanding of Gramsci present in work that portrays hegemony as essentially "below the surface" (e.g., Alonso 1994; Comaroff and Comaroff 1991: 22–32; Pauketat and Emerson 1999). More difficult are the implicit questions Kurtz (1996: 116) raises regarding the locus of hegemonic activity. To what extent is hegemony to be located in the conscious actions of political and cultural agents? In particular, imagining a world divided into manipulators and dupes (or prophets and followers) seems to dissipate hegemony's significance as a culturally constitutive force.

Here we are reminded of the problematic convergence in the writings of Bourdieu and Foucault on the issue of power and its reproduction in everyday life. Both scholars focus on the nonagentive workings of power that are reproduced by producing specific kinds of subjects. Bourdieu's position begins from his concept of a h*abitus*,[2] as a lived material context where one learns cultural dispositions necessary to get on in the world and, at the same time, reproduces and potentially changes those dispositions due to the improvised nature of living through such structures in historical time. Bourdieu argues that under normal circumstances habitus reproduces power structures subliminally by constituting them as part of the natural order of being.[3] So, for example, in his famous study of Kabyle Berber houses Bourdieu (1970) shows how associations in the spatial division of the houses inscribe gender- and age-based power relations into the embodied experience of everyday life.[4] In other words, as stated in Bourdieu's own aphorism, "what is essential *goes without saying because it comes without saying*: the tradition is silent" (Bourdieu 1977: 167; emphasis in original). Bourdieu (1977: 164–71) terms this unconscious subordination *doxa* and claims that doxic taxonomies remain unarticulated until moments of crisis which break "the immediate fit between the subjective structures and the objective structures" (168–69). Such moments result in significant cultural and historical change and are marked by the formation of a field of opinion in which previously taken-for-granted power structures are debated through what Bourdieu calls orthodox and heterodox discourse.[5]

Bourdieu's argument solves one problem in the analysis of power and political domination, namely the need to imagine duplicity and hypocrisy as paired character traits of subordinate and dominant actors respectively. However, as critics have pointed out (e.g., Smith 2001: 155–61), Bourdieu's concept of doxa alienates subjects from their actions to such a degree that motivations cease to have even contextual relevance and change is strictly limited to revolutionary moments of heroic emancipatory insight. In this light, Bourdieu's concept of doxa begins to look very much like the ideal type that it is. Indeed, if we ask when such perfect unspoken order has actually occurred, Bourdieu gives us the interestingly oblique answer "in ancient societies " (Bourdieu 1977: 164).[6] In fact, what we see in Bourdieu's own accounts of Kabyle social life is not silence but regular interventions in the form of scorn, truisms, advice and admonitions.[7] These are intellectual products aimed at influencing the behavior of others, something that is more or less necessary as the limits of doxa are realized in the resistance of some to various collective projects. Such interventions hover at the intersection of habitus and discourse, as those with authority and cultural skill are able to frame the inarticulate structures of the habitus in the form of appropriate speech or action.

While Bourdieu's concept of habitus locates power in the specific practices of the everyday, his concept of doxa implies a collective and unitary system of domination. Foucault, in contrast, assiduously avoided this leap from practice to system, focusing on the "infinitesimal mechanisms of power" (Foucault 1980: 99) dispersed in a capillary fashion through all human relations (141–42). Power is therefore dispersed and fragmentary, located in specific sites with particular genealogies and embodied in specific technologies. Yet, this also creates a problem for Foucault. How does power as the relational aspect of locally incoherent discursive practices cohere to form global patterns of power relations that are at leas partially constituted by the strategic agency of the powerful (see Jessop 1990: 233–41; Mitchell 1999: 87–89)? Foucault's (1977: 204–8) initial solution was that of the "diagram," that is to say a specific and shared formula or technology of power that pervades relations in given epochs and hence produces particular kinds of social subjects (i.e., surveillance, self-discipline, and the "Panopticon" in modern times). Yet, as Bob Jessop (1990: 231) notes, "For Foucault the danger is that the specificity of different social relations is dissolved through their common use of the same techniques of power." Because Foucault views power as a quality of all human relations, a singular global diagram of power effectively fuses micro- and macroscale social relations in a manner analogous to Bourdieu's doxa. Hence, much as with Bourdieu, when power is made habitual and nonagentive, agency, resistance and strategy become problematic issues. Foucault clearly recognizes this, offering resistance as an innate quality of the social body, a "plebeian quality" of disengagement that serves as the counterstroke to every advance of power (Foucault 1980: 138). Similarly, Foucault (1980: 99–108, 141–42) moves from the global diagram to speak of a certain strategic coherence in the interconnections between social relations. However, for Foucault power is always immanent rather than structurally determined (i.e., it is "just there") and neither resistance nor global strategies result from specific agencies, hence his attempts to discuss global patterns fluctuate between underspecified metaphors and monolithic techniques (see Jessop 1990: 230–41).

It is precisely this problem that is critiqued by Kurtz (1996) in certain common uses of the concept of hegemony within anthropology. Jean and John Comaroff (1991: 22–32), for example, suggest that a continuum exists from hegemony as an unconscious (nonagentive) order to ideology as the conscious (agentive) constitution of power. Essentially, for the Comaroffs, political systems attempt to move power along this continuum, making it

"disappear" in a taken-for-granted hegemonic form. At the same time, ideology can also confront hegemonic orders by bringing to the light of consciousness the hidden principles of power on which that hegemony rests.
Again, one sees not only a misrepresentation of Gramsci's work but also a
deep tension between micro and macro social relations and between strategic and systemic workings of power.

Alternatively, Laclau and Mouffe (2001: 105–45) have provided an influential discourse-centered reading of Gramsci that emphasizes the dual
nature of state hegemony (constructed and constitutive).[8] They propose
that such hegemony is constituted by specific discourses that seek to transform widely available "elements" (what I would term cultural resources)[9]
by fixing their meaning as "moments" within a particular discursive formation. Laclau and Mouffe systematize and develop Gramsci's discussions of
the role of intellectuals in articulating the consciousness of "the masses,"
which is latent, but incoherent, in "common sense" understandings of lived
experience (Gramsci 2000: 324–49). In doing so, hegemony represents as
universal (i.e., of value to everyone) the particular interests and orientations of one segment of society (Laclau 2000: 55–57). For example, when a
king is represented as the father of his people a series of cultural resources
are articulated and their meanings are fixed in relation to kingship (e.g.,
fatherhood, peoplehood), such that the king's rule is presented as of intrinsic value to all defined as "his people."

Here we might also consider Bruce Kapferer's comparative study of Sri
Lankan (Sinhalese Buddhist) and Australian nationalism, which is conceived in the vein of interpretive anthropology, rather than neo-Gramscian
state theory. In contrasting the radically different forms that nationalist
ideologies take in Sri Lanka and Australia, Kapferer (1988: 78–84) argues
that routine cultural practices of the sort that make up a habitus, in
Bourdieu's sense, help constitute widely shared "ontologies" that can provide moral force for ideologies. These are neither "norms" nor doxic
orders, in that they provide raw materials for improvised articulations,
rather than rules to be repeated. Consequently, the efficacy of the resultant
intellectual products is never guaranteed, with their legitimacy open to
challenges drawn from the same body of cultural resources. Insofar as they
are successful (i.e., accepted, rather than necessarily effective) these interventions constitute a moral order, one that implies a link between a particular taxonomy of identity and particular behavioral expectations.

I would suggest the need for a terminological shift from Kapferer's
"ontologies" to what I believe is the more preferable term, "cultural
resources." In Kapferer's work there is a degree of unresolved tension in
the structuralist logic of his argument, such that his use of the term
"ontologies" implies an underlying essential pattern from which specific
nationalist acts, rhetoric, or ideologies are generated as surface phenomena. That this need not be the case is noted by Kapferer himself when he

writes, "Sinhalese nationalism selects within the many possibilities of Buddhism in practice and realizes a particular logic, a logic made integral to Sinhalese nationalism and forceful to its process" (Kapferer 1988: 6). To my mind, this point is of the utmost importance. The cultural resources activated in the formation of specific moral orders may give power, legitimacy, and conviction to those orders, but they do not necessarily determine their form or content. Indeed, the same cultural resources can be (and in the case of the major world religions often are) deployed in moral orders that are quite different, or even directly opposed.

This is precisely the point made by Laclau and Mouffe (2001: 110–14) when they argue that the meanings of cultural resources ("elements") cannot be wholly fixed in any specific discourse; hence they are always available for rearticulation in alternative, even opposed discourses. Consequently, a variety of possible social orders can be derived from specific microlevel relations of power, while any particular social order requires specific practices to embed these microrelations in particular chains of meaning and disembed them from others (Jessop 1990: 242). Furthermore, as Jessop notes (242), one need not posit social orders such as states as unified, globally calculating subjects. Instead, he (1990: 243) writes that

a "global calculating subject" is no more (or less) than a real social agent which formulates a "global" strategy. And the latter is a strategy which tends to subtend and articulate a number of smaller sites of power relations within its orbit. . . . These smaller sites none the less continue to have an independent existence . . . and to constitute potential sites of structural recalcitrance and/or social resistance to the global strategy.

Hegemony and State Formation

We can now pull these ideas together to flesh out our discussion of state formation in Chapter 1. First, the state is not a "thing," nor is it a social totality (i.e., society itself). The state is the effect of a process embedded in a specific historical bloc that unites (by time/space proximity) a discordant ensemble of social forces and positions (habitus in Bourdieu's terminology). This process is what we have chosen to call hegemony, which in a clear modification of Gramsci's views we consider to be the result of force and consent operating together. More specifically, hegemony is the selective and strategic articulation of cultural resources embedded in this ensemble by means of specific intellectual products (texts, rituals, institutions, administrative procedures) that seek to fix their meaning in relation to an overarching moral order or "global" identity (i.e., the state). Hegemony, therefore, is the cumulative and not wholly intended effect of specific projects carried out by particular agents. Besides articulation, these effects include the bounding of the social space of the state and the differentiation of those who rule from those who are ruled. Furthermore, when we speak of state formation, we are talking about the gathering together and subordination of smaller sites of power (family, village, temples and shrines, myths and symbols, etc.) which to varying degrees in different contexts, retain an independent existence and hence form concrete (and nonessentialized) sites of potential resistance. It is in this sense that we used Bourdieu's image of state formation as the cumulative concentration of capital in Chapter 1.

Beyond Gramsci?

While we have already modified Gramsci's ideas and put them to work is a very particular direction, two problems remain that require us to break more clearly with Gramsci's own position. These are the necessary (a priori) class character of hegemony, and the exclusive modernity of the hegemonic state. A particular concern of Laclau and Mouffe (2001) is to root out any essentialism that locates hegemony outside of the discursive practices by which it is formed. In this sense they claim to go beyond Gramsci by rejecting the prior existence of economic classes as fundamental social groups already defined in the realm of production and only articulated and made conscious in the realm of political activity. In other words, hegemony is not the result of a ruling class convincing subaltern classes to accept its rule, as Gramsci often suggests, since the very identities involved (i.e., the subject positions) are what hegemony constructs. However, if we refuse to locate the division between ruler and ruled outside of state hegemony itself, we face a real problem in understanding how any particular state came into existence. As Jessop notes (1982: 200–202; 1990: 288–304), Laclau and Mouffe give no attention to the conditions of acceptance for state hegemony and focus almost exclusively on identity and ideological discourse. In point of fact, the state has a class character insofar as it articulates economic production within itself as one of the "smaller sites of power" we mentioned above. What it does not have is an a priori or necessary class character, as the articulation of production within state hegemony is context, history, and polity specific. Furthermore, as neoWeberian sociologists such as Giddens (1985: 22–60) and Mann (1986: 1–34) have pointed out, one must give attention to the means of violence as well as the means of production. Hence, with Gramsci we can say that state formation is a project of domination that has its origins in specific, already existing social relations, including most particularly relations of production. However, such preexistent social relations do not fully encompass and define the relations of domination articulated by state hegemony.

Our second problem is peculiar to the archaeological orientation of this book, namely can we presume that Gramsci's construct of hegemony is a meaningful analytical framework for studying premodern contexts? On this issue Gramsci was rather clear in stating that his was a theory of the modern state.[10]

In the ancient and mediaeval State alike, centralisation, whether political-territorial or social . . . was minimal. The State was, in a certain sense, a mechanical bloc of social groups . . . within the circle of political-military compression, which was only exercised harshly at certain moments, the subaltern groups had a life of their own, their own institutions, etc. The modern State substitutes for the mechanical bloc of social groups their subordination to the active hegemony of the directive and dominant group. (Gramsci 1971: 54, n. 4)

Gramsci's position is an idiosyncratic version of Marx's Asiatic Mode of Production, and virtually identical to Anthony Giddens's (1985: 35–82) characterization of "traditional" states as "class-divided." Gramsci's insistence on the unitary and unified nature of hegemony, over and against his own image of "a contradictory and discordant ensemble," predisposes him to adopt a primitivist position on the nature of premodern states. In short, with many other scholars, Gramsci imagines ancient and medieval states as tiny ruling classes that relate to large, fragmented subject populations in a limited and sporadically exploitative manner. In the absence of a unified public culture, there is for Gramsci no hegemony.

We have already raised some objections to this modern/premodern divide in Chapter 1.[11] Certainly, modernity has been constructed to a large extent through such rhetorical oppositions with "traditional" society (see Carrier 1995). Yet, even if one were to grant (which I do not) that the ancient state was simply a "mechanical bloc" in the Durkheimian sense, one cannot presume that such weak integration was straightforward to achieve or that rule could be defined solely by the use of force. As Kertzer noted, the exercise of force rests on the symbolic power through which people (e.g., the army, henchmen) are mobilized. Hence, even polities that appear to be based simply on the irregular extraction of tribute must be constituted and represented in a cultural form.

In these first two chapters we have explored theoretical issues that problematize the traditional trait-based definition of the state widely employed in both processual and cultural historical archaeology. At the same time, by engaging the work of Antonio Gramsci, we have seen that a cultural theory of the state, or at least of state formation, is both necessary and possible. This positive contribution has been largely lacking in the so-called postprocessual engagement with political theory within archaeology.

When understood in this manner, the explication of state formation makes rather significant empirical demands, as it is only through historically specific practices, which articulate specific cultural resources, that any particular state is given substance as a hegemonic effect. We will, therefore, turn our attention in the remainder of this book to the case of Iron Age Moab, in order to provide substantive illustration of the rather complex processes of state formation passed over with the lightness of abstraction in these first two chapters. In keeping with the neo-Gramscian position developed in this chapter, particular attention will be given to defining key cultural resources embedded in the "common sense" experiences of family and community life in the Iron Age. We will also look closely at how specific intellectual products (esp. texts and architecture) served to select and artic- ulate these cultural resources in constituting the hegemony of Moab as a moral order with a spatial presence. Finally, we will give careful attention to contextual question of when, why and how this occurred in order to high- light the strategic and historically contingent nature of state formation.

Chapter 3

Land and Story

> *Thus the two daughters of Lot came to be with child by their father. The older one bore a son and named him Moab; he is the father of the Moabites of today. And the younger also bore a son, and she called him Ben-ammi; he is the father of the Ammonites of today.*
>
> —*Genesis 19: 36–38*

Moab, as we noted, contains in its semantic field an elision of place, people, and polity. In this chapter we will consider the first of these referents, and will explore the significance of Moab as a place. We have already seen that a spatial presence is one of the fundamental effects of state hegemony. Here "effect" is the key word, as the geographic referent of Moab is not a neutral container or a "natural" backdrop for the more political aspects of Moab as a polity or a collective identity. In evoking the "land of Moab," people called forward and privileged specific features from among the many possibilities present within the physical landscape. Hence, the "land of Moab" was simultaneously a place and an argument about that place. This point can be made most clearly if we begin by considering the spatial representation of Moab in the Hebrew Bible.

Biblical Moab

For the author of Genesis 19 the origin of Moab lay in the punch line of an off-color joke. Here, in the story of Lot's incestuous relations with his daughters, the "true" etymology of Moab and Ammon is revealed. Moab, particularly in its gentilic form *Mo'abi* (Moabite) can be parsed in Hebrew as *Me-* [from]; *'ab-* [father]; *i-* [my]. In other words, "From my father." Similarly, the eponymous ancestor of the *Benay-'ammon* (sons of Ammon; Ammonites) is here rendered as *Ben-'ammi*—"son of my (close patrilineal) kinsman." Moabites and Ammonites, therefore, in their very names bore the mark of (what the heading in my NRSV Bible calls) their "shameful origins."

It may seem odd to begin a discussion of the spatial boundaries of Moab with reference to this rather clever but clearly antagonistic bit of wordplay. However, understanding the uses the Bible makes of Moab is of central importance to examining how we are to understand this entity. It must be remembered that Moab is not an archaeological culture in any meaningful sense. That is to say, it is not an entity defined in the first instance by patterns of continuity/discontinuity in the spatial distribution of material culture. Rather, Moab is a predefined historical identity that is given a spatial dimension by textual references, primarily from the Bible and secondarily from indigenous and Neo-Assyrian inscriptions.[1] In this way, Moab acts as a container such that the archaeology of the Iron Age within certain geographical boundaries becomes the archaeology of Moab. I should add that this is not merely a question of time and accumulating evidence, since the historical category of Moab is prefigured by texts and cannot be "discovered" in patterns of material culture.

Like most things related to the Bible, understanding its uses of Moab is far from simple. More than two centuries of critical scholarship have stressed the Bible's lengthy and complicated "prehistory" of compilation and redaction, as well as its incorporation of divergent theological concerns and emphasizes. At the same time, the Bible retains a high level of internal intertextuality (quotation, cross-reference, repeated themes) and literary coherence. I do not here wish to engage in the well-established debates over whether the Bible is to be mined (by dissection) for historical nuggets or read (and counterread) holistically as a literary gem. In my reading, Moab is portrayed relatively consistently across the chronologically disparate units of the canonical text of the Bible. This is not to imply that the Bible is univocal; it most definitely is not, as is illustrated below by the story of Ruth. However, insofar as the Bible contains multiple perspectives, these positions play off each other, showing a textual awareness that benefits from a holistic approach. Drawing historical conclusions about the specific referents of specific passages is a separate matter, but one that is aided by an understanding of the generic themes that seem to underlie the Bible's portrayal of Moab.

Let us begin with the "genealogical imagination" (see Shryock 1997) witnessed in Genesis 19. In the Bible, genealogy presents itself as a total system, explaining substance by means of patrilineal descent (Wilson 1977). In representative practice, this system has many parallels with the logic of "closeness" (Arabic—*qaraba*) as used by ethnographers in describing kinship within so-called tribal societies in Middle East (Eickelman 1989: 156–61). Yet, at the level of "nations" (*goyim*) this logic is curiously inverted. For the Bible, danger lies not in the foreign 'Other" but in the alterity of the familiar with its threat of assimilation. Genealogical "closeness," a symbol of mutual trust and responsibility in personal life, becomes a marker of conflict in the universal genealogies of Genesis (Crüsemann 1996; Kunin 1995: 178–204). This is "part and parcel" of the larger biblical project of constructing Israel as a collective identity in both its more horrific (e.g., Deut. 20: 16–18) and humane (e.g., Exod. 19: 5–6) forms.

For the most part, Genesis is built around a genealogical core that is universal in scope but progressively narrows its focus and expands its biographic detail in tracing the specific lineage of Jacob/Israel. Eighteen generations after Adam one reaches Terah, Abraham's father, who marks a key moment in the Bible's understanding of history. Terah leaves Ur, bringing his family to the Levant, thereby opening a new phase in human history. If one counts forward three generations from Terah (Abraham-Isaac-Jacob) one reaches the end goal of the genealogies, the father of the tribes of Israel. Interestingly, virtually every time you count forward three generations from Terah you end up with the eponymous founder of a polity, or "tribe," that interacted closely with the kingdom of Judah between the eighth and sixth centuries B.C.E. For example, Haran-Lot-Moab and Haran-Lot-Ben Ami results in the polities of Moab and Ammon. Abraham-Isaac-Esau/Edom results in the polity of Edom; Abraham-Ishmael-Kedar results in the Qedarite Arabs; and Nahor-Kemuel-Aram results in the kingdom of Damascus (the usual referent of Aram in the Bible). It seems clear, therefore, that the political and cultural landscape of the Late Iron Age is understood in Genesis as the result of a branching genealogy. For the most part, this branching ends with the third generation after Terah, fixing the boundaries of the polities in question. Only the line of Jacob/Israel (fifth generation) and his brother Esau/Edom (fourth generation—including the always nasty Amalekites) continues further.

Numerous attempts have been made to unlock the logic of this genealogical approach to world history (e.g., Crüsemann 1996; Oded 1986), particularly by scholars working within various traditions of structural anthropology (e.g., Kunin 1995: 178–204; 1999; Leach 1969; Pitt-Rivers 1977: 126–71; Prewitt 1981; 1990). Most such approaches note the significance of marriage, sexual reproduction, and inheritance in these stories, especially regarding the question of exogamy vs endogamy as applied to the descendants of Terah in relation to the children of Israel/Jacob. However, the dynamic of negative closeness is not easily reduced to transformations of an underlying structural logic based on the contradictions of alliance through marriage. For example, Philistine city-states are placed at considerable genealogical distance from Israel (Gen. 10: 13) despite playing an antagonistic role similar to that of other neighboring cultures. Here the genealogies seem to recognize cultural similarity as a product of genealogical proximity, as the Philistines are placed in a genealogically close relationship to the Aegean world. This "Aegean connection" is well illustrated in the earliest Iron Age contexts at Philistine sites on the coastal plain of Israel (Dothan 1982; Stager 1995).

At the same time, outside the genealogical material, the Philistines are placed with Ammon, Moab, and Edom as nations "close" to Israel in the sense of sharing a common history of movement, conquest, and possession of their current territory. In Deuteronomy 2: 1–23, Yahweh states that he gave each of these nations their territories as a possession. Hence, Ammon, Moab, Edom, and the Philistines are imagined as emerging in the land of Canaan on the same model as that of Israel. Each claims its territory by displacing an indigenous population of "giants," all of whom the Bible states were equivalent (all were *Rephaim*) despite their distinct local names. For example, Deuteronomy 2: 9–12 provides the following parenthetical historical commentary:

I have assigned Ar as a possession to the descendants of Lot. (It was formerly inhabited by the Emim, a people great and numerous, and as tall as the Anakites. Like the Anakites, they are counted as Rephaim; but the Moabites call them Emim. Similarly, Seir was formerly inhabited by the Horites; but the descendants of Esau dispossessed them, wiping them out and settling in their place, just as Israel did in the land they were to possess, which the LORD had given to them.)

Unlike the trope of radical difference, common to racist, nationalist, and colonial discourse of the modern era, the Bible is concerned with drawing contrasts across a field of acknowledged similarity. Distance from the main line of Jacob is not absolute, but achieved through unusual, and by turns farcical or tragic, events. This not only includes the incestuous origins of Moab and Ammon but also Jacob's (and Rachel's) tricking of Esau/Edom to gain his birthright, and Sarah's expulsion of Hagar and Ishmael into the desert and away from Abraham's tent. It is this context of familiar alterity that we need to read references to Moab in the Bible.

Biblical references (see Miller 1989b; Van Zyl 1960: 5–29) to Moab can be divided into five major groups: (1) simple expressions of antagonism; (2) extended narratives with Moabite characters; (3) prophetic predictions of coming destruction, labeled by biblical scholars as the "Oracles against the Nations;" (4) simple geographic references, referring to boundaries, topographic features and settlements; (5) multiple recitations of the capture of Sihon's kingdom, used to justify an Israelite claim to the northern portion of Moab. The first three categories illustrate the relatively consistent treatment of Moab as the familiar "Other" and help set the stage for interpreting the last two, which raise more directly the question of the spatial presence of Moab within biblical narratives.

Boundaries, Places, and Landscape

Biblical references to the physical territory designated as Moab show an interested and uneven geographic knowledge on the part of biblical authors. There is clear knowledge of the main travel routes to Moab from Judah on either end of the Dead Sea. The northern route is best known, with the *'Arâbā* ("Plains") of Moab being consistently placed in the basin of the Jordan Rift Valley north of the Dead Sea, south of Wadi Ḥisban/Wadi Kafrayn and directly east of Jericho. As the setting for Moses' conveyance of the Torah to the children of Israel, the "Plains of Moab" is referred to rather frequently in the Bible. The southern route, described as the "ascent of Luhith" (Isa. 15: 5; Jer. 48: 5), is less frequently mentioned and confidently delineated, although it seems safe (see Ben-David 2003; Mittmann 1982; Schottroff 1966; Worschech and Knauf 1986) to associate it with one or more of the *widyan* (henceforth anglicized as wadis) that descend to the Basin of the Dead Sea from the southwest corner of the Karak Plateau, in the vicinity of the city of al-Karak (e.g., Wadi Isal, Wadi al-Karak, Wadi an-Numayra).

The Arnon Valley almost certainly refers to the modern Wadi Mujib and serves as the principal topographic reference point in biblical discussions of Moab. This is not surprising, as Wadi Mujib, with a maximum width of some 6 km and a depth of up to 1,100 m, is one of the most dramatic features of Jordan's topography. Extending north approximately 40 km from the Arnon/Mujib to the towns of Heshbon (modern Ḥisban) and Elealeh (modern al-'Al) is the area known in the Bible as the *Mishor* ("tableland"). It is here that one finds the vast majority of Moabite settlements referred to in the Bible, and indeed there would appear to be a dramatic difference in the knowledge and interest biblical authors express in settlements located north and south of the Arnon/Mujib (see Jones 1991). To the south, the Bible shows a slightly fuzzy awareness (see Miller 1989a) of the Zered as a major wadi system, most probably Wadi al-Ḥasa (cf. Zared in the sixth-century C.E. Madaba Mosaic Map – see Piccirillo and Alliata 1999). To the east, biblical authors are aware in a fairly nonspecific sense that Moab borders on steppic and desert land. As a general characterization, Moab is seen as fertile and productive associated alternatively with livestock (Num. 32: 4; 2 Kgs. 3: 4), viticulture (Isa. 16: 10; Jer. 48: 33) and abundant grain fields (Isa. 16: 10; Jer. 48: 33).

Biblical references, therefore, connect the name Moab with territory extending from the Wadi al-Ḥasa in the south to the "Plains of Moab" and Wadi Ḥisban in the north. Yet, when specifically delineating the territory of Moab, the Bible insistently denies this extended spatial definition. Most particularly, the Bible repeatedly draws the northern border of Moab at the Arnon (Wadi Mujib) by telling and retelling a single story to justify this claim. Numbers 21 and Deuteronomy 2 tell the story of the defeat of Sihon, the Amorite king of Heshbon, by the Israelites while traveling en route from Egypt to Canaan. [2] Sihon is said to have "won" control of the *Mishor* from the Moabites. Numerous subsequent references to this story (especially Josh. 12: 2; 13: 9–10; Judg. 11: 19–21; Ps. 135: 11–12; 136: 19–22; Neh. 9: 22) make clear that the biblical argument is aimed at justifying an Israelite claim to this territory. Hence, Judges 11: 17–18 is careful to state that the Israelites were denied permission to transverse Moab and so skirted it to the east before defeating Sihon who had already defeated the Moabites. [3] From the Bible's perspective this eliminated any Moabite claim on the Mishor. The entire complex of passing through/around Moab without inflicting harm and without receiving hospitality, of capturing the Mishor from Sihon rather than Moab, and of the Moabite king hiring Balaam to curse Israel, is repeatedly cited as both cause and justification for antagonism between Israel and Moab (Deut. 23: 4–5; Neh. 13: 1–2). Hence, we cannot separate the textual representation of the territory of Moab in the Bible from its antagonistic stance toward Moab.

The contradiction between the explicit claims of a territorially limited Moab and the regular association of the area north of Wadi Mujib with Moab is compounded by confusion over just which component of Israel laid claim to this area. Joshua 13: 15–28 clearly assigns the Mishor to the tribe of Reuben, while the area north of Heshbon is assigned to the tribe of Gad. However, in Numbers 32: 34–38 Gad rebuilds and occupies cities in the southern Mishor (Dibon, 'Aṭarot, Aroer) while Reuben rebuilds and occupies cities to the north (Heshbon, Elealeh, Nebo, Baal Meon, etc.) In Numbers 33: 46 Dibon (modern Dhiban) is referred to as Dibon-Gad. Furthermore, in the Mesha Inscription (see Chapter 7) the men of Gad are said to have dwelt in 'Aṭarot "forever," while Nebo is associated with the king of Israel and Dibon is a Moabite center.

Reuben, it must be said, is a rather obscure tribe, a fact which clearly confused some later biblical authors (1 Chron. 5: 1–2), due to Reuben's premier genealogical position as the first-born son of Jacob. Frank Moore Cross (1988) has built a case for an early rise and fall for the tribe of Reuben, which is reflected in both its structural/genealogical importance and its obscurity. However, this begs the question of the coherence, autonomy, and spatial integrity of the groups with conflicting textual claims of priority in northern Moab.

This picture of multiple competing claims is compounded if we remember that the recounting of the Sihon story in Judges 11 is directed not against Moabite claims to the Mishor, but against the Ammonite king, based further north in Rabbath-Amman (the Qal'a, or "Citadel," of modern Amman). Furthermore, although the city of Heshbon is normally associated with Moab in biblical texts, in Jeremiah 49: 3 it is associated with Ammon. Some archaeologists see these references as pointing to an expansion of Ammon into the Mishor late in the Iron Age (Daviau 1997; Herr 1992b, 1999b). Their argument pivots on a relatively coherent set of material culture dating to the late seventh and sixth centuries that can be traced outward from the area of Amman, and is identified by these archaeologists as the product of ethnic "Ammonites." [4] The boundaries of this "Ammonite" complex are tentatively said to extend south to the Wadi Wala/ Wadi ath-Thamad drainage system, north to the north side of the Wadi az-Zarqa, west to the Jordan River and east to the Syrian Desert. In other words, in this model, by circa 600 B.C.E. about two-thirds of the Mishor was Ammonite. A serious analytical study of the assemblages involved has yet to be done, and there are a number of problematic issues with the definition of this complex (see Routledge 1996c: 520–23). Some scholars have argued that the references in Judges 11 and Jer. 49 are scribal errors or editorial corruptions (Hübner 1992: 303–5; Knauf 1992c) or that examples of so-called Ammonite script cannot be attributed coherently to Ammon (Hübner 1988). Such arguments are largely ad hoc and hardly fatal to the Ammonite model. What is hugely problematic is that the scholars relating national/ethnic identities to the distribution of material culture provide no conceptual road map to explain how we get from one to the other. Not only is it unclear why we should expect either Ammonite hegemony or Ammonite ethnicity to map to material culture, we also cannot answer why this should have only happened at the very end of the Iron Age.

As we watch scholars juggling Moab, Ammon, Gad, and Reuben while moving between various biblical and (at least one) extra-biblical texts, we might ask if the problem lies in the starting point. The assumption that discrete groups existed independent of discursive practices that sought to enact them, and textual practices that sought to fix them, is deeply problematic and obscures the complex and contested situation suggested by the available evidence. Manfred Weippert, for example, notes some rather practical, yet destabilizing, conclusions to be reached from the textual evidence:

> It is probable that further, more or less significant, ethnic groups or regional groups existed in Transjordan. Their names have disappeared because they could not assert themselves against the "national" states that dominated the history of the first half of the first millennium B.C. on both sides of the Jordan; in this manner they were integrated and became [part] of the Arameans, Israelites, Ammonites, Moabites, or Edomites. All this is not pure speculation as we see in the very eventful case of Gad, who is better known in this regard than the other tribes. Its example permits us to learn that tribal identity and nationality (i.e., the condition of belonging to a state) must not be confused; since Gad must have, depending upon the political situation in the southern *Belqā* and the *Kūrā*, by turns become Israelite or Moabite. This is probably also true for Reuben. (Weippert 1997: 26; my translation)

We can conclude, therefore, that defining Moab is not as simple as knowing its spatial boundaries. The Bible localizes Moab rather consistently in the region between Wadi al-Ḥasa and the northern end of the Dead Sea (Wadi Ḥisban or Wadi Kafrayn), yet it does so in a manner that always raises questions of conflict and competing claims. Indeed, although the date of composition and final editing for the biblical references to Moab is uncertain, both the consistency of the Bible's oppositional stance to Moab and its reflection in the independent witness of the Mesha Inscription make it reasonable to take the Bible's theme of conflict with Moab as reflecting an actual Iron Age social context. Rather than beginning from Moab as a fixed space and/or collective identity, we need to consider its construction and assertion within a space where it is not the only possibility. We need to recognize a territory within which arguments for absolute opposition between ethnonational entities were made against the silent arguments of both local autonomy and regional similarity.

An Actual Place

In spite of itself, the Bible provides us with a geographic frame within which rivals actively and retroactively sought to define the land of Moab. The land of Moab is therefore a political argument in which landscape is simultaneously physical and metaphysical. It is vain to hope that we could somehow recover the totality of this spatial experience in its multiple, and local, manifestations. What, for example, was Moab for a specific pastoralist or subsistence farmer? We do, however, have access to more than one version of this land. We have already seen that the Bible itself contains distinct understandings of just what the land of Moab incorporated, and we have hinted that indigenous inscriptions, especially the Mesha Inscription, suggest a somewhat different Moab as well. If we change gears and move from biblical studies to the earth sciences, we can bring forward several other versions of the land of Moab.

If we look at the Bible's geographic frame today, we see that Moab is part of the uplifted plateau that runs north-south from the Yarmuk River basin to the escarpment at Ras en-Naqb. This plateau is approximately 6,000 km^2 in area, representing about 6 percent of Jordan's current national boundaries but containing more than 95 percent of its population. Moab constitutes approximately one-third of this plateau, in the north incorporating the southern portion of the administrative district of al-Balqa and in the south all of ard al-Karak (the Karak Plateau).

This plateau is divided by major and minor wadi systems that drain westward to the Jordan Rift Valley (Arabic Ghawr), the largest of which (Yarmuk, az-Zarqa, al-Mujib, al-Ḥasa) have usually marked administrative subdivisions since Late Antiquity (Figure 3.1). These wadis are particularly prominent features of south central Jordan. Wadi al-Ḥasa (max. 1,000 m deep and 7 km wide) and Wadi Mujib (described above) are the largest and most striking, framing the Karak Plateau as a distinct unit. In northern Moab, smaller, but still impressive wadis such as Wadi Wala (including Wadi Haydan and Wadi ath-Thamad) and Wadi az-Zarqa-Ma'in represent significant breaks in the landscape on the western side of the plateau. The deep incision of these wadis is relatively recent in geologic time, beginning in conjunction with episodes of very rapid subsidence of the basin of the Dead Sea in the early Quaternary (from ca. 2 mya).

The uplifting, warping, and subsidence that resulted from the strike-slip faulting of the Jordan Rift Valley means that south central Transjordan initially rises very rapidly from the Ghawr to the plateau.[5] Beginning from the

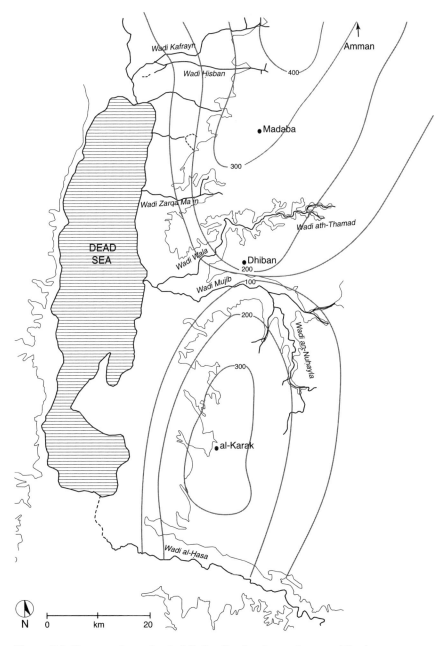

Figure 3.1. Topography and rainfall distribution in south central Jordan.

Dead Sea surface (currently 410 m bsl—i.e., below sea level) to a maximum
of 1,305 m asl (above sea level) at Jabal Dubab, near al-Karak in the south
over a distance of only 13 km, and to about 900 m asl in the north overlooking Wadi Ḥisban. The plateau slopes gently downward to about. 700 m
asl from both north and south toward Wadi Mujib and from west to east
as the plateau gives way to the rolling steppic terrain that is transitional to
the Syrian Desert.

   The principal exposed bedrock was laid under marine conditions during
the Upper Cretaceous period (Senomian, ca. 88–65 mya) and hence is characterized by the interbedding of soft (e.g., chalk, marl, limestone) and hard
(dolomite, coquina, chert) sedimentary rock (see Bender 1974; al-Hunjul
1995; Koucky 1987; Powell 1988; Shawabkeh 1991). This has created a
karstic landscape that is susceptible to erosion. Precipitation is readily absorbed through surface marls and limestone and transported horizontally,
forming underground channels that run at the interface of rock beds. This
water emerges in the form of springs in the wadi bottoms and on the eastern face of the basin of the Dead Sea. When combined with the region's
high evapotranspiration rates, this means that there is very little surface
water available on the plateau proper despite its relatively higher levels of
rainfall (see Agar-und-Hydrotechnik 1977). Before the twentieth century,
human settlement away from the wadi edges was dependent on cisterns, as
the available aquifers are mostly too deep to be reached by wells drilled
with nonmechanized technologies.

   Prevailing weather systems move from west to east. Predominant summer
air masses are northeast African in origin and are subject to thermic inversion over the Mediterranean inhibiting the formation of precipitation-
bearing clouds and resulting in virtually no summer rain (LaBianca and
Lacelle 1986: 11). Consequently, precipitation in Jordan falls almost exclusively between November and May. Predominant winter air masses are
North Atlantic in origin and drop their precipitation on the uplifted western rim of the basin of the Dead Sea in Palestine, and again (in smaller
quantities) on the eastern rim, which is the western side of Moab. The
result is a rain shadow over the basin of the Dead Sea (and southern Jordan
Valley). On the plateau, rainfall is highest in areas of highest elevation
along the western side. On the eastern side, precipitation drops rapidly. In
practice, this means that only territory at the southwestern and northwestern ends of the territory encompassed by Moab receives more than 300 mm
of precipitation per year on average (see Figure 3.1). Both the basin of the
Dead Sea and most of Wadi Mujib lie below the 100 mm isohyet. To the
east, the edge of the plateau is marked most effectively by a drop-off in precipitation rates and accompanying changes in climax vegetation.

   Conventionally, an average precipitation rate of 250 mm per annum is held
as an absolute minimum for the successful dry farming of barley, while 300
mm or more is held as necessary for the reliable production of wheat, most

legumes, and olive trees (Arnon 1972; Buddenhagen 1990; el-Hurani and Duwayri 1986). In practice, actual land use is highly dependent on micro-environmental conditions, especially topography, soil, and runoff catchments. Furthermore, as in most arid to semi-arid zones, the volume and distribution of rainfall fluctuates widely on both an inter and intra-annual basis.

Vegetation in south central Jordan has been dramatically modified by agriculture and livestock grazing and in most places must be reconstructed from bioclimate models and relic plant communities. The eastern fringe is classified as an Irano-Turanian steppic vegetation zone, characterized by dwarf shrubland, now heavily degraded from livestock grazing and trampling. On the west side of Moab, the rapid descent into the basin of the Dead Sea is accompanied by rapid changes in climate and vegetation by elevation, from Mediterranean to Irano-Turanian to Sudanian (sandy Hamada desert) to a Saline (Halophytic) environment on the Dead Sea shores (see al-Eisawi 1985; Kürschner 1986).

In the central plateau, land currently not under cultivation is generally colonized by thorny shrubs and herbaceous plants. However, temperature, precipitation, and elevation define the central plateau as a Mediterranean nonforest vegetation zone, suggesting a now-degraded Evergreen Oak-Pistachio maquis (al-Eisawi 1985: 54; Kürschner 1986: 52–53) as the climax vegetation. The extent of this woodland and the precise chronology of its destruction are problematic questions for which we currently have little data. Despite skepticism (e.g., Harlan 1985: 128), it seems likely that the higher rainfall areas on the northwestern and southwestern ends of the territory of Moab were once covered by such a maquis.

Øystein LaBianca (n.d.) has modeled a possible sequence for this deforestation, using the location and number of archaeological sites by period in the vicinity of Ḥisban to simulate rates of tree clearance. LaBianca suggests a series of reductions and partial recoveries of the forest beginning in the Early Bronze Age (third millennium B.C.E.) and resulting in a progressive retreat until the Late Roman-Byzantine era, when a major collapse occurs. This model matches macroregional patterns in tree pollen in the Sea of Galilee (Lake Kinneret) and Dead Sea cores published by Baruch (1986, 1990). The Galilee core points to a long-term trend of declining deciduous oak species, increasing plantain species (an invasive weed), and a series of peaks and troughs in the prominence of olive species (Baruch 1986: Fig. 4). Somewhat similar trends can be noted for the Dead Sea cores (Baruch 1990: Figs. 3–4), although in the Ein-Gedi core deciduous oak declines less rapidly until its traumatic collapse in the first millennium C.E. Overall, as Baruch notes (1986: 47; 1990: 292), these pollen cores point to the establishment of near-modern plant communities at the end of the fourth millennium, followed by a long history of human-induced vegetational change (clearing of oak forests, cultivation of fruit trees). As we shall see below, a drying of the climate at the end of the third millennium may account for some of the decline in oak pollen, but the long-term replacement of oak by fruit tree pollen can only be explained anthropogenically. The Iron Age likely occupied an intermediary position in this process.

Deforestation and large-scale soil erosion are intimately related in the highlands of Jordan (Christopherson and Guertin 1995; Christopherson 2000: 188–224). Following Moormann (1959) we can classify the principal soils of south central Jordan as Red Mediterranean (RM), Yellow Mediterranean (YM), and Yellow Steppic (YS).[6] RM soils are similar to the *terra rosa* soils found throughout the Mediterranean Basin, being clay-rich with well-developed A and B horizons and high water infiltration rates and water storage capacities (LaBianca and Lacelle 1986: 53). However, RM soils are a good deal more calcareous than *terra rosa* soils, perhaps reflecting the erosion of an original noncalcareous A horizon (Horowitz 1979: 167). This is possible because of the age of the RM soils, which are relics formed under more humid conditions during the Pleistocene (Cordova 2000: 560–62; Horowitz 1979: 167–68). YM soils are shallower and more calcareous, having been formed on slopes and in more arid areas (LaBianca and Lacelle 1986: 45–57). YS soils are associated with the arid transition to the desert. They are very thin, poorly developed and slightly coarse with low clay content and very low agricultural potential (LaBianca and Lacelle 1986: 45–57). Both, the poor aggregation and the low stability of these soils make them susceptible to erosion, this being exacerbated by their tendency to form surface crusts that decrease water infiltration and increase runoff (Singer 1991: 102). The low rainfall in this region means that microbial activity in these soils is low and nitrogen cycling tightly controlled by plants, hence limiting the nitrogen content of the soils (West 1991: 299–304). Increasing with the calcareousness of the soils, from RM to YM to YS soils, is the chance that subsoil horizons of cemented $CaCO3$ will form through evaporation, limiting root access to subsoil moisture (Singer 1991: 95–96). Furthermore, under certain conditions, calcareous soils can tie up soil phosphorus in insoluble forms, making it unavailable to plants despite a relative abundance in the soil (West 1991: 305).

Currently, RM soils are associated with the best agricultural land in Moab. They are found mostly within the 300 mm[+] isohyet zone, in areas with low to moderate slopes. Geomorphological analysis (Cordova 1999; 2000) suggests that RM soils once extended further east into the Wadi ath-Thamad, where alluvial and colluvial deposits dating up through the Pottery Neolithic appear to have been constituted by eroded RM soils. In contrast, later deposits are consistent with the Yellow soils currently found on the adjacent plateau, or with sediments weathered from exposed marl or bedrock. Similarly, in the Wadi an-Nuḥayla, a colluvial terrace capped by a late Natufian or Khiamian site (ca. 10,000 B.C.E.) appears to be constituted by RM soils despite the current dominance of YS and YM soils in this region (Field 1999). In short, the semiarid to arid regions that encircle the principal area of RM soils on the plateau may represent the former limits of RM soil distribution prior to massive erosion episodes in terminal Pleistocene and early Holocene times. The timing of these erosion sequences is not entirely clear. However, the morphology of wadi terraces suggests a decline in soil erosion rates and the predominance of incision (with the notable exception of Vita-Finzi's "Younger Fill"—see below) since the end of the Early Bronze Age (ca. 2300 B.C.E.), if not earlier. This suggests that the massive erosion of RM soils on the arid margins of Moab was long completed before the Iron Age began (Cordova 1999: 195–98).

Climate Change

The above sketch of climate and ecology in the land of Moab points to a marginal setting for dry farming in the sense that over the long term, agricultural production is uncertain even in those areas capable of yielding significant returns. Of course, the low level and instability of rainfall is a major factor in this situation, but so too is the intimate relationship between aridity, land-use, ground cover, and erosion. Human degradation of the landscape has been the central dynamic within the current territory of Jordan since the mid-Holocene and remains one of the primary agricultural research and policy issues in the country today (e.g., Khresat et al. 1998). In light of the evident volatility of this ecosystem and its current highly stressed state, we must ask how comparable present climatic and environmental conditions are to those of the Iron Age.

The reconstruction of past climates is dependent on the identification of residual signatures that are several steps removed from the process being reconstructed (e.g., pollen spectra in relation to rainfall). As Goodfriend notes, all such proxies are "affected by more than one factor, therefore [their] paleoclimatic interpretation contains some degree of ambiguity" (Goodfriend 1999: 501). In the Mid-Late Holocene (ca. 3000 B.C.E.-present), human agropastoral practices have been *the* nonclimatic factor, impacting key intermediary steps between climate and signature in many cases. Hence in the southern Levant, erosion rates, the composition of plant communities, and the cycling of groundwater have all been significantly altered by human action over the past 5,000 years.

A good deal of geomorphological analysis has been conducted in both Jordan and the state of Israel on Holocene alluvial and colluvial terraces deposited in wadi bottoms. Here, changes in watershed dynamics are marked by shifts from alluvial deposition to massive hillslope erosion to streambed incision. While alluvial deposition is frequently associated with more humid conditions than pertain today, close inspection suggests that all three of these processes are often related to climate change in very localized and ambiguous ways (see Wilkinson 1999; Yair 1994). Regional (e.g., Mediterranean Basin) generalizations, of the sort made most particularly by Vita-Finzi (1969), usually breakdown within specific wadi systems (cf. van Andel *et al.* 1990 for Greece).

This said, there do appear to be two major episodes of alluvial deposition during the past 5,000 years (dated by ^{14}C and embedded artifacts) that are probably regional in scale. Within Moab, alluvial terraces in Wadi Wala (Cordova 1999, 2000), Wadi al-Karak, and Wadi an-Numayra (Donahue 1985; Donahue et al. 1997) were deposited during the fourth to third millennium (Chalcolithic–Early Bronze Age) and subsequently covered by colluvium and incised by downcutting of the streambed. In the state of Israel, very similar third millennium sequences have been studied by Rosen (1986, 1991) in the Nahal Lachish. Less certainly, Copeland and Vita-Finzi (1978) have published a date of 3950 ± 150 B.P. (2878–2118 cal B.C.E. 2 σ) from a Holocene alluvial terrace in Wadi al-Ḥasa in Jordan (Fill III). Schuldenrein and Clark (1994: 44–45) report a date of 990 ± 120 B.P. (805–1268 cal C.E., 2 σ) from what they believe is the same deposit, namely the latest of two Holocene fills that constitute the alluvial plain flanking the current streambed of the upper Wadi al-Ḥasa. Interestingly, the earlier fill in this terrace is said to be constituted by low-energy fine sand and silts (Schuldenrein and Clark 1994: 50), perhaps indicating a stable flood plain such as has been reconstructed for the fourth-third millennium deposits in Wadi Wala and Nahal Lachish. Brett Hill (2000: 15) has recently noted evidence from the Wadi al-Ḥasa survey (MacDonald 1988) showing both a Byzantine deposit (WHS 725) and the base of a Roman bridge in the channel bed against Fill III. This, he suggests supports Vita-Finzi and Copeland in dating the downcutting of the channel bed much earlier than the date obtained by Schuldenrein and Clark. While possibly coincidental, it is interesting that the radiocarbon dates from these two superimposed terraces are, as we shall see, each dated to the two most significant periods of deposition during the mid-to-late Holocene. Hence, it might be worth considering if the third millennium B.C.E. ^{14}C date published by Vita-Finzi originated in the lower terrace, while the upper fill was both late, and deposited in a complex and discontinuous manner.

The second major depositional event is Vita-Finzi's so-called Younger Fill (Bintliff 1992; Vita-Finzi 1969; Wagstaff 1981), associated with Schuldenrein and Clark's Early to Middle Islamic era date (805–1268 cal C.E.) for the latest alluvial fill in the Wadi al-Ḥasa. This is also represented in the Wadi ath-Thamad and Wadi Wala (Cordova 1999, 2000), where ^{14}C dates in the late first and early second millennium C.E. were obtained (705–980 cal C.E. 2 s, and 980–1055 cal C.E./1085–1150 cal C.E. 2 σ). This episode of alluvial deposition may have begun during the Byzantine period (fifth to seventh century C.E.; see Cordova 1999: 197). Preliminary work in the Wadi an-Nuḥayla (Field 1999) in Moab discovered a Hand-Made Geometrically-Painted Ware sherd in the latest alluvial terrace, suggesting that deposition continued until at least the eleventh to fifteenth century C.E. (see Brown

1992: 243–56). Cordova estimates that stream-bed incision in Wadi ath-Thamad and Wadi Wala ended this episode of sediment deposition sometime after the eleventh century C.E., while evidence from the Negev in Israel (Goldberg 1986; Goodfriend 1987) suggests that the current regime of incision began about 400–500 years ago.

Arlene Rosen (1995) has argued that the late third-millennium B.C.E. shift in many wadis from an agrading alluvial environment to one of hillslope erosion and/or streambed incision marks a dramatic drying of the climate at the end of the Early Bronze Age. This would coincide with the large-scale deurbanization of the southern Levant during the Early Bronze IV period (ca. 2300–1950 B.C.E.—see Palumbo 1990). Although this may well have been a global climatic event (see Dalfes et al.1997) Rosen cogently argues, that this environmental change does not in itself explain the end of EB urban society, as the subsequent reurbanization of Middle Bronze took place under these same very dry conditions. Rather, Rosen argues that climate change provided circumstances within which the contradictions of Early Bronze Age urban social formations became critical and unresolvable. At the same time, as Wilkinson (1999) notes, because the third millennium was also a period of significant settlement density throughout the Near East, the assumed independence of climatic and anthropogenic change needs to be examined critically.

Vita-Finzi's "Younger Fill" is even more problematic for precisely these same reasons. Most of these fill deposits are cross-bedded and poorly sorted, suggesting deposition in abrupt flood events. While Vita-Finz suggested climatic change, others (e.g., Wagstaff 1981) have suggested a strictly anthropogenic origin. Certainly, the fifth to seventh centuries C.E. saw widespread and intensive agricultural activity on marginal lands in the eastern Mediterranean, as did the first two centuries of Islamic expansion (Bruins 1986; Nevo 1991). Whether the "Younger Fill" is to be credited directly to erosion triggered by this agricultural activity or secondarily to the subsequent abandonment of terraces and other soil conservation installations after the eighth/ninth century remains uncertain.

Some confirmation for these major environmental shifts comes from studies of Dead Sea levels, which as a salt lake with no outlet and a very large drainage area is closely correlated with regional hydrology. Salt caves in Mt. Sedom, overlooking the western shore of the Dead Sea (Frumkin et al. 1991; 1994), have been shown to correlate by elevation and passage morphology (width/length ratio) with the elevation of the Dead Sea's surface. This work suggests that the some of the highest Dead Sea levels of the Holocene occurred during the late fourth and third millennium B.C.E. (based on ^{14}C of wood trapped in the caves when last active). This apparently wet phase is followed by a dramatic drop in the Dead Sea level beginning ca. 3900 ± 90 B.P. (2562–2280 cal B.C.E. 1σ) and bottoming out at ca. 3580 ± 80 B.P. (2112–1819 cal B.C.E. 1σ). High Dead Sea levels are also recorded during the Late Bronze Age (3100 ± 55 B.P. and 3030 ± 50 B.P.), the entire Roman Era (1990 ±50 B.P. to 1690± 50 B.P.), and again in the Early to Middle Islamic period (1100± 45 B.P. to 720 ± 40 B.P.).

The Early Bronze Age and Early/Middle Islamic highs in Dead Sea levels correlate with episodes of wadi alluviation noted above. Because Dead Sea levels reflect the amount of water entering the Basin of the Dead Sea they are potentially affected by runoff rates as well as precipitation rates. Hence again the independence of climatic and anthropogenic change is open to question.

The two periods of high Dead Sea levels not well represented in dated alluvial terraces are strikingly different from one another. The Late Bronze is amongst the least, and the Roman era is among the most, prominent post-Neolithic cultural-historic periods in south central Transjordan. Further evidence for more humid conditions in the vicinity of the Dead Sea during the Roman Era has been suggested. Fossil wood buried in the Roman siege ramp at Masada shows slightly depleted levels of ^{18}O and ^{13}C (Yakir et al. 1994; Issar and Yakir 1997) when compared to modern samples, suggesting reduced evaporation enrichment and hence a more humid climate.

It seems clear that at some point in the Middle Holocene, precipitation levels were a good deal higher than they are today, and that a significant drying of the environment occurred in late prehistoric or early historic times. Most likely, as Rosen (1995) has already argued, this change was a contributing factor to the dramatic end of Early Bronze Age urban culture. After this point, however, it becomes very difficult to distinguish confidently between climatic and anthropogenic change in the landscape of Moab. The Iron Age (ca. 1200–525 B.C.E.) appears to have been a dry period, relatively comparable to the recent past in terms of precipitation rates and weather patterns. One can reasonably suggest that the Iron Age landscape of Moab presented more surface vegetation, and hence a less depleted soil profile, than is found today. It is also likely that relic forest stands formed part of the Iron Age landscape of Moab, as they still do today further south and north in the vicinity of Shaubak and 'Ajlun respectively. Overall, however, it seems that modern environmental conditions are at least reasonable proxies for conditions during the Iron Age.

From these environmental conditions we can derive certain probable structures of life in the Iron Age. Agricultural production would of necessity involve a winter-cropping system, with a single grain harvest in the late spring. Farming would have involved significant risk of crop failure, and outside of the 300 mm+ isohyet zone such events would have been regular. In such zones agriculture would require intensive strategies such as runoff harvesting and floodwater farming in wadi bottoms or extensive strategies such as multiyear fallows and seed conservation through strategic late planting. Viticulture would have been limited to intensely prepared hill-slopes in higher rainfall zones. Pastoralism was likely to have been very important and to have involved seasonal mobility. Both in the recent past (Lancaster and Lancaster 1995) and perhaps also in the Roman (Banning 1985) and Chalcolithic periods (Henry 1992) this involved movement from the wadi bottoms, the slopes of the *Ghawr* and the steppe in the winter to the central plateau in the summer.

Environmental conditions helped ensure the perpetuation of certain forms of practical knowledge and structured practice over several millennia. At the same time, these very environmental conditions ensured that the "land of Moab" as an inhabited landscape was both synchronically and diachronically diverse. Everywhere there were paradoxes and conditional circumstances. Rainwater was more abundant in the central plateau, but groundwater was more abundant on the edges of the major wadi systems. The productivity of land, and particularly hillslopes, varied directly with the production strategies being employed (intensive/extensive; agriculture/pastoralism). Mobility and spatial continuity were deeply embedded in broader questions of regional political organization, extractive exploitation, and personal security.

Similarly, Alex Joffe (1993: 24) has argued that in the premodern era the southern Levant was dominated by small kinship groups that served as fundamental units into which other entities were decomposable. This, he argues, is an adaptation to the risk and diversity of the southern Levantine environment. At one level, this is an undeniably insightful suggestion, as extensive, low-density, highly mobile occupation of the land is a clear and oft-attested approach to living in the marginal environment of the southern Levant. At the same time, the landscape of Moab has supported episodes of dense settlement and intensive agriculture (e.g., Byzantine and current "Hashemite" periods), as well as periods in which year-round settlement was sparse and agriculture sporadic (e.g., Late Bronze Age and Late Ottoman period). Small kin groups are significant in all of these cases. However, when examined closely the specific articulation and social position of these groups varies considerably. Hence, one cannot explain the landscape of Moab at any particular moment in this history of change as the by-product of a single formula. Even if considered only in terms of production, the landscape of Moab has always been historically embedded in specific political economies that are contextually defined (Routledge 1996a).

Of course, landscape cannot be reduced to the realm of production. In juxtaposing biblical and environmental perspectives on the land of Moab, we have sought to highlight the land of Moab as more than the space between borders on a map. Moab was not constructed in a vacuum, nor was its hegemony a mere product of the mind's eye. Rather, the land of Moab was an active claim about an actual place, a violent assertion of the right to name this land and tell its story as ones own. In the following chapters we will explore this claim, the conditions under which it was made, and the consequences of its assertion in specific historical circumstances.

Chapter 4

Beginnings I: The Late Bronze Age

> *Kill your lord and be like us: then you will have peace!*
> —*Attributed to Abdi-Ashirta* Amarna Letter *EA 74.*

Retrodiction and selective amnesia are among the state's primary histori-cal tools, making Pilgrims into Americans and Gauls into Frenchmen. As a counterstroke, Bourdieu (1999) suggests that we define the moment before the state in all of its historical possibilities (i.e., paths not taken or even forcibly suppressed) as a strategy to avoid "thinking the state" when theo-rizing the conditions of its existence. Moab presents us with some peculiar difficulties in this regard. The term first appears in ancient Near Eastern texts during the Late Bronze IIB period (ca. 1300–1200 B.C.E.). Yet, as we saw in Chapter 3, this "land of Moab" had contested meanings and mul-tiple possibilities. Hence, retrodiction from the Iron Age polity to a Bronze Age ancestor is neither straightforward nor necessary. Indeed, in this chap-ter I will argue that the hegemonies of Late Bronze Age "city-states" con-trasted markedly with those of Iron Age ethnoterritorial states, highlighting the distinct ability of state hegemony to recast old terms in reference to new social forms.

Moab, Egypt, and Ramses II

In the Upper Egyptian Temple of Luxor, at the north end of the east wall of Ramses II's court, Moab enters the extant documentary record in a scene typical of what might be called Ramses II's "minor wars" (Kitchen 1964; Gaballa 1976: 108–12). Here Ramses II faces an abandoned fortified set-tlement, from which prisoners are being removed. The latest in a palimp-sest of two superimposed texts names this city as Shabtuna in central Syria; however, the original label reads, "Town which the mighty arm of pharaoh, life prosperity health, plundered in [the] land of Moab: B[w]trt."

There is no year formula or any other indication of a specific calendrical date preserved in this scene, although a consideration (Haider 1987: 119–22,

Kitchen 1992: 28, 31 n. 42; contra Timm 1989: 20–21) of the known campaigns of Ramses II suggests a date in the ninth year of this pharaoh's reign (ca. 1270 B.C.E.). The location of B[w]trt is also uncertain. Ever since Kitchen (1964: 64–65) drew attention to the south Transjordanian toponym Rababatora in the Byzantine gazetteer *Taubla Peutingeriana*, scholars have looked to place the site in the vicinity of modern ar-Rabba (Areopolis/Rabbat Mo'ab), or at least south of Wadi Mujib (Görg 1989: 115–17; Knauf 1985; Timm 1989: 16–19; Weippert 1995; Worschech 1990a: 126). However, these suggestions remain tentative at best (Weippert 1995: 338).

Working outward from the scene, one must note its generic nature. The giant Ramses before a captured city, with downturned bow, spear, or extended arm repeats itself numerous times at Luxor, Karnak, the Ramesseum, et cetera. The fortified settlement with two superimposed ramparts seems to represent an Egyptian iconographic category "Levantine fortified town" (see Badawy 1954: Type 2[b]). Similarly, the prisoners themselves are given a certain "ethnic" specificity as Syrians (Haider 1987: 109), but this is contained within Egypt's rather limited iconographic options for representing foreigners (Baines 1996; Leahy 1995; on literary representations, see Loprieno 1988). The scene, therefore, is specific only to the point of depicting the capture of a generic Levantine settlement, witnessed by the ease with which the referent of the scene could be changed by plastering over a new name (from B[w]trt to Sbdn/Shabtuna). The inscriptional elements are similarly generic, both in the language of Ramses' victory ("Town which the mighty arm of pharaoh, LPH, plundered . . .) and in the themes of rebellion and moral failure presented as implicit causes for Ramses II's actions (Grimal 1986: 649–702, esp. 670; Liverani 1990: 126–59).

As for more specific social and economic information, we can note that Moab is written with the determinative sign for a foreign land or hilly country. Generally, this sign marks a spatial totality, that is to say a geographical or political entity, rather than a regional subdivision or a group of people (Gardiner 1957: 488 n. 25). Furthermore, the settlement B[w]trt is designated as a *dmi* (town), which seems, in the New Kingdom at least (Gardiner 1947: II 205*), to be contrasted with *whywt* (village/hamlet) on the basis of scale, although inconsistency in the Egyptian use of these terms suggests that syntactical factors besides scale are involved in these word choices. The title *niwt* (city) is usually denied to foreign settlements (Redford 1997: 211 n. 5).

So what does this mean, especially given Manfred Weippert's (1979: 27) conclusion that we cannot establish "whether Ramses II conquered a fortress, a fortified city, a village or only a nomad's camp in Moab"? Redford (1997: 217 n. 17) notes that despite variable use within Egypt, New Kingdom Egyptian texts are consistent in using *dmi* and *whywt* to distinguish between central and dependent settlements in Canaan.[1] Yet here the key factor may well be the role of the settlement in the visual or written narrative under consideration, rather than scale per se. Hence, although we can conclude that B[w]trt (Butartu) was almost certainly a settlement, rather than a nomad's camp, we cannot assume any specific scale for this settlement. It was likely important relative to its surrounding territory, but this may simply reflect an absence of rivals, rather than any absolute qualities of the settlement itself.

Finally, if correctly reconstructed, Ramses II commands the royal prince to speak with the *wr* (lit. "great one") of the foreigners.[2] This title is relatively general, but with connotations of significant rank (Erman and Grapow 1926: 326–31). In this sense *wr* contrasts with titles implying a lower standing or contexts with less stratification, such as *ʿ3* often used for "shaykhs" of Shasu nomads (Giveon 1971: 257–58; Redford 1990: 70). So, while the scene itself is generic, it does serve to categorize the events involved within a specifically Egyptian taxonomy of world order. Ramses II campaigns against a Levantine walled town (as opposed to a village or a Nubian settlement), inhabited by "Syrians" (as opposed to "Shasu nomads," "Hittites," or "Libyans"), ruled by a *wr* (as opposed to an *ʿ3*) in a territory (as opposed to an *ethné*, or province) named Moab. The question remains, however, whether this Egyptian taxonomy can be meaningfully converted to the categories and measures of modern academic discourse.

Beyond this wall relief, only two further references to Moab are known from ancient Egyptian sources,[3] both being found in lists of Western Asian toponyms dating to the reign of Ramses II (see Kitchen 1969: 185, 215–16).[4] The preambles to these and other similar toponymic lists from the New Kingdom indicate that they served to evoke the boundaries of the known world as the proper terrain for the realization of the pharaoh's dominion. As Mario Liverani (1990: 51–65) has pointed out, in the royal ideology of the New Kingdom, the pharaoh is continually attaining the outer limits of these boundaries by conquest and submission, establishing order at the very frontier of chaos. Therefore, while the presence of Moab on these lists may indicate a heightened awareness of this territory during the reign of Ramses II, we should not read too much into its co-presence with contemporary superpowers such as Assur or Hatti.

Evidently the scribes of Ramses II knew of a place named Moab by the second quarter of the thirteenth century B.C.E.; indeed, Ramses II himself seems likely to have been there on a military campaign. What we do not know from the Egyptian evidence is precisely what sort of Moab Ramses II visited. To what extent is this Moab historically continuous with and equivalent to the Moab of some four centuries in the future, a polity that seems to be just beginning the transformative process of state formation?

Egypt and Northern Transjordan

As a result of his pioneering surveys of Transjordan in the 1930s, Nelson Glueck (1970) famously suggested that the plateau south of Wadi az-Zarqa was largely devoid of sedentary occupation during the Middle and Late Bronze Ages (ca. 1950–1200 B.C.E.). Critics have frequently pointed out the empirical inadequacies of Glueck's synthesis (e.g., Mattingly 1983; Sauer 1986). However, after almost seventy years of further archaeological research one must at least admit that the Middle and Late Bronze Ages are not particularly obtrusive in the archaeological record of Transjordan in comparison with either the Early Bronze Age or the Iron Age (see Palumbo 1994). Furthermore, this apparent abatement is more notable in the south than in the north (including the Jordan Valley), provided one defines "south" as south of Wadi Ḥisban or Madaba rather than Wadi az-Zarqa.

We do well at this point to remember the position of Transjordan within the empire of New Kingdom Egypt. Egyptian involvement in the Levant shifts from sporadic military campaigns to a more fixed position with regularized tributary relations sometime soon after Thutmose III conquers a coalition of local rulers at Megiddo in approximately 1457 B.C.E. (Redford 1992: 148–60). The northern border of the empire is rather loosely defined, although Egypt's ability to extract tribute declines rapidly in Syria/Lebanon north of the Lebanese Biqa', where first Mittanian and then Hittite kings effectively dominate local rulers. As Hittite power in Syria expands, Egyptian rule in the southern Levant enters a new phase in the reigns of Seti I (1294–1279 B.C.E.) and his son Ramses II (1279–1213 B.C.E.), marked by an increased and more densely networked physical presence of Egyptians "on the ground" (Hasel 1998; Morris 2001: 802–8; Oren 1984; Redford 1990; 1992: 192–213; Weinstein 1981; cf. Higginbotham 2000). However, even during this last phase (Nineteenth to mid-Twentieth Dynasty, about 1300–1140 B.C.E.), Egyptian rule is relatively loosely organized and focused primarily on a limited number of key settlements located along trade and travel routes (e.g., Deir al-Balah, Gaza, Tell esh-Sharia, Aphek, Jaffa, Beth Shean, Kamid al-Lodz; see Redford 1990, 1992: 203–7). These Egyptian outposts are generally located at settlements proximate to major Canaanite regional centers, rather than at the regional centers themselves (cf. Finkelstein 1996a: Maps 1 and 2).

It appears that northern Transjordan was on the periphery of direct Egyptian imperial concern and southern Transjordan was outside of it altogether. However, it is probably incorrect to speak of borders in relation to the Egyptian presence in northern Transjordan. Egypt's focus was nodal and parasitic, apparently aimed at extracting tribute and controlling travel and trade routes rather than governing per se. Ideologically, of course, Egypt acknowledged no "outside" to its empire, no space that the pharaoh did not in theory command (Liverani 1990: 44–58). In practice, however, the outside was defined either by strong opponents that had to be acknowledged (e.g., Mittani, Hatti, Assyria) or by a dwindling of interest brought on perhaps by some ratio of logistic difficulty to evident loot. In this latter sense most of the Transjordanian Plateau was outside of the empire most of the time, brought in sporadically by unusually adventuresome campaigns. At the same time, this area was deeply embedded in the economic, political, and social relations that spun outward from the historical conjunctures of Egyptian imperialism.

Pella (Akkadian Piḫil—modern Ṭabaqat Faḥl) is the only city-state east of the Jordan River and south of the Yarmouk River unequivocally mentioned in the Amarna letters (EA 255, 256; see Albright 1943; Knapp 1993: 42–48; Moran 1992: 308–19; Smith 1973: 23–33).[5] Trade routes to the north evidently passed through Pella, since Mut-Baḥlu the city ruler, defends himself against the accusation of having raided an Egyptian caravan bound for Mittanni (Ḫanagalbat; see EA 255) and swears that he is not harboring the fugitive ruler of Ashtarot, with whom he is evidently a close ally (EA 255). Ashtarot, probably located just across the modern Jordan-Syria border at Tall al-Ashtara, was on the route to Damascus, suggesting that international trade was at least one of the links between these two rulers.

Pella's importance is not surprising, as it is positioned in the foothills of the plateau near one of the principal crossing points of the Jordan River (Koucky 1992), opposite the major Egyptian outpost of Beth Shean. The recent downdating of the "Palace" at Pella[6] from LB IA to LB IB/LB IIA means that this building, along with its carved ivory boxes (Potts 1987), two cuneiform tablets, lapis lazuli beads, and Mycenaean and Cypriot pottery, overlapped with the era of the Amarna letters (Bourke 1997: 107–10; Bourke et al.1994: 104–9; 1998: 196–201).

Stelae erected by Seti I[7] and Ramses II[8] show that by the early Nineteenth Dynasty Egyptians found it necessary to campaign on more than one occasion in northern Transjordan. Indeed, one of the Seti I stele (Rowe 1930: 24–29; Smith 1973: 28–29) explicitly names Pella as the partner of Hamath (in Syria) in a coalition threatening the sites of Beth Shean and Rehob. More vaguely, a second stele of Seti I refers to defeating 'apiru (see below) in northern Transjordan (Rowe 1930: 29–30).

This increased military concern may be reflected at Tall as-Sa'idiyya, about 26 km southwest of Pella in the Jordan Valley. Here, Jonathan Tubb (1988: 40–43; 1995: 140; Tubb et al. 1996: 24–30) has excavated what he classifies as an Egyptian "governor's residency" dating from the late Nineteenth through mid-Twentieth Dynasties (1250–1140 B.C.E.). This category of LB II–IR IAbuilding is well known from Palestine (Oren 1984, 1992), and best illustrated at Beth Shean (buildings 1500, 1700) where hieroglyphic-inscribed door-posts actually name the occupants as titled Egyptian officials (Ward in James 1966: 160–79). As with most examples, the published evidence from Tall as-Sa'idiyya is less compelling then that of Beth Shean, although large quantities of Egyptian style storage jars are reported from this strata (Tubb 1988: Fig.19: 14; Tubb 1995:140).[9] A Twentieth Dynasty outpost would help explain the site's LB IIB–IR IA cemetery (Pritchard 1980; Tubb 1988: 73–80; 1990: 29–37, 38–42; Tubb and Dorrell 1991: 67–72; Tubb et al. 1996: 36–39), where both grave goods and individuated burial practices are closely paralleled at the Egyptian outpost of Deir al-Balaḥ (Dothan 1979).

Precious Things: Offerings, Gods, and Dead Relations

Across northern Transjordan, Late Bronze Age sites are consistent in defying expectations. Overall, these sites are generally rather small (see Figure 4.1 and Table 4.1), and although one can define settlement clusters in a number of cases (e.g., Dayr 'Alla—van der Steen 1996; Jerash—Braemer 1992; Amman—McGovern 1992; Younker 1999), these do not seem to resolve themselves into more than a two-tiered hierarchy of site sizes. At the same time, most of the excavated LB sites have revealed either a major "public" building and/or a temple or significant ritual deposit. "Wealthy" communal (multiple successive burials) tombs are quite common,[10] as are imported objects, especially Cypriot and Mycenaean pottery, Egyptian silicates and related jewelry, and Syro-Mesopotamian cylinder seals.

Insofar as we are able to examine the find-spots of these imported items,[11] they are overwhelmingly associated with funerary,[12] ritual,[13] and "palatial"[14] contexts, probably in that order (cf. Hankey 1981 and Leonard and Cline 1998 for Palestine). In general, temple and tomb assemblages parallel each other in their focus on what might be termed presentation vessels.[15] Primary (bowls and kraters) and elaborate (pedestalled bowls and chalices) serving vessels are very common, as are vessels for the decanting of liquids (jugs, pilgrims'/lentoid flasks). Faunal remains within tombs show that these vessels were often presented in conjunction with, and at times contained, food offerings that seem intended for the dead (Horowitz 2001; Lev-Tov and Maher 2001). Containers for aromatics (juglets, alabastron, stirrup jars) and oil lamps are also common, as are objects carried on the body, such as jewelry, toggle pins, cylinder seals, and small weapons.

Temple assemblages compare reasonably well[16] to Late Bronze Age texts from Syria describing both whole and burnt offerings (e.g., Clemens 2001; Fleming 2000; del Olmo Lete 1999). For example, the calendrical texts (fourteenth-century B.C.E.) marking ritual observances by month, found in the so-called 'Diviner's Archive' at Emar in northern Syria, include the following offerings to be made on the twenty-seventh day of the month of Abî: "one gallon and one quart of (barley-) mash, a jar, one presentation vessel of barley beer, one presentation vessel of wine, one sheep, one dove, honey, oil, ghee, beef, venison, fish, apricots, soured milk, figs, all kinds of fruits, four Hurrian(?) birds" (Fleming 2000: 287, Emar 452, ll. 43–45).

This particular text is also interesting, as it raises the question of the relations between temple and tomb offerings. The twenty-fifth day of Abî includes an offering ceremony at the gate of the cemetery, which is then sealed, perhaps in preparation for the disappearance of the waxing moon

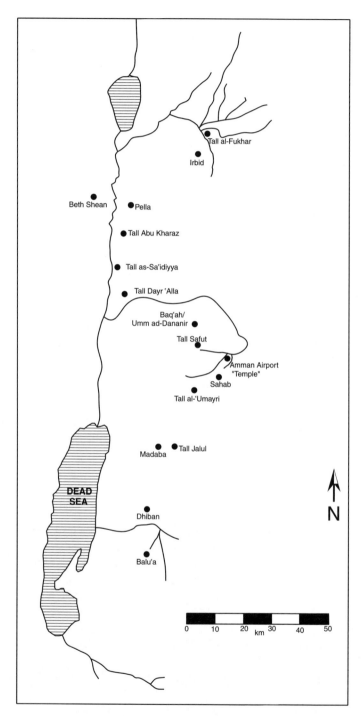

Figure 4.1. Excavated Late Bronze Age sites in Transjordan.

TABLE 4.1. Late Bronze Age site sizes and features

Site	SIZE (Late Bronze)	"Palatial" building	"Temple" assemblage	City wall	Mycenean/Cypriot pottery
Pella/Tabaqat Fahl	≈ 10.0 ha[1]	Yes	Yes	No?	Yes
Irbid	≤ 10 ha.	Yes[2]	Yes[3]	Yes	Yes
Dayr 'Alla	≈ 4.5 ha.[4]	No?	Yes	No?	Yes
T. al-Fukhar	≈ 1.0 ha.[5] Acropolis	Yes		Yes	Yes
Abu Kharaz	≈ 1.1 ha.[6]/ 2.75 ha.[7]	?	Yes	Yes	Yes
Safut	≈ 1.73 ha.	Yes?	?	Yes	?
T. al-Umayri	≈ 1.17 ha.	Yes	?	?	Yes
Umm ad-Dananir	< 2.5 ha.[8]	No?	Yes?	?	Yes
Sahab	≈ 2.0 ha.[9]	Yes	?	Yes	Yes

1. Assuming the MB-LB city wall in Fields IV and II forms a rough oval following present contours of the tall.
2. Lenzen (1989); Lenzen et al. (1985).
3. Lenzen (1988); Lenzen, et al. (1985: 155).
4. If settlement reached as far as LB material in units C/P13 + 14 at the base of the tall on the southwest side (Ibrahim and Kooji 1997: 107-8)
5. Assuming the LB wall surrounding the acropolis delineates the limits of LB settlement.
6. Assuming the LB on the acropolis delineates the limits of LB settlement.
7. Total area of mound.
8. McGovern (1989) assumes LB occupation upslope from the excavated *Quadratbau* structure, but this was not demonstrated in excavation. Whatever the case, the LB occupation seems smaller than the maximum extent of the site.
9. Ibrahim (1987).

before the new moon of Dagan (chief deity of Emar) rose at the beginning of the next month (see Fleming 2000: 192–95). The equivalent month of Abu in the Mesopotamian calendar is associated with veneration of the dead (Cohen 1993: 319–21; Tsukimoto 1985).[17] As Fleming (2000: 188–89) notes, although the Mesopotamian month name does not seem to have derived from Akkadian *abu* = "father," at least one scribe at Emar understood it in this sense raising the possibility that the offerings at the *abû* of various temples on the twenty-fifth and twenthy-sixth days of the month (in conjunction with the sealing of the cemetery gates) were understood as offerings made to ancestors.

Here I do not wish to digress into the sticky issue of whether or not the dead were worshipped in Syria-Palestine or whether phrases attested at Emar, Ugarit, and Nuzi, such as "god of the father" or "my gods and my dead," referred to the elevation of ancestors to the rank of deities.[18] What we can say is that the presentation of things was a central component of ones relation to both deities and the dead. Furthermore, the very repetition of these presentations structured a world of human experience. The constant returning to the same tomb implies its latent presence in the life one lived between deaths. In short, remembering the tomb and reusing it are logically inseparable acts. The leaving behind of precious things only intensifies this experience, making both temple and tomb the site of sacrifices not everyone could make.

We should, however, qualify the role we have just assigned to communal tombs. In all periods, but particularly in the Late Bronze Age, people were buried in a variety of ways (see Gonen 1992). Hence, although the use of caves for multiple successive burials was common in the southern Levant from the Chalcolithic through the Persian period (4500–330 B.C.E.), it does not follow that most people were buried in this fashion. For one thing, we have evidence for only a tiny portion of the Late Bronze Age population. Israel Finkelstein (1996a: 244) estimates the Late Bronze Age II population of Palestine at about 90,000 (89,500—Finkelstein 1996a: Table 1) on the basis of the size and number of known archaeological sites. While this figure certainly varied over the course of the Late Bronze Age (cf. Bunimovitz 1995; Gonen 1984) it seems a workable and conservative rough running average. Presuming a high mortality regime, reasonable demographic models suggest that in a stable population of 90,000 about 985,871–1,422,576 people would have died over the 356 years of the Late Bronze Age (1540–1186 B.C.E.).[19] Rivka Gonen (1992) notes the excavation of at least 815 Late Bronze Age tombs in Palestine, of which at least 173 were multiple successive burials in caves.[20] This suggests that perhaps 2,000–10,000 bodies are accounted for archaeologically, so clearly we are missing a good number of the dead.[21] Something like 36–49 percent of the expected dead would have been children under the age of five, so perhaps we might account for their absence from the archaeological record in terms of age specific burial customs and taphonomic processes. However, this still leaves us an estimated 633,027–722,384 dead to account for. Doubling, tripling, even quadrupling the archaeologically known tombs will not significantly change this situation.

What, then, were these communal tombs? In Bronze Age contexts single tomb populations vary considerably (from only two to as many as three hundred individuals) and in large samples (e.g., McGovern 1986: 295–314) show no consistently systematic selection (across tombs) for age or gender with the exception of neonates. Hence, in any particular tomb criteria for the inclusion of burials are unclear, as are the reasons for its final closure. In the case of Ugarit, in northwest Syria, many houses have tombs for multiple burials directly beneath their floors accessible by a stairway internal to the house (Salles 1995). This fits well with contemporary textual evidence indicating that tombs played a significant role in family identity, whatever one concludes regarding the divinity of ancestors (see above). Although a small number of similar tombs have been found in urban Middle and Late Bronze Age contexts in Palestine (Gonen 1992: 139–41), the direct connection between houses and communal tombs is not so clear in the southern Levant. Still, a domestic or descent group of some sort remains the most contextually reasonable referent for the continued use of the communal tombs we have been considering. When such groups are predicated not merely on descent but also on honor, property, name, and tenuous class privilege, continuity and identification across generations are centrally important. Such identities are of necessity enacted, and hence historical and indeterminate in their implications and reproduction. It seems likely that tomb use, funerary feasts, and funerary offerings were very much part of this enactment, with their scale and longevity tied, perhaps, to the fate of particular names across generations (cf. Gillespie 2000).

Aegean Pottery and the Amman Airport "Temple"

Along these lines, we can learn several interesting things by looking specifically at the pottery imported from the Aegean. Leonard (1987; cf. Leonard 1994) notes that of Furumark's 336 Mycenaean pottery shapes (Furumark1941; cf. Mountjoy 1986) approximately 70 have been found in the Levant, of which 24 are found in Transjordan. However, 14 of these forms are found only at the highly unusual Amman Airport "Temple" and DAJ Tomb 1 at Pella (see below). Outside these two contexts, variations on the so-called squat stirrup jar (FS 171–80) are by far the most common Mycenaean shapes, and in general Mycenaean imports are focused rather narrowly on small containers likely used for aromatic oils and unguents (Leonard 1987: 264). This is interesting, as it is precisely these same forms (stirrup jars, pyxis and alabastra, pilgrim's/lentoid flasks) that are imitated in large quantities both in tombs that contain Mycenaean imports (e.g., Dajani

1970) and in those that do not (e.g., Fischer 1997). Hence, it seems clear that vessel and content were closely associated and significant to funerary rituals in a manner that goes beyond their status as imported exotica.

One of the larger caches of Aegean pottery in the Near East comes from one of the most unusual Late Bronze Age sites yet excavated in Transjordan. The Amman Airport "Temple" was a single building measuring 15 × 15 m in the so-called Quadratbau style (Figure 4.2; see Fritz 1971; Ottoson 1980: 101–4; Wright 1966; Yassine 1988: 61–64). It was located about 5 km northeast of central Amman at the Amman Civil Airport and was subject to three salvage excavations (Harding 1958; Hennessy 1966, 1985, 1989; Herr 1983a, b) before being destroyed by runway expansion in 1978. The building appears to have been isolated[22] and was distinguished not only by large quantities of imported pottery,[23] bronze weapons,[24] jewelry, scarabs, cylinder seals (Tournay 1967; Ward 1964), and imported stone vessels,[25] but also by several thousand small fragments of burned human bone (Hennessy 1985: 97; Little, in Herr 1983a: 47–55).

Despite the density of finds, the structure's four phases covered a brief period (somewhere between 1300 and 1200/1150 B.C.E.).[26] In contrast to the chronologically homogeneous local pottery, the imported material ranges widely in its date of manufacture from perhaps 3500 to about 1200 B.C.E.,[27] raising the rather obvious question of why so many old objects were offered together. The Levantine trade in Egyptian stone bowls during the Middle and Late Bronze Ages included many Predynastic and Early Dynastic examples that may have represented the fruits of tomb robbing, rather than a concern for antiques per se (e.g., Brandl1984: 61–62). However, the fact that objects several centuries old at the time of deposition were found in most of the artifact categories at the Amman Airport "Temple" suggests that curation was a major aspect in the formation of this assemblage.

As burned human bone and small items of personal adornment were found along with ash pockets in foundation trenches and subfloor fills,[28] it is assumed that both bones and objects were deposited as part of the construction of the building as well as during its use. J. Basil Hennessy (1985, 1989) interpreted the remains as evidence for a cult of human sacrifice, while Larry Herr (1983a, b) suggested that the building was a crematorium.[29] Hennessy relies on a limited, selective, and (frankly) idiosyncratic presentation of textual evidence. Herr invokes the influence of ethnic Hittites to explain the cremation but seems to ignore the intimate relationship between the initial deposition of human bones and offerings and the construction of the building. Both explanations divert our attention from the primary fact of this short-lived complex, namely that it is quite odd. Rather than explaining it away, we should incorporate this oddity into our understanding of the site.

As noted above, a number of architectural analogues for the Amman

Airport "Temple" have been identified from Middle and Late Bronze Age contexts in the southern Levant under the label of Quadratbau structures. At least two and perhaps three of these[30] are located in the greater Amman area (McGovern 1989; Yassine 1988: 61–64; Waheeb 1992), although only one has produced evidence that is at all comparable to the Amman Airport "Temple."[31] In excavations at the LB IB-IIA site of Ḥirbat Umm ad-Dananir, about 24 km northwest of the Amman Airport "Temple," Patrick McGovern excavated approximately one-third of what he considered a Quadratbau structure (McGovern 1989: 128–34).[32] Here McGovern found a thick subfloor and foundation trench deposit of animal bones,[33] pottery,[34]

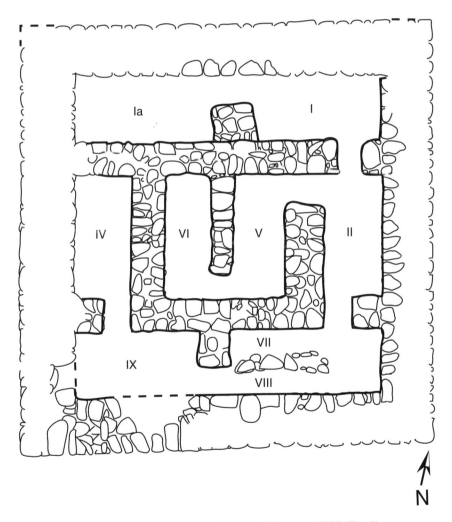

Figure 4.2. The Amman Airport "Temple" (after Hennessy 1966: Fig. 2).

and miniature vessels, but no human bone or imported objects. A direct comparison of Umm ad-Dananir to the Amman Airport "Temple" emphasizes the degree to which the latter is a transformation of the former (human bone vs. animal bone; curated imported objects vs. local wares).

If we accept with Herr (1983b) that the Amman Airport "Temple" is a funerary site, then the curated artifacts could be explained by the exhumation of bodies and offerings for renewed deposition. Alternatively, whether temple or tomb, we could assume that the imported offerings were objects long held back from the gods and the dead. In either case, it seems evident that in addition to the aesthetic qualities and exotic origins of the objects, their specific histories were also significant. The Amman Airport "Temple" seems to ratchet up, if you will, the basic Late Bronze Age themes of offerings and the dead. In this sense, the Amman Airport "Temple" represents the extreme possibilities resident in the ritual complex of the Late Bronze Age. However, as we shall see below, the extremes of the Amman Airport "Temple" are not an aberration and serve rather to make clear the logic of ritual practices carried out elsewhere on a smaller scale.

Pella DAJ Tombs

If not for the political turmoil of 1970–71, the finds of the Amman Airport "temple" may not have seemed quite so unique. In 1963 and 1964, the Jerash office of the Department of Antiquities carried out salvage excavations of about fifteen tombs at Tall al-Husn, adjacent to Pella (Ṭabaqat Faḥl). This included a cluster of eleven tombs dating to LB II–IR IA in what is now area XI of the University of Sydney excavations (Bourke and Sparks 1995: 149–50). The very large assemblage of finds from these tombs was dislocated and largely lost during the civil unrest that culminated in open fighting between the Palestine Liberation Army and the Hashemite government. A 1971 inventory documented 612 surviving objects, of which 229 still retained some provenance information when study by the Sydney team began in 1985 (Bourke and Sparks 1995: 151).

Study notes by visiting scholars and eyewitness accounts (e.g., Smith 1973: 13–14; Yassine 1988: 41 n. 11) indicate that the original assemblage included at least 2 anthropoid sarcophagi which no longer survive,[35] as many as 35–50 Mycenaean vessels, of which 5 survive,[36] and over 100 Cypriot Base Ring and White Slip Ware vessels, of which 12 survive. The surviving collection (Bourke and Sparks 1995: 159–66) also includes Egyptian-style pottery (8 vessels) and gypsum, alabaster, and finely worked basalt bowls (21 vessels). Perhaps most astonishingly, excavations by the Sydney team have uncovered the entry shaft (Sydney Tomb 106) to what appears to have been the wealthiest tomb complex (the interconnected DAJ Tombs 1 and 2). Laid in the *dromos* of this entry passage were three adults, including one male whose ankles were shackled with copper/bronze manacles and who appears to have been executed in situ (see Bourke et al. 1994: 116–17; Bourke and Sparks 1995: 166; Bourke 1997: 109–10; Walmsley et al. 1993: 190).[37]

Given the potentially long life of these tombs, and the possibility of artifact curation, we cannot reconstruct their precise date on currently published evidence.[38] What we can say is that at some point after the middle of the fourteenth century B.C.E. one of the richer assemblages of tomb offerings yet know from Late Bronze Age Canaan began to accumulate in DAJ Tombs 1 and 2 at Pella. Yet, these tombs do not simply signify wealth. Much as in the Amman Airport "Temple," a ritual "poetics" of offerings and death envelops the unusual quantities of imported items. Furthermore, the internment and execution of the shackled man,[39] makes clear the exclusionary logic of elite mortuary ritual that we have otherwise only inferred from absences (e.g., insufficient numbers of tombs, few "poor" tombs, etc.). While this figure is unusual in a Late Bronze Age context, DAJ Tombs 1–2 otherwise contain the same categories of objects we have already enumerated for northern Transjordan. Hence, in one sense these tombs simply extend the logic of offerings from things to people, thereby highlighting rather graphically the different relations people might have with these LB tombs (e.g., offerer versus offering).

Exchange, Consumption, Alienation

We can better appreciate how these piecemeal observations come together if we look at the relationship between the offering of objects and the particular social formations evidenced in the Late Bronze Age of northern Transjordan. International exchange and long-distance trade are, of course, classic themes of the Late Bronze Age in the eastern Mediterranean (e.g., Knapp and Cherry 1994; Cline 1994). Scholars (Bleiberg 1996; Liverani 1979a, 1990: 205–73; Pintore 1978; Zaccagnini 1973, 1987) who have focused on royal exchange, particularly as reflected in the Amarna letters, have produced a rather elegant model of a Maussian reciprocal gift economy (Mauss 1990 [1925]), as refracted through the writings of Karl Polanyi (Polanyi 1957). Scholars (Sherratt and Sherratt 1991) who have focused on the archaeological evidence for long-distance trade have constructed an equally elegant model of market expansion by means of conspicuous consumption. Neither position is total in the sense of producing a coherent, logically closed account of the evidence, but then again, closure itself seems inimical to the evidence.

The "Rome school" (i.e., Liverani and Zaccagnini) clearly recognizes that Mauss's model of gift exchange as simple reciprocity does not fully capture the realities of royal gift exchange in the Late Bronze Age (Liverani 1990: 206–23; Zaccagnini 1973; 1987). A lack of interest in acquisition is seldom even feigned, and an unrecompensed gift seems (against Maussian expectations) to threaten shame for the one who gives without receiving. These apparent aberrations are explained rather ingeniously by Mario Liverani (1990: 206–23; see also Zaccagnini 1987: 58–60) as the result of two ideologically distinct spheres of local and international exchange, only partially integrated and possessing distinct logics and discourses. As the domain of prestige, marked by the unreciprocated accumulation of goods (i.e., tribute) at a cosmological center (i.e., the palace), the local/internal sphere is the focal point and end goal of acquisition. Ideologically, in the local sphere both goods and honor are obliged to move in only one direction—inward to the king. From this perspective, the acquisition of foreign goods, desirable for their workmanship, aesthetic qualities and categorical exoticism, entail significant risks. They must be acquired by entering into relationships and giving things away. Reciprocity is vital, as it is this (and only this) that distinguishes gifts from tribute and colleagues from vassals (Liverani 1990: 255–66). The primacy of the local sphere and the threat of symbolic incorporation (i.e., treating gifts as tribute) form the subtext for the not-so-subtle emphasis on reciprocal acquisition in the international sphere.

Clearly, however, international exchange was more than the movement of gifts between kings. Most dramatically revealed in the Ulu Burin shipwreck (Pulak 1998), archaeological evidence shows quite clearly the large scale, and diverse origins, of goods shipped around the eastern Mediterranean Basin. Both Liverani and Zaccagnini accept the existence (even commonness) of private merchants and suggest that, in many cases, the rhetoric of gift exchange is an ideologically necessary screen for what amounts to commercial trade between kingdoms. Hence, one might be justified in wondering if Mauss's model (in its Polyanian form) is a hindrance to understanding Late Bronze Age trade, or at least a convention whose applicability is limited to a small number of official transactions.

From this perspective, Arjun Appadurai's (1986) influential reorientation of anthropological interests from production and exchange to consumption is rather attractive. In particular, Appadurai argues that a focus on desire/demand, rather than reciprocity, provided a way of transcending the gift/commodity—primitive/complex dualism that plagues the anthropology of exchange. Appadurai (1986: 30) suggests that consumption is productively considered as a means of both sending and receiving social messages, of both being fashioned as a person in a particular sociocultural context and creatively fashioning oneself within that context. In this regard, he gives particular attention to luxury goods (Appadurai 1986: 36–41) as objects with rhetorical and symbolic uses that meet essentially political needs, and yet often precipitate significant changes in the production and circulation of utilitarian goods. Here, quite clearly, we see all the elements of what has subsequently become the anthropology of consumption (Miller 1995).

As David Graeber (2001: 32) points out,[40] Appadurai's focus on consumption and demand fits poorly with agonistic forms of exchange such as potlatch or Homeric gift giving (what Appadurai terms "tournaments of value"), aimed at outgiving rivals (cf. Beidelman 1989; Morris 1986; Parry 1986). However, this problem does not apply to the case of Late Bronze Age exchange where demand is quite palpable. Not surprisingly, therefore, we find in the work of Andrew and Susan Sherratt a direct adaptation of Appadurai's discussion of luxury goods to Late Bronze Age trade in the Mediterranean Basin.

The Sherratts argue that the conspicuous consumption of luxury goods was the central feature of a lifestyle pursued by elites around the eastern Mediterranean in the second millennium B.C.E. Both unequal development and regional diversity in available luxury items at the beginning of regular long-distance sea transport in the Middle Bronze Age spurred a spiral of intensifying production and exchange that continued upward through the Late Bronze Age. In particular, they follow Appadurai (1986: 39) very closely in arguing for the top-down impact of the demand for luxury goods on the scale and specialization of local production (Sherratt and Sherratt 1991: 359).

However, the Sherratts' atomistic focus on the desires of elite actors, and their realization in international exchange, misses the totality of exchanges that both underlie and encompass conspicuous consumption. In the case of northern Transjordan this most certainly includes offerings to the gods and the dead, and it most likely includes the movement of taxes, tribute, rent, or labor from commoners to elites. The social formations imagined by the Sherratts are in this sense very curious. Relations between elites and local primary producers are simplistically exploitative, marked by a one-way flow of bulk goods with no clear reason for its continuity over time. Besides stimulating international exchange, the role of luxury goods in this system is reduced to the simple (indeed transparent) signification of wealth or power along the lines sketched long ago by Thorstein Veblen (1979 [1899]). The problems entailed in reproducing such a system of unequal exchange do not seem to concern the Sherratts. Yet, on reflection, these would seem to be the central problems evoked by their model.

To begin, the gods and the dead seem rather important partners in Late Bronze Age exchange, a fact made clear by the distribution of Mycenaean pottery in northern Transjordan. Indeed, in this region at least, one can hardly speak of conspicuous consumption, unless it is the gods and the dead who are the consumers. Mycenaean sherds have been found in so-called palace contexts (e.g., Tall al-Fukhar, Pella, Tall al-'Umayri). However, the find contexts and fragmentary condition of these sherds tell us little about the use or deposition of the original vessels. If relevant to northern Transjordan, one might note that at Megiddo, where one actually finds significant quantities of Mycenaean vessels in nontemple, nontomb contexts (Leonard and Cline 1998), these vessels appear to be stored in caches, perhaps meant to be retained rather than consumed. Of course, we cannot be certain about the contents of these vessels, as they could easily be refilled. However, as noted above, local imitations were also used in tomb contexts, suggesting either the importance of offering specific products or the valuing of Mycenaean vessels in themselves.

Interestingly, Liverani (1990: 223) suggests that consumption was largely negated in the ideological systems of the second millennium Near East. Instead, he argues that accumulation stood in an opposed tension with exchange; the former representing the local ideal of an abundant center and the latter the international ideal of reciprocal circulation. I would go farther and suggest that, at least in the case of northern Transjordan, the central local dynamic was one of accumulation in the face of the very special demands of offering to the gods and the dead.

Offerings to gods and ancestors invoke an exchange relation that cannot be reduced to the "norm of reciprocity" (Godelier 1999: 179–98). Debts to gods and ancestors (for life, food, progeny, etc.) are such that they cannot be repaid. Offerings, therefore, are closer to tribute than to gifts, although the former is in some sense a transformation of the latter within asymmetrical relations of power. In this sense, offerings incessantly re-create relations between the living, their deities and their ancestors. However, offerings also re-create relations within the community of the living, a fact brought home if we consider the distinct implications of offerings made in temples and those made in tombs.

Late Bronze Age temples are small and often isolated in their location, suggesting that ritual may have been physically exclusive. Yet, those making offerings represented the community in some sense, if only (as in the case of major kings) because they ideologically embodied the community within themselves as a personal possession. Offerings in tombs or to family gods are quite different in that they are specific to houses and lineages and hence serve to partition, rather than encompass, the community. These two seemingly distinct modes of offering come together if we follow the implications of artifact distributions (especially Mycenaean pottery) and assume that both temples and the wealthiest tombs were supplied by the same people.

Annette Weiner (1992) has highlighted the importance of the retention of inalienable possessions in the constitution of hierarchy within groups directly engaged in the world's most famous reciprocal exchange network— the Kula ring of the Trobriand Islands (cf. Malinowski 1922). Weiner focuses in particular on sacred objects that are passed down within lineages. By retaining these objects over time while meeting fully their reciprocal exchange obligations, lineages materialize their superior rank, wealth, and history. Weiner terms this phenomenon "keeping-while-giving," and, while we are concerned with exotic trade goods rather than inalienable sacred objects, this concept has important implications for understanding Late Bronze Age Transjordan.

Rather than simply consuming exotic foreign goods, it seems that those with access to such goods accumulated them to be circulated in very specific contexts. In northern Transjordan this involved deep-seated values of deity and ancestor veneration that, in the form of temple and tomb offerings, were cultural resources articulated within a particular social hierarchy. By successfully engaging in both the community-encompassing act of temple ritual and the community-partitioning act of tomb ritual, elite lineages in northern Transjordan materialized their status, wealth, and international connections. Importantly, acquiring rarer goods like Mycenaean pottery required one to be present in the international circuit of commercial and gift exchange. This implied both access to desirable products to offer for trade and tribute and/or the ability to protect trade caravans and provision Egyptian troops in a given territory (e.g., EA 255). This in turn required the mobilization of people, something that appears to have been achieved without a significant redistribution of the valued objects themselves.

What is missing from our equation is the flow of labor and surplus that constituted this mobilization of people. Archaeological evidence from northern Transjordan is currently too uneven (and unpublished) to allow us to say much about economic relations at specific sites. We have clear evidence for specialized pottery production in the central Jordan Valley at the very beginning of the Late Bronze Age (Fischer 1999; Knapp 1993). However, we know little about the organization of this production (e.g., scale, location, and status of workshops). More tellingly, we know very little about the storage and distribution of bulk agricultural products, especially grain.

Potentially helpful in this regard are certain of the Amarna letters, particularly those originating on the Lebanese coast, that make use of Akkadian social taxonomic terms. Besides the terms for town and city rulers (usually *ḫazannu*), the most important are *ḫupšu, maryanu,* and *'apiru.* *Ḫupšu* seems to refer to a free peasant, subject to taxation and labor service and often holding land that he directly worked (von Dassow 1997: 393–400; Dietrich and Loretz 1969; Gelb et al. 1956: 241–42). The voluminous and at times shrill correspondence of Rib-Adda, ruler of Byblos, suggests that: (1) *ḫupšu* was used to described the primary cultivating population within the territory of Byblos; (2) reciprocal expectations of some form existed between Rib-Adda and "his" *ḫupšu* people (e.g., EA 81: 31; EA 85: 10–15), perhaps relating to military protection and grain subsidies on one hand (e.g., EA 118: 23; EA 125: 35–31), and labor service[41] or in-kind taxation on the other; (3) members of the *ḫupšu* class could abandon their fields, switch allegiances (EA 81: 41–47), or rise up against the *ḫazannu* of a city-state (EA 77: 37; 117: 90).[42]

As elsewhere in the second millennium Near East the term *maryanu* is used in close association with chariots in the Amarna letters (e.g., EA 107: 42). North Syrian (Alalaḫ, and Ugarit) and north Mesopotamian (Nuzi) evidence suggests that the *maryannu* were of a high social status and often owned significant property worked by dependents attached through various full- or part-time labor obligations. Most debate involves "chicken and egg" problems regarding the primary or secondary nature of either of these two characteristics (chariotry vs. landed status; see von Dassow 1997: 258–331; Rainey 1965; Wilhelm 1989: 17–19).[43]

If evidence from north Syria can be extended to the southern Levant, then it appears that chariot ownership was limited to this group, although *maryannu* were also granted chariots and horses by local rulers (von Dassow 1997: 319–24). At both Ugarit (Nougayrol 1955: 140–41) and Alalaḫ (Smith 1939: 43–44), one could either be born a *maryanu* or be made one by royal decree (cf. von Dassow 1997: 287–91). *Maryannu* at Alalaḫ may have been exempted from certain forms of labor service levied on *ḫupšu*; however, they were obligated to provide military service to the king (von Dassow 1997: 307–9). We therefore see what amounts to both status group and economic class distinctions between *ḫupšu* and *maryanu*.

The term *'apiru* has long been a source of controversy.[44] Second millennium textual references from northern Syria and Mesopotamia suggest that *'apiru* refers to someone uprooted from their place of origin (by war, debt, blood guilt/feud, drought, etc.), that is to say, an "immigrant" (see Bottéro 1954, 1972; and Greenberg 1955 for texts). Often, such figures appear in military contexts, perhaps as mercenaries (but see von Dassow 1997: 204–8). However, in the Amarna letters this term takes on explicitly negative connotations. Here we are potentially victims of Rib-Adda's prolific stylus, as the majority of references to *'apiru* come from his many letters to the pharaoh and his officials. However, the same rhetorical opposition of an orderly, obedient, city-state vassal and the chaotic *'apiru* can be found in the letters of other *ḫazannu*, such as those of 'Abdi-Ḥeba of Jerusalem (e.g., EA 288: 29). Indeed, this contrast is so formulaic[45] as to lend itself to a structuralist representation along the lines of *ḫazannu*: *'apiru* :: inside : outside :: good : bad. It seems clear therefore, that although *'apiru* in the Amarna letters may have the specific denotation of a mercenary, or freebooter, etc. (Rainey 1995), its connotational significance is that of signifying the outside of proper patron-client relations (see Moran 1987).[46]

This image of inside and outside, of properly attached *ḫupšu* and dangerous *'apiru* (with whom a *ḫupšu* could well join) fits well with the archaeological evidence presented above. Late Bronze Age settlements in north Transjordan emerge as a series of nodal points built around the residences and ritual activities of elites tied into the Eastern Mediterranean trade system and the empire of New Kingdom Egypt (Knapp 1993: 85–90). At the level of representation, scale seems to be of little relevance, as the rulers of tiny settlements in highland Transjordan accumulated and offered similar objects in a similar manner to their counterparts at larger centers in lowland Palestine and the Jordan Valley. At the level of practice, the Transjordanian centers seem most comparable to Shechem and particularly

Jerusalem in the highlands, which seem to have been small strongholds claiming dominion over a sparsely settled area with a significant nonsedentary population (Finkelstein 1996a; Na'aman 1996).

Hegemony in this case is constituted by a loose centrifugal focus on dominant families/lineages in small political/ritual centers with attached cultivators. Offerings to deities and ancestors, drawn from luxury goods with limited paths of circulation, both bound a ritual community (temple) and differentiated it internally (tombs). In this manner, Late Bronze Age hegemonies "universalized" the particular actions and experiences of ruling classes. To speculate, Late Bronze Age ritual complexes were built around the shared values of ancestor and deity veneration, but articulated these values such that elite offerings to the deities and the veneration of their ancestors could seen as encompassing the entire community.

Articulated and made meaningful within this configuration is the specific asymmetrical relationship of economic and social obligation between ḫazanu and ḫupšu. Here ritual is no simple opiate, as both Rib-Adda and Abdi-Ḫeba seem well aware (even tortured) by their conflicted and precarious position of power, their ultimate dependence on the retention of ḫupšu in a context where the self-interest of cultivators propels them outward. Indeed, the extremely small size of Late Bronze Age settlements, their limited hierarchical clustering and their disproportionate focus on temples, palaces, and wealthy tombs suggest that the attachment and subordination of labor was the site of considerable stress and latent conflict (see Bunimovitz 1994). Perhaps it is this context of perpetual crisis that renders comprehensible the extremes of ritual display witnessed at both the Amman Airport "Temple" and DAJ Tomb 1 at Pella. Interestingly, both of these cases involve mortuary, rather than temple, rituals, suggesting that perhaps status and class distinctions by lineage were the sites of particular conflict and stress.

Southern Transjordan

If we shift our attention to southern Transjordan, we encounter a somewhat different situation, particularly in terms of available evidence. Besides Ramses II's brief references to Moab, the majority of Egyptian textual references to southern Transjordan relate to people the Egyptians term shasu and to a vaguely defined territory termed shasu-land (Giveon 1971; Hasel 1998: 217–39; Redford 1990: 68–75, 1992: 269–80; Ward 1972; Weippert 1974). Scholars usually identify shasu as pastoral-nomads, somewhat akin to modern Bedouin[47] in their economic reliance on livestock and their association with arid regions (Giveon 1971: 2–3, 240–41).[48] However, while shasu are frequently associated with tents, camps, movement, and livestock, the shasu-land is also on occasion portrayed as having towns (dmi; Giveon 1971: Doc. 32). On occasion, this shasu-land or the point of origin of a specific *shasu* is specified as "Seir" (Giveon 1971: Doc. 16a, 25, 38) or "Edom" (Giveon 1971: Doc. 37), terms used in the Bible to refer to the portion of Transjordan south of Wadi al-Ḥasa and perhaps also the southeastern portion of the Negev. However, *shasu* are regularly encountered by Egyptians outside of this area, especially in the Sinai, northern Negev, and eastern Egyptian Deserts, but also in Lebanon, Syria, and the central highlands of Palestine (Giveon 1971: 235–39; Ward 1972: 50–53). Finally, Egyptian iconographic conventions seem to depict *shasu* with some consistency, namely with pointed beards, headscarves and a tasseled kilt (Giveon 1971: 241–54), although the exclusivity of these features has been questioned (Ward 1972: 45–50).

Once again, we find ourselves struggling to "translate" an ancient Egyptian taxonomic category into the sort of comprehensive and mutually exclusive category employed in academic discourse. This is inevitably a losing proposition. Importantly, we should not confuse Egyptian taxonomies for self-identification and thereby ascribe to *shasu* an ethnic unity that is in no sense attested in the available evidence. What we can say is that as Egyptians encountered people from the Levant in the context of New Kingdom imperial expansion (with all that implies regarding the nature of these interactions), they categorized these people in a manner that blended mode of production, social structure, bodily appearance, geographic location, ethnicity, and context specific relationship to Egypt (mercenary, enemy, vassal, guide, brigand etc.). Not surprisingly, in the case of *shasu*, this taxonomy suggests that the arid southern portions of Transjordan, Palestine and the Sinai were associated with pastoral nomads. Yet, again not surprisingly, this naming is not exclusive. Everywhere that Egyptians encountered people who in some sense could be fit within this category, the term *shasu* could potentially be employed (cf. Ward 1972: 54–56). What we do learn from the Egyptian association of the term *shasu* most particularly with southern Transjordan is that Egyptians noted a difference in the lifestyle and landscape of this region. Most probably, this reflects the sparse Late Bronze Age settlement and importance of pastoral nomadism suggested by archaeological evidence.

Late Bronze Age Settlement on the Karak Plateau

Looking at the final report of the Central Moab Survey (Miller 1991) one might wonder about the apparent rarity of Late Bronze Age settlement in south central Transjordan. The CMS, directed by Maxwell Miller, conducted a purposive vehicular survey of the Karak Plateau in which they recorded 443 Chalcolithic to Late Ottoman period (ca. 4500 B.C.E.–1917 C.E.) sites in an area of 875 km². Of these, 109 (ca. 25 percent) are said to have yielded at least one diagnostic Late Bronze Age sherd. However, as Israel Finkelstein (1998a: 125) has pointed out, this extremely high number of Late Bronze Age sites compares very poorly with the results of method-ologically similar surveys carried out in immediately adjacent regions (Table 4.2).[49] Unfortunately, the Late Bronze Age sherds published in the CMS report (Miller 1991: 273–74) are not clearly diagnostic and in most cases could be found in Iron I contexts. Indeed at least some of the mate-rial dated to the Late Bronze Age by the Central Moab Survey is very prob-ably Iron I in origin.[50] Several of the sites identified as containing Late Bronze Age pottery have been subject to excavation or further surface col-lection subsequent to the CMS team visit and provide us with at least some means of evaluating the CMS attributions. Most damning have been Piotr Bienkowski's soundings at Ḥirbat Dubab (Bienkowski 1995a; Bienkowski et al. 1997; Bienkowski and Adams 1999), where the CMS survey recorded thirty-eight LB sherds, one of the highest concentrations they recorded on the plateau. Bienkowski's soundings revealed no pottery earlier than the Iron II period and no in situ occupational remains earlier than the Nabat-aean period. Furthermore, Bienkowski examined the sherds collected by the CMS at Ḥ. Dubab and concluded that they had been misidentified, sug-gesting that the ceramic analysts' notes indicated a high level of uncertainty regarding the identification of LB and Iron I pottery (Bienkowski and Adams 1999: 168–170). Bienkowski concludes that "it is no longer possible to accept uncritically the survey results and the description of settlement patterns that arose from them" (Bienkowski and Adams 1999: 170).

The combination of Finkelstein's and Bienkowski's critiques calls into question all the LB identifications made by the CMS. Yet we cannot as a result simply return to a modified form of Glueck's thesis of an empty land-scape. Bienkowski himself admits that the CMS sherd collection includes legitimate LB forms (Bienkowski and Adams 1999: 168). Furthermore, at the site of al-Misna, east of ar-Rabba, where the CMS recorded 12 LB sherds

TABLE 4.2. Site tallies by period for archaeological surveys of south-central Jordan

Name of survey	Late Bronze	Iron I	Iron II
Hesban[1]	6	30	63
Dhiban Plateau[2]	10	19	53
Central Moab[3]	109	72	97
Limes Arabicus[4]	0	5	105
NW. Arḍ al-Karak[5]	1?	6	11
Wadi Isal[6]	0	0	27
North Bank—Wadi al-Ḥasa[7]	0	12	97

1. Ibach (1987).
2. Ji and 'Attiya (1997); Ji and Lee (1998, 2000).
3. Miller (1991).
4. Koucky (1987).
5. Worschech (1985a, b, 1990a); Worschech et al. (1986)
6. Jacobs (1983).
7. Clark et al. (1992, 1994).

(Miller 1991: 64–65), a team directed by Udo Worschech recently reported a mixed layer of MB and LB pottery stratified, as one might expect, between Early Bronze and Iron Age deposits (Worschech and Ninow 1999: 172).

One option for dealing with the LB sites of the Central Moab Survey would be to move away from a focus on sites and site tallies. Taking the CMS's own criteria of five or more sherds as a significant occupation, we find 30 sites that meet this standard in the CMS catalogue (Figure 4.3). Not surprisingly, these sites cluster in the southwest sector of the Karak Plateau,

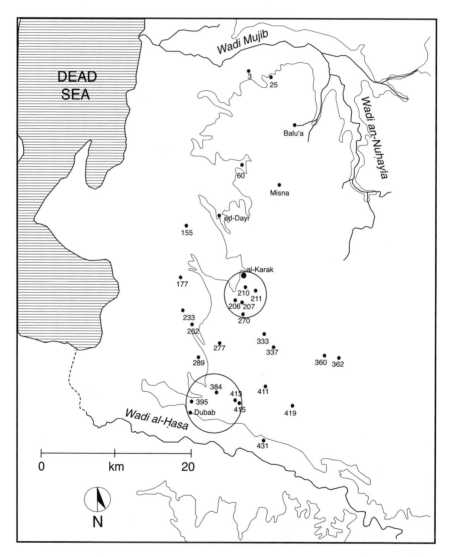

Figure 4.3. *K*-means clusters of Late Bronze Age sites on the Karak Plateau.

where as we saw in Chapter 3 both rainfall and soils are most favorable for agriculture. In fact, if we cluster these sites into spatial groups using a least-squares algorithm (*K*-means clustering—Legendre 2001)[51] we find one very robust cluster[52] of six sites that includes al-Karak and measures about five km in diameter. A second, less coherent cluster of five sites, measuring about six km in diameter, is located in the extreme southwest corner of the plateau.[53] If we compare the proportion of sites identified with five or more LB sherds found in the al-Karak cluster to the proportion of all sites discovered by the CMS within this same cluster boundary, the LB sample can be shown to differ from the population to a statistically significant degree ($p < 0.0001$) by means of a one-sample Z-test. Hence, there is no immediate reason to suspect that the concentration of sites with more than five recorded LB sherds is the simple product of regionally unequal site discovery rates.

All of this suggests some interesting things about the nature of LB settlement on the Karak Plateau. Most particularly, while we cannot be certain as to which sites were actually occupied in the Late Bronze Age without further field investigation, we can say that Late Bronze Age occupation took one of two forms. Put simply, LB occupation occurred either in relatively isolated settlements widely dispersed on the landscape or it occurred in one of the settlement clusters concentrated in the southwest portion of the Karak Plateau. Obviously, these settlement clusters are themselves dependent on sites at which Late Bronze Age settlement may well have been erroneously identified. However, regional settlement trends make it unlikely that significant numbers of new LB settlements will be discovered (see Finkelstein 1998a).[54] Hence, these two forms of LB settlement seem likely to remain our best characterization of the period on the Karak Plateau.

Outside of the Karak Plateau, Late Bronze Age occupation in the territory of Moab is somewhat uncertain, due to limited survey and excavation coverage. The neighboring sites of Tall Jalul and Madaba in the northern portion of Moab are currently the excavated sites with Late Bronze Age material.[55] Hence, current evidence suggests that for most of the Late Bronze Age substantial sedentary occupation was concentrated in the less marginal southwest and northwest sectors of Moab. It seems, therefore, that in the territory of Moab, settlement was nodally concentrated, as in the north, albeit with even less intensity and more dispersal between settlement clusters. The degree to which a similar nexus of ritual, mortuary, and exchange relations also pertained in the south cannot be determined on current archaeological evidence, as no Late Bronze Age occupation phases have been excavated south of Jalul. Given the clear graded decline in Late Bronze Age settlement density from north to south, and the Egyptian association of the south with *shasu*, one might reasonably wonder if we should not think in terms of a north/south division of Transjordanian social formations. In other words, should we contrast a mobile, pastoral, and "tribal" south with a settled, cosmopolitan north?[56] In truth, the lack of excavated in situ Late Bronze Age deposits makes it impossible to answer this question. However, one piece of evidence does stand out in favor of linking northern and southern Transjordan on the issue of politics and ideologies. Indeed, despite its ambiguity, the Balu'a Stele may well replicate certain hegemonic themes from the north, especially ritual display, connection to deities, and access to/knowledge of foreign images and material culture.

The Balu'a Stele

In 1930, a 1.73 × 0.7 m stele, carved on a basalt block (see Figure 4.4), was serendipitously discovered on the surface of the site of Balu'a at the north-eastern end of the Karak Plateau (Horsfield and Vincent 1932). The stele is constituted by a scene consisting of three figures cut in high relief, with a four-to-six-line inscription engraved above their heads. The scene itself is a familiar one in royal art of the Egyptian New Kingdom, showing a male deity on the left investing the central, presumably royal figure with divine authority by means of the *was*-scepter and what is probably a second short-scepter grasped in his left and right hands respectively. To the right, a female figure grasping an ankh-symbol presents the "king" to the male deity. In Egyptian art this female figure can be either a goddess or a queen.

While this general scene is familiar in Egyptian art, many of its details are not. The male deity wears the expected "double-crown" of Upper and Lower Egypt; however, the crown is encircled by a band just below the pinnacle, as is typical[57] in Egyptian depictions of the Canaanite gods Ba'al and Reshef (Cornelius 1994: 246–48).[58] The female figure wears an 'atef' crown, which is not worn by Egyptian goddesses or queens but is witnessed on Canaanite goddesses (e.g., Rowe and Fitzgerald 1940: Pl. 49A.1, Pl. 66A.1). The headdress of the central male figure is unusual in Egyptian art, being similar to the depiction of headscarves worn by the *shasu* in Egyptian reliefs (Drioton 1933: 360–65; Ward and Martin 1964: 14–15; Giveon 1971: 202–4). Further non-Egyptian features in the dress, execution and physical proportions of the figures, as well as the lunar and "sun-disk in a crescent" symbols that flank the central figure, compound these discrepancies. All of this evidence strongly suggests that the scene on the Balu'a Stele was carved in imitation of Egyptian artistic traditions, rather than from within that tradition.

The inscription is very poorly preserved, with little more than text base-lines visible today. Comparing photographs taken shortly after the stele's discovery (Horsfield and Vincent 1932: Pl. 9) and in the early 1960s (Ward and Martin 1964: Pl. 1) with a recent visual inspection of the stele in the Amman Citadel Museum, it would seem that the text has deteriorated continually since its discovery. This being said, even at the time of the discovery the text was considered unreadable (Horsfield and Vincent 1932:

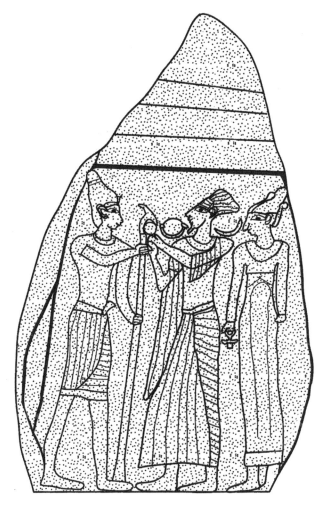

Figure 4.4. The Balu'a Stele.

423–24). Indeed, even the nature of the script cannot be identified with confidence, and scholars have alternatively suggested that it is a variant of: Cretan Linear B (Alt 1940; Weill 1938); the undeciphered Late Bronze Age script from Deir 'Alla (Masson 1976: 30–31); pseudohieroglyphic Byblite (Albright 1949: 186); Egyptian hieratic (Horsfield and Vincent 1932); and graffito Egyptian hieratic (Ward and Martin 1964). With the exception of Ward and Martin (1964), these proposed script identifications are based on Horsfield and Vincent's very preliminary transcription of the inscription rather than direct observation of the stele itself. Similarly, with the exception of Ward and Martin, no scholars have been able to propose serious readings of the stele's signs in terms of the script that they have proposed. For these reasons, Ward and Martin's interpretations have generally been cited as authoritative for the past thirty-five years.

Basically, Ward and Martin (1964) look to graffiti from the Theban necropolis (Černý 1956) in order to identify signs on the Balu'a Stele. Although never clearly stated, the examples cited from Černý's (1956) study imply that Ward and Martin view the Balu'a inscription as being written in an Egyptian hieratic, rather than hieroglyphic, script. Frankly, given the current state of the stele there seems to be little point in addressing their proposals on a sign-by-sign basis. However, Carolyn Routledge (C. Routledge 2000) has recently argued quite convincingly that there are numerous basic problems with Ward and Martin's approach to reading that text that make their proposed reading of the stele highly unlikely.[59] Given the tendency of some to miss Ward and Martin's repeated emphasis[60] on the tentative nature of their proposed readings,[61] Routledge's observations are worth stressing.

The details of the relief scene are much less debated than those of the inscription, although even here we are not without controversy. From Horsfield and Vincent's initial publication, it was recognized that this was a relatively standard investiture scene, although one marked by distinctly un-Egyptian execution in terms of bodily proportions and physical details. Drioton (1933) highlighted three key features of the dress of these figures that remain central to the issue of dating the stele: (1) the female figure's sheath dress with a front-tied sash; (2) the "gala" robe of the central male figure; (3) the headdress of the central male figure. The most recent of these is the *shasu* headdress, which first begins on Egyptian reliefs in the reign of Seti I (1294–1279 B.C.E.) and is closest to the example from Balu'a in the reign of Ramses III (1184–1153 B.C.E.).

Drioton sees great chronological significance in this, since he believes a local ruler would only have dared to adopt the pharaoh's "gala" robe in the years immediately after Ramses III's death when Egypt's Levantine empire began to crumble. However, the Balu'a Stele is an Egyptianizing object, one that uses the iconographic language of Egypt to its own ends. The central figure, with its "foreign" features, is already one that cannot exist in the pharaoh-centric world of Egypt. Hence, given that earlier *shasu* head-dresses are not so radically different from those in the reign of Ramses II (e.g., Wente 1963), it seems prudent to follow the rest of our evidence, and date the stele broadly to the post-Amarna period, especially the Nineteenth to Twentieth Dynasties.[62]

As Marion Feldman (1998) has argued, the question of meaning in an Egyptianizing piece like the Balu'a Stele is not a question of what the artist got wrong but rather of the choices that have been made in using the iconographic language of Egypt. From this perspective we can see two outstanding features of the Balu'a Stele. The first is the choice of an investiture scene, illustrating not simply the cosmologically legitimate investiture of power (*was*-scepter, "gala" robes, etc.), as would be the case in Egypt, but importantly the legitimate investing of power by means of a specifically Egyptian cosmology. The second is the fact that this is no mere imitation. In both the features of the central figure and the iconography of the deities a consistent effort is made to depict this as an explicitly Canaanite scene. Hence, oddly enough, the Egyptian iconography for "foreigners" is here used by those foreigners for the purpose of self-representation.[63]

Moab in the Late Bronze Age

Moab's appearance as a toponym in the texts and reliefs of Ramses II presents us with an archaeological problem. Surveys and limited excavations suggest a low-intensity settlement landscape of small sites, either isolated or in small clusters. Whatever or wherever B[w]trt was, it was evidently small and isolated. Despite its probable mention in Ramses II Luxor reliefs (see above), any Late Bronze occupation at Dhiban is likely to have been both ephemeral and small.[64] At the site of Balu'a, excavations have yet to discover Late Bronze Age occupation, and they indicate only limited early Iron IA occupation (Worschech and Ninow 1999). Yet, we encounter the Balu'a stele with its striking appropriation (and inversion) of Egyptian iconographic conventions for local ends.

These contradictions are not particularly contradictory when we consider what we already know from northern Transjordan. As we saw, in the Late Bronze Age extremely small settlements served as a sort of nucleus, with actors and social groups revolving in a valence of loose and friable relations of dominance. The center defined itself through display, access to the "outside," and above all else the ability to "do right" by the gods and the dead, especially as "doing right" was something not everyone had the means to do. Something similar may be visible in the Balu'a Stele, which taken at face value is a scene of piety that inevitably assumes power as a condition of its existence.

While certain of these themes (e.g., divine approval) carry through to the Iron Age, this Late Bronze Age hegemony is notable as a point of contrast.

In the Late Bronze Age we encounter Moab as a geographic territory encompassed by the irregular patchwork of the Egyptian Empire. Within this space, little centers of power hung like constellations. As we shall see, the Iron Age is defined by the collapse of this system of hegemony, which is based on the local reproduction of power and status through ritual display by numerous centers. In its place, a discourse of unity and an encompassing territoriality arise that draw their cultural resources more directly from the internal dynamics of communities. This Moab is quite different from the geographic Moab of the Late Bronze Age. Understanding this difference will occupy us for the next four chapters, taking us from the unraveling of one hegemony to the fixing of another in the ninth century B.C.E.

Chapter 5

Beginnings II: The Early Iron Age

In those days there was no king in Israel;
a man did what was right in his own eyes.

—Judges *21: 25*

The transition from the Late Bronze Age to the Iron Age in the eastern Mediterranean is one of the archetypal cases of social rupture in the ancient world (see Gitin, Mazar, and Stern 1998; Ward and Joukowsky 1992). The political and economic systems that decompose between 1250 and 1150 B.C.E. and those that emerge between 950 and 850 B.C.E. are, in certain important ways, discontinuous in terms of both cultural content and their organizing principles. The very scale and extent of this transformation seem to demand grand theories, and scholars have seldom beenshy in responding (e.g., Coote and Whitelam 1987; Drews 1993; Liverani 1987; Sherratt and Sherratt 1991; Stiebing 1989). Yet global "causes" (migration, trade, environmental change, class conflict) can only be realized in relation to specific communities, and it is in such small things and local concerns that the raw material of state hegemony is found. In this chapter we will consider the Late Bronze II–Iron I transition, not as one more instance of a global event, but rather as a reordering of the modes and practices binding people to communities. In particular, we will spell out key cultural resources born in the common sense experiences of these new domestic orders that were thereby available for articulation in subsequent Moabite state formation.

From Bronze to Iron

In Transjordan we see much that is familiar at the end of the Late Bronze Age. The transition to the Iron Age is uneven, extending from the end of the thirteenth century through at least the end of the Iron IA period, when evidence for an Egyptian imperial presence ceases (ca. 1140 B.C.E.). In all regions,[1] one sees a significant increase in the number of Iron I sites over those attested from the Late Bronze Age (see Table 4.2). In Moab, this is marked in particular by the spread of settlement into more agriculturally marginal areas. In northern Transjordan, there is a cessation of Aegean imports and the abandonment of the probable Egyptian outpost at Tall as-Saʿidiyya. Most notable, however, is the evidence for significant changes in the symbolic and representational practices of power.

As we saw in Chapter 4, the wealth and frequency of funerary displays, ritual assemblages, and palaces in Late Bronze Age northern Transjordan seems unusually high given the evident scale of the communities in question. Indeed, the evidence suggests a moral order dependent on public spectacle to reproduce its own hegemony. The beginning of the Iron Age marks a decisive shift away from this personalized ritual and elite display. While communal burials continue, they no longer contain imports, and the elaborate funerary displays of the Amman Airport "Temple" and Pella DAJ Tombs 1 and 2 have no parallel in Iron I. Temples and palaces, though frequently abandoned in the LB, now cease to be founded altogether.[2] In several cases "palaces" and/or temples are destroyed or put out of use and directly succeeded by domestic deposits.[3]

The collapse of pan-Mediterranean trade was certainly a factor in this transformation (Coote and Whitelam 1987), but it was not an independent factor (Sherratt and Sherratt 1991). Trade was inseparable from local practices in which the fruits of this trade (e.g., Mycenaean pottery) were central to reproducing political hegemony (gift giving, temple and tomb ritual, etc.). Local hegemony was in turn central to the reproduction of trade relations, as it was the means by which raw materials, finished goods, and labor were accumulated for exchange. In other words, the interdependence of eastern Mediterranean elites (with each other and with trade) was constituted not by the scale of trade, which varied considerably, but by the shared fact that access to trade goods and networks of allies and partners had been made integral to both the ideology and the practice of rule.

The increased extractive burden and interdependence of local town rulers and Egyptian officials that came with a heavier Egyptian presence in the southern Levant during the Nineteenth and early Twentieth Dynasties is another likely factor in Late Bronze Age collapse. Yet again, it is important to stress that the impact of Egypt was not independent of the internal organization of Late Bronze Age polities, as these did not rebound after the Egyptian empire withdrew. Rather, over the century in question (ca. 1250–1150 B.C.E.) we see a sequence of events (military build-up, famine in Anatolia, migrations, collapse of the Hittite Empire, breakdown of trade networks etc.) that exacerbated centrifugal tendencies already evident in the relationship between Late Bronze Age political centers and their subject populations.

To be clear, the uncertain hegemony of these Late Bronze Age polities was not a system that became destabilized (contra Portugali 1994). It was from the beginning built on contradiction (cf. Liverani 1987). Most notably this involved the foundational assumption that surplus labor and product would be expropriated in perpetuity, even though flexible and mobile production strategies were central to the long-term well-being of primary producers in this drought-prone environment. The counterbalance was the provision of security against warfare and famine, as well as the mediation of relations with deities, ancestors, and external powers. This relationship was not masked by ideology, it was embedded in a moral order that included a variety of specific resources (patronage, imported objects, ancestor veneration, temple ritual, and possibly kinship) articulated in specific projects (honoring noble lineages, attracting cultivators, legitimizing succession, etc.). In other words, those interested in expropriating the labor of others were engaged "directly, daily and personally" (Bourdieu 1977: 190) in reproducing relations of dominance by means that, under certain terms of reference, made sense of the world. As we know from the Amarna letters, this was a precarious business that frequently failed. As we know from archaeology, it eventually failed altogether.

In the transition between the Late Bronze Age and the Early Iron Age, the logic by which community life was organized changed in a relatively radical manner. This transformation was not simply ideological or economic, as it involved changes in both modes of production and modes of identification. If one were looking for operative symbols to characterize this transformation, it would be the shift from "palace" to house. As David Schloen (2001) has shown with great insight, it is not that the Late Bronze Age lacked domestic metaphors for organizing political society; indeed, quite the opposite was true. Kings in the northern Levant, and, as we surmise from small hints, petty rulers in the southern Levant as well represented their rule and their political relationships in the domestic terms of family and household. In this sense, the palace stood as the exemplary house at the center of society.

In contrast, Iron I sites are characterized by the modular repetition of pillared houses. This "family" of house designs consists of elements (pillars and rectangular rooms) and spatial arrangements[4] that are variably realized but always recognizable as transformations of each other. Due to their size, consistent domestic installations, and ubiquitous presence at Iron Age sites in Palestine, pillared houses have come to be associated with primary domestic groups, thought to be extended or joint families (Bendor 1996; Schloen 2001: 135–85; Stager 1985; cf. Holladay 1992, 1997). Hence, it is clear that Iron I communities were also about family and household, but here these powerful cultural resources have been reclaimed and rearticulated in a spatial syntax that emphasizes autonomy and equivalency over the exemplary center of LB settlements. Indeed, in the Iron Age the display of status distinctions (i.e., ritual offering of trade goods, sponsorship of craft production) becomes muted, even when economic distinctions are clearly demonstrable (see below). At the same time, a focus on forms of power centered on the internal dynamics of agropastoral communities (e.g., kinship, segmentation, patriarchy, and patronage) becomes the most promising means of describing political society. In all of this we see a key point from our discussion of Gramsci, namely that the formation and dissolution of hegemonies involves struggles over the meanings of central symbols and familiar practices.

Comparing Highlands

Sketched in this broad manner, it clear that the changes wrought during the LB II–IR I transition were not unique to Transjordan. Highland settlement in Palestine possesses all of these characteristics, as well as a clear spatial displacement in the center of gravity of settlement from lowland to highland areas (see Finkelstein 1995a; Stager 1998). Indeed, scholars have long seen this transformation rather specifically as the result of some version of the biblical account of Israel's settlement in Canaan. After all, it is in the LB II–IR I transition that ancient Israel first appears in the historical record,[5] while the "simplicity" and "egalitarianism" of Iron I settlements seemed to fit the theological expectations that many scholars held for early Israel.

The past twenty years have seen these assumptions shift rather significantly. The notion of a "historical kernel" underlying biblical accounts of the Israelite conquest and settlement has been seriously challenged (e.g., Na'aman 1994b), a new appreciation of the complexities of ethnic identification has made the ethnogenesis of Israel a problem for investigation rather than an explanation for change (Edelman 1996; Finkelstein 1997; Hesse and Wapnish 1997), and the panregional character of the LB II–IR I transition has come to be stressed (Stager 1998). Hence, recent research has shifted away from the classic competing explanations of conquest,[6] peaceful infiltration,[7] and peasant revolt,[8] each of which focused particularly on the emergence of Israel as a historical (and theological) question. Instead, current scholarship is heavily focused on the interpretation of settlement patterns as the product of long-term structural change in the organization of production (e.g., Finkelstein and Na'aman 1994). In particular, Israel Finkelstein has focused on the sedentarization of "enclosed nomads" (Rowton 1974) as a cyclical feature of production strategies in the marginal environment of highland Palestine (Finkelstein 1988; 1995a; Finkelstein and Na'aman ed.1994; cf. LaBianca 1990 for Transjordan). Alternatively, a variety of scholars have focused (in rather different ways) on the disengagement of primary producers from fixed relations of production in the lowlands in the face of an open highland frontier and declining wealth, stability, and security in urban areas (Coote and Whitelam 1987; Dever 1991; Marfoe 1979; Stager 1998: 104–5).

Overall, these developments have had a salutary effect on the sophistication and breadth of research carried out on the Iron I period. However, Syro-Palestinian archaeology remains wedded to an essentialist view of human society, now favoring a version that is functionalist rather than romantic in orientation. While ancient Israel has been problematized as an identity in formation, its place has been taken in explanatory narratives by static cross-cultural categories (e.g., peasants, pastoralists, tribesmen, etc.). These categories usually serve to fill in the gaps in our knowledge rather than to test the empirical adequacy of their universal claims. [9] Hence, Iron I communities are often portrayed as possessing intrinsic social structural attributes (e.g., lineage organization, egalitarianism, corporate orientation) that ultimately derive from their membership in ethnographically defined social types. While appeals to anthropology (and sociology) are common in this literature, they are still primarily to classic functionalist work on social structure (e.g., Fortes 1953; Lenski and Lenski 1978). In particular, very little attention has been paid to the reorientation of kinship studies toward representation, discourse, and strategy (e.g., Schneider 1984). Consequently, the enumeration of "essential" characteristics tends to displace a concern for the strategic engagement of people with structures, values, and material conditions, encountered from different subject positions within specific historical circumstances (i.e., life as we know it).

To be clear, there are many excellent statements within this literature on the flexibility of kinship, unilineal descent, and collective identity (see McNutt 1999: 75–94). Yet somehow, despite these moments of recognition, we always return to social masses (e.g., tribes and lineages) in the process of becoming (e.g., ethnogenesis). In other words, we start out talking about identity but end up talking about groups. Ironically, in a study that is widely cited in the recent rethinking of the LB II–IR I transition, Leon Marfoe (1979) clearly detailed the failure of abstract social structural forms to account for the diverse historical possibilities of flexible and fragmented local identities. While Marfoe ultimately grounded this dynamic in the multiplicity of local microenvironments in the Lebanese Biqa', he stressed that southern Levantine social history involved the constant unmaking of fixed positions, and he pointed to the explicitly strategic and ideological process of binding people together.

Evidence for the LB II-Iron I transition emerging from Transjordan differs from that of Palestine in a number of ways that seem to undermine the fixed categories of recent syntheses, suggesting that Marfoe's observations need to be pursued further. For example, in contrast to Palestine (Finkelstein 1988, 1995a; Stager 1998) the Late Bronze Age to Iron Age transition in Transjordan is not marked by a spatial displacement of settlement away from the traditional centers of Late Bronze Age culture. Settlement expands and is found in new areas, but these areas are generally the marginal, yet still accessible, fringes of the plateau (see Palumbo 1994).[10] Similarly, one cannot reasonably characterize this transition as a shift from an urban to a rural society, as most of the Late Bronze Age centers are hardly urban (see Table 4.1) and in some cases (e.g., Sahab and Ibrahim 1987: 77) are smaller than the Iron I occupations that succeed them. Hence, the themes of withdrawal and isolation, often used in Palestine to treat highland and lowland populations as distinct (and hence ripe for ethnogenesis) have little relevance in Transjordan.[11]

Furthermore, there is no necessary reason to presume that pastoralism and agriculture correlated with politically or socially bifurcated populations in Late Bronze Age Transjordan. The interdependence of pastoralism and agriculture is well known and can be resolved in a variety of ways, in terms both of the division of labor and of the social organization of this labor. As we have already suggested, the small Late Bronze Age centers of northern Transjordan drew on a regional population that likely included pastoralists of variable seasonal mobility (van der Steen 1995, 1999). Archaeological, environmental, and textual data do suggest that pastoral nomadism grew significantly in importance from north to south. This is notable, for example, in the Egyptian association of the south of Jordan with *shasu*. However, as we saw in Chapter 4, Egyptian texts also recognized towns and villages within *shasu*-land. Indeed, the very iconography used by the Egyptians to represent *shasu* is appropriated for a royal investiture scene in the case of the Balu'a Stele.

Finally, Iron I settlement is highly episodic, marked by frequent disruptions and abandonments (see Table 5.1). Survey data, which of necessity lump all of the Iron I period together, create a picture of large-scale contemporary settlement events that followed in close succession on the end of the Late Bronze Age.[12] However, many of the Iron I sites in Transjordan (and Palestine) are short-lived and sequentially, rather than contemporaneously, occupied. Hence, settlement foundation was not a single event that began an era of rooted village communities. Rather, village foundation and abandonment were continuous aspects of potentially transitory Iron I communities. In short, none of the dichotomies (lowland/highland, urban/rural, agriculture/pastoral nomadism, cosmopolitan/traditional) used to create collective actors (and to imply their prior unity)[13] in the now-familiar syntheses from Palestine have a necessary, or even obvious, relevance to Transjordan.

My point is not to argue that "tribes" or "lineages" did not exist. Rather, I wish to shift our focus away from reifying collectives that were in reality the actively negotiated and contingent products of human action. Instead, I would suggest that we break these categories down by interpreting the so-called classic characteristics of Middle Eastern "tribal" societies as cultural resources that could be combined and articulated in a variety of ways. In particular, (1) segmentation as a mode of identification; (2) domestic autonomy, especially as embodied in the house as both a structure and a metaphor; and (3) genealogy as an idiom for representing extrahousehold relations are all well recognized as key resources for constituting identity under the rubric of "tribalism" (see Eickelman 1989).

Analytically we could conceive of these resources in terms of a kind of inverse structuralism. Rather than positing deep structures that generate surface manifestations as transformations of themselves, we might think instead of these cultural resources as being carried along historically by surface manifestations (e.g., rituals, folk sayings, spatial arrangements) to be encountered, appropriated and differentially reproduced by specific agents under specific circumstances. Such resources are therefore reproducible in a recursive and largely unconscious manner but are also interpretable and adaptable to new circumstances. Such cultural resources are available for the fashioning of lives, as in their familiarity they allow the self-narration of continuity through time and across social contexts (i.e., I am "X"). At the same time, this potential for meaningful interpretation is what makes cultural resources the object of hegemonic struggle to "deconstruct some chains of meaning and power and to construct others" (Jessop 1990: 242). Indeed, in subsequent chapters I will argue that segmentation, genealogy, and domestic metaphors are among the most prominent cultural resources articulated in Iron Age state hegemony in general, and Moab in particular.

Reading the Margins of Moab

A further benefit comes with shifting our focus away from corporate groups, in that such groups (e.g., "tribes") can only be linked to archaeological materials by employing rather simplistic or mechanical assumptions regarding their consistency and coherence (Hayden and Cannon 1982). In contrast, principles of collective identification (like segmentation, or domestic

TABLE 5.1. Occupation histories by century for selected early Iron Age sites

Site	Century				
	12th	11th	10th	9th	8th
ḤMA	—	X	A	—	—
ḤMM	—	X	A	—	—
Lahun	X	X	A	—	X
Ḥisban	X / A	L	X	A / L	L
Dhiban	X	X	?	X	X
'Umayri	X	X / A	—	L	?
Sahab	X	X	D / X	X	X
Sai'diyya	X / A	—	L	X	X
Dayr 'Alla	X / D	X	X / D	X	X
al-Mazar	—	X	X / A	—	X
al-Fukhar	X / A	—	—	—	—

X=occupied; A=abandoned; D=destruction; L=limited ocupation.

autonomy) are potentially registered in a semiotic sense by a wide variety of intellectual products, including material culture (see Herzfeld 1992). This, however, requires detailed contextual analysis of Iron I communities emphasizing variability and site structure over our traditional focus on similarity and classification. In the case of Moab, the available excavated contexts limit our options for analysis to some extent. However, several single-period sites with very coherent surface remains dating towards the end of the Iron I period provide evidence suited to our analytical needs.

Survey and excavation have revealed a concentration of extremely well preserved Iron I sites overlooking the Wadi Mujib and its major tributaries (Table 5.2; Figure 5.1). All of these sites are located in an agriculturally marginal zone, where average annual precipitation rates range between 150–300 mm per annum (see Chapter 3). To say that these sites overlook wadis is an understatement. Most are dramatically positioned on ridges or promontories with steep slopes on at least one side of the site that often reach several hundred meters in height. Furthermore, where determinable these sites tend to be fortified, with a casemate wall that conforms to the topography of the ridge or promontory on which the site is located. The isolation, marginality, and fortification of these sites are very striking. Yet, while early researchers like Nelson Glueck (1939: 73, 79, 88–89) con-structed rather fanciful circuits of Moabite border fortresses from these data, they are, on closer inspection, fairly typical Iron Age villages.[14] Hence, accounting for their location and form promises specific insights into the Iron I communities of Moab.

Placing these sites in a larger regional context is made difficult by the available survey data. On the north side of Wadi Mujib, an extensive survey of the Dhiban Plateau has only recently been completed and only prelimi-narily published (Ji and 'Attiyat 1997; Ji and Lee 1999, 2000). South of Wadi Mujib several overlapping surveys have been published (Koucky 1987; Miller 1991; Worschech 1985a, b, 1990a; Worschech, Rosenthal, and Zayadine 1986), but these were all low intensity and purposive in nature, lacking consistent information on site size by period. On current evidence,

TABLE 5.2. Iron I sites adjacent to Wadi Mujib

Site	Size (ha)	Casemate wall
Ḥal-Mudayna al-'Aliya	2.2	yes
Ḥal-Mudayna al-Mu'arradja	1.0	yes
Lahun	1.6	yes
Ara'ir	?	yes (Iron II)
Abu al-Ḥaraqah	0.36	yes (Roman?)
Balu'a	< 4.0	yes (Iron II?)
Ḥal-Mudayna ala al-Mujib	0.36?	?
ar-Rumayl	0.80	yes (Iron II?)

we can note that, while clustered around a common topographic feature, these sites do not form in themselves distinct clusters. Excavated sites show no clear evidence of intimate links to any larger center, nor that they were themselves at the center of a settlement cluster.[15] Indeed, neither survey nor excavation evidence clearly indicates the existence of any Iron I site in Moab significantly larger than the 0.36–2.2 ha ranged indicated by the sites in Table 5.2.[16]

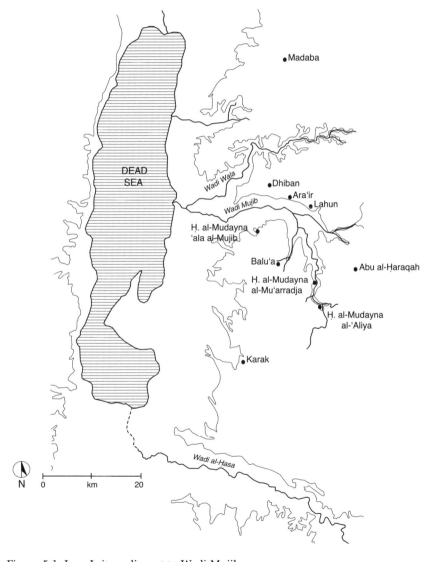

Figure 5.1. Iron I sites adjacent to Wadi Mujib.

The location and clustering of these sites make a certain degree of sense if we return to our discussion of environment and topography in Chapter 3. The semiarid karstic conditions of Moab mean that springs are largely restricted to wadi bottoms, and groundwater on the plateau proper is very limited in those areas below the 300-mm isohyet. Furthermore, soil erosion rates are high and soil quality low in this marginal zone, making the alluvial and colluvial terraces of the wadis more attractive for farming. This is rather dramatically illustrated by the preliminary results of Chang Ho-Ji's survey of the Dhiban Plateau (Ji and Lee 2000: Fig. 1), all of which falls below the 300-mm isohyet. As Figure 5.2 shows, during all time periods prior to the twentieth century, sites were heavily clustered along the edges of the Wadi Mujib and the Wadi Wala/Wadi ath-Thamad, as well as their tributaries, while the center of the plateau was very sparsely settled.

Paleobotanical evidence from my own excavations at Ḥirbat al-Mudayna al-ʿAliya (Routledge 2000a) suggest that the barley used at the site was grown in the wadi bottom, as wetland weed species (*Cardamine* cf. *hirusta*; *Suueada asphaltica/aegyptica*; *Phalaris* cf. *minor*) were found mixed with the grain stored in bins (Simmons 2000). Similarly, fresh water crab, which are still found below the site in the Wadi an-Nuḥayla, constitute the second most frequently attested species in our faunal sample (Lev-Tov n.d.).

We can therefore suggest that there is no great mystery in the clustering of sites along the edges of the central plateaus of Moab, as water and arable land were more accessible in the wadi bottom than on the plateau in the 100–300-mm isohyet zone. This does not, however, explain why these marginal zones were settled at all, nor why sites in these zones tended to be heavily fortified and so securely positioned. To answer these questions we need to look more closely at the sites themselves. Of the five sites in Table 5.2 that have been excavated, Baluʿa and Araʿir have yielded pottery but no coherent architecture from the Iron I period The remaining three sites, namely Ḥirbat al-Mudayna al-ʿAliya (henceforth ḤMA), Lahun, and Ḥirbat Mudayna al-Muʿarradja (henceforth ḤMM) have been investigated in sufficient detail to allow us to look closely at site form, foundation, internal structure, and abandonment. Taken together, these issues highlight a number of key factors in community political organization during the Iron I period.

Site Form: Architecture and Layout

ḤMA, located 19 km northeast of al-Karak, is a relatively large Iron I village of 2.2 ha situated on a promontory 250 meters above the juncture of the Wadi al-Muḥayris and the Wadi an-Nuḥayla (Figure 5.3). The site is surrounded by a casemate wall and further protected by a short moat and a massive tower on its vulnerable western side. An estimated 35–45 houses are attached directly to the town wall, forming a ringed enclosure with an

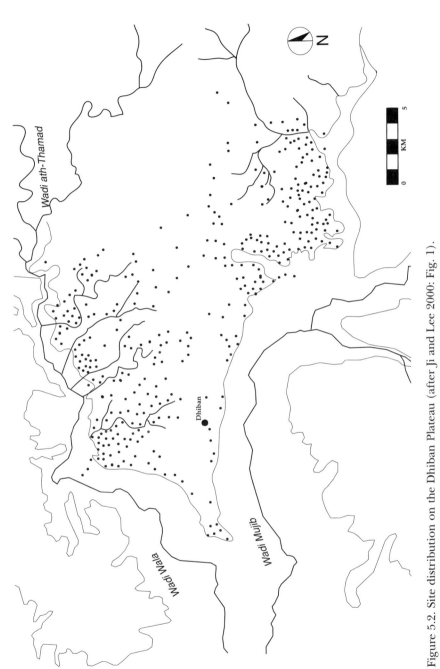

Figure 5.2. Site distribution on the Dhiban Plateau (after Ji and Lee 2000: Fig. 1).

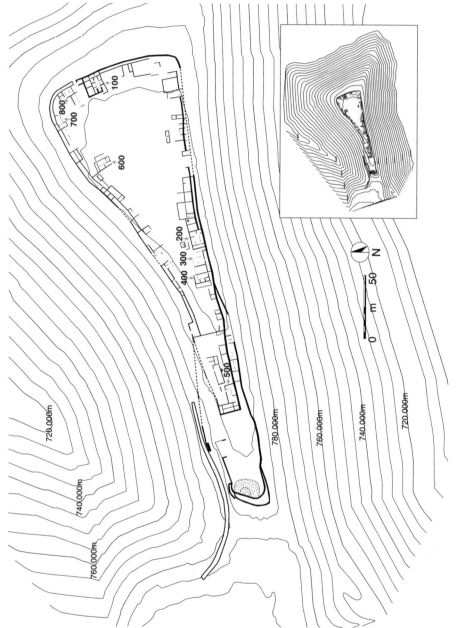

Figure 5.3. Hirbat al-Mudayna al-ʿAliya.

open plaza in the center. Excavations so far indicate only one primary phase of occupation, contemporary with the extensive architectural remains visible on the surface of the site. The ceramic assemblage is homogeneous and seemingly short-lived (see Routledge 2000a: Fig. 5–7), fitting best with assemblages dated between 1050–1000 B.C.E. in the traditional regional chronology.[17]

ḤMM (Figure 5.4) and Lahun (Figure 5.5) are also fortified by a casemate wall system and are located on steep promontories. Unlike ḤMA, both Lahun (Homès-Fredericq 1997: Fig. 41) and ḤMM (Olàvarri 1977–78: 138) have a block of houses in the center of the casemate enclosure in addition to those attached directly to the fortification walls. Hence, despite their smaller size these two sites are more densely occupied than ḤMA. At Lahun, parts of 21 structures have been identified in excavation (Homès-Fredericq 1997: Fig. 41; van Hoof 1997: 21–58), allowing one to estimate a total of about 50–60 houses at the site.[18] At ḤMM portions of two, or perhaps three, houses were excavated (Olàvarri 1977–78: 138, 1983: Fig. 4), with room for a total of perhaps 25–35 houses.

The dimensions and characteristics of the less intensively investigated sites in Table 5.2 seem to be in line with those of ḤMA, ḤMM, and Lahun. Hence, in each case we seem to be dealing with fortified villages with perhaps 100–400 inhabitants. In terms of layout, these villages are identifiable as "enclosed settlements" of the sort best attested in Iron I sites from the northern Negev and central highlands of Palestine (Herzog 1994), but evident in rural

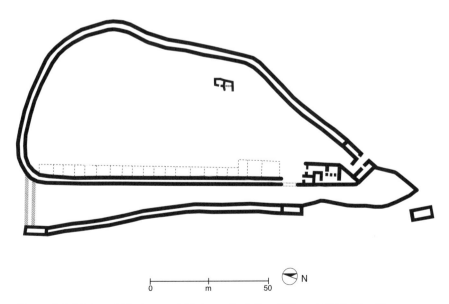

Figure 5.4. Ḥirbat al-Mudayna al-Muʿarradja (after Olàvarri 1983: Fig. 3).

villages of the later Iron Age as well (e.g., Riklin 1997). Where pottery has been published (Crowfoot 1934: Pl. 2, Fig. 2: 5–6, 14; Olàvarri 1965: Figs. 1: 1–6, 9–10; 2: 1–3, 7, 11; 1977–78: Fig. 2; 1983: Fig. 6; Worschech 1990a: Abb. 16–17), it matches the homogeneous late-eleventh-century assemblage from ḤMA. The only exception is Lahun, where a small number of vessels found in association with the base of the outer casemate wall are distinct and seem to be late thirteenth or twelfth century in date (Homès-Fredericq 1992: 193–94; 1997: Fig. 33–34). Therefore, the village at Lahun may have been founded already in the twelfth century but was significantly rebuilt in the eleventh.

Site Foundation

Simply on the volume of stone visible on the surface of ḤMA, ḤMM, and to a lesser extent Lahun, one is forced to conclude that the construction of each of these sites was a major undertaking. Furthermore, bonding patterns between walls show that large proportions of each site were laid out in a single building operation. This is most evident in the fortification walls, which in the case of ḤMA form two continuous sections of 700 m (casemate) and 380 m (single wall) each. However, large-scale construction is also attested by the block of houses in the center of Lahun, which seems to have been built as a continuous row of casemate rooms (Homès-Fredericq 1997: Fig. 29) to which the remainder of each house was then

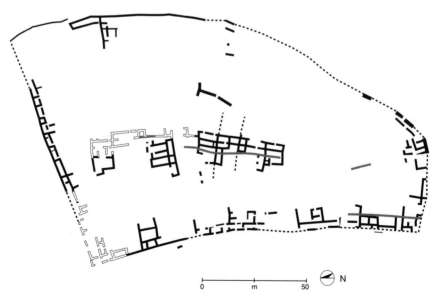

Figure 5.5. Lahun, Iron I period (after Homès-Fredricq 1997: Fig. 41).

added. Hence, we appear to be dealing with founding events rather than organic growth in the sense of a progressive agglomeration of independent houses.

When we factor in human labor, site foundation on the margins of Iron I Moab becomes a rather striking phenomenon. Just to construct the outer fortification wall at ḤMA required something like 9,558 person-days (i.e., 100 people × 96 days) of labor.[19] Given probable site populations, each site foundation seems to represent a near-total collective effort on the part of the entire community, if not the participation of a wider population.

Site Structure: Houses and Storage

While the consistency of domestic architecture varies from site to site, twenty out of the twenty-two houses for which layout can be determined represent some variation on the pillared house. At ḤMA houses can be oriented either parallel or perpendicular to the outer wall, constrained primarily by the local rule that entrances open onto the central plaza and are distant from the broadroom at the back of the house. This creates two common spatial zones (house interior/central plaza) within the community. Repetition of design and a common bipartite spatial relationship to the community as a whole emphasize the conceptual autonomy of each house. In other words, people moving through this community transgress direct physical barriers at two points; upon entering the village through a gate and at the entrance to each house.

Despite the consistency of this shared design, these houses exhibit a good deal of variability, most particularly in terms of size. For example, the investigated houses at ḤMA[20] range in area from 71.5 to 238.8 m², a difference of 334 percent between the smallest and largest recorded examples.[21] However, the two largest houses (buildings 500 and 100) are distinguished by more than their size, being both prominently located and equipped with an unusual quantity of storage space.

Building 500 (Figure 5.6) is located on a high point at the western terminus of the casemate wall system, overlooking both the monumental tower and a probable gate (see Routledge 2000a: 48–49). While less ambiguous in Figure 5.3 than it is on the ground, wall lines suggest that this entire western section may have been walled off from the rest of the site. Certainly, unlike all of the other houses examined thus far, the entrance to building 500 is not oriented to the central plaza. The core of building 500 is a standard house, which on its own is not unusually large for ḤMA (133 m²). However, attached directly to this core unit is a rectangular block of long rooms accessed by a single path. In fact, these rooms are extremely deep within the house in the sense that one had to pass through almost every other room in order to reach them. The form and inaccessibility of this block of rooms suggest that they were used for storage. Of the two rooms

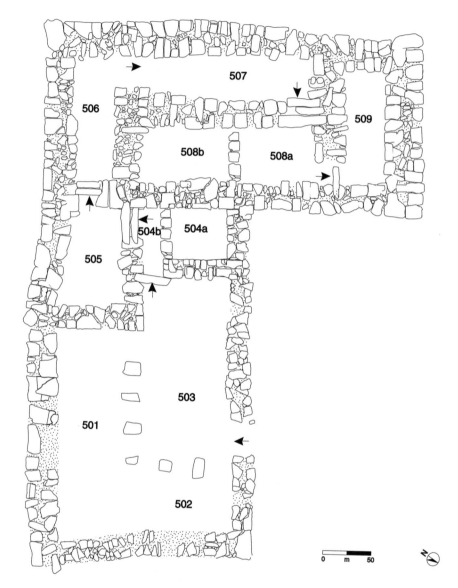

Figure 5.6. ḤMA—Building 500.

excavated thus far, one (508) contained a modified bedrock depression (508b) framed by a low wall and comparable to storage installations in rooms 504a and 102 (see below). The other room (504) contained a bin (504a) that had been thoroughly burned in antiquity and contained large quantities of stored barley (Figure 5.7).

Building 100 (Figure 5.8) is located at the far eastern end of the site adjacent to a postern gate that gives access to the wadi bottom and to the site's primary cisterns. Excavations in two of the building's side rooms (102 and 106) have shown that both contained storage installations (Figure 5.9), one of which (room 106) was burned in antiquity, allowing the recovery of another large sample of carbonized barley. The composition of the stored barley assemblages from buildings 100 (Simmons 2000) and 500 (Simmons n.d.) suggests that the grain was most likely intended for animal fodder.[22]

An emphasis on fodder should not be surprising at ḤMA, since supplemental feed would have been essential if village-based flocks reached any appreciable size, especially in the period between the end of postharvest stubble grazing and the first autumn rains (see Tully et al. 1985). Given mean annual precipitation rates in the vicinity of ḤMA (200 mm/yr) and the limited land available for cultivation in the wadi bottom, sheep and goats were almost certainly central to the village economy (see Cribb 1991: 23–43; Dahl and Hjort 1976; Routledge 1996a: 272–338).[23] At the same time, sustainable grazing was likely to be a significant concern if village-based flocks averaged more than 10–15 animals per house, requiring the use of grazing land more than five kilometers from the village[24] and making supplemental feed an important component of long-term herd viability. Interestingly, the central plaza in enclosed settlements is often thought (Finkelstein 1988) to have been used for the communal herding of village flocks, while Halstead (1987: 81–83) has argued that nucleated settlements tend to communalize animal herding to facilitate transport to distant grazing land. In all of this the "house-bound" manner in which this fodder was stored stands out as significant.

In summary, the largest houses at ḤMA (500 and 100) are also the most prominently located, being positioned at opposite ends of the site, adjacent to both the main and postern gates of the settlement. A considerable proportion of both of these houses appears to have been given over to storage, particularly of barley. If our analytical models are correct, then the stored grain assemblages were processed with the goal of supplementing the feed of village-based herds, allowing the year-round presence of larger herds than could be sustained on free-range grazing alone.

The same specificity of evidence is not yet available from Lahun and ḤMM, hence it is difficult to compare their internal site structure to that of ḤMA. At ḤMM only one house was completely exposed (Olàvarri 1983: Fig. 4), although it was both large (ca. 155 m²) and located immediately adjacent to the gate,[25] making it potentially comparable to buildings 500 and

Figure 5.7. ḤMA—Building 500, rooms 504a and b looking south.

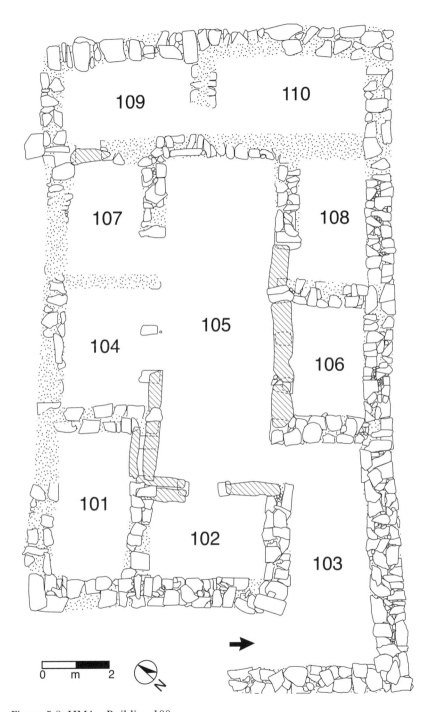

Figure 5.8. ḤMA—Building 100.

100 at ḤMA. For Lahun, Denyse Homès-Fredericq has labeled House 1 the "Shayḫ's house," claiming that it is larger, better constructed, and better preserved than other houses at the site, possessing a unique stone-slab roof (Homès-Fredericq 2000: 182; 1997: 65). However, it is difficult to compare the features, variability, or locational aspects of the Lahun houses on current evidence.[26]

Site Abandonment

On visiting ḤMA one is struck by an evident dichotomy in the preservation of buildings visible from surface remains. Visible architecture indicates seven houses with walls preserved at least 1.5 meters in height, while the remaining houses (n ≈ 28–38) appear to be preserved to heights of 0.50 meters or less. Excavation seems to support this observation. Units excavated in buildings 500 and 100 have revealed walls preserved up to nine courses and 2.3 meters in height. In contrast, units excavated in buildings 200 and 700 (Figure 5.10) have revealed no walls preserved more than three courses and 0.50 meters in height. Topographically, this dichotomy appears to be randomly distributed and not obviously attributable to differential erosion or slope aspect etc. In fact, in the four excavated houses

Figure 5.9. ḤMA—Building 100, room 102, looking north.

there are notable differences in stratigraphic sequence and artifact distribution that correlate with wall preservation. The well-preserved houses 500 and 100 show a straightforward sequence of burning and roof collapse with a fairly low density of artifacts and a single use phase. In both houses, rooms that do not show evidence of burning (102 and 508b) exhibit an even simpler sequence of massive rock collapse over some compressed clay roof detritus and a single floor surface with a low artifact density. Houses 200 and 700, in contrast, contain no roofing material, nor do they present sufficient stone collapse to account for their original wall heights. Floor surfaces are fragmented and poorly preserved, and the above floor soil matrices are composed of fine-grained weathered or redeposited soils. Fully 80 percent of the pottery sherds, 88 percent of the bones, and 100 percent of the metal thus far excavated come from postoccupation deposits in units within these two houses, where artifact densities are at least three times higher than elsewhere on the site. Furthermore, palaeobotanical samples from these contexts show the highest level of species diversity on the site (Simmons 2000, n.d.).

Based on this evidence, the most reasonable conclusion seems to be that, after their abandonment, houses 200 and 700 were used as garbage dumps and their walls were at least partially disassembled for building stone. This in turn suggests that HMA was still occupied after buildings 200 and 700

Figure 5.10. ḤMA—Building 700, looking northeast.

were abandoned. In contrast, the lack of postabandonment deposits in buildings 500 and 100, as well as the extensive preservation of their walls, suggests that the abandonment of these houses coincided closely with the final abandonment of ḤMA. Hence, at ḤMA we seem to have evidence for a piecemeal abandonment of the site in which the inhabitants of the two most prominent houses were amongst the last to leave.

Like ḤMA, site abandonment at circa1000 B.C.E. is probable for most of the sites in Table 5.2 for which one can estimate a reasonable occupational sequence (i.e., ḤMM, Lahun, Ara'ir, Abu al-Ḥaraqa). Sites that are reoccupied soon thereafter, such as Lahun, and Ara'ir, are rebuilt on entirely different lines that directly overlie, rather than reuse, the Iron I architecture (see Chapter 9).[27] From a broader perspective, Table 5.1 presents attested occupation at excavated Iron I and Iron IIA sites in Transjordan, where this can be reasonably broken down by century. Most particularly, from circa 1200–900 B.C.E. settlement in Transjordan is highly unstable, marked by de novo settlement foundation, settlement destruction/disruption and large-scale abandonment. This is perhaps most clearly captured in the prominence of single period sites in the archaeological record. However, even excavated sites with stratigraphic sequences spanning this time show evidence for multiple episodes of settlement disruption and abandonment. The specific sequence of both site structure and abandonment proposed for ḤMA cannot be demonstrated on current evidence from any of the other sites in Tables 5.1–2.[28] However, the potential of this site-specific model is illustrated when we turn to consider several well-known Iron I sites from Palestine.

Palestinian Parallels

'Izbet Ṣarṭah, on the eastern edge of the Shephelah in the state of Israel, is a small Iron I site founded as a simple casemate enclosure with no internal houses (Str. III—Finkelstein 1986: 5–12). It is then rebuilt in Str. II (Figure 5.11) as an irregular circle of small and mid-sized houses (ca. 41.0–67.0 m²) enclosing a courtyard that contained one extremely large (ca. 195 m²) pillared house (109b) and 43 stone-lined pits (Finkelstein 1986: 12–23). Such stone-lined pits are generally thought to have been used for grain storage (Currid and Navon 1989). If true, then the total capacity of the Str. II pits was quite significant, equaling about.150 m³, that is, about 115.5 metric tons of wheat or 91.5 metric tons of barley (see Rosen in Finkelstein 1986: 171–74).[29] In Str. I, the large house(109a) is rebuilt, but it is accompanied by fewer silos and the surrounding houses have been abandoned (Finkelstein 1986: 23–28). Although realized in a quite different manner, the association between prominence of location, size, and storage facilities in the case of house 109 at 'Izbet Ṣarṭah has obvious parallels for our discussions of ḤMA. Similarly, the abandonment in Str. I of the smaller peripheral houses before that of house 109 suggests a set of relations between houses and community similar to that at ḤMA.

The Str. VII–VI sequence at the site of Tel Beer-Sheba (Tell es-Seba') is also quite relevant (Herzog 1984: 8–36). After two initial phases of Iron I settlement consisting of pits and semisubterranean dwellings (Str. IX) and a poorly preserved stone house (Str. VIII), Str. VII is founded as a settlement of perhaps 20 houses arranged as an oval enclosure (Herzog 1984: 15–28). A well-planned fortified town (Str. V) replaces this settlement in the course of the tenth century, marking a clear break with the Iron I sequence. In between, Str. VI continues the layout of Str. VII, but shows extensive evidence for piecemeal abandonment. Some houses are completely abandoned, others are subdivided into smaller compartments (Herzog 1984: 28–36) and only one new house is built (building 2072). Ze'ev Herzog suggests that Str. VI is a transitional stage used during the preparations for the

Figure 5.11. 'Iẓbet Ṣarṭah, Stratum II.

construction of the Str. V town (Herzog 1984: 84–85). Yet, as we have seen, piecemeal abandonment on a house-by-house basis is not uncommon in Iron I settlements, and hence the case of Beer-Sheba Str. VI might best explained in the same terms as that of ḤMA and 'Izbet Ṣarṭah.

Points of Attachment

If we pull this evidence together by asking how people were attached to communities and collectives in Iron I Moab, several factors stand out. In particular: (1) Relatively large groups of people (possibly numbering in the hundreds) were brought together to constitute or reconstruct communities. (2) These communities were marked by inequalities of scale, if not of kind. This seems especially true in terms of bulk storage space and hence perhaps land and livestock as well. (3) Intracommunity social ties were evidently friable. In particular, community spatial structure emphasized the autonomy of dwelling groups, as is also witnessed by the piecemeal abandonment of the site. (4) Ties to the settlement were perhaps strongest for the inhabitants of the largest, most prominent houses, as these were among the last abandoned.

Already we can see evidence for some of the cultural resources deployed both in the constitution of both people and communities. In their form, spatial relations and abandonment, houses substantiate the autonomy of domestic groups, making domestic architecture the primary material component of these communities. The contrast between the large groups founding sites and their piecemeal abandonment, suggests that segmentary modes of identification (see Chap. 6) were prominent in Iron I communities, allowing aggregation without effacing the autonomy of domestic groups or their potential to disperse.

There is, however, much more than this going on. At the center of these communities would seem to be domestic groups with access to, or control over, more agricultural resources than others. The houses in question are not merely those of the wealthy, as they are also strategically located in relation to the settlement as a whole and, in at least some cases, their inhabitants show a stronger attachment to the settlement than those of other houses. In the case of ḤMA, we do not know if the control of storage evidenced by buildings 100 and 500 indicates larger landholdings, preferential access to land or to its products, or only a greater right to store and dispense those products. What is clear is that this storage was extremely house bound, requiring one to enter deeply into the house in order to access storage facilities. At the same time, there are no obvious indicators of class distinctions within these communities in the sense that each house seems to encompass a relatively self-contained unit of production and consumption with its own storage and work areas.

Given the long-term instability of these communities and the evident focus on the recruitment and attachment of domestic groups in their formation, it seems unproductive to explain the evidence for hierarchy in terms of fixed positions within a kinship structure. If one had to choose between the old anthropological chestnuts of "big man" and "chief" (e.g., Sahlins 1963), one would have to opt for the former, if only because stable lineages with ascribed privileges (i.e., "chiefs") could hardly account for these unstable sites. Instead of noble lineages, it appears that we are looking at core domestic groups who attain authority and privilege by attaching others to themselves in the process of founding a community.

This image of founding houses at the center of a community does not come out of the blue. As is well known, a number of biblical place names contain lineage or family names in combination with some form of site descriptor (e.g., Hazaraddar = "enclosure of Addar," 'Abel Bêt-Ma'akah = "meadow of the house of Ma'akah"), and the suggestion that this relates to the lineage or family who founded the settlement has been made on many occasions (e.g., Faust 2000: 31; Stager 1998: 101–102; cf. Bendor 1996: 98–107). Similarly, the ninth or early eighth century "taxation" ostraca from Samaria contain place names that match names in the genealogies of Joshua 17: 2–3 and Numbers 26: 30–33 (Aharoni 1979: 356–68; Schloen 2001: 156–65). Hence, it is not unreasonable to posit either founding "houses" or a genealogical idiom at the center of community identification in our Iron I sites. Typically, this recognition is seen as evidence for the stabilizing role of unilineal descent in a traditional context, with villages existing as the spatial realization of kin groups and hence, barring trauma, fixed in place and identity.[30] This image hardly sits well with the evidence for settlement instability, human displacement, and newly emerging identities that characterizes the Iron I period in the southern Levant. We need, therefore, to imagine these same factors in new ways to account for the empirical evidence from Iron I Moab.

Frontier Settlement: An African Model

The southern Levantine Iron Age is hardly the only time and place where settlement volatility and flexible descent reckoning have come together in important ways. Igor Kopytoff (1987) has provided an innovative discussion of settlement formation in Equatorial Africa that provides a useful alternative for thinking about communities in Iron I Moab.[31] Kopytoff revises Turner's famous "frontier" model of American historical development (Turner 1920) in a context dominated by flexible kin groups, high levels of mobility, and a focus on "wealth-in-people." "Wealth-in-people" refers to the overriding political importance of recruiting and attaching people and rights-to-people (rather than controlling resources) in the formation and development of African polities.

Historically, in western and central Africa, new settlements were frequently founded in the interstices of established settlements through the "spitting-out" of individuals, and particularly descent groups, as the result of conflict and lineage fissioning. Low population densities made territorial coloniza-tion a viable strategy for such disenfranchised people. Furthermore, being first in colonizing a territory carried with it ideological claims to the rights and privileges of leadership (Murphy and Bledsoe 1987), in part because these are embedded in the process of recruiting other settlers, usually through marriage, lineage grafting, military protection or clientship. Endre Nyerges (1992) has shown the rather pragmatic aspects of this process in the case of swidden agriculture, where aspiring village headmen must recruit people and organize their labor in order to clear new swiddens, then work to keep people attached to the village, especially as soil pro-ductivity declines. The resultant pattern is one of highly fluid settlement histories, characterized by high rates of village abandonment and, less fre-quently, the long-term development of autonomous polities, where "founders" retain subsidiary settlements as clients. Kopytoff has characterized the crit-ical differences between the open social relations of frontier settlement with classic views of tribalism in the following manner:

This pattern of social formation is incompatible with the model of ethnogenesis im-plied by the classical notion of the tribe. Instead of a primordial embryo—a kind of tribal homunculus—maturing through history while preserving its ethnic essence, what we have here is a magnet that grows by attracting to itself the ethnic and cul-tural detritus produced by the routine workings of other societies. (Kopytoff 1987: 6–7)

The Iron I Frontier

Kopytoff's characterization of the African frontier is relevant to the case of Iron I Moab in more ways than one. First, it allows us to imagine alter-natives to fixed collective identities and stable rural settlements without denying the salience of genealogy, domestic autonomy, or segmentary identification. This in turn allows us to imagine contexts where recruit-ment, rather than putative point of origin (e.g., nomad, peasant), was the key dynamic in forging new identities, economic relations, and political modalities. Indeed, given that the boundaries between sedentarism and nomadism, and agriculture and pastoralism, are not likely to have been firmly drawn at the end of the Late Bronze Age, the logic of recruiting peo-ple to newly "equalitarian" settlements seems the most significant aspect of the social changes marking the Iron I period.

Second, and more directly, it provides a model for the expansion of set-tlement into the margins of Moab's plateaus. Insofar as we have evidence, the earliest Iron I communities appear to have been formed in areas already occupied during the Late Bronze Age.[32] Indeed, the longer Iron I sequences at sites on the west and north of Moab suggests that these core sites,[33] despite their own disruptions and instabilities, were the source from which at least some of the population for the marginal late Iron I sites was drawn.

To summarize, it is clear that Late Bronze Age hegemonies never filled the landscape they inhabited and hence were always marked by a significant "exterior" social space where people by turns nominally acknowledged or openly resisted elite claims. Indeed, as Marfoe (1979: 15–17) has argued, physical mobility and flexible identities mean that one cannot effectively divide those under and those beyond elite patronage and control. As the ability of Late Bronze political centers to lay claim to territory declined, people from both within and without these centers began to gravitate to new communities focused on mutual defense and subsistence security. In contrast to the "palace" or temple focus of LB sites, these new communities stressed domestic autonomy and an ideology of categorical equality between domestic groups. This is not to say that such villages were either egalitarian or economically homogeneous. Indeed, we have linked significant differences on both fronts to a "founder's privilege" that set some lineages apart from others. However, the formation of these villages involved new economic relations as the tributary relations of the LB centers were not perpetuated. These villages also entailed new forms of identification, as the ritual complex that affirmed social difference through offerings made at the "center" was supplanted by the effacement of difference through the replication of like units.

In Moab, the earliest and most successfully established sites were located on the western portion of the plateau. However, site foundation was not a single event. Indeed, the potential for village fissioning was built into the segmentary modes of identification that bound domestic groups to communities. Hence, families retained high levels of mobility, and site foundation continued as a path to local leadership. These realities must have underlain even the most continuously occupied sites, not only constituting a limit on the exertion of coercive force, but also structuring the dynamics and priorities of communal life.

In this chapter, we have suggested that the LB II–IR I transition was marked by the dissolution of LB hegemonies, with people gravitating to communities founded on new principles. The LB focus on an exemplary center that cares for the gods and the dead is displaced by a focus on domestic autonomy materialized in the house and, I would argue, in segmentary modes of identification and genealogical idioms. When articulated to compose Iron I communities, these cultural resources conspired to provide strategies for leadership and also to place limits on hierarchy. However, as we shall see in subsequent chapters, these same cultural resources were also available for rearticulation in Iron II state hegemonies, making "moral" and "orderly" a moral order of class stratification and asymmetrical power relations.

Chapter 6
Structures and Metaphors

Even the Nuer are not like The Nuer.
—*Adam Kuper*, Lineage Theory: A Critical Retrospect

My insistence on breaking down structural models of social organization in the last chapter may seem the product of a perverse desire to obscure. After all, we have abundant ethnographic models of patrilineal descent as a political system. These in turn allow us to make sense of a good deal of our textual and archaeological evidence. Everyone knows that such models are imperfectly realized in a messy world, and I myself have admitted that I believe the component parts of these models (segmentation, genealogy, domestic autonomy) to be central to the constitution of Iron Age states. Furthermore, regionally oriented scholarship has used these models to construct innovative and interesting pictures of Iron Age polities that escape from the often-trivializing universality of neoevolutionary stages. So what is the problem?

The problem, I would argue, lies in the search to discover an irreducible essence of society such that history becomes the realization of a social form grounded outside of history itself.[1] In this chapter I will examine two of the most sophisticated nonevolutionary approaches to Iron Age state formation in order to illustrate the importance of treating state hegemony as historically contingent in both content and form, even while recognizing that it deploys deeply embedded and potentially powerful cultural resources. The first approach plays on the theme of "tribalism," looking to unilineal descent systems as the principal form of political cohesion underlying Transjordanian Iron Age states (Bienkowski and van der Steen 2001; Knauf 1992a, b; Knauf-Belleri 1995; LaBianca 1999; LaBianca and Younker 1995; Younker 1997a, b, 1999). The second develops Weber's concept of "patrimonialism," looking to the household as a model of social relations replicated at multiple scales of inclusion in constituting the state (King and Stager 2001: 4–5; Master 2001; Schloen 2001; Stager 1985: 25–28; 1998: 149–51, 171–72). Both of these approaches provide us with essential interpretive insights particularly suited to the case of Moab. However, in both cases a rigid formalism fails to account for the contingent, creative, and contested process by which state hegemony is constituted.

Tribal States

As part of a long-term research project focused in the Madaba Plains, south of Amman, Øysten LaBianca has sought to detail structural continuities in settlement and social organization in the highlands of Jordan from the third millennium to the present day. Like many scholars (Adams 1978; Finkelstein and Perevolotsky 1990; Hopkins 1985; Joffe 1993; Marfoe 1979), LaBianca has emphasized the role of flexible productive strategies and social relations as a means of reducing and spreading risk in this agriculturally marginal environment. In particular, this flexibility is realized in a continuous history of fluid movement by residents of highland Jordan along sedentary-nomadic and agriculture-pastoralism continua. Such movement may find its catalyst in external economic, political, and environmental change, but it is facilitated by flexible suprafamily descent systems that provide structural continuity across these shifts in subsistence practices.

Both LaBianca and his colleague Randall Younker (LaBianca 1990, 1999; LaBianca and Younker 1995; Younker 1997a, b, 1999) have developed the idea of tribalism as a structural constant in Transjordanian social history into an explanation for both the form and the formation of state level polities in Iron Age Jordan (Ammon, Moab, and Edom). Somewhat similar arguments have been made independently by E. A. Knauf (1992a, b; Knauf-Belleri 1995)[2] and explored most recently by Piotr Bienkowski and Eveline van der Steen (2001).

Minimally, the tribal state model constitutes a negative position focused on what the state is not (i.e., centralized, hierarchical, bureaucratic), characterizing Ammon, Moab and Edom as a "thin veneer of central administration" (Knauf 1992a: 52), laid over a relatively untouched base of kin relations. More positively, the tribal state model argues that the Iron Age states of Transjordan lie at one end of a segmentary continuum as supratribal confederacies. These are seen as clusters of tribes united under the idiom of kinship in opposition to external threat and under the leadership of a king who is little more than an elevated kin-group leader. From this perspective, segmentation and the idiom of descent, the two classic components of segmentary lineage systems (e.g., Evans-Pritchard 1940; Gellner 1969; Smith 1956), remain at the center of all Transjordanian social formations. Hence, in the case of Iron Age Transjordan, state formation becomes a question of changes in scale rather than kind.

Certain aspects of the tribal state model do account well for empirical evidence. Bienkowski and van der Steen (2001), for example, have pointed out the rather extreme decentralization of Edom in the far south of Jordan.

Even during the peak of Iron Age occupation in the late eighth through sixth centuries B.C.E., the capital of Busayra (biblical Bozrah) is virtually the only settlement that one might classify as something other than a hamlet, and approximately 40 percent of this site is given over to the temples/palaces of the acropolis. According to Bienkowski and van der Steen (2001: 26–28), ceramic assemblages vary greatly between "Edomite" sites, indicating local production and minimal intersite exchange. Economically, there seems to be a focus on the acquisition and movement of raw materials, including both the copper mines in the Wadi Faynan, south of the Dead Sea, and the newly emergent trade routes from the Arabian Peninsula, probably focused on aromatics (Edens and Bawden 1989; Singer-Avitz 1999).[3] Hence, scholars have emphasized the "derivative" nature of the Edomite state as a product of the external demand for raw materials in an interregional economic system (e.g., Knauf 1992a; Knauf-Belleri 1995: 108–11).

Texts and inscriptions also provide a good deal of evidence that could be cited in favor of the tribal state model. As we shall see in the next chapter, the recognition of multiple levels of identification beneath that of Moab (and potentially in competition with it) in the Mesha Inscription has also been used as evidence for the tribal nature of political society in Iron Age Transjordan (Bienkowski and van der Steen 2001: 38–39; Younker 1997b). Furthermore, we know that genealogies played an important role in the formation of social and political identities in the Iron Age Levant. Ammon, the Iron Age polity with which LaBianca and Younker are most immediately concerned, is consistently referred to in biblical, Neo-Assyrian and indigenous texts as "the Sons of Ammon" (*benay-'ammon*—see Hübner 1992: 243–45). A genealogical reading of this name is well supported, though the specific implications of this and similar polity naming is neither clear nor simple (see below). The formula "X son of Y (male name)" (or less frequently "X daughter of Y [male name]") is the principal form of self-identification in inscriptional evidence from the Iron Age Levant, indicating that patrilineal descent played an important role in personal identity (see Avigad and Sass 1997: 469–70; Clines 1972). Finally, of course, one should remember that the Hebrew Bible/Tanak portrays the neighboring Iron Age polities of Judah and Israel as societies segmented into genealogically and territorially defined tribes (de Geus 1976; Gottwald 1979; Lemche 1985).

At the same time, LaBianca and Younker in particular presume that while the particular scale at which tribalism is realized varies historically, the generative structure itself exists outside of history, grounded in a largely changeless set of environmental conditions. In short, the state is tacked on to political relations, rather than transforming them. As "secondary states," Ammon, Moab, and Edom are defined by external stimuli, rather than through the construction of state hegemony within a given historical bloc (to use Gramsci's terminology). Hence, in this model tribal states are presumed to be latent in the generative genealogies of tribalism.

For example, one finds Ammonite tribes referred to as a prior unitary identity, of which the state of Ammon is merely a particular expression (Younker 1997a, 1999). Similarly, one finds all Jordan's tribal states (i.e., Ammon, Moab, Edom) treated as variable expressions of a single tribal form (LaBianca and Younker 1995: 405–10).

The trouble with the tribal state model, as well as potential paths beyond it, becomes clearer if we look in detail at its two constituent components, namely flexible unilineal descent as an expression of interpersonal relations and ecological conditions as the determining cause of this descent system. My goal is not to evoke the rather well-known dismissals of the tribe as mere colonialist exoticism.[4] Instead, I want to problematize it, to make tribalism a historical question, rather than an answer. Dissecting, rather than dismissing, tribalism in this manner is ultimately productive, since it brings forward many of the key cultural resources and dispositions from which Moabite state hegemony was forged.

LaBianca and Younker (1995: 403–4; LaBianca 1990: 39) follow Emmanuel Marx (1977)[5] in defining a tribe as a unit of subsistence that exhibits "strong in-group loyalty based on various fluid notions of common unilineal descent" (LaBianca and Younker 1995: 403). This minority position saves them from some of the more problematic aspects associated with structural-functionalist understandings of the tribe as a kind of balanced anarchy (e.g., Fortes and Evans-Pritchard 1940; Gellner 1969). However, it also leaves many empirical and theoretical issues unaddressed.

Most obvious is the fact that the majority of Middle Eastern agrarian communities of the recent past were not organized into larger genealogically integrated units, that is to say 'tribes." Notable are the villages of Palestine and northern Jordan that practiced collective landholding (*masha'a*) and mutual defense by means of small-scale alliances between households (*hamula*—see Asad 1975; Atran 1986; Cohen 1965). The households of a *hamula* were usually integrated under a single patronym and ranged from those that were largely autonomous to those densely interconnected to both equivalent and larger groups by genealogy and alliance, as in the nineteenth–early twentieth century multivillage defense alliance centered on the village of Tibne in northern Jordan (Antoun 1972: 16–19, 44–49).[6] However, unless one wishes to gloss tribalism simply as the political use of kinship idioms, these are not tribes. Hence, if tribalism is an ecological adaptation then one must ask where the threshold lies that separates tribal from nontribal residents in the same region.

Here the case of northern Yemen becomes relevant. In the area north and east from San'a, as many as 500,000 sedentary farmers practicing run-off irrigation are integrated into one of two large tribal confederacies[7] (Hashid and Bakil) that act essentially as political blocs (Dresch 1989: 3–6, 22–29). Paul Dresch (1989: 336–40) is at pains to note that tribal territories in northern Yemen are not determined in any obvious way by ecological or economic considerations. In terms of subsistence, arable land is privately held by extended or joint families (al-Bayt), which form the primary units of production and consumption. Grazing land is held in common by villages, which also form the primary unit of jural authority (Dresch 1989: 276–86; Mundy 1995: 62–80). Neither the tribal confederacies nor their major constituent tribes seem to play a significant role in agropastoral production (see Mundy 1995: 89–119). Hence, it seems difficult to argue for either a subsistence role or an ecological threshold that can stand on its own as a sufficient definition or explanation for tribalism.

Finally, LaBianca and Younker (1995: 406–8), as well as Knauf (1992a: 50), make some rather specific claims regarding the sequence of tribal state formation on the basis of ecological criteria. In particular, they claim that tribes coalesced into tribal states from north to south (i.e., from moister to drier climate zones), in keeping with the degree of investment in plow agriculture. Yet, if this is so, one must ask why no such tribal states formed in the northern Transjordan, where both Late Bronze and Iron I settlement was much denser than in Ammon, Moab or Edom (see Braemer 1992; Kamlah 2000). To give the usual reasons, namely that this region was trapped between, and contested by, the regional powers of Israel (to the west) and Aram-Damascus (to the north) is to introduce issues of history and politics that undermine the ahistorical assumptions of adaptation and equilibrium.[8]

Ultimately, this kind of point-counterpoint critique does not take us very far. The case against ecological determinism is already well known and needs little bolstering. Furthermore, because adaptation mainly comes into play as an initial explanation for tribalism, it could be replaced by some other cause with little impact on the overall form of LaBianca and Younker's arguments. Instead, it is much more important to explore the basic conceptual issues that are involved when we say that tribalism is adaptive and that the Iron Age polities of Jordan were tribal.

Quite rightly, LaBianca and Younker emphasize with most Middle Eastern ethnographers that unilineal genealogies are metaphors of closeness that do not in the first instance depend upon genetic relationships (Eickelman 1989: 154–61). Kinship terminology is above all the language of alliance and cooperation. To put it simply, in the languages that concern us as either object (i.e., Biblical Hebrew, Moabite, Aramaic) or analogue (i.e., Arabic), terms like "brother" or "uncle's son" encompass "ally" in their semantic field.

Metaphors of closeness, however, automatically entail their opposite, that is metaphors of distance and to say that genealogies "do" something (i.e., facilitate flexible subsistence strategies) requires that we ask just what distance might do. In other words, if genealogy as closeness constructs a world of flexible alliances that facilitate particular subsistence strategies, what kind of world does genealogy as distance construct? This question is more than mere sophistry, since these two aspects of genealogy are, of course, inseparable. Hence any attempt to identify tribalism as an essence in Transjordanian social life, to make it a principle prior to history itself, grounded say in ecology or a presumed *mentalité,* must account for both closeness and distance, alliance and conflict. I will illustrate what I mean in relation to three issues: the gendering of closeness in patrilineal genealogies, the construction of hierarchy by means of genealogy, and the definition of group boundaries.

Gendered Genealogies

First, it must be remembered that marriage is the principal form of incorporation and alliance formation under an ideology of patrilineal descent. Large-scale genealogical reorganization (telescoping, grafting, etc.) is secondary and often serves in conjunction with marriage ties. Furthermore, ethnographic accounts show time and again that affinal (by marriage) relations and matrilineal connections are central to sociality and social action (e.g., Antoun 1972: 114–16; Lancaster 1981: 58–72; Peters 1972: 185–96).[9] At the same time, an ideology of patrilineal descent continually denies affinal/matrilineal links or seeks to convert them to agnatic/patrilineal ones (see Gingrich 1995: 163; Bonte 1994).[10]

From here springs the extended literature on "parallel cousin" marriage in Middle Eastern ethnography. As Bourdieu (1977: 30–71) discusses at length with regard to North Africa, the ideal of endogamous "Father's-Brother's-Daughter/Father's-Brother's-Son" (FBD/FBS) marriages partakes in the contradiction between public representations of male descent and practical recognition of female centrality in marriage, procreation, and family alliance. Lila Abu-Lughod (1986) has suggested that this contradiction can take the form of dual but coextensive social domains. For example, Awlad 'Ali women from Egypt's Western Desert maintain strong social alliances with their birth families, and they counterpoise epic poetry—one of the major venues for replicating the patrilineal values of honor and conflict (see Meeker 1979; Caton 1990; Shryock 1997)—with a genre of love poetry that employs otherwise dishonorable language and is explicitly recognized as belonging to the domain of women and youths.

Hence, patrilineal descent may serve to form alliances suitable for the pursuit of flexible subsistence strategies, but it also reconfigures those alliances in order to reproduce specific gender relations. Furthermore, these gendered relations are subject to contestation and resistance, which can manifest itself both in specific acts (e.g., abandoning a marriage) or in counterpoised practices, like love poetry or women's social alliances. Here, then, is the first point of complexity in the uses of genealogy. Any explanation for unilineal descent must also explain the gendered domains that this descent system creates in contradiction with the conditions of its own reproduction (i.e., the centrality of women in patrilineal descent).

Equality and Hierarchy

Unilineal descent is also generally viewed as a framework for egalitarian social relations, since both the underlying premise of common substance (e.g., Arabic *asabiyya*) and the ease with which it justifies partible social groups means that leadership is tightly constrained by followers who regularly vote with their feet (e.g., Salzman 2000). Yet, such social formations often give rise to relatively marked inequalities, as indeed is implied in the concept of a tribal state (see Bradburd 1987; Digard 1987). From a typological perspective this fact is discomfiting, hence the acts of contortion some scholars commit to claim that tribal inequalities are in fact illusory, as they are dependent on consent in the absence of a monopoly on coercive force (Lancaster 1981: 80–94; Salzman 2000). Yet, as we have already seen, coercion is only half the story of power, ignoring very real differences in the cultural capital available to individuals for the purpose of collective persuasion (Caton 1987).[11]

As Pierre Bonte (1991: 146–48, 2000) points out, the unilineal genealogical structure of a tribe provides both a (male) egalitarian model and a hierarchical model of social relations. The metaphor of common substance via a common ancestor is a powerful egalitarian model, especially when used in contrast to nonmembers. At the same time, this "genealogical imagination" allows for hierarchical models that distinguish between primary and collateral lineages, and between those with "noble" genealogies and those who belong to "half," "foreign," or "slave" lineages grafted through relations of protective clientship or even servitude (see also Munson 1989). Indeed, commonality of substance through descent can itself be a principle of differentiation, most notably in the Islamic world in the case of descent from the Prophet (see Bonte, Conte, and Dresch 2001; Tapper 1997: 343–48).[12] These marks of difference are cultural capital that can serve to distinguish ruling lineages from those being ruled (Digard 1987; Hamès 1991), or dominant tribes from subaltern ones. As Andrew Shryock notes regarding two such tribes in his rich discussion of oral history in Jordan:

When 'Abbadis challenge the 'Adwan, they assert an equality of honor that 'Adwanis fail to discern. The language in which the two tribes confront each other is intrinsically unbalanced and the rhetorical tools needed to build historical truth—namely, poetry and genealogy—have accumulated, over time, in the hands of dominant shaykhs. Thus, in the Balga today, colloquial memory is composed of speech acts that reimpose power differentials located in a real historical past. (Shryock 1997: 211)

Genealogies, therefore, are at once egalitarian and hierarchical. To say that a given tribe is ranked or unranked is to miss the point. Genealogies provide the cultural resources with which both equality and hierarchy can be asserted and contested, though often from dominant and subaltern positions. Hence, genealogies are not merely pragmatic tools for alliance, reorganized to match current realities (e.g., new subsistence relations). Rather, genealogies are historical assertions marking closeness and distance, equality and difference, that are both witnessed in present realities and at least partially constitutive of those realities (see Shryock 1997: 212). This then is our second point of complexity. The political use of genealogies does not necessarily produce a particular kind of society (i.e., tribal), and hence one cannot extrapolate from genealogical language (e.g., "the Sons of Ammon") to other presumably correlated traits.

Segmentation and Boundaries

The tribal state concept asserts that Iron Age polities find their roots in tribal confederacies that banded together to defend common interests against external threat (LaBianca and Younker 1995: 405, 408–11; LaBianca 1999: 20–21; Younker 1997a: 120–26; 1999: 206–9). This commonality of interest and identity is held to be latent in the genealogical structure of the tribe, namely in its ability to provide a common point of cohesion through a common apical ancestor. Normally, it is here, on the question of how tribes aggregate and disaggregate in terms of a politics of opposition, that segmentary lineage theory is brought into play. Our authors, with the exception of Younker (1997a: 60–63), do not give segmentary lineage theory more than passing comment. However (justly or not), the concerns of ethnographic literature on Middle Eastern tribal societies over the past 150 years make it impossible to discuss the politics of tribalism without discussing segmentary lineage theory in some form or another (see Bonte and Conte 1991; Eickelman 1989: 131–38; Kraus 1998; Kuper 1982; and Smith 1956 for literature).

In classic formulations, tribes were structured by the combination of unilineal descent and segmentation (Evans-Pritchard 1940: 94–248; Fortes and Evans-Pritchard 1940: 5–15; Fortes 1953; Gellner 1969: 35–69; Smith 1956). Segmentation refers to a conceptual hierarchy whereby equivalent social units are opposed at one level of reckoning but subsumed or united in a larger social unit with its own set of oppositions. A segmentary lineage system is one in which, at each level of reckoning, equivalent descent groups (e.g., lineages) are structured in competitive opposition while being joined through descent from a common ancestor at the next highest level of reckoning. The logic of this system portrays society as a pyramid of nested social groups, increasing in number at each successively lower level of organization. Such systems are said to be characterized by a process of "fission and fusion," whereby segments aggregate and disaggregate in accordance with the scale at which disputes occur and loyalties are mobilized. Furthermore, this system was seen as existing in balanced opposition, in that at each level of descent reckoning corporate groups were confronted by opposing groups of roughly equivalent size and power. This was said to provide a framework for managing conflict in a society without institutionalized government, as offenses against individuals potentially implicated an ascending spiral of larger groups with responsibility for vengeance or redress (esp. Gellner 1969: 53).

While conceptually tidy, as a model by which to understand collective action in the real world segmentary lineage theory has run into trouble at almost every turn. Ethnographers observed that tribal subdivisions were often not balanced, descent groups were not always coherent, lines of conflict did not always follow genealogical principles, and genealogical position did not always determine personal action (Eickelman 1989: 134–38; Kraus 1998; Kuper 1982; Munson 1989; Peters 1967; Rosen 1979; Salzman 1978). Already in 1956, Michael G. Smith noted the conceptual importance of distinguishing segmentation from descent. In seeking alternatives to segmentary lineage theory, a number of scholars took up this suggestion (Dresch 1986; 1988; Herzfeld 1987; Karp and Maynard 1983; Maynard 1988) and focused on segmentation as an aspect of social and political identity, rather than as a type of political society (Herzfeld 1987: 158).[13] Paul Dresch (1986, 1988) in particular, has emphasized that segmentation is a structure of meaning (what he later calls more specifically a "structure of privacy"; Dresch 2000), which in a Middle Eastern context is built around honor as a limited good that must be defended. Dresch (1986: 312) argues that because the shared or opposed nature of honor must be evoked in a given case, the course of events in any given circumstance is never predetermined by the "social masses" (family, lineage, clan, tribe, etc.) potentially involved. Tribes, Dresch (1989: 97–106) suggests, must be called forth, activated, and given shape by oratorical persuasion.

Segmentation, in this sense, can be understood as a taxonomic categorizing of social distance based on contrast ("us vs. them"), which involves: (1) logical principles of differentiation (such as honor); (2) the cultural idioms in which this is expressed (such as descent); and (3) the practices in which differentiation (or cohesion) is realized (oral history, blood feuds, legitimate marriage, political allegiance, etc.; see Dresch 1986; Karp and Maynard 1983: 484; Maynard 1988).[14] This means that segmentation is not, in the first instance, about what corporate groups (tribes, lineages, etc.) do, but rather about how identity (and hence expectations and actions) is formed in a given context. These segmentary identities are formed by creating equalities through distinction and hierarchies through incorporation.

One problem remains in imagining tribalism as the playing out of a segementary logic rooted in personal identity. Dresch in particular has been criticized for presenting segmentation as a structural principle or a collective disposition that in effect generates Middle Eastern tribalism.[15] In other words, he seems to suggest that a tribesman is a priori a particular kind of person, what Abu-Lughod (1989: 283) has facetiously termed *homo segmenticus* (cf. Dresch 2000). What is obscured in Dresch's work is that key practices, such as the composition and recitation of epic poetry or genealogies, the contracting of marriages, and the mediation or execution of feuds, are not manifestations of a prior segmentary logic but are the construction and reproduction of that logic in itself (cf. Caton 1990; Shryock 1997). Segmentation, therefore, is constituted as a historical disposition within a specific lived material context.

This brings us to our third point of complexity in the meaning of tribalism. The boundaries and definition of a tribe do not simply exist; they must be called into existence by historically and culturally specific practices. Part of what we recognize in the phenomena of tribalism is a segmentary logic of identification realized through a genealogical idiom. However, this is not a timeless *mentalité* or a convenient adaptive mechanism. While difficult to recognize when carried out successfully over time, we should never forget that tribes never exist, rather they are constantly being made.

My goal in reviewing ethnographic literature from the Middle East has not been to construct rules or even regularities that govern tribal societies in Jordan or elsewhere. Indeed, my goal has been quite the opposite. In showing the complexity and historical contingency of apparently tribal social forms, I am arguing that we cannot treat tribalism as a stable category. Genealogy and segmentation are cultural resources that can be configured and interpreted in a variety of ways, hence we cannot infer a whole (i.e., tribalism) from the appearance of any particular part (e.g., genealogical language). If we are looking for an interpretive path to understanding Iron Age state formation, tribalism is a short-cut that does not take us where we want to go.

Patrimonial States

Though not presented as an alternative to tribalism, the exploration of Weber's "patrimonial state" (Weber 1978: 1010–1014) initially by Lawrence Stager (1985: 25–28), and more explicitly by his students David Schloen (2001) and Daniel Master (2001), has produced a rather distinct model of Levantine polities. Following Weber, these scholars focus in the first instance not on social collectives, but on the subjective orientations of individuals (cf. Weber 1978: 13–18). In particular, for Weber societies cohered around subjective understandings of political authority that actors employed in constituting legitimate domination. He recognized three forms of such authority (rational, traditional, and charismatic) that engendered three forms of legitimate domination (bureaucracy, patrimonialism and hierocracy).

Of these forms of legitimate domination, patrimonialism is modeled explicitly on the household. It employs traditional authority, meaning that a subject's "obedience is owed not to enacted rules but to the person who occupies a position of authority by tradition or has been chosen for it by the traditional master" (Weber 1978: 227).

The particular form of traditional authority involved is what Weber terms "patriarchalism," namely the filial obedience owed by a household to its master, but here realized at a suprahousehold level. Again, to quote Weber (1978: 1013): "The establishment of a "political" domination, that is, of *one* master's domination over *other masters* who are not subject to his patriarchal power implies an affiliation of authority relations which differ only in degree and content, not in structure" (emphasis in original).

In practice, for Weber this meant that in societies of a particular kind (i.e., patrimonial ones) all relations of domination were modeled on those learned in the household. Hence, for example, patrimonial states were imagined as the personal household of the ruler. Such rulers exercised the absolute authority Weber ascribes to the patriarch but were also constrained by tradition and the personal, loyalty-dependent nature of household authority.

The argument made by Schloen (2001) in relation to Late Bronze Age Ugarit (and a variety of other Bronze Age Near Eastern polities), and by Stager (1985: 25–28; 1998: 149–51, 171–72) and Master (2001) in relation to Iron Age Israel and Judah, is that these states were organized on the model of patrimonial authority. In other words, these scholars shift the focus of state formation from institutional arrangements and administrative structures to the metaphors and models of legitimate domination employed by subjects in the formation of a state. Most particularly, they argue that in the patrimonial states of the Near East both rulers and ruled conceived of the state as a singular household in which the realm formed the private domain of the king in his role as the premier patriarch.[16] Underlying this argument is the assertion that under the substantive rationality of a "traditional" Mediterranean society it could hardly have been any different, as the household was the only model of legitimate domination readily available. Indeed, Schloen (2001: 71–72) goes so far as to argue that ancient Near Eastern social formations are distinguished only by their scale and not by their political organization.

There is in fact some rather compelling evidence for the idea of the state as a household in the Iron Age Levant. In the Bible and in Neo-Assyrian and Northwest Semitic inscriptions from the ninth–seventh centuries B.C.E. one finds polities named as the "House of X," with "X" being a male personal name (Table 6.1; see Dion 1997: 225–28). Persons attached to these polities are often referred to as the "Sons of X," of which the above mentioned example of the "sons of Ammon" (*benay-'ammon*) (Hübner 1992: 243–45) has figured prominently in discussions of Transjordanian states. This pattern cannot be reduced to the conventions of any one textual or linguistic tradition, as examples occur across such traditions and in both self-descriptions and the descriptions of others.

Table 6.1. Polity naming patterns in the Iron Age Levant

Polity	Dynasty	Ancestor	Other	bit-X	byt-X	mār-X	bmy-X
Ammon	—	House/Sons of Ammon	—	yes[1]	—	—	yes[2]
Israel	House of Omri	House/Sons of Israel	Samaria (royal city)	yes[3]	yes	—	yes
Judah	House of David	House/Sons of Judah	—	—	yes[4]	—	yes
Bit-Agusi	House of Gush	—	Yahan, Arpad	yes[5]	yes[6]	yes[7]	yes[8]
Bit-Adini	—	House/Sons of Idini	—	yes[9]	—	yes[10]	—
Bit-Bahiani	—	Sons of Bahiani	Gozan (royal city)	yes[11]	—	yes[12]	—
Sam'al	Sons of Gabbar	—	Sam'al, Y'DY	—	—	yes[13]	—
Bit-Zamani	—	—	—	yes[14]	—	yes[15]	yes[16]
Damascus	House of Hazael	—	Aram-Damascus, "Land of the Asses"	yes[17]	—	—	—

bit = house and *mār* = son in Akkadian; *byt* = house and *bmy* = "sons of" in Hebrew and Aramaic.

1. See Parpola (1970: 76).
2. See Aufrecht (1989: 154–64, 203–11).
3. See Parpola (1970: 82–83).
4. See Lemaire (1994a, b).
5. See Parpola (1970: 76).
6. See Lemaire and Durand (1984: 123, L. 11, 127, L. 10); Puech (1978).
7. See Parpola (1970: 76).
8. See Lemaire and Durand (1984: 113, L. 16, 114, L. 3).
9. See Parpola (1970: 75–76).
10. See Parpola (1970: 75–76).
11. See Parpola (1970: 78).
12. See Parpola (1970: 78).
13. See Parpola (1970: 81).
14. See Parpola (1970: 91).
15. See Parpola (1970: 91).
16. See Fales (1996: 92–93).
17. See Tadmor (1994: 138–39, L. 7′, 186–87, L. 3).

Hélène Sader (1987: 272–73) has noted that for several of the polities named "House of X" (Bît X) in Neo-Assyrian texts it is possible to identify the key figure (the X of the phrase) as an actual historical person. This is true for the Aramean state of "Bît-Agusi" (the House of Gush), apparently founded by "Gush the Yahanean" (cf. Grayson 1991: 218 col. iii ll. 77b–78), as well as for the kingdom of Israel, known as "Bît-Humri" (The House of Omri) and Aram-Damascus, known as "Bît-Haza'il" (The House of Hazael), these latter two being the dominant, rather than founding, kings in the history of their respective states.

This same naming pattern recurs in Northwest Semitic inscriptions. Both "House of Gush" and "Sons of Gush" occur in Aramaic, as well as Neo-Assyrian, inscriptions (Lemaire and Durand 1984; Puech 1978). The discovery of the Tel Dan Inscription (Biran and Naveh 1993, 1995), and the re-reading of the Mesha Inscription that this discovery inspired (Lemaire 1994a, b), provide two examples of the state of Judah referred to as the "House of David." Finally, Shalmaneser III refers to Hayya, the king of the northern Syrian state of Sam'al, as the "Son of Gabbar" (Grayson 1996: 18 col. ii ll. 24b) the dynastic founder of Sam'al, even though, as the Kilamuwa Inscription makes clear (Tropper 1993: 27–46), the former is not a descendant of the latter.

On the basis of this information, Sader (1987: 273) concluded that the formulas "Sons of X" referred to dynastic founders after whom polities were named.[17] This stands in contrast to the more typical position that such formulas are eponymous in nature and hence evidence for the tribal origins of the societies in question (Brinkman 1980: 465; Postgate 1974b: 234). Certainly, the concept of a royal "house" figures very prominently in several of the long inscriptions from Zincirli (Panamuwa and Bar-Rakib–Tropper 1993), from Sefire (Lemaire and Durand 1984), and in the Hebrew Bible.[18]

Paul Dion (1997: 228–31), however, argues that certain collectives, such as the "Sons of Adini," are given " House of X"/"Son of X" designations before they appear to have been organized into a hereditary monarchy and hence are likely to be named for eponymous figures in a tribal genealogy. Ammon presents us with another such case, as the named figure (Ammon) appears to be eponymous (Hübner 1992: 243–45). The Bible (Gen. 19: 36–38) suggests as much by satirizing such an ancestral figure as the offspring of Lot's incestuous relations with his daughters. Dion (1997: 231), therefore, suggests that these naming formula included both dynastic founders and eponymous ancestors.

To these two forms of naming we can add a third, nongenealogical formula, where the polity is designated by a territorial or place name (e.g., Moab, Edom, Sam'al). One might be inclined to argue from this evidence that polities across the Iron Age Levant were organized in distinct ways, some focused on royal houses, some on tribal genealogies, and some on traditions of place. However, these naming formula are not exclusive. Single polities can possess both dynastic and ancestral names ("House of David"/"House of Judah," "House of Omri"/"House of Israel"/"House of Joseph"), or dynastic and territorial names ("Sons of Gabbar"/Sam'al). Here we can begin to see some of the problems that arise in asserting that Iron Age states were always imagined as patriarchal households. If the household was the "root metaphor" (Schloen 2001: 46) or underlying structure ordering possible subjective understandings of political relationships, how, then, do we account for this diversity in naming formula? How is it that individual polities, which collectively share numerous parallels in the form and structure of their domestic domains, can be referred to in these distinct, often multiple, ways? To answer this question requires us to break with the central a priori assumption of the patrimonial model, namely the conceptual irreducibility of the patriarchal household.

For both Stager and Schloen the root of patrimonialism is the central and irreducible role of the complex (extended or joint) patriarchal household in Levantine societies of the Bronze and Iron Ages. Particularly influential has been the archetypal example of the biblical *bêt 'ab*, or "House of the Father." Indeed, both Stager (1985) and Schloen (2001: 135–83) make the *bêt 'ab* central to their arguments. The *bêt 'ab* is traditionally seen as a complex patrilineal/patrilocal household occupying the lowest rung in a three-tiered system that included the *mishpaha* (lineage or section) and the *shebet/mattah* (tribe) (See Bendor 1996; de Geus 1976; Gottwald 1979; Lemche 1985). Its moral and ethical status relates to the land it holds in common as a patrimony (*ḥeleq* "plot/share"; *naḥala* "common inheritance") and to the name of the patriarch that it perpetuates over several generations (Bendor 1996: 124–33; Lewis 1991). There is also textual evidence that family name and property were connected with the maintenance of an ancestral tomb (e.g., Gen. 23; 2 Sam. 2: 32; 2 Sam. 21: 12–14; cf. Brichto 1973; Lewis 1989; Schmidt 1994). Indeed, this may well underlie the long-term importance of communal tombs (i.e., multiple successive burials) in the Bronze and Iron Age southern Levant (Bloch-Smith 1992; Chesson 1999).

The central contribution of Stager (1985), which is developed by Schloen (2001: 135–83), was to provide a material and archaeological context for the otherwise exclusively textual phenomenon of the *bêt 'ab*. In particular, Stager argued rather elegantly that the repetitious agglomeration of pillared houses so characteristic of Iron Age settlements in the southern Levant was in fact the material trace left by the *bêt 'ab*. More correctly, he argued that the pillared houses contained the component nuclear families that composed the *bêt 'ab* as a complex family.[19] This is because pillared houses were, by Stager's analysis, too small to house a complex family using standard person-to-living space ratios (e.g., Naroll 1962). Hence Stager attempted to show that a small but significant proportion of pillared houses could be said to form multihouse compounds, as one might expect of a successful *bêt 'ab*. Stager's particular innovation was to recognize that domestic life cycles, high infant mortality rates, and gendered age gaps at marriage made the realization of a multigenerational *bêt 'ab* relatively rare (see Roth 1987; Saller 1994).

Subsequent work (e.g., Faust 2000: 19; Routledge 1996b; Schloen 2001: 150–51) has pointed out both the extreme rarity of good candidates for multihouse compounds and the even bleaker demographic regime likely to have obtained in the Iron Age.[20] Yet, for the most part (but see Faust 1999, 2000), this has simply made the connection between the pillared house and the *bêt 'ab* as a complex family seem stronger, taking the form of a one-to-one relationship. Hence, the fact that Iron Age sites are principally composed of repetitive agglomerations of domestic structures would seem to confirm the complex patriarchal family as the fundamental social unit in the southern Levant. Palaces, which begin to be seen in the Iron II period, appear from an archaeological perspective to sit atop this collection of relatively undifferentiated domestic structures with few if any institutions or collective spaces intervening (see Holladay 1995: 392). In this context, the use of house metaphors in the self-representations of rulers would seem to confirm Weber's insights into patrimonialism as the extension of household relations to the state in the absence of alternative subjective understandings of legitimate domination. However, if we take seriously the basic building blocks of the argument for patrimonialism, namely the extensibility and power of the house as a metaphor and its material grounding in a lived human context, we find that neither house nor household can be maintained as the essentially ahistorical foundation that patrimonialism demands. To illustrate what I mean we will first consider an ethnographic example in which patrilineal households occupy an ostensibly comparable position to that laid out by Stager and Schloen. In doing so we will see not a structural analogy, but rather the complexity possible in actual historical contexts. From there we will return first to the biblical uses of *bêt 'ab* and then to the arguments of Weber himself.

An Ethnographic Caveat

Martha Mundy's ethnographic study of domestic groups in al-Wadi, northern Yemen, focuses explicitly on the historical, economic, and strategic aspects of households, kinship and marriage (Mundy 1995). Here 316 households attest 127 patronymics, in the pattern "House (*bayt*) of –X" (Mundy 1995: 93). If organized by landholdings, one finds that the patronymic groups with the most land also tend to have the most constituent households. Indeed, these differences are quite striking, ranging from landless families that are virtually nuclear to large landholding houses that contain over 100 individuals. Mundy (1995: 97–101) goes on to show that, although this is a census-based snapshot of the settlement, these differences in house composition cannot be explained by life cycle differences alone. Indeed, in comparing the size of each household with the age of its head, consistent patterns only emerged when she controlled for differences in wealth and occupation (Mundy 1995: 99).

Though Mundy does not provide a detailed discussion of residency patterns, these patronymic groups also seem to show striking differences (Mundy 1995: 93). The thirteen households of the largest landholding group (*Bayt 'Akish*) are concentrated entirely within one of the settlement's eight wards, which also bears the name of this house. On the other hand, the ten households of the second largest landholding group (*Bayt al-Abyad*) are spread over four of the settlement's wards. *Bayt al-Abyad* in particular maintains its unity through dense marriage alliances across the three main genealogical stems of the "house" (Mundy 1995: 187–95).[21]

Despite the differences in size, these various houses cannot be said to be operating at different levels in society (as a lineage, patronymic association, a complex family, a nuclear family, etc.), since the largest groups are not composed of the smallest but are separated from them by wealth, personal history and structural complexity (Mundy 1995: 95, 223 n. 27). Indeed, Mundy shows that wealth, status and house size are not accidents of demographic success but instead are closely interwoven features of "close marriage" alliances in this settlement. Large, wealthy houses can work through marriage to consolidate or expand their landholdings and retain conjugal couples from one generation to the next. By contrast, many landless craftsmen and agricultural workers must practice neolocal residency, often at some distance from their fathers, simply to maintain a viable household. As Mundy (1995: 95) notes: "we should not hope romantically that among the poor it is simply their mobility which hides their cousins from our tabular representations . . . the links of the poor with distant kin are often anything but intense."

In al-Wadi, certain people were able to successfully assert and maintain a patronymic house with significant genealogical depth, while others were not. This provided some people, and not others, with the ability to retain and expand their landholdings, to contract favorable marriages, and to garner significant factional support. Hence, despite an ideology of unilineal descent, individuals in al-Wadi were not embedded like Russian dolls in a genealogical structure of increasingly inclusive social groups. Instead, people encountered cultural resources and dispositions (e.g., genealogy, patrilocal residency) with markedly unequal abilities to exploit them. As Mundy (1995: 93) notes: "for some people a *bait* is just a house. But not for all."

Al-Wadi is not in any sense archetypal. Like any settlement it has its own history and its own specific conditions of existence. However, Mundy's study highlights what we miss when we reduce cultural constructs like the *bêt 'ab* to an essential social group. In al-Wadi, houses were not simply the conceptual building blocks for other social relations. Rather, property, status, class, and gender were all strategically at play in the meanings and implications of naming a house. In a similar manner, one must historicize rather than essentialize the *bêt 'ab* and analogous domestic groups in the Iron Age. This in turn has direct implications for the metaphorical extension of the house to other political relationships.

The Variable Houses of David

Consider, for example, the use of *bayit* (Hebrew "house") in the so-called Succession Narratives of First and Second Samuel. At the very moment that the "houses" of David and Saul are battling over succession, the "house of Judah" anoints David as its king (2 Sam. 2: 1–11). This not only casts political unity in the language of kinship with David, who is from the tribe of Judah (2 Sam. 19: 42–43), it clearly excludes Israel (the northern tribes), drawing, as it were, a line in the sand. In defecting to the "house of David," Abner promises that all Israel and the "house of Benjamin" (Saul's tribe) will follow him (2 Sam. 3: 19), implicitly incorporating the "house of Saul" under David's rule. Finally, with his rule over both the north and south of the country secured, David brings the Ark of the Covenant back to Jerusalem in a procession with the whole "house of Israel" (2 Sam. 6: 15), meaning now both north (Israel) and south (Judah) together as one. In each case, the house serves as a powerful metaphor. However, if the salient feature of this metaphor is strictly a particular understanding of legitimate domination (patriarchalism), we lose the important imagery of incorporation and exclusion that pervades these passages. Just as the walls of a house both incorporate and exclude, so too does the metaphor of the house, making possible its extension or contraction in all directions.

Weber Revisited

This brings us back to Weber's original formulation of patrimonialism and to the limits of its focus on a fixed and abstract set of power relations. One need hardly mention that Weber treated his social categories as ideal types, and hence intended them to be used in comparison with, rather than in place of, lived historical contexts. Yet, even acknowledging this, his typology remains problematic. His focus on the absolutism of patriarchal authority may say more about Weber (and the Germany of Bismarck) than it does about domestic relations in cross-cultural perspective. Furthermore, his implicit suggestion that subjective understandings are singular and shared at the level of entire societies would seem to demand a feminist critique that acknowledged diversity and modes of resistance in addition to the constitution of domination.

What is valuable in Weber's work is the recognition that, in many cases, the domestic domain is a site where domination is learned and produced. Weber does not pursue this observation further, accepting the perceived naturalness of patriarchal authority as sufficient justification for its application at more inclusive social levels. On this point Weber's words are (perhaps unintentionally) insightful and worth quoting at length:

In the case of domestic authority the belief in authority is based on personal relations that are perceived as natural. This belief is rooted in filial piety, in the close and permanent living together of all dependents of the household which results in an external and spiritual "community of fate." The woman is dependent because of the normal superiority of the physical and intellectual energies of the male, and the child because of his objective helplessness, the grown-up because of habituation, the persistent influence of education and the effect of firmly rooted memories from childhood and adolescence, and the servant because from childhood the facts of life have taught him that he lacks protection outside the master's power sphere and that he must submit to him to gain protection. (Weber 1978: 1007)

Contemplating the "normal superiority" of the male, the hard lessons life has taught the servant, or even the "habituation" of the grown-up immediatly leads us to ask just what cultural, economic and political practices help produce and reproduce these "natural" perceptions with some consistency through time. Indeed, the entire structure of Weber's argument invites an analysis of what Foucault (1980: 99) would term the "infinitesimal mechanisms of power" as realized in these housebound relations.

To draw inspiration from Foucault (1980: 97–98), we might modify Weber's arguments to conclude that the domestic domain is a place where subjects are formed. Hence Weber's focus on the household as an irreducible social unit is already too abstract, missing as it does the practices situated within and between households that ensure the reproduction of such social units by means of persons acting as historically constituted subjects. For Weber, constituting the household as an imagined political community was analogous to, and hence equally natural as, the constitution of the household as a material entity.[22] Yet, in questioning the naturalness of household relations, we are also questioning the naturalness of their replication at the level of a political community. The house as a metaphor does not simply arise from the bottom up. Just as the house produces subjects, so to do subjects produce the house.

Throughout this chapter I have been arguing against the easy substitution of abstract forms (tribe, household) for historically specific cultural patterns. Here I should be clear. I have no doubt that much can be learned from the domestic domain about the logic and order of Iron Age monarchies. I am equally convinced that both genealogical and domestic metaphors were central resources exploited in the constitution of these Iron Age states. In fact, in the next two chapters I will go further by focusing on segmentation as a principle of identification basic to the constitution of

Iron Age states like Moab. What I find more difficult is the idea that tribes or households have essential forms that place them outside of history, or meanings so fixed as never to be contested. What I find impossible is the idea that these timeless forms can generate state hegemony in their own image monolithically, noncontingently, and outside of the articulation of specific cultural resources in specific hegemonic projects.

To return to the title of this chapter, human social life is organized around metaphors and structures that shape particular ways of being and render them meaningful. This much, perhaps, is universal. Conceptual abstractions (like tribe and household) help us to approximate the ordering principles of specific contexts and appropriate them to the analytical language of academic discourse. Yet, in doing so we should never confuse the elegance of our abstractions for the messy business of real life. Genealogical and domestic metaphors were important to Iron Age state formation, not because ecological adaptation or a traditional *mentalité* determined their necessity, but because they were effectively and at times forcibly articulated against other possible meanings with distinct implications. This is the process of hegemony.

Chapter 7

Mesha and the Naming of Names

> *The ability to name is at the center of political power, at the heart of political innovation. It entails not only the creation of new symbols but the redefinition of the old.*
>
> —*David Kertzer,* Politics and Symbols
>
> *I am Meš'a' son of Kemoš[yat] king of Moab the Dibonite*
>
> —*the Mesha Inscription*

On August 19, 1868 Frederick Klein and Zaṭam son of Findî' al-Fāyiz arrived at Dhiban, in south central Jordan. Klein was an Anglican missionary employed by the Church Missionary Society, Zaṭam the son of a shaykh of the Banî Saḥr tribe serving as Klein's host and protector. Dhiban was then a ruin seasonally occupied as a camp of the Banî Ḥamîda tribe. While drinking coffee with their Banî Ḥamîda host, they were told of an inscribed stone "that no Frank" (i.e., European) had ever seen. On being shown what later became known as the Mesha Inscription (henceforth MI), Klein copied down some of its signs and then left for al-Karak early the next morning. On his return to Jerusalem, Klein showed his notes to Heinrich Petermann, the North German consul. Thus began a frenzied fifteen-month battle to acquire the MI waged between Prussian, French and British representatives in Jerusalem (see Graham 1989; Horn 1986; Silberman 1982: 100–112). This ended with the Banî Ḥamîda breaking-up the inscription, perhaps in reaction to the intervention of Rashid al-Pasha, the Ottoman *wali* (governor) of Damascus, who was particularly unpopular among the Bedouin of Transjordan. Charles Clermont-Ganneau (1875) reconstructed the stone from surviving fragments and an imperfect squeeze made from the complete inscription. The result is the incomplete 34-line inscription currently on display in the Louvre (AO 5066; see Figure 7.1).

In the story of its acquisition, the MI is a veritable monument to the blending of colonial ambition and a pious mania for "biblical" antiquities that characterized European, and eventually American, engagement with the Ottoman Empire in the late nineteenth and early twentieth centuries

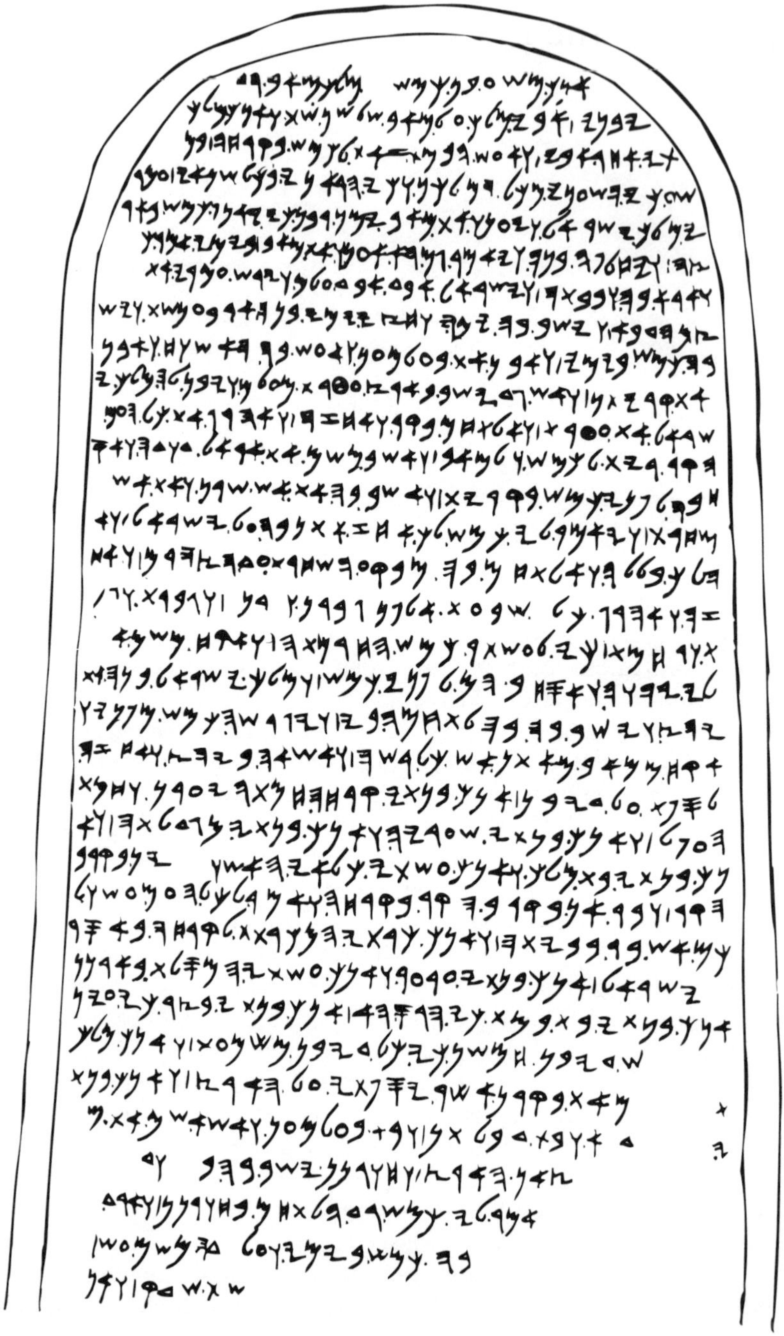

Figure 7.1. The Mesha Inscription.

(see Silberman 1982). Yet, while many other finds from this era of frantic acquisition have been overshadowed by the subsequent discoveries of controlled excavation, the MI has remained an object of significant scholarly attention. In brief, the MI memorializes the exploits of one "Mesha, King of Moab," who drives the "King of Israel" out of the "land of Moab" at the command of the god Kemosh, to whom the land of Moab belongs.[1] Today, 135 years after its discovery, the MI remains the longest and most informative Iron Age (1200–550 B.C.E.) document known from the southern Levant. For this reason, the inscription has a certain importance defined by the absence of rivals. On its own terms, however, it is also a text that rewards careful reading; one that provides a unique glimpse into political discourse at a key turning point in the historical development of the Levant. This political discourse is our central concern, as it opens a window onto the structure and rhetoric of Moabite state hegemony.

The Mesha Inscription (author's translation)

1. I am Meša' son of Kemoš[yat] king of Moab the Dibonite/
2. My father ruled over Moab thirty years and I ruled
3. after my father/ And I made this "high place" for Kemoš in Qarḥō / a "high [place"
4. of sal] [2]vation, because he saved me from all the kings[3] and because he caused me to prevail over all my enemies / Now Omr[i]
5. King of Israel oppressed Moab many days, for Kemoš was angry with his land /
6. And his son succeeded him and he also said "Behold I will oppress Moab" / In my days he said th[is][4]
7. but I prevailed over him and over his house / Now Israel perished, perished forever, but Omri took possession of the land[5]
8. of Madaba/ And he dwelt in it in his days and half of the days of his son, forty years, but
9. Kemoš returned it in my days / and I built Ba'al-Ma'on and I made in it a reservoir and I built
10. Qiryatēn / Now the men of Gad (had) dwelt in the land of 'Aṭarot from of old and the King of Israel built for (them)[6]
11. 'Aṭarot / And I fought against the city and I took it / and I killed all the people.
12. The city was[7] for Kemoš and for Moab / And I brought back from there the 'ryl of its dwd[8] and I
13. hauled it before Kemoš in Qiryat / and I caused men of Šaron and men of Maḥarot to dwell in it /
14. and Kemoš said to me, "Go. Take Nebo from Israel." / And I
15. went in the night and I fought against it from the break of the morning until noon/ And I

16. took it and I killed all: seven thousand male citizens and foreign men/ female citizens, foreign

17. women and female slaves / For Aštar Kemoš I made it an inaliena-ble possession (through destruction) / And I took from there the vessels

18. of Yahweh and I hauled them before Kemoš / Now the King of Israel had built

19. Yahaṣ and he dwelt in it while fighting against me / But Kemoš drove him out from before me and

20. I took from Moab two hundred men, its entire unit[9] / And I took it up against Yahaṣ and I captured it

21. to annex it to Dibon / I myself built Qarḥō, the wall of the wood lot and the wall

22. of the acropolis / and I myself built its gates and I myself built its towers / and I

23. myself built the palace and I myself made the retaining walls of the reservoir for the spring[10] inside

24. the city / And there were no cisterns inside the city at Qarḥō and I said to all the people "Make for your-

25. selves each (one) a cistern in his house / And I myself dug the ditches for Qarḥō with prisoners

26. of Israel / I myself built ʿAroʿer and I myself made the highway through the Arnon [/]

27. I myself built Bet Bamot for it was destroyed / I myself built Bezer, for [it was] ruins [/]

28. [And] the men of Dibon were in battle-array[11] for all of Dibon were subjects / And I ruled

29. [over the] hundreds in the cities that I annexed to the land / And I myself built

30. [. . . . Mad]aba and the temple of Diblaten / and the temple of Baʿal-Maʿon. And I took up there [. . .]

31. [. . .] sheep of the land / Now Ḥawronen, the House of [Da]vid[12] dwelt in it [. . .]

32. [. . .] Kemoš said to me, "Go down. Fight against Ḥawronen / And I went down and [. . .]

33. [. . .] Kemoš [retur]ned it in my days. And I brought up from there ten[13] [. . .]

34. [. . .] [. . .š]t. šdq/ And I [. . .]

Historical Context

Across the Levant, the Iron I period ends with the formation of small-scale polities in the course of the tenth and early ninth centuries B.C.E. (see Finkelstein 1999; Dion 1997; Sader 2000). In the southern Levant, debates over the historicity and archaeological status of the biblical "United Monarchy" (Saul, David, and Solomon) continue to rage (see Bruins, van Plicht, and Mazar 2003; Dever 2001; Finkelstein and Silberman 2001). One can, however, establish two minimum statements of general agreement. First, the biblical image of a Davidic empire conquering all of Transjordan and southern Syria to the Euphrates river[14] is historically and archaeologically untenable. Indeed, whatever its ultimate political status, Jerusalem in the tenth century was a small, locally oriented site (Finkelstein 2001; Knauf 2000; Na'aman 1996; Steiner 2001), rather than a major imperial center. Second, as we saw in Chapter 6, the naming of Judah as the "House of David" in two ninth-century inscriptions (the Tel Dan and Mesha Inscriptions) fits very well with Levantine patterns for naming polities. In fact, the Bible's claim of a tenth-century founder for this polity finds parallels in the historical figures of Gush the Yahanean and Gabbar of Sam'al. Hence, as Finkelstein and Silberman themselves admit (2001: 128–30), the question is not whether the "House of David" existed, but rather the nature and scale of this entity.

In terms of Moab, the debates over the United Monarchy lose some relevance once we recognize that the tenth-century polities of Palestine, whether unified or not, were likely only one of many small-scale competing forces in a period marked locally by a low ebb in settlement distribution and probably also in settlement security. This situation changes early in the ninth century, when both the northern kingdom of Israel and the kingdom of Aram-Damascus emerge as regional powers capable of imposing themselves upon neighboring polities and territories (see Dion 1997; Finkelstein 1999, 2000; Pitard 1987). As the Mesha Inscription states, Omri king of Israel "oppressed" Moab and appears to have occupied specific strongholds, as well as having supported what may have been the ethnically distinct "Men of Gad" in the "land of 'Aṭarot" (see below). The exact chronology of the occupation by, and expulsion of, Israel is subject to continual debate, as the Bible and the Mesha Inscription seem to disagree over the specific timing of these events (e.g., Dearman 1989: 164–67; Lemaire 1991a: 146–50; Rendsburg 1981).[15] In truth, the insolubility and uncertain importance of the issues involved give these debates a rather scholastic air. For our purposes it is enough to recognize that by most reasonable scenarios (see Dearman 1989: 163) the king of Israel dominated the Mishor from some point around 880 B.C.E. until anywhere between the last years of Ahab (ca. 855–853 B.C.E.) and the earliest years of Jehu's dynasty (ca. 841–830 B.C.E.).

Already at the time of the events recounted in the Mesha Inscription, a major historical transformation of the southern Levant had begun. Between 853 B.C.E. and 838 B.C.E. Shalmaneser III of Assyria conducted six campaigns into southern Syria, in which a coalition of leaders representing the southern portion of the Levant (Phoenicia, Hamath, Damascus, Israel, Egypt, Kedarite Arabs, etc.) first faced the expanding Neo-Assyrian Empire

(Tadmor 1975; Weippert 1987: 97). This sequence of events was transformational in two respects. First, it marked the beginning of the end for the local great powers of the southern Levant, namely Hamath, Damascus, and Israel (Tadmor 1975: 39–40), who had dominated trade and politics in the first half of the ninth century. Indeed, as Tadmor (1975) emphasizes, the diverse makeup of the coalitions that fought against Shalmaneser III, bringing together Egypt, Phoenicia, and Kedarite Arabs in addition to the main local powers, points to the general concern of all parties to maintain the current political and economic structure in the south, most particularly with regard to interregional trade.

Second, Shalmaneser III's campaigns begin a relatively new phase in the western expansion of the Neo-Assyrian Empire, one of incorporation and consolidation that was to continue with ups and downs until the last years of Assurbanipal. Although fully realized only in the reign of Tiglath-Pileser III (744–727 B.C.E.), the ninth century saw the beginning of Assyria's consolidation of north Syrian polities (Liverani 1988: 91) leading eventually to their incorporation into the "Land of Assur" as provinces rather than as distinct political entities (Liverani 1988: 90–91; Postgate 1992: 251). As a result, the eighth century saw the formation of a southwestern frontier of polities exterior to these incorporated lands, and now a clear target for expansion.

Assyria's conquests were not, however, a smooth or continuous process. Assyria is unattested west of the Euphrates between 830 and 803 B.C.E., with military efforts apparently focused on consolidating rule close to home. Despite bearing the brunt of Assyrian attacks in 841 and 838, Hazael the usurper and most prominent king of Damascus used his reign (ca. 843–803 B.C.E.) to subjugate northern Transjordan, Palestine and central Syria (see Dion 1997: 191–204; Lemaire 1991b; Pitard 1987: 145–51). Hence, the Mesha Inscription is positioned at a significant point in time, as small states, regional powers, and "global" empires vied to fix their hegemony on as yet indeterminate political terrain, with each polity impacting the trajectory taken by the others.

Previous Scholarship

Scholarly interest in the politics of the MI has been largely limited to the strategic and historical issues of Mesha's military campaigns, particularly as they relate to the biblical account of Mesha's "revolt" in 2 Kings 3 (e.g., Liver 1967; Murphy 1953; Rendsburg 1981; van Zyl 1960). In this literature, a number of interpretive dilemmas regarding the MI have been isolated but not resolved (see Dearman 1989). In particular, the inclusive nature of Mesha's claims for the territorial extent of Moab and his kingly authority contrasts markedly with his need to campaign both north and south of Dibon in the course of his reign. Furthermore, parts of the MI seem to assume a simple military occupation by Israel of lands legitimately claimed by Mesha as king of Moab. However, these claims seem to be confounded by the segmented nature of northern Moab and the overwhelming centrality of Dibon in Mesha's activities and identity. In addition, statements such as line 10, where the men of Gad are said to have lived in 'Aṭarot since "of old," suggest that Mesha faced a complex ethnopolitical landscape. At the root of these tensions is a set of problematic assumptions regarding the relationship of political authority, territory, and national identity in the Iron Age states of the southern Levant. In particular, scholars have shown a tendency to work as if political authority, territory and nationhood were coterminous and indivisible.

More recently, there has been a shift in scholarly emphasis. This shift is characterized on one hand by an increased interest in the rhetorical, literary, and ideological nature of the MI as a public text (e.g., Auffret 1980; Drinkard 1989; Irsigler 1993; Miller 1974; Müller 1994; Niccacci 1994; Smelik 1992) and on the other hand by a new emphasis on the fragile, emergent, or even non-existent nature of Moabite statehood as witnessed in the MI (Dearman 1992; Knauf 1992a; LaBianca and Younker 1995; Miller 1992; Na'aman 1997; Younker 1997b). Indeed, in reaction to the interpretive dilemmas noted above, it has become commonplace to point out the rather local points of reference and sources of power expressed by Mesha and the absence of unequivocal evidence in either the MI or the Hebrew Bible for a territorially integrated state of Moab before Mesha (Dearman 1992; Knauf 1992a; Miller 1992; Routledge 1997a; Younker 1997b). Most concretely, it has been suggested that Moab was a tribal confederacy or tribal state, dominated by relations of kinship and charisma rather than class or institutions (Knauf 1992a; LaBianca and Younker 1995; Younker 1997b).

These recent trends in scholarship have not always worked in concert. Our new understandings of Moabite social and political organization have not always benefited from the close readings of the MI that typify literary studies, while literary approaches have yet to show themselves fully cognizant of recent discussions of politics and society in the MI. As I hope to demonstrate, a new reading of the text can provide significant evidence pertaining to issues of politics and social organization, while a nuanced appreciation of politics and society suggests new ways of reading the MI.

Moab the "Unstate"

Recent commentators have pointed to two aspects of the MI that serve as evidence for the dominance of a decentralized, tribal form of social organization in Moab at the time of Mesha. These are the prominence of the town of Dibon in Mesha's activities and identity and the segmented political landscape suggested by the recurrent phrase "land of [city name]" in the MI (Dearman 1992: 75; Knauf 1992a: 49–50; Younker 1997b: 242–43).

While these points are well made, they do not exhaust the evidence for political structure in the MI. Furthermore, as we have already discussed in the last chapter, there is no easy or obvious meaning to be attached to the term tribal. In other words, we cannot presume to move easily and without argument from certain traits in the MI, such as a segmented political structure, to an overarching social type like the tribal state. Rather than fitting Moab within the confined parameters of a particular ideal type, we must work to understand the locally relevant forms of political and social discourse that circulated within this polity.

We begin with the central fact that the MI is a royal inscription, belonging to a well-established genre labeled by scholars as memorial inscriptions (Miller 1974). In general, first-millennium B.C.E. royal inscriptions from the Levant share a striking number of physical, organizational, and thematic features (see Chapter 8). Most were erected at the dedication of a structure or monument (often funerary or religious). Of these, two broad categories (dedicatory and memorial) have been identified (Drinkard 1989; Miller 1974). Not surprisingly, both dedicatory and memorial inscriptions make reference to the building or monument being dedicated, as well as to the king and the deity who are on the giving and receiving ends of the dedication respectively. However, memorial inscriptions go farther in using the occasion as a pretext for memorializing the major achievements of a king's reign. Consequently, the MI as a memorial inscription is bound up in the ideological project of legitimizing and reproducing kingship in Moab.

At the same time, the MI cannot be reduced to mere stereotyped propaganda. Memorial inscriptions represent a culturally specific, rather than generalized, royal ideology—something that becomes clear on comparison with other royal inscriptions from the ancient Near East. For instance, claims for world dominion and singular superiority are strikingly absent. Rather, Levantine rulers are surprisingly candid about the existence of competitors of near equal (or even superior) rank and power against whom they struggle. This contrasts markedly with contemporary Neo-Assyrian inscriptions (Liverani 1979b), as well as the internal/external "prestige and interest" dichotomy that Liverani (see Liverani 1990) has noted for royal inscriptions and international correspondence during the Late Bronze Age.

In this light, it seems productive to consider the MI as an intellectual product in the sense discussed in Chapter 2. By this I mean that the MI can be effectively analyzed in terms of the cultural resources it selects and articulates within the hegemonic project of constituting Mesha's rule, and indeed (as we shall see below) of Moab itself. Here a reasonable objection could be made that as a single inscription that likely had a rather limited audience it may well have been either idiosyncratic and/or of little significance. In response, one could note that the MI does not exist in isolation. For example, the fragment of an Iron Age royal inscription (possibly a second Mesha Inscription)[16] was found built into a house wall at al-Karak

(Freedman 1964; Reed and Winnett 1963; Swiggers 1982; Timm 1989: 269–77). Several other Iron Age lapidary inscriptions have also been found within the territory of Moab, although these are much less certainly royal in nature.[17] This said, it must be admitted that no "Moabite" inscription provides sufficient content to allow an independent comparison with the MI. Hence, if viewed simply as a message (i.e., propaganda) that "functions" by directly convincing its readers, the importance and impact of the MI cannot be determined.

The MI, however, is more than a simple message. Its conformity with the general conventions of Iron Age royal inscriptions in the Levant means that beyond its specific content it signifies a larger body of textual practices associated with kingship. As we shall see in the next chapter, this same signification of royal practices extends in particular to Iron Age architecture and sculpture. Hence, the MI existed in a constellation of intellectual products with broadly similar points of reference. At the same time, as I shall argue below, the MI also draws from, and transforms, local cultural resources as the tools and raw materials of its narration. Hence, its argument for royalty is neither irrelevant nor imposed. As such the MI is not about the narration or falsification of an event-based history aimed at convincing a credulous audience. Rather, the MI is about historymaking; bringing into being a certain understanding of the world by the context and manner in which it recounts events. To put this more pragmatically, it has often been recognized (Dearman 1989: 209–10) that the MI makes a case for the legitimacy of Mesha's rule over an enlarged geographic territory. In what follows, I will demonstrate that in making this case, the MI both incorporates and attempts to transform a preexisting model of political identity based on social segmentation and local affinity.

Syntax and Narration in the Mesha Inscription

Our starting point, from an analytical perspective, is the text of the MI itself. In analyzing the MI, I follow those semiticists influenced by text linguistics (e.g., Bodine 1995) in seeing a significant link between systematic variation in syntax (especially at the paragraph level) and the marking of topical units within a text.[18] Therefore, I assume that both syntax and semantics should play a role in communicating conceptual structures and topical emphasis within the MI. Recently A. Niccacci (1994) has offered an extended analysis of the syntactical organization of the MI. This study systematizes and extends Andersen's observation that there are two different types of paragraphs in the MI (Andersen 1966: 115–16). Put simply, the main line of the story in the MI is initiated and continued in two different ways. One paragraph type is initiated by the verbal construction "*waw*-x-*qatal*"[19] and continued by the construction "*wayyiqtol*,"[20] while the other is initiated by the verbal construction "x-*qatal*" and continued by the construction "*waw-x-qatal.*" More specifically, Niccacci (1994: 226) proposes that the first paragraph type is introduced by *waw* plus a noun phrase, followed by a verb in the finite third person (termed "noun phrase + finite verb"). Niccacci (1994: 226) proposes that the second paragraph type is introduced by the first person independent pronoun (normally) followed by a verb in first person singular perfect form (termed "*'anāk + qatal*"). In most cases the first paragraph type is continued by a *wayyiqtol* construction, while the second is continued by the verbal construction "*w'anāk + qatal,*" or a subordinate *ky* clause.

The two verbal constructions noted by Niccacci structure the MI at two different levels. At the paragraph level, these constructions mark new units each time they are used. At the text level, it is clear that the MI is organized in several large sections marked by shifts from the dominance of one verbal construction to the other.[21] What is interesting from our perspective is that at both the paragraph and the text level a consideration of semantics and topical focus supports the integrity of the units marked by these verbal constructions.

Beginning with the text level, "noun phrase + finite verb" constructions are associated almost exclusively with the narration of military campaigns. "*'anāk + qatal*" constructions, on the other hand, are associated with biographical statements regarding Mesha and his performance of kingly acts, especially acts of construction and piety. While not without some uncertainties,[22] alternation between these two paragraph types divide the MI into five main sections:

1. lines 1–4 (Biography
2. lines 5–21a (Narrative)
3. lines 21b–31a (Biography)
4. lines 31b–34 (Narrative)
5. Lines 34–? broken (Biography?)[23]

The regular shifting between paragraph types is a particularly striking feature of the text-level structure of the MI and suggests intentional variation. Consequently, these syntactical shifts should carry information of importance to the narrative. The content of these sections raises the possibility that the repeated syntactical shifts pivoted on a north/south division of Moab (marked by the Arnon/Wadi Mujib). Indeed, our five major sections can be described as follows:

1. Introduction (Biography)
2. Campaigns north of Wadi Mujib (Narrative)
3. Kingly construction north of Wadi Mujib (Biography)
4. Campaigns south of Wadi Mujib to Ḥawronen[24] (Narrative)
5. Kingly construction (?) south of Wadi Mujib (Biography?)

In other words, the MI proceeds by detailing Mesha's military campaigns and then his building projects in the north of Moab, before repeating this pattern for his activities in the south (Figure 7.2).[25] Of course, with the exception of the campaign against Ḥawronen, the nature of Mesha's activities in southern Moab is lost in the damaged portions of the text and must remain conjectural.

If we look closely at the paragraphs within the narrative sections of the MI we see an interesting pattern that is directly relevant to interpreting the "land of [city name]" phrases. New paragraphs are introduced with "noun phrase + finite verb" constructions in lines 5 ('*mry.mlk.ysr'l. wy'nw*, "Omri, king of Israel, and he oppressed . . ."), 7b (*wysr'l. 'bd*; "Now Israel perished . . ."), 10 (*w's.gd.ysb*; "Now the men of Gad dwelt . . ."), 19 (*wmlk.ysr'l.bnh yhṣ*; "Now the king of Israel built Yahaz . . ."), and 31b (*whwrnn.ysb.bh*; "Now Ḥawronen, he lived in it . . .").

Line 5 introduces the overall theme of the narrative, namely that Omri had oppressed Moab but Kemosh, working through Mesha, had reversed this situation. Following this introduction, each of the new paragraphs introduced by a "noun phrase + finite verb" construction seems to contain information about Mesha's activities in the area of a particular geographic region. In particular, lines 7–8, 10, 19 and 31b each introduce narratives regarding the subjugation of distinct cities or regions by Mesha (lines 7–8 = '*rs.mhdb*', "land of Madaba"; line 10 = '*rs. 'trt*, "land of 'Aṭarot"; line 19 = *yhṣ* "Yahaz"; line 31b = *hwrnn*, "Ḥawronen"). Furthermore, Mesha's building activities at Ba'al Ma'on and Qiryaten in lines 9–10 are syntactically subsumed in the paragraph dealing with "the land of Madaba" (lines 7b–10a). Since both of these sites are to be located near Madaba (see Figure 7.2; Dearman 1989: 175–77), it suggests that the paragraph was structured to cover all of Mesha's actions within a distinct geographical territory.

The only problem site is that of Nebo. Syntactically the campaign against Nebo, narrated in lines 14–18, is not marked. It is introduced by a *wayyiqtol* construction, and hence would seem to continue the paragraph begun at line 10b. In terms of geography, Nebo is not likely to have been part of "the land of 'Aṭarot," nor is this suggested by its prominence in the narration. However, Nebo and 'Aṭarot are linked conceptually in the use of parallel phrasing to detail the process of capture, wholesale slaughter and removal of key ritual objects. This parallel phrasing, as well as the clear ideological significance of the events it relates, sets the campaigns against 'Aṭarot and Nebo apart from all the others.[26]

Interpretation

Returning to the questions of politics and social organization, we now can see that the syntactical structure of the MI both complements and expands on recent suggestions regarding the significance of the phrase "land of

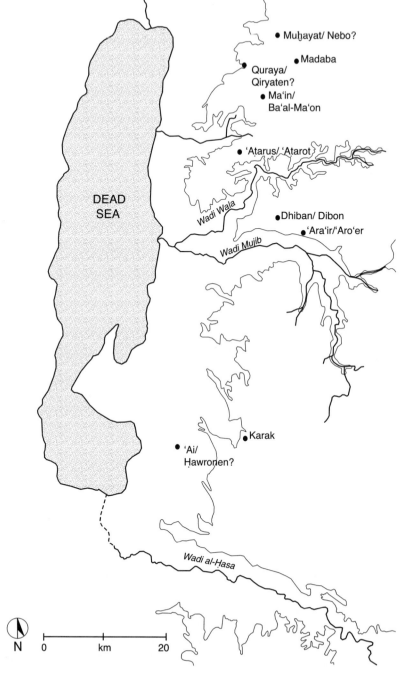

Figure 7.2. Major settlements in the Mesha Inscription.

[city name]." Overall, the MI seems to be syntactically organized around hierarchically linked geopolitical units that follow the pattern shown in Figure 7.3.

Section 1 (lines 1–4) presents Moab as the prime geopolitical unit, based on Mesha's legitimacy and Kemosh's aid. The syntactical shift at line 31b seems to hinge on the north/south symmetry mentioned above, while the paragraphs within the narrative sections are built around major city regions that themselves incorporate lesser settlements. Here the phrase "land of [city name]" denotes a major territorial unit. Perhaps equivalent in meaning is the phrase "all Dibon" in line 28, indicating a territorial designation associated with the settlement of Dibon and conceptually equivalent to the units designated as "land of [city name]" (Dearman 1997; Younker 1997b).[27]

As for individual settlements, we have already mentioned a lower organizational level incorporating individual "satellite settlements," as in the case of Ba'al Ma'on and Qiryaten in the "land of Madaba." Similarly, it is interesting to note that the MI seems to distinguish in lines 10–13 between the "land of 'Aṭarot" and the settlement itself, referred to as *qr* ("city"). Therefore, while all settlements within a "land of [city name]" region were not equal, they do seem to occupy the same taxonomic level with regard to the region as a whole (i.e., a region is made up of a collection of settlements, including the dominant one after which the region is named).

If one takes *qr* in line 13b to be the referent of *bh* in *w'sb.bh.'t.'s.srn. w't.'(s).mhrt* ("and I put in it men of Sharon and men of Maḥarot"), then it would appear that these settlements themselves may have been segmented into social groups, defined perhaps by metaphors of blood-relatedness (i.e., ethnicity or kinship). This creates a fourth level of hierarchical distinction beneath that of Moab.

Running contrary to this neat pyramidal structure is the recurrent importance of the town (or region) of Dibon (see Miller 1992; Knauf 1992a; Dearman 1992; LaBianca and Younker 1995; Younker 1997b). References to Dibon appear in both narrative and biographical sections of the MI, always conveying important and surprising information that seems to call into question the hierarchical relationship of Dibon and Moab. In line 1 Mesha identified himself as both "king of Moab" and "the Dibonite," suggesting that both were identities of some importance for the purposes of the MI. In line 21, the section narrating Mesha's campaigns in the north closes with the annexation of Yahaz to Dibon. This occurs despite the fact that Mesha's military force is said to be from Moab (line 20). This runs counter to the opposition of Moab : Israel:: Mesha : king of Israel used up to that point; an opposition that implies Moab, rather than Dibon, should be the entity to which territory taken from Israel is annexed. In line 28 Mesha explicitly points out that all of Dibon was subject to him[28] in a manner that suggests this suzerainty is one of the bases of his power.

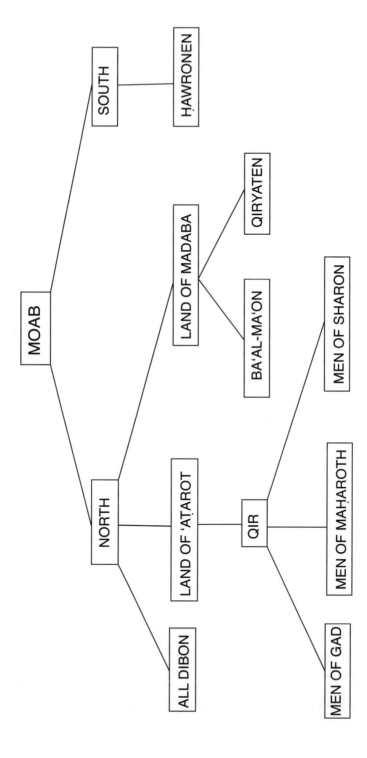

Figure 7.3. The segmentary structure of political units in the Mesha Inscription.

Qarḥō is clearly the focus of Mesha's building activities in the MI. This applies both to the conceptual significance of the *bamah* ("high place") in Qarḥō, the dedication of which provides the *raison d'être* for the MI in lines 3–4, and to the greater detail and attention given building activities in Qarḥō when compared to the other sites mentioned in lines 21b–30. The relationship of Dibon to Qarḥō in the MI remains problematic (see Dearman 1989: 171–74). As already noted, the phrase "all Dibon" in line 28 suggests an ethnoterritorial designation, within which Qarḥō could be seen as a settlement. However, territorial designations in the MI are named after the principal settlement within that territory, and the Hebrew Bible knows Dibon only as a settlement. Therefore, it seems best to follow those who see Qarḥō as a designation for a citadel within Dibon.[29] Hence Dibon, through Qarḥō, is also central to Mesha's building program.

In summary, the MI incorporates two seemingly competing representations of Moabite political society: Moab as a hierarchically segmented system of territories ruled by Mesha, in which Dibon is one of several major subdivisions; and Dibon as Mesha's expanding power base, one that comes eventually to incorporate all of Moab by conquest. Understanding the logic and relation of these two representations brings us back to recent characterizations of Moab as tribal, and requires some reflection on the principles of politics and social organization running through the MI.

Moabite Segmentation

For those who use the MI as a prime example of Transjordanian tribalism there is a rather significant tension that remains unresolved in their arguments. Throughout the MI, the primary units of identification and social action are based in locality rather than descent. Of course, groupings based on metaphors of blood certainly exist. If one follows biblical evidence, then the "Men of Gad" are clearly a descent group. Furthermore, according to the MI, the Men of Gad compose the population of "the Land of 'Aṭarot." However, it is the Land of 'Aṭarot that is constituted as an effective political unit through comparison ("Land of Madaba," "All Dibon"), rather than the Men of Gad. Indeed, the only other possible descent groups in the MI (Men of Sharon, Men of Maharath) are relocated by Mesha to replace the massacred Men of Gad and appear to be incorporated into the Land of 'Aṭarot.

Descent and locality are, of course, not necessarily opposed. Adam Kuper (1982) has traced the long history of conceptual tension between territory and descent as principles of socio-political organization, and especially the tendency to associate the former with state societies and the latter with non-state (i.e., tribal) societies. As Kuper points out, such a position assumes a structural exclusivity of principles of association that simply does not exist in real life. Certainly, Evans-Pritchard (1940: 203–5) himself recognized that the Nuer did not distinguish clearly between lineage and locality except in ceremonial contexts. However, Evans-Pritchard insisted that descent was the idiom through which territorial politics was expressed. As he states: "The assimilation of community ties to lineage structure, the expression of territorial affiliation in a lineage idiom and the expression of lineage affiliation in terms of territorial attachments is what makes the lineage system so significant for a study of political organization" (Evans-Pritchard 1940: 205). This is precisely what does not happen in the MI, and one can only conclude that descent is there in territorial guise if one presumes that it has to be, that descent was of necessity the only idiom for the expression of political relationships.

Ironically, what those who support a tribal reading of the MI actually point to is not an idiom of descent but rather its overlooked partner, segmentation. The MI's "Land of [city name]" terminology, its multicentric focus with the recognition of political units beneath that of Moab, and its contrastive politics are all comprehensible in the terms of segmentation but have no clear connection to the idiom of descent. What makes this difficult to perceive clearly is that traditional structural functionalist literature on Middle Eastern tribalism always portrayed segmentation and descent as inseparable characteristics of relations between concrete social groups (but see Smith 1956). As noted already in Chapter 6, this position has proven itself rather problematic, not least due to its failure as a description of those contexts it purports to represent. Instead, segmentation seems more productively considered as a form of subjective identification predicated on opposition and incorporation rather than as a structural quality of relations between groups.

In this sense, positing segmentation as an analytical abstraction does not mean positing an exotic disposition, that is to say a "tribal mind." As Michael Herzfeld (1987: 159) notes: "The question is not whether a given society *is* segmentary or not. All societies must be segmentary inasmuch as they recognize more than one level of social differentiation. It would be more useful to inquire instead whether the prevailing ideology makes the presence of segmentary relations explicit or attempts to suppress it." Hence, segmentation as a means of forming and relating multiple political identities is a widely available cultural resource, but it is not everywhere articulated in the constitution of state hegemony.

Using the issues discussed thus far, we can now return to the problem of political discourse in the MI in an empirically and theoretically more sophisticated manner. If we look at our schematization of Moabite political society as presented in the MI (see Figure 7.3) we see a taxonomy of political units that is the logical outcome of a process of segmentation. In Chapter Six we characterized the segmentary representation of political relationships in terms of the principles (e.g., honor), cultural idioms (e.g., descent) and practices (e.g., feuds) through which it was realized. Neither the principle nor the practices of segmentation in the MI are particularly clear. However, if we consider line 28, where *mišmaʿat* (one made subject) is offered as the state of being that caused the battle readiness of the Dibonites, we might argue that *mišmaʿat* refers to a principle of loyalty or obedience against which contrasts in political identity were drawn. From this, warfare emerges as the practice in which this identity was realized in the MI. Indeed, the MI as a whole supports the importance of warfare as the means by which contrasting political identities take material form.

Unquestionably the cultural idiom through which the experience of being *mišmaʿat* is expressed in the MI is that of territorial affiliation. As we have already pointed out, the Land of ʿAṭarot (ll.10–14) incorporated peoples with different ethnic/kin designations (Men of Gad, Men of Sharon, Men of Maharath) rather than being coterminous with, or defined by, such identities. This indicates that the territorial divisions cannot be treated as descent groups by another name. Also interesting in this regard is the fact that the anger of Kemosh in line 5 is specifically directed against "his land" rather than "his people."

In summary, the state of being *mišmaʿat* with regard to specific territorial units (and leaders) was the means by which people were mobilized to take part in particular conflicts. At the same time, the successful mobilization of people for warfare helped substantiate, and hence reproduce, this same segmented hierarchy of political identity based on territorial location. In this hierarchy of contrasting territorial units, Moab takes on particular significance in its position at the pinnacle. It is notable that Moab and Mesha are constantly opposed to Israel, and the king of Israel (or Omri), while Kemosh is the principal catalyst for the events that unfold. Given the tension between the role of Moab and Dibon that we have already noted, one might ask why the explicit opposition of Israel and Moab (rather than Dibon or some explicitly recognized coalition) is so central to the narrative.

The necessity of Moab in the MI lies, I believe, in the logic of segmentation. The creation of equivalency through differentiation is, as we noted, one way in which segmented political identities can be defined. Identities distinguished in this way are significant because they cannot incorporate one another, as is the case for those that are related hierarchically (e.g., the "land of Madaba" and "Moab"). From this perspective the events narrated in lines 10b–18a, where Mesha invokes *ḥerem* (explicitly against Nebo, perhaps implicitly against ʿAṭarot) in killing the inhabitants of the two cities he captures, take on a new significance. Without developing the argument fully here, it is helpful to remember certain features of *ḥerem* ("the Ban" in King James English) as it is used in the Hebrew Bible. On one hand, *ḥerem* serves to make something irredeemable (or inalienable) through its dedication as the property of Yahweh (Lev. 27: 26–29). On the other hand, it is something to be invoked against non-Israelites living in the territory

Yahweh gives to Israel, ostensibly to avoid religious exchange between Israelites and non-Israelites (Deut. 20: 16–18). As has been clear at least since Mauss (Mauss 1990 [1923]) exchange is the basis for a good deal of human sociability between those who are not close kin. I would argue that conceptually, the key to invoking *ḥerem* is the prevention of exchange through the insertion of the deity, who holds booty and captives as inalienable (nonexchangeable) possessions. In preventing exchange, one prevents the formation of a mutually recognized relationship. That conquest, booty, and the implications of resultant tributary relations were viewed as a form of sociable exchange[30] is made clear in 1 Kings 20, which recounts the inversion of tributary relations between Ahab of Israel and Ben-Hadad of Aram Damascus. Interestingly, the unnamed prophet in this passage condemns Ahab for entering into tributary relations with Ben-Hadad rather than invoking *ḥerem* against Aram-Damascus.

In the case of the MI, the invocation of *ḥerem* emphasizes the oppositional (and hence equivalent) nature of Moab and Israel by denying the possibility either of incorporating subunits associated with Israel (e.g., Men of Gad) into Moab[31] or of mutual recognition via exchange (as in the case of tributary relations). Hence, it is in opposition to Israel that Moab emerges as a workable, and independent, national identity. The dynamic element in the MI may be the underlying risk that Moab would not prove a meaningful rallying point and instead denote "a level where, as it were, no one lives" (Dresch 1986: 12). For this reason, Kemosh as a national deity of Moab, whose will is realized through the actions of Mesha, plays a vital legitimizing role in the argument put forward by the MI.

At the same time, Mesha did not invent "the land of Moab" as a convenient vehicle for his rise to power. We know that as a geographic designation, if nothing else, the term dates back at least to the reign of Ramses II (see Chapter 4). Furthermore, Mesha claims that his father ruled Moab before him, and the MI treats Kemosh as the god of Moab. Therefore, it seems safe to assume that "the land of Moab" was well established as a collective identity available to inhabitants of Moab during the ninth century. However, being Moabite in this sense was likely only one of many intersecting identities that could have been claimed by inhabitants of the land of Moab in the ninth century. Therefore, the novelty of the MI lies in Mesha's apparently successful mobilization of this identity as the organizing principle for a territorial polity. Certainly the events of the MI suggest that the nature, extent, and basis of his father's authority were much more limited than Mesha's.

What I am suggesting is that the MI presents a novel view of the land of Moab as a politically unified territory. Evidence for this novelty lies in the conflicting roles of Moab and Dibon noted above. Certainly, recalling the words of Herzfeld, in the MI social divisions below that of the state are suppressed only weakly. More specifically, according to the MI, social segmentation and political organization in Moab were conjoined in a structurally significant manner. This use of segmentary modes of identification illustrates our oft-repeated dictum that state hegemony is dependent on the articulation of deeply rooted cultural resources. The MI also provides a concrete example of how this articulation is not simply the repetition of established forms but rather involves the creative transformation of common logics (e.g., segmentation) for uncommon ends (e.g., establishing "legitimate" political domination).

Segmentary States

The image of Moab portrayed in the MI is multicentric in that it recognizes political identities below that of the state and seems to incorporate them into, rather than replace them with, the concept of Moab. In this way, Moab in the MI differs from the classic model of the nation-state as a unified entity, possessing a monopoly on coercive force and a centralized, institutionalized, and internally specialized administrative body. The very uncertainty of Moab's efficacy as a mobilizing metaphor, as well as the need to explicitly recognize lower-order territorial units, emphasizes the importance, relative independence, and conceptual equivalency of these units. At the same time, we have also seen that the MI is very much a "statist" text in that it argues strongly for the validity and legitimacy of the centralizing triad of Moab, Kemosh, and Mesha.

I have already argued that the MI articulates segmentary forms of identification as a cultural resource in constituting the hegemony of Mesha's rule. Thus far I have also been at pains to distance this argument from taxonomic approaches to premodern states (tribal, patrimonial) arguing that such categories bypass the reality of state formation as a historically contingent process grounded in the constitution of hegemony. Yet, many scholars have already visited the topic of social segmentation in relation to the state and have proposed the segmentary state as a distinct taxonomic category.[32] In particular, the most carefully developed applications of the term segmentary state have focused on some form of social segmentation (e.g., segmentary lineages) as the structuring principle of an ideologically centralized polity. However, much like the tribal and patrimonial states, the segmentary state is limited by the a priori necessity with which it is conceived. Under the segmentary state model polities are, or are not, segmentary as a structural condition of their existence. As critics of the use of this model in relation to medieval India have pointed out, the segmentary state presents a rather static and exoticized structural model of non-Western polities (Dirks 1993: 403–4; Kulke 1995) into which historical change and political strategy are not easily inserted.

In contrast, our concern is to highlight the strategic and contested articulation of segmentation within the immediate context of the MI as an intellectual product. Certainly, our consideration of the early Iron Age in Chapter 5 has already suggested that segmentary modes of identification played an important role in social life within Moab. Hence, we can begin to understand how the logic of rule enunciated in the MI may have found conditions favorable to its acceptance through these modes of segmentary identification, even as these modes were transformed through their subordination to the state. However, this is not an argument for the underlying generative role of segmentation in Iron Age political formations. As our discussion of Late Bronze Age polities in Chapter 4 highlights, alternative logics of political hierarchy were certainly possible. Hence, Iron Age polities that articulate a logic of segmentation in constituting their hegemony do so contextually and strategically, rather than naturally or necessarily. Furthermore, as is made clear by the horrific use of what amounts to large-scale ritual murder after the capture of Nebo and ʿAṭarot, the particular segmentary understanding of Moab presented in the MI was asserted violently against local resistance. Hence, in keeping with the expectations of Gramsci, we see Moab formed in a particular struggle where force and consent combine to constitute the moral order, that is to say the hegemony, of Mesha's state.

Elsewhere similar ends were pursued by different means. For example, in other Iron Age contexts the house was a metaphor that could both envelop genealogical commonality and achieve dynastic singularity without any linguistic contradiction. It was in this sense extraordinarily powerful and well suited to the task of encompassing and subordinating the fragmented components of the Iron Age social landscape. As we saw in Chapter 6, the overlapping use of house, genealogy and segmentation in reference to the same polity indicated that these were not the generative principles of distinct kinds of Iron Age states but rather interrelated cultural resources differentially deployed in specific cultural and historical contexts.

Synopsis

Mesha emerged at some point in the middle of the ninth century as someone able, through military success, to convert his position of dominance within the town of Dibon to a position of dominance over the land of Moab. Yet, in doing so, the nature and meaning of Moab changed. Certainly, the specific historical circumstances of conflict operated in a fairly classical manner to make possible both the emergence of a new form of hierarchy under the guise of military necessity and perhaps also a new oppositional identity (i.e., Moab versus Israel). However, the content, form, and implications of Moab newly conceived are not separable from, fully determined by, nor secondary to the practical issue of securing power and mobilizing bodies. Here we might note two important considerations derived directly from Gramsci's own notes. The first is his argument that social groups must already exercise "leadership" before assuming governmental power (Gramsci 2000: 249). Mesha's reference to the rule of his father over Moab, his characterization of the men of Dibon as *mišmaʿat*, and his fully developed conception of Kemosh as the national god of Moab with himself as the deity's chief agent suggest that many of the core ideas of the MI were already established in Dibon. Perhaps this image of Moab as a land encompassing a collection of nested territories to be bound together on behalf of Kemosh by the king was already established among those loyal to him as the moral principle justifying Mesha's expansionist military campaigns.

The question of the spread of this "Dibionite" view of Moab raises the second of Gramsci's issues. He argues that hegemony is constituted through "spontaneous" attraction, generated when intellectuals are able to articulate priorities, desires, and experiences rooted in the immediate historical conditions of given social groups (Gramsci 2000: 251). Along these lines, Jones (1997: 92–105; cf. Comaroff and Comaroff 1992) has suggested that ethnogenesis can be located in the distinct experience of cultural contact and conflict, when the forcible encounter with "foreignness" results in the explicit reflection on cultural differences and hence "ruptures" the taken-for-granted nature of daily practice. Whatever its merit as a universal explanation for ethnogenesis, Jones' argument may well describe the conditions of acceptance that made Mesha's vision of Moab as a state identity spontaneously relevant. The immediate experience of Israel's oppression of Moab provides a context were the contrast between Israel and a unified "land of Moab" could gain particular saliency. Made natural by its employment of a segmentary logic and embedded in acts of violence and a structure of force, we might posit that Mesha's hegemonic claim successfully narrowed the meaning of Moab to refer specifically to a land that he ruled.

My argument in this chapter has placed a good deal of weight on the concept of segmentation as a form of identification. I believe that this emphasis is justified by the content of the MI, but it is also strategically important in necessitating a clear conceptual break with ahistorical social forms (tribe, state, etc.). It remains to be demonstrated that segmentation can bear the interpretive burden I have placed upon it once we move beyond the MI. I have already suggested that the MI would have been interpreted both by its content and by its position within a system of signifiers. Indeed, I would argue that a large part of the meaning ascribable to the MI would have been derived in just this manner from its distribution within a constellation of other "kingly things." Ultimately, this comparative form of generating meaning is grounded in segmentary modes of identification. In the next chapter we will take up this theme, looking closely at how the content of the MI brought forward in this chapter compares to the larger impression drawn from its relation to a variety of object categories specifically marked as "kingly things."

Chapter 8

Replicative Kingship

We want a king over us. Then we will be like all the other nations with a king to lead us and to go out before us and fight our battles.
—*1 Samuel 8: 19–20*

The Mesha Inscription provided us with an unusually detailed example of how a specific cultural resource could be articulated in the constitution of state hegemony. In particular, we saw how the dynamics of segmentary identification, in which equivalency was marked by contrast and hierarchy by incorporation, could be appropriated from the domain of kinship and community in order to render familiar the asymmetrical relations of an emergent state. The comparative logic of segmentation was not limited, however, to the single case of the MI.

We noted, for example, that the MI itself would have been interpreted comparatively, as the member of a category of objects and as a sign in a collection of signifiers. The context for this comparison was both local (i.e., other "kingly things") and global (i.e., other royal inscriptions), and indeed movement between these two domains was likely to vary by subject position and personal experience, leading to divergent interpretive possibilities. Here I should be more explicit about the practical implications of this argument before moving on to look in detail at what was being compared, by what means and to what ends.

In the Iron Age Levant, kingship cannot be separated from the specific performative acts (warfare, building projects, temple dedications, etc.) by which kingliness was made manifest. Through such actions, kings coopted to themselves culturally resonant symbols, values, and metaphors. In doing so several things happened. First, specific genres of representing and expressing kingship were widely circulated, most likely through the creative replication of concrete models. In other words, actual buildings, actual inscriptions, and actual statuary provided the media for the transmission of the common themes, styles, and phrases that we can recognize across the relatively significant spatial and cultural divides of the Iron Age Levant.

Second, these intellectual products seem to have gained indexical value beyond the "internal" meanings they conveyed. Here I use indexical in Peirce's sense (Peirce 1931: 4: 445–48), as a meaning elicited by a sign through its regular association with particular objects or conditions.

Locally, this seems clearest in the interrelationship between "kingly things." As we shall discuss in detail below, the various markers of kingship in the Iron Age Levant were often directly implicated with one another, as inscriptions were located on, or referred to, architecture and statuary, and statuary was made integral to architecture. Both in their association with each other and in their common status as objects marked off from the everyday, "kingly things" gained indexical value as signs of kingship. Hence, one need not be literate, for example, in order to comprehend the specifically royal reference of an inscribed stele,[1] as the context of its erection usually associated it with a range of signs signifying roughly the same thing. Globally, one must presume that, in at least certain circles, the generic aspects of these intellectual products were sufficiently known as to make them identifiable as members of specifically royal categories; categories that were explicitly replicated in distinct polities as marks of equivalency.

Hence, we see contrastive comparisons working in at least three ways. (1) In the actual content of certain intellectual products (e.g., the MI) we see segmentary identification articulated as a cultural resource to naturalize the state; (2) in the local context we see the indexical association of particular sets of objects with kingship; (3) globally we see the indexical association of particular categories of objects with kingship. Specifically what was being compared as "royal" remains to be seen.

Royal Inscriptions

While large-scale inscriptions on stone in the Iron Age Levant are not exclusively royal in theme and putative authorship, kings are by far the dominant figures encountered in this medium. In this simple sense, the MI belongs by definition to a specific category of objects, royal lapidary inscriptions. While hardly ubiquitous, such royal inscriptions are not uncommon, especially if we are willing to consider fragments as likely examples of once-complete royal inscriptions. From Moab we have already noted the MI, the Karak fragment (Reed and Winnett 1963), and the Dhiban fragment (Murphy 1953). Elsewhere in the southern Levant, clear or possible examples are also known from the neighboring states of Ammon, Israel, Judah, Aram-Damascus, and the Philistine city-state of Ekron (Tel Miqne/ Ḥ. al-Muqanna').[2] In the northern Levant, royal lapidary inscriptions abound from the tenth century B.C.E. down through the fourth century (under the Achaemenid Persian Empire).[3] The spatial distribution of these stelae from one end of the Levant to the other indicates their important role as a common medium for the representation of kingship.

Genre, Structure, and Themes

In Chapter 7 we followed Maxwell Miller (1974) in characterizing the MI as a "memorial inscription," implying thereby that it belonged to a well-established genre. As Miller pointed out, in common with the Kilamuwa, Panamuwa I (Hadad), and Bar-Rakib inscriptions from Zincirli; the Azatiwada inscription; and the Zakkur Inscription, the MI (1) is introduced by the name of a king;[4] (2) proceeds in the first person; (3) uses the occasion of a building/shrine dedication to memorialize the achievements of the king. Absent from the MI, perhaps lost in the missing bottom portion, is the concluding recitation of curses against those who might deface the inscription in the future. In this manner, Miller distinguished "memorial' from "dedicatory" inscriptions as the latter (1) are introduced by a description of the object being dedicated; (2) refer only secondarily to the king; (3) conclude with a request for blessings for the king.

A taxonomy of fixed genres is, however, somewhat problematic, as one can note examples, such as the Zakkur Inscription or the Panamuwa II Inscription, which combine or imperfectly exhibit the defining traits of these two genres. Therefore, it may prove more informative to focus on the distribution and use of actual generic elements (i.e., phrases, syntactical structures, and themes), which tended to be used consistently for distinct purposes (hence the "memorial" and "dedicatory" patterns) but which could also be employed actively and creatively by specific authors. These tools were clearly in circulation as technical knowledge available to local scribes for the expression of local events. However, by this very fact they also served as structuring principles that ensured the replication of royal inscriptions within recognizable forms.

As we have already seen in the case of the MI, this could include the embedding of particular models of identification in the organization and syntax of the inscription itself. Hence, one need not postulate deep structures or ineffable essences to account for common themes and cultural forms in Iron Age state formation.

In addition to the general characteristics already noted for memorial inscriptions, Miller discusses several others that can be developed further as structural features shared by specific texts. First, there is a marked temporality in these inscriptions. As Miller (1974: 15–16) noted, the phrase "in my days" is used to establish a temporal contrast between past and present conditions. Mesha, for example, contrasts Omri's successful oppression of Moab in the past with his son's unsuccessful attempt to do the same "in my days" in line 6 of the MI. Similarly, Mesha contrasts Omri's occupation of the land of Madaba in the past with Kemosh's returning of this land "in my days" in line 9.[5] As Miller notes (1974: 15–16), both the Azatiwada and Kilamuwa Inscriptions use the phrase "in my days" to similar effect. To this we may also add an identical usage in the Panamuwa I (Hadad) Inscription

(Tropper 1993: 67). Interestingly, in the Panamuwa II inscription, where the putative author is the son of the figure being memorialized, the phrases "in his days" (Tropper 1993: 116, S184) and "in the days of my father" (Tropper 1993: 117, S187) are used in the same contrastive manner as "in my days" in the autobiographical inscriptions.

This temporal contrast of a difficult past to a present made better by the king extends beyond those inscriptions that use the "in my days" formula.[6] Interestingly, it is not only the events of the past that are cast in a poor light but often the previous kings of the polity as well. At times, as in the case of the MI, this critique is left implicit by stating that the author's father or other predecessor ruled before the author and then detailing the terrible conditions in place when the author came to the throne. However, others are more direct. Azatiwada states that he conquered strong lands in the West "that no king before me ever humbled" (Hallo and Younger 2000: 149). Most dramatically, Kilamuwa states: "Gabbar ruled over YʾDY, but he achieved nothing, then BNH but he achieved nothing, and then my father Ḥayya, but he achieved nothing, and then my brother Ṣaʾil, but he achieved nothing, but I, Kilamuwa son of TML, what I achieved (my) predecessors had not achieved" (Tropper 1993: 31–33).

In addition to contrasting past and present, the temporal element in these inscriptions is also carried forward. From a bad past through an improved present, these inscriptions look to an unchanged future. As Klaas Smelik (1992: 69) notes with regard to lines 4–7 of the MI, one can see this temporal progression in the shift from "Now Omri oppressed Moab many days" in lines 4/5 (bad past) through "In my days he said this, but I prevailed over him" in lines 6–7 (improved present) to "Now Israel perished, perished forever" in line 7 (changeless future). A similar sequence is evidenced in the Sefire Treaty (Sefire III: 23–25—Lemaire and Durand 1984: 119–121), where Talʾaym and its villages are said to have belonged "of old" to the "father's house" of Bir Gaʾyah and been lost(bad past), then restored "now" to Bir Gaʾyah (improved present) and "to his son and to his grandson and to his descendants forever" (unchanged future).

More commonly, the changeability of the future is acknowledged as a threat to be countered by a curse. Hence, many Iron Age royal inscriptions end with a curse directed against any future person (especially a future ruler) who would efface the inscription, particularly by removing the name of the inscription's putative royal author. In the case of the Panamuwa I (Hadad) Inscription, the author assumes that succession to his throne will be a bloody affair,[7] with a significant chance that his name and "dead spirit" (nbš) will not be remembered by his own descendants (Tropper 1993: 81–82). Interestingly, just as contrast with the past opposes the king to his ineffectual predecessors, the curse recognizes that he too could occupy this position with regard to his successors. Hence, the hope for a changeless future includes an assertion of competitive contrast opposing the king to both past and future. While the king outdid his predecessors, his successors should not be able to outdo him.

Kings, of course, occupy a privileged position in all ancient Near Eastern royal inscriptions. However, Iron Age Levantine inscriptions are distinguished by the cosmology and theology through which this privilege is achieved. In Chapter 7 we noted that in the MI, the god Kemosh is the primary catalytic force. Moab exists as "his land," and its history is a question, not of struggle with other deities, but of his own pleasure or displeasure ("Kemosh was angry with his land"—MI l. 5; cf. Müller 1994). Mesha acts as the principal agent of Kemosh and hence partakes of divine authority not as a personal quality, but as a by-product of his distinct relationship of service to the deity. Kemosh speaks directly to Mesha, and Mesha acts accordingly and hence successfully.

Besides the well-known case of the Bible,[8] a similar encompassing of history by the will of a deity is shown in a brief statement in the Sefire Treaty (Sefire III: 23–25), where the royal house of KTK's loss of the hegemony over Tal'ayim is credited to the gods "beating down" the royal house,[9] while the restoration of this same land is credited to the god's restoration of this royal house. Elsewhere in these inscriptions, deities do not play that same total role with regard to causation. However, deities, and occasionally powerful patrons as well, typically occupy catalytic roles in these inscriptions, empowering, directing and legitimizing the actions of kings. Very commonly, kings credit deities, or occasionally a powerful patron, with placing them on the throne.[10] Closer still to the MI, Panamuwa I states that he was specifically invited by the god Hadad to execute a building project (Tropper 1993: 74–75, S. 72–73), while Azatiwada states that the deities Ba'al and Resheph of the *sprm* (stags?) commissioned him to build a city (Hallo and Younger 2000: 150, col. ii. ll. 9–12). Like Kemosh with Mesha, Ba'alshamayn addresses Zakkur in direct speech (Hallo and Younger 2000: 155),[11] as does the god Milkom to the unnamed Ammonite king, if we are to take the Amman Citadel Inscription to be royal (Aufrecht 1989: 154–63; Hübner 1992; 17–21). The Levantine king, therefore, is picked out and commissioned by higher forces without partaking directly in the qualities of those forces (divinity, omnipotence, omniscience, etc.). As we noted in Chapter 7, the role of Kemosh in the MI is structurally and ideologically important, as it provides an encompassing "national" level not immediately evident in the military actions of Mesha the Dibonite. Other Levantine royal inscriptions seem also to evoke deities (and powerful patrons) to go over the heads of kings, as it were, to turn divisive local conflicts into a unity with legitimate and illegitimate contestants. Indeed, these inscriptions are surprisingly frank about such conflict and the need for powerful external intervention. Zakkur is rescued by the god Ba'alshamayn from an enemy siege because, he is told, Ba'alshamayn made him king and will stand beside him (Hallo and Younger 2000: 155). Kilamuwa, Panamuwa II,[12] and Bar-Rakib of YˀDY all turn to the king of Assyria as a higher power because of strong rivals who could not be overcome. This acknowledgment of equivalent (or even more powerful) peers against whom one struggles (rather than overwhelms) and over whom one usually succeeds only through supernatural, or at least superpower (i.e., Assyria), intervention, gives Levantine royal inscriptions a two-sided, conflicted quality less commonly found in other royal inscriptions from the ancient Near East.

In sum, throughout the royal inscriptions of the Iron Age Levant, various themes, phrases, and syntactical structures are replicated such that contrast and comparison can be creatively employed in fashioning a new space, or social plane, in which state hegemony is manifest. As noted in the case of the MI, the logic employed is segmentary, and while less obvious in other royal inscriptions, contrast and an incorporative hierarchy can still be identified. Certainly, other cultural resources were also employed, especially domestic metaphors, images of piety, martial prowess, and an active building program. However, the articulation of all these resources occurred with reference to a comparative gaze, in which hegemony was constituted at the intersection of both local and global domains.

Form, Location, and Associations

Often lost in the transcription and translation of royal inscriptions is the fact that they are physical objects whose form and original context were significant components of their communicative possibilities. The most common pretext for carving such an inscription was the dedication of a particular architectural feature or statue. Hence, these inscriptions often explicitly name the object, structure, or complex with which they were to be associated. In the MI, Mesha explicitly mentions making "this high place for Kemosh" in line 3. The Ekron, the Yaḥmilik of Byblos, and the Bar-Rakib inscriptions name the building of "this[13] *bt/byt* (lit. "house")[14] as the occasion for each of these inscriptions. Azatiwada of Karatepe cites the building of "this city," while Yeḥawmilk of Byblos describes in detail by means of a list of deomstrative pronouns ("this X . . . this Y . . . this Z") what seems to be a colonnaded temple with gold and bronze accouterments.

In certain cases, the inscription is on a self-contained object in which the iconography and inscription seem to cross-reference one another. The Tall al-Faḥariya Inscription (Abou-Assaf, Bordreuil, and Millard 1982), the Panamuwa I (Hadad) Inscription (Tropper 1993: 54–97) and the Panamuwa II inscription (Tropper 1993: 98–131) are all inscribed on statues to which each refers directly in its opening lines. The Zakkur Inscription and the Melqart Stele (Hallo and Younger 2000: 152–53) simply refer to themselves as a stele or monument in honor of a particular deity, who seems to be portrayed in an accompanying relief. These statue and relief inscriptions may be of particular significance for Moab, as the Karak fragment (Reed and Winnett 1963) appears to include a fringe of clothing, suggesting that it was originally part of some sort of figurative monument.

Unfortunately, most of the royal inscriptions we currently know were found in tertiary contexts, reused as building stone in later structures, found on the surface of sites, or purchased with limited knowledge of the original find-spot. However, the few cases where inscriptions are found in primary, or unambiguous secondary, contexts indicate that spatial location supported the information we have already gleaned from the self-referencing of the texts. For example, the Azatiwada Inscription from Karatepe was written bilingually in Phoenician and Hieroglyphic Luwian (NeoHittite) and repeated in at least three locations on the site: (1) on orthostats and a stone lion built into the Lower (North) Gate; (2) on orthostats built into the Upper (South) Gate; and (3) on the skirt of a colossal divine statue located just inside the Upper Gate (see Çambel 1999). If we remember that the inscription not only claims as its object of dedication "this city," but also names the site for Azatiwada himself ("Azatiwadaya"; col. ii l. 10), it is clear that the liminal experience of entering this hill-top fortress through its monumental gateways was not lost on Azatiwada.[15]

The Tel Miqne Inscription was found on a limestone block, evidently adjacent to the wall from whence it fell. This wall is the rear (western) wall of a colonnaded cella that forms the primary room of a large (57 × 38m) open-court complex, identified in the inscription as a temple for *ptgyh* (an otherwise unknown goddess). Immediately in front of the find-spot of the inscription is a stepped stone threshold, suggesting a raised dais at the western end of the cella, directly opposite the doorway. Hence, as the excavators note (Gitin et al. 1997: 7), the inscription is likely to have been located at, or very near, the spatial and visual focal point of the entire complex.

Overall, it is clear that royal inscriptions were not intended to exist as texts in the abstract. In a context where writing itself was associated primarily with official activities and the class from whom state officials were drawn, the physicality of monumental inscriptions was perhaps as important as their content. Hence, our tendency in analysis (encouraged by the conditions of discovery) to treat word, image, and space independently by partitioning inscriptions from their architectural and artistic contexts misses something significant.

Here it is relevant to note the emphasis on building campaigns, and particularly on the founding, or dramatic reconstruction, of cities as a royal project in these inscriptions (cf. Ahlström 1982). Furthermore, in addition to the MI (l. 13), both the Azatiwada (Hallo aand Younger 2000: 149; Rollig in Çambel 1999: 64–65, l. 12) and Panamuwa II (Tropper 1993: 122, S.196–97) Inscriptions list the movement and resettlement of populations as one the king's achievements. Hence, at least in the realm of ideological representation, the king was someone who inscribed himself on the landscape by both creating built environments and inhabiting them with people (see Mazzoni 1994). Therefore, it is not surprising that architecture provides us with some of our best evidence for the kinds of comparative identities I have outlined in relation to these inscriptions.

Architecture

Mesha's Palace?

If, like child actors and precocious musicians, an archaeological site could be scarred by early success then the site of Dhiban undoubtedly would be in need of a therapist. Within a year of the discovery of the Mesha Inscription, Euro-American scholars began visiting the site regularly and registering with equal regularity their disappointment at its lack of potential (e.g., Palmer 1881: 69; Tristram 1873: 146–49). The main mound of Dhiban is a mid-sized *tall* of approximately five hectares at its base (3 ha on its summit), located about 60 km south of Amman at a bend in the Wadi Dhiban. A saddle separates the unoccupied mound from the modern town located to the south, although it is evident that in at least some periods settlement extended into the area of the modern town. Systematic exploration of the site in the form of topographic mapping and surface collection was first undertaken in 1910[16] by Duncan Mackenzie, under the auspices of the Palestine Exploration Fund (Mackenzie 1913). Even as he approached the site, Mackenzie recognized that the substantial architectural remains visible from a distance were vaulted, and hence likely Medieval in date. Recognizing that the Iron Age Dibon of Mesha was likely to be deeply buried and heavily damaged by later construction, Mackenzie (1913: 59) writes: "As we settled in camp for the night we had to confess to a feeling of disappointment, if not of actual dismay, at the discovery."

This sense of frustration at the equivocal nature of Iron Age occupation at Dhiban carried through to the final reports of the ASOR-sponsored excavations of 1950–53 (Winnett and Reed 1964; Tushingham 1972). In point of fact, these (and subsequent) excavations uncovered important and understudied examples of domestic architecture of the twelfth to fourteenth centuries C.E. (Ayyubid-Mameluke), significant public buildings of the Nabataean period (occupied ca. 10–106 C.E.), and two churches and several interesting tombs from the Byzantine era. However, as with Mackenzie's work, because the MI formed the principal justification for the excavation project, it looms over these reports as if taunting the excavators with their lack of success. For example, Douglas Tushingham (1972: 26) writes: "One must confess that even after three seasons' excavation at Dhiban the amount of new light thrown on the history and civilization of the Moabites is very meagre."

William Morton, a senior staff member of the ASOR project was particularly disconcerted by what he saw as the near-complete failure of these excavations to illuminate the content of the MI (Morton 1989: 239). He therefore opted to continue the excavation project after its first three directors (Fred V. Winnett, William L. Reed, and A. Douglas Tushingham) had completed their successive terms.[17] Morton conducted a series of soundings to locate areas with the highest potential for yielding Iron Age remains, focusing in particular on the summit of the *tall* (Area L) and the northern side (Area H), where topography suggested the possible existence of a gateway (Morton 1989: 239). In three seasons of fieldwork (1955, 1956, and 1965), Morton was very successful in discovering significant Iron Age remains. Unfortunately, numerous adversities, including ill health, limited funding, heavy institutional responsibilities, and the 1967 War, prevented him both from conducting his planned fourth season of excavation and from producing a final report on his work at the site. At the time of his death from cancer in 1988, only brief notices on these excavations had been published (Morton 1955; 1957; 1989). In 1997 I assumed responsibility for publishing this material,[18] the partial results of which are presented below for the first time.

Most important in Morton's mind was his belief that he had uncovered the palace that Mesha claims to have built in Qarḥō in line 23 of the MI. As one might suspect, such a sensational claim cannot be directly proven from the archaeological evidence, nor is it necessarily all that important for the aims and interests of this study. What we can say is that Morton uncovered a major public building on the summit of the site that, with some uncertainty, seems to have been built in the ninth century B.C.E. (Figure 8.1). Whether or not we identify this building with Mesha, its presence and form raise a number of issues already introduced in our discussion of royal inscriptions.

The element of uncertainty in the analysis of this building comes from the fateful combination of Area L's dense and very complicated stratigraphy, the relative inexperience of the excavators in the so-called Wheeler-Kenyon method of stratigraphic excavation, and the ravages of time and numerous displacements on the excavation archives. Hence, at several key points it is evident that either we are missing documentation (esp. balk section drawings) or that the existing documentation is insufficient or likely incorrect.[19] Furthermore, while the archives include large quantities of well-labeled pottery, we do not know for certain what selection criteria were used for the retention and registration of sherds. Hence, while analysis suggests that most diagnostic sherds (rims, decorated sherds, etc.) were retained from most loci, we cannot in fact control completely for systematic bias in the assemblage as it exists today.

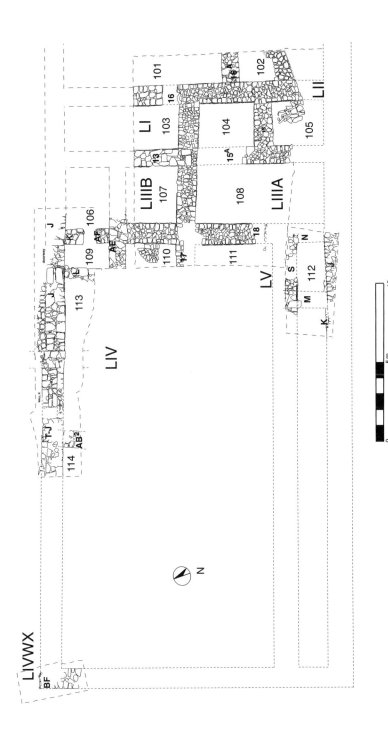

Figure 8.1. Dhiban, Area L "palace 1."

This said, we can sort out in a relatively general manner the sequence of construction, modification, and abandonment of the Area L building. We can also identify a number of its architectural features and thereby consider it from a comparative, as well as a site-specific, perspective. Our most coherent evidence comes from areas LI, LII, and LIIIB, which constitute the eastern and northeastern portions of the building as exposed in excavation. In particular, the north-east corner, marked by rooms 101–4, provides the best starting point, both because a major renovation (see Figures 8.1 and 8.2) in this area provides a clear stratigraphic benchmark and because both of the two surviving balk section drawings from Field L come from this area (Figures 8.3, 8.4).[20]

Table 8.1 presents a highly simplified version of the stratigraphic sequence lumped into five broad phases in the occupational history of this building. This sequence is established first for the area of rooms 101 and 103, where paving stones (loci 26 and 29), a drain (locus 35) with a rubble platform (locus 32), and the insertion of new walls (15a and 12a) clearly distinguish what we have called Palace 2 from the earlier Palace 1. This sequence is then extended on a room by room basis along the eastern side of the building (Areas LI and LII), where we have at least some hope of reconstructing the building's internal occupational history. Figures 8.5–8.7 present the pottery that accompanies our stratigraphic phases.

Phase 1: Subfloor fills into which the primary walls of Palace 1 are inserted, or upon which they rest,[21] consistently contain pottery from the Early Bronze Age and Iron Age I. *Phase 2*: Above this, one finds occupational deposits associated with the primary walls of Palace 1 that seem to date from the mid to late ninth century B.C.E.[22] *Phase 3*: Above this we find fill/occupation layers whose latest material dates to the eighth century B.C.E. *Phase 4*: This is followed by a relatively clear upper living surface that appears to date to the end of the eighth century B.C.E. This renovation included the construction of the above mentioned drain in room 103, as well as a plastered cistern and drain/conduit in room 107. *Phase 5*: Thick fill deposits that completely cover this building indicate that it was out of use by the late seventh or early sixth century B.C.E., with new buildings not evident on this spot until perhaps the first century C.E.

If the wall corner in the far northwest excavation unit (LIV WX) is actually part of this building, as Morton suggests,[23] then the building is relatively large, measuring more than 21 × 43 meters with major walls of up to 1.25 m in thickness. Finds from this structure are not particularly unusual, consisting primarily of pottery. However, pieces of a largely reconstructable "cult-stand" (Morton 1989: Fig. 14, now lost) were found in rooms 101 and 104 of Phase 2. Also, a three-letter ostracon fragment (Morton 1989: Fig. 12, reading *ḥm*)[24] was found in a probable Phase 4 context in room 102.

Due to the partial exposure of the Field L building at Dhiban, we cannot be confident as to its complete form. However, we can compare the remains

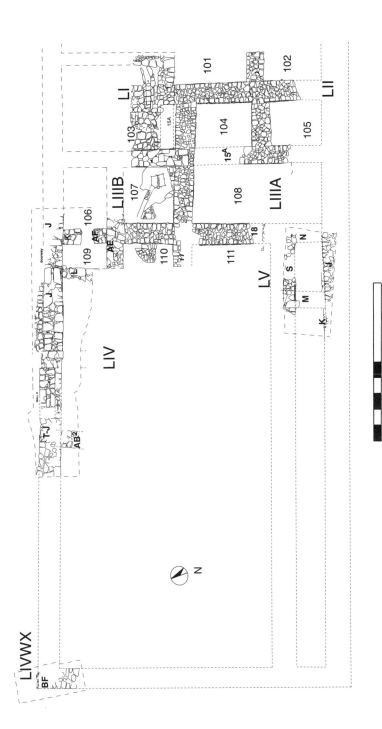

Figure 8.2. Dhiban, Area L "palace 2."

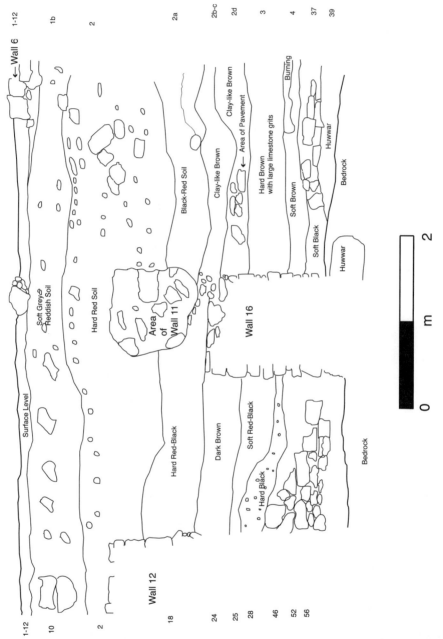

Figure 8.3. Dhiban, Area LI south balk.

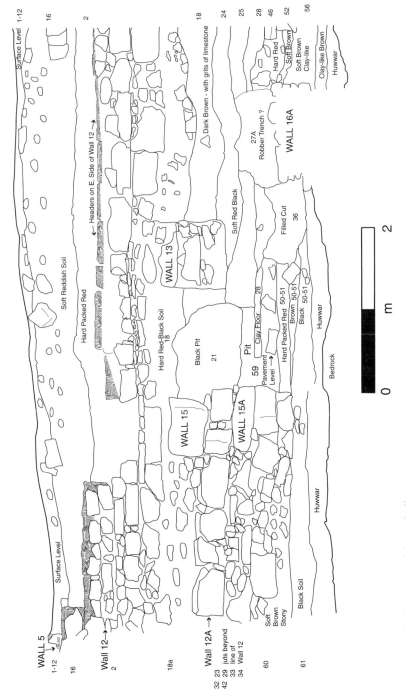

Figure 8.4. Dhiban, Area LI east balk.

as exposed to roughly contemporary public buildings elsewhere in the southern Levant. In this manner, we can at least suggest the extent to which the Dhiban Field L building does, or does not, conform to more-or-less standard design features found in these other public buildings. Most large, well-constructed Iron Age buildings from the southern Levant appear from their features and associated finds to be "palaces" rather than "temples" or strictly administrative buildings. [25] In contrast to the Bronze Age, obvious evidence for cultic activity in the Iron Age is most typically found in small, single-room shrines (see Holladay 1987; Zevit 2001). The recent discovery of one such shrine within the territory of Moab at Ḥ. al-Mudayna ath-Thamad (Daviau and Dion 2002; Daviau and Steiner 2000; Dion and Daviau 2000), complete with limestone altars and an elaborate inscribed incense burner, shows that this same pattern may well hold true for Moab as well for Israel and Judah. Regardless of how we interpret specific buildings, comparative study makes it evident that during the Iron Age scale and spatial segregation were used to distinguish a limited set of buildings in what are otherwise not particularly large, nor highly differentiated, sites.

TABLE 8.1. Major Iron Age stratigraphic phases in Area L, Dhiban

Phase	Context	Key loci (visible in Figs. 8.3–8.4)
1	Subfloor fills and pre-"palace" deposits dating to the Early Bronze II–III and Iron Age I periods.	LI. 37, 39, 46, 50–51, 52, 56, 60, 61
2	Floors and related deposits associated with construction and initial use of Palace 1, dating to the ninth-century B.C.E.	LI. 4, 28, 34, 36, 44
3	Deposits above Phase 2 but beneath Palace 2 renovation. Ca. first half of the eighth century B.C.E.	LI. 3, 25, 33, 41, 42
4	Deposits associated with Palace 2 renovation and occupation. Ca. end of eighth/ beginning of seventh-century B.C.E.	LI. 2d, 24, 26, 27a, 29, 32, 35
5	Deposits laid over the tops of Palace 2 walls. Ca. late seventh-century B.C.E.	LI. 2b–c, 18

Iron Age Palaces

In general, scholars have identified three primary "palace" forms in Iron Age contexts from the southern Levant (see Fritz 1983a; Nigro 1994: 193–323; Reich 1992). The so-called *bît-ḫilani* style is identified by a sequence of two "long rooms" whose longitudinal axis is parallel to the building's facade (see Frankfort 1952). The outermost long room forms a columned entrance porch approached by a stairway. *Bît-ḫilani* are well attested as the primary palace form in north Syria in the tenth–eighth

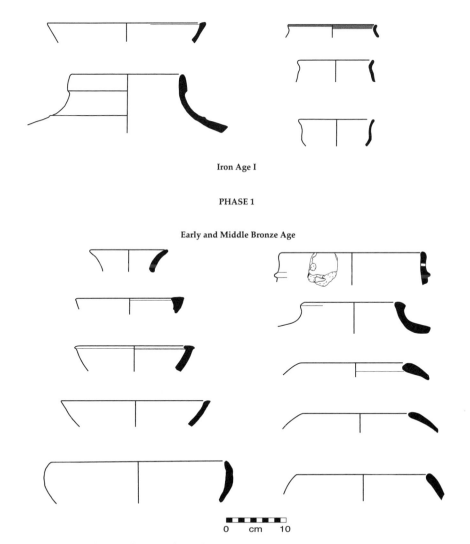

Iron Age I

PHASE 1

Early and Middle Bronze Age

0   cm   10

Figure 8.5. Dhiban, Area L Phase 1 pottery.

centuries, with antecedents going back to the Late Bronze Age. These palaces begin to be replaced by Assyrian-style palaces from the eighth century on, apparently in conjunction with the conquest and incorporation of NeoHittite and Aramean polities of Syria into the Neo-Assyrian Empire. In the southern Levant the *bît-ḫilani* style is used more briefly, being limited largely to the tenth century B.C.E. (Arav and Bernett 2000; Reich 1992: 202–6; Ussishkin 1966, 1973) and exhibiting a number of idiosyncratic features (Fritz 1983b). Thus far, no *bît-ḫilani* style buildings have been identified in Transjordan.

More typical for Palestine are the dense arrangements of small rectangular rooms found in monumental ninth through eighth century buildings

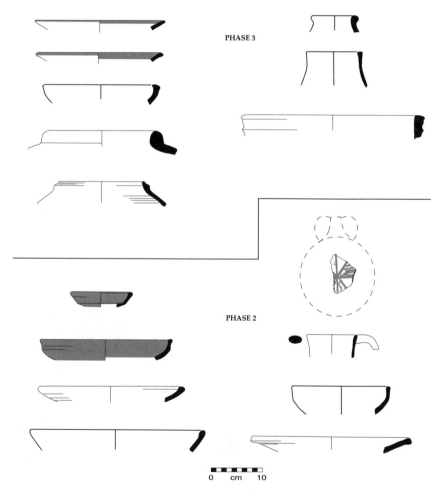

PHASE 3

PHASE 2

0   cm   10

Figure 8.6. Dhiban, Area L Phase 2 and 3 pottery.

at Lachish (Palace phases A–C—Nigro 1994: 239–50; Reich 1992: 208–10; Ussishkin 1978: 27–42), Samaria ("Omri's Palace"—Nigro 1994: 229–80; Reisner et al. 1924: 98–114, Pl. 5), and to a lesser extent Megiddo building 338 and the Hazor citadel. [26] While these buildings may have begun from a roughly square core unit with a long narrow court (esp. Lachish Palace A), they grew primarily by the addition of irregularly subdivided blocks of rooms.

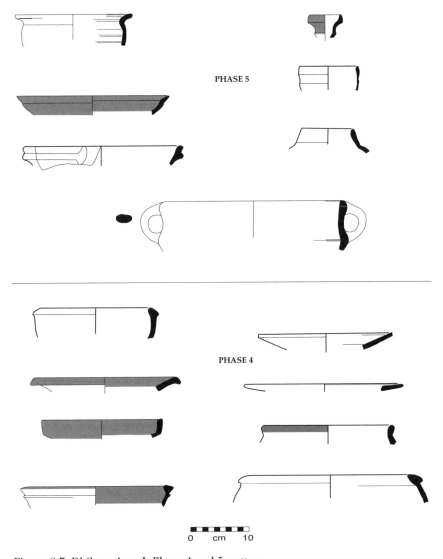

Figure 8.7. Dhiban, Area L Phase 4 and 5 pottery.

Finally, at the end of the eighth century, one sees the introduction of Assyrian-style palaces, with large open courts and reception rooms. Here a distinction needs to be made. The general category of "open court" buildings is broadly Mesopotamian in origin and found from Iran to Palestine (e.g., Amiran and Dunyavesky 1958) under the hegemony of the Neo-Babylonian (609–539 B.C.E.) and Achaemenid Persia (539–333 B.C.E.) Empires. Assyrian palaces are a subset of these open court buildings but have a much more consistent and precisely defined set of attributes (Loud 1936; Turner 1970). In the southern Levant, at the outskirts of empire, one finds "open-court" buildings that adhere to greater or lesser degrees with the specific details identified for the Assyrian-style palaces. This has led to lengthy discussions regarding both the correct chronological ascription of particular structures (e.g., Lipschitz 1990; Reich 1975) and the desirability of distinguishing "authentic" Assyrian-style palaces from those that employ certain design elements in a locally distinct manner (Fritz 1979; Nigro 1994: 452–56; Reich 1992: 214–15, 218–19). For our purposes, it is sufficient to recognize that, from the end of the eighth century on, the construction of monumental buildings in the southern Levant drew on models with global, rather than local or regional, points of reference.

The Dhiban Area L building does not fit easily into either end of this proposed architectural sequence. Most specifically, the Dhiban building contains at least four rows of adjacent rectangular broad rooms on its eastern (excavated) side before one encounters flanking long rooms that may have outlined a courtyard in the unexcavated portion of the building. This layout lacks both the simple broad rooms of the *bît-ḥilani* and the symmetrical orientation to a large central court that characterizes open court structures. It does, however, show parallels to the dense clusters of peripheral rooms found at Lachish (Phase C; see Figure 8.8) and Samaria. These parallels are, in turn, roughly contemporary with the ninth-eighth century period of occupation we have suggested for the Dhiban Area L building.

In contrast, "palatial" buildings have been partially excavated in seventh-century contexts at the principal centers of Moab's immediate neighbors, namely in Area C at Busayra (biblical Bozrah) in Edom (Bennett 1974, 1975, 1977, 1983; Bienkowski 1990, 1995b, 2001b: 354–58; Bienkowski et al. 2002; Reich 1992: 219–20) and on the third terrace of the Amman Citadel (biblical Rabbat Ammon) in Ammon (Humbert and Zayadine 1991; Zayadine et al. 1989). Despite their limited exposure, these two buildings share extremely similar layouts, an unusually enthusiastic use of plaster, and similarly positioned and constructed bathrooms with stone toilets and subfloor drains. These same features are also shared with small-scale examples of seventh-century Assyrian-style palace architecture, such as Megiddo building 1039 (Lamon and Shipton 1939: 69–74, Fig. 89).

This suggests that: (1) for each of the Iron Age polities of Transjordan (Ammon, Moab, Edom), buildings larger than ten times the area of a typical domestic dwelling have been discovered at sites arguably to be identified as capitals, or at least royal/administrative centers; and that (2) relatively consistent regionwide shifts in palace styles occurred across political boundaries in the southern Levant. This is in turn suggests that palaces were not merely local aggrandizing gestures. Rather, these major building projects were planned and executed with an awareness of what had been done, and what was being done, in neighboring polities. Hence palaces were marked locally by scale (their incomparability to domestic architecture) and globally by their conformity to recognized models (their comparability to other palaces).

Gate Complexes

Palaces and their citadels represent the public face of kingship in rather obvious ways. However, while relatively clear, these architectural messages are hardly unique to the Iron Age Levant. Much more specific are a number of architectural features that are closely replicated across polities, both in form and in the context and mode of their deployment.

Fortified gateways are one such feature, As biblical texts make clear, the gateway was a key locale in Iron Age settlements. As van Gennep (1960 [1909]) pointed out almost a century ago, it is not surprising to find human beings attaching significance to a liminal space, such as the entrance to a walled settlement. However, the Iron Age evidence goes beyond this in offering a rich, culturally specific context in which the gate served as the focal point of extra household sociability and sociality. In the Bible, while not predicated on the public/private divide found in the modern concept of civil society, the gate was clearly the primary space for communal discourse, where key inside/outside relationships (e.g., foreign/familiar; community/family; male/female) were constituted through enactment and public acknowledgment. This is marked most dramatically by the fact that the gate (and the open space in front of it—2 Chronicles 32: 6) was where strangers slept or waited to be invited home as guests (Gen. 19: 1–3; Judg. 19: 15–21). It was also in the gate that the city elders gathered (Gen. 34:20; Deut. 22: 15; Ruth 4: 2; cf. Reviv 1989), that informal dispute resolution and legal transactions took place (Gen. 23: 10–16; Ruth 4: 1–12; Amos 5: 15), and that commercial exchange was conducted (2 Kings 7: 1). This significance is potentially supported archaeologically by the elaborate nondefensive features, and especially plastered stone benches, found within the chambers of Iron Age gateways (Herzog 1992: 271–72). Also interesting are three eighth-century inscribed objects (a stone weight and two jars) designating these items as "of the gate," perhaps referring to a specific standardized measure (Eph'al and Naveh 1993).

Perhaps most importantly, the gate was a primary public space for the constitution of masculine honor through peer acknowledgment.[27] It is here that the father of a recent bride presented the bloodied nuptial cloth to defend the virginal status of his daughter if wrongly accused of prior sexual activity by her new husband (Deut. 22: 13–19). According to Proverbs 31: 23, the husband of a virtuous (read hardworking) wife was "known in the city gates, taking his seat among the elders of the land." To have a place in the gate was to be a member of the male cohort of the community and to carry in public the limited good of family honor. To be known in the gate was to be acknowledged and thereby to possess social capital. Hence, the gateway provided a consistent stage on which honor, status, local identity, and masculinity were mutually constituted in daily performance. No less so were dishonor, poverty, foreignness, and femininity constituted by their displacement from this space.

In this light, it is perhaps significant that Tamar disguises herself as a prostitute and waits for Judah at the "entrance" to Enaim (Gen. 38: 14). In this story male honor is restored (Levirite obligation fulfilled) by means of its public antithesis, unregulated female sexuality (Gen. 38: 24–26). The direct parallels drawn within the Bible between this story and that of Ruth and Boaz (e.g., Ruth 4: 12), in which the Levirite obligation is properly handled by Boaz among the elders in the gate (Ruth 4: 1–12), are striking and hardly coincidental. More bluntly, a group of lepers is explicitly located immediately outside of the city gate in 2 Kings 7: 3, highlighting the insider/outsider significance of this space in relation to "proper" masculine social identities.

Masculine honor was also a cultural resource articulated by kingly hegemony in the Iron Age (and at many other times and places). As wise judges, brave warriors, pious worshipers, and active builders, kings appropriated the public signs of masculinity to themselves. In doing so, they rearticulated these signs into new models of masculine honor that were inseparable from the theory and practice of kingship itself. Hence, it is not surprising to see the active inscription of kingship (literally in certain cases) on a social space like the gate. Indeed Iron Age royal inscriptions and monuments were often erected in gateways (e.g., Karatepe, Carchemish, Zincirli, Samaria, and Tel Dan—Bernett and Keel 1998; Mazzoni 1997; Ussishkin 1989a). Similarly, one is not surprised to see biblical kings taking their seat in the gate, on the model of the city elders (e.g., 2 Sam.15: 2, 19: 8; 1 Kings 22: 10). Indeed, at Tel Dan the ornamental column bases and ashlar-built platform found in the gateway may well represent just such a royal seat that was covered by a canopy (Biran 1994: 237–41). We have, therefore, every reason to attach a good deal of significance to this architectural space in our discussion of hegemony and to interpret its form and distribution accordingly.

At Dhiban, Morton (1989: 242–43) was convinced that he had uncovered an Iron Age gateway on the north side of the site (his Field H). Unfortunately, later remains completely obscure the architectural features in question, making it difficult to evaluate this claim in any detail. However, two well-defined Iron Age II gateways have recently been excavated within the territory of Moab at Ḥirbat al-Mudayna ath-Thamad and Ḥirbat al-Mudaybiʻ. Considered together, these gates provide interesting evidence of particular relevance to our argument.

Ḥirbat al-Mudayna ath-Thamad is a small site (ca. 1 ha) located some 16 km northeast of Dhiban that appears to have been rebuilt and heavily fortified at the beginning of eighth (or end of the ninth) century B.C.E. An excavation project directed by Michèle Daviau has been active at the site since 1996, completely exposing an exceptionally well-preserved "six-chambered" gateway measuring 15.80 × 16.35 m (Chadwick et al. 2000: 258–67). In keeping with the textual image of gates as social spaces, this gate complex appears to have had built-in stone benches lining the entry-way (i.e., the street) as well as inside the gate chambers. One of these benches appears to have a game board etched on its surface (Chadwick et al. 2000: 263). The first four chambers and flanking towers of the gate form a single unit to which the rear (southern) two chambers are abutted. This, as well as the irregular orientation of the southern chambers' walls, sug-gests that the gate was expanded from a four- to a six-chambered gateway at some point in its history. However, the excavators (Chadwick et al. 2000: 266) maintain that the current six-chambered configuration, including the benches and roadway, is a stratigraphically integral unit.[28]

Ḥirbat al-Mudaybiʻ is a rectangular fort (83.5 × 88.75 m; see also Chap-ter 9), located in an agriculturally marginal zone, about 20 km southeast of al-Karak. Known to Western scholars at least since its appearance in Charles Doughty's travelogue (Doughty 1888: 20), the site has been under excavation by the Karak Resources Project since 1997 (Mattingly et al. 1999; Mattingly 1997). Thus far, excavations seem to confirm that the outer enclosure of the fort, with its corner towers, midwall buttresses, and a monumental gateway, dates to the Iron Age II period. In Field B a four-chambered gateway has been discovered but not yet fully exposed. Much like H. al-Mudayna ath-Thamad, the entryway of this gate is slightly inset with a stone threshold and appears to be flanked by solid towers. The gate proportions at al-Mudaybiʻ appear to be very close to those of four-cham-bered gates known from Palestine, while those of al-Mudayna would fit only among the smallest Palestinian examples (cf. Herzog 1992: Table 2).

Decisive dating criteria, especially pottery from the foundation levels, have yet to be published for either gateway. However, radiocarbon dates (see Chadwick et al. 2000; Drinkard 2002) from roof beams and floor mats in both gate complexes would appear not to be distinguishable in a statis-tically significant manner. Both gates, therefore, may have been founded close together in time, perhaps in the first half of the eighth century B.C.E.[29] Furthermore, both excavation projects report contexts with late seventh- or early sixth-century material in and/or associated with their respective gate complexes.[30] Hence, it seems at least possible that these two gateways shared a relatively similar history of construction, use, and destruction.

Both six-chambered and four-chambered gates are well known from Palestine, where heated debate over chronological ascription has overshadowed a general agreement as to their association with royal building programs (see Herzog 1992: 265–74; Shiloh 1980; Ussishkin 1980; Yadin 1970). For present purposes we can put typological and chronological issues to one side and focus instead on the obvious, and hence often ignored, implications of these gate complexes. It is evident that gateways in the Iron II period were major edifices constructed to share a relatively common appearance. Assyrian wall reliefs depicting cities under siege, textual references to rooms above the gate (2 Sam. 18: 33), burned beams and roof matting found collapsed within gateways, and the analogy provided by the exceptionally well-preserved mudbrick superstructures of Middle Bronze Age gateways at Tel Dan (Biran 1994: 75–90) and Ashkelon (Stager 1991) all indicate that Iron Age gate complexes are likely to have stood six meters or more in height. The use of the same gate design at the entry to the city and at the entry to the citadel (e.g., Lachish III—see Ussishkin 1978; 1983), as well as the erection of royal monuments in the gateway (Bernett and Keel 1998; Ussishkin 1989a), points to a direct connection between these monumental edifices and the other building activities of kings. Of course, four-chambered gates are quite old, being "standard issue" in the fortified city-states of the Middle Bronze Age Levant. However, as this design was revived, rather than continuous over the intervening six hundred years, one cannot conclude that it was simply the only model available within this particular cultural context. Indeed, as is witnessed by the simple gate with benches found at the Iron I site of Ḥ. al-Mudayna al-Mu'arradja within the territory of Moab (Olàvarri 1983: Fig. 4), other designs were known and had been employed in the more recent past. Hence, the common use of multichambered gates with piers forms another category of kingly things consciously deployed in a common manner across political boundaries in the Iron Age southern Levant.

Proto-Aeolic Capitals

The importance, and specifically royal reference, of monumental gateways becomes clearer when we consider an architectural feature occasionally utilized withn these gateways. So-called Proto-Aeolic or Volute capitals are typically carved from limestone blocks and seem to have sat atop columns or pilasters bearing the weight of beams or lintels (Figure 8.8). These capitals are characterized by two symmetrical volutes, separated by a bud, usually stylized as a triangle, framed on the bottom and top by leaves, the latter of which is topped by a flat, rectangular abacus that serves as the weight-bearing surface of the capital (Shiloh 1979: 14).

In his extended study of these capitals, Yigal Shiloh noted thirty-three examples from Palestine, found in particular at Hazor, Megiddo, Samaria, Ramat Rahel, and Jerusalem (Shiloh 1979: 15. Table 2). In each case, when it is possible to reconstruct the original location of these capitals they are inevitably associated with citadels and palatial structures, particularly outer gates or inner entrances.

Since Shiloh's publication, three more examples have been published from Tel Dan (Biran 1994: 254, Figs. 201, 209) and a fourth has been claimed for Gezer (Brandl 1985). However, the largest number of new capitals has come from Transjordan. The existence of at least one "Proto-Aeolic" capital at Ḥ. al-Mudaybi' had been known since Glueck (1934: 13) visited the site in 1932. Current excavations have confirmed the existence of at least five such capitals at the site, all located within the four-chambered gateway (Drinkard 2002; Negueruela 1982). Another Proto-Aeolic capital has been found within the territory of Moab at 'Ayn Sara near al-Karak, where it is in secondary use (built into the wall of a restaurant parking lot!—Donner and Knauf 1986: Abb. 116). On the Amman Citadel, at least two examples have been found reused as building stone in later walls (Drinkard 2002; Najjar 1999: Fig. 4.8). Also reused on the Amman Citadel was a decoratively carved round column base (Najjar 1999: Fig. 4.9) very close in design to those that seem to have supported a throne canopy in the gateway at Tel Dan (Biran 1994: 237–41). Similarly carved column bases were also widely used in northern Syria (e.g., Carchemish, Tell Tayinat, Zincirli—Shiloh 1979: Fig. 71).

While Proto-Aeolic capitals seem to represent a highly stylized palm tree as rendered in a widely attested ancient Near Eastern iconographic tradition (Shiloh 1979: 26–35), they also form a distinct and coherent group in terms of their specific form and function. We have seen that they were used

Figure 8.8. Proto-Aeolic capital.

in at least four adjacent Iron Age states (Moab, Ammon, Judah, and Israel) in a manner that suggests a common deployment within the local hegemonic practices of kingship.

In point of fact, the use of rather similar volute capitals in funerary and temple contexts from the seventh- through fifth-century B.C.E. in Cyprus, as well as their common appearance on Phoenician and Punic stelae and model shrines, suggests that the Proto-Aeolic capital was also firmly established among the Phoenician city-states and colonies of Lebanon and Cyprus (Betancourt 1977; Shiloh 1979: 35–41). Once again we see signs that have common, cross-polity references being used to mark local distinctions.

Sculpture and Reliefs

The visual depiction of kings and deities in stone was a key component in the representation of ancient Near Eastern kingship from its very inception (e.g., Narmer Palette, ca. 3050 B.C.E.). Sculpture and stone reliefs would seem, therefore, to be among the most obvious media for constituting and representing state hegemony. Given its extensive archaeological exploration, the relative paucity of such objects from Palestine has led to the view that the southern Levant was unusual within the Near East in its limited use of monumental artwork in stone. In fact, we do have quite good evidence for stone sculpture and relief work from Moab, as well as its immediate neighbor Ammon. However, as this material has accumulated piecemeal over more than a century, often with very uncertain provenance, the evidence from Moab has never been fully gathered together or discussed.

Most famous is the Rujm al-'Abd Stele (Warembol 1983 with bibliography), discovered by Felix de Saulcy in the vicinity of Jebel Shihan in 1851 (de Saulcy 1854: 324, 333 Pl. 17), acquired by dubious means by the duc de Luynes in 1864 (de Luynes 1874: 170–82) and now on display at the Louvre (AO 5055; see Figure 8.9). This stele depicts a figure with a cap from which a curled streamer descends, wielding a spear in a downward-thrusting position and accompanied by, what appears to be, a lion. This stele is sometimes dated to the thirteenth–twelfth centuries B.C.E. (Zayadine 1991: 36–37), although without detailed argument. In my opinion, the theme ("serpent-slayer") and Egyptianizing execution are better placed in the Iron II period, as witnessed in the motifs of both "Phoenician" ivories and gold and silver bowls (cf. Warembol 1983; Weippert 1988: 667–68).[31]

An unpublished and unprovenanced basalt statue fragment, currently on display at the Karak Castle museum, seems to demonstrate that the Rujm al-'Abd stele did not exist in splendid isolation. This approximately 0.25–0.30 m tall fragment represents the knees to midhip of a straight-armed figure carved in the round. Both the figure's *sndty* kilt and thigh muscles(?) are executed in a manner nearly identical to that of the Rujm al-'Abd

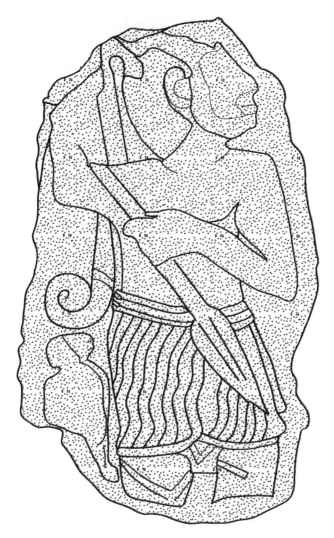

Figure 8.9. Rujm al-'Abd stele.

figure. Indeed, it is hard to imagine that they did not come from the same workshop, if not the same hand. Another unprovenanced statue fragment said to come from al-Karak is the head and torso of a male figure with an Egytianizing coiffure published in 1907 (Germer-Durand 1907: fig. 32; Hübner 1990) from the collections of Notre Dame de France à Jerusalem (now the Notre Dame de Jerusalem Center). The size and style of this piece identify it as an Iron Age statue akin to the more numerous and better-known examples from Amman (see below). Similarly, a basalt arm fragment excavated at Dhiban (Tushingham 1972: 25, Pl. 23: 8, Fig.38: 15), though carved in the round, is similar in its bent position to the corpus of so-called Ammonite statues (see below).

Stone stelae and statuary depicting individual figures are well known in both NeoHittite and Aramean contexts in the northern Levant (e.g., Genge 1979: Abb. 1–5, 8, 15–22, 26–28, 44, 52–53, 65–66, 75, 103–4; Orthmann 1971: 233–97). Inscriptions accompanying these stelae often identify the figures as royalty, or more frequently as deities in whose honor a royal personage has offered the stele or statue. The Rujm al-'Abd figure with its downward-thrusting spear, cap with streamer, and accompanying lion fits iconographic features used to identify the Canaanite god Ba'al, especially when fused with Seth as the slayer of Apophis the serpent in Egyptian art (Cornelius 1994: 161–68; Keel et al. 1990: 320–21) and more particularly in Egyptianizing art of the Iron Age.[32] Some scholars have speculatively identified this figure as the god Kemosh (see Mattingly 1989: 223), a suggestion that cannot be completely discounted, as local deities were frequently represented as the hypostasis of Ba'al as storm god.

Closer to Moab is the well-known corpus of Iron Age statuary from the vicinity of Amman. In 1980, Ali Abou-Assaf published a catalogue of twenty small full-body figures (0.33–0.81 m high),[33] near life-size busts (0.20–0.46 m high), and a similarly proportioned torso with a neck hole, evidently to allow the insertion and removal of such busts. To this corpus one can now add four more busts ('Amr 1990: Taf. 7a, 8a–b; Ornan 1986), one full-body statue (Zayadine et al. 1989: Pl. 51: 1–2), and a much-damaged head like those of the busts but carved in relief on a limestone block (Humbert and Zayadine 1991: 235, Pl. 9: a).

The number of examples from Ammon is sufficient to allow us to consider the internal structure and variability of this corpus. Overall, a number of stylistic axes serve to distinguish the Ammonite statues in fairly systematic ways (Figure 8.10). Notably, these axes are the presence or absence of: (1) an atef crown, (2) a beard, (3) the bent-arm position, and (4) a grasped lotus blossom. As Daviau and Dion (1994) point out, there is good iconographic precedence in the Levant for depicting a deity in the atef crown, especially El (contra Horn 1973). This corresponds very well with the Amman statuary. First, one of the figures without an atef crown (Abou-Assaf 1980: 25–27, Taf. 6) is inscribed as "Yarh'azar son of Zakir son of Shanib/p," perhaps the grandson of the Ammonite king Sanipu mentioned in the annals of Tiglath-Pilser III (Tadmor 1994: 170–71, l.7'), and hence likely royal himself (Aufrecht 1989: 106–9; Hübner 1992: 23–26 both with bibliography). This same figure grasps a drooping lotus blossom, as does at least one other (headless) figure from the Amman Citadel (Abou-Assaf 1980: 27–28, Taf. 7),[34] while the two full-body statues with atef crowns do not. While grasping a lotus blossom is an Egyptian iconographic feature associated with rebirth (Brunner-Traut 1980) it seems to have doubled as a symbol of kingship in the Levant, already in the thirteenth–twelfth century Megiddo ivory plaque (Loud 1939: Fig. 4) and quite commonly in

A   B

Figure 8.10. Ammonite statuary (drawing by Thomas Norman).

Aramaean reliefs and stelae.[35] We therefore have an interesting pattern where deities and kings are paralleled in their body treatment (bent-arm position, bearded), but distinguished by specific features (atef crown, lotus).

This shared body position (bent arm) is one widely attested in ancient Near Eastern statuary,[36] and used in particular to convey kingly authority in NeoAssyrian statues, where the figure grasps a scepter and a flail (Strommenger 1970: Taf. 1a–d, 2a). However, while the Ammonite statues employ motifs with international resonance, the logic of their arrangement into a system of differences (i.e., presences or absences) is local in its structure and points of reference.

Finally, another chance find from al-Karak stands out thus far as unique in the southern Levant, though it is quite at home in northern Syria/southern Turkey. This is a basalt orthostat skillfully carved in relief with the hindquarters of a lion (Canova 1954: 8–9, Fig. 4; Horsfield and Vincent 1932: 438, Pl. 15: 4). Lions are a mainstay of Neo-Hittite and Aramean art, most dramatically in the lions that flank gates and doorways as guardian figures or who serve as footrests for deities and kings in statuary and stelae. The representational link between king and lion was widespread, both in the metaphorical substitution of one for the other (Cassin 1987) and in the staged drama of conquest that constituted royal lion hunts (e.g., Weissert 1997).

Closest to the al-Karak orthostat are the individual slabs placed in series to create narrative wall reliefs lining gateways, large-scale courtyards, and processional avenues at sites such as Karatepe, Carchemish, Zincirli, Tall Halaf, and Sakçe-Gözü (see Orthmann 1971: 459–553). These running scenes contain familiar themes of kingship (especially warfare, hunting, chariots, tribute processions, and enthronement scenes), as well as religious scenes (ritual processions, mythical beasts, offering scenes). Particularly close to the al-Karak orthostat in terms of style and skill is the eighth-century lion-hunt relief from Sakçe-Gözü (Humann and Puchstein 1890: pl. 46; Orthmann 1971: Taf. 51c). Indeed, in terms of technical execution, the al-Karak orthostat compares very favorably to the most skillful northern Syrian examples. Hence, despite its isolated status as the lone Iron Age wall panel from the southern Levant, the al-Karak orthostat seems to witness the existence of experienced and skillful relief sculptors active in Moab during the Iron II period.

Hegemony, Replication, and "Kingly Things"

Examined in isolation, the material manifestations of kingship in Moab are fragmentary and uncertain. However, for each of these fragments we have found a place within broader categories of "kingly things" well attested elsewhere in the Levant. Hence, written over local cultural contexts, which could vary considerably across ecological zones and linguistic boundaries, we find the signs of kingship continuously replicated.

Although the semantics of this language of kingly things was international, its syntax was local. To assert that Moab was a kingdom through its comparability to other such polities was also to assert that Moab stood above and encompassed a variety of local identities. Hence, just as in the MI we see segmentary modes of identitification appropriated for the task of constituting state hegemony.

There is, however, one other point that becomes clear by considering the indexical value of kingly things. In many cases we do not in fact know if particular buildings or gates or works of art were created under the auspices of the king or the guidance of state agents. This would be problematic if we were to argue that hegemony is entirely the product of strategic action on the part of state agents. If, for example, a council of town elders built a four-chambered gate of their own volition, then the argument linking state hegemony and material culture would be seriously weakened. However, we can show that particular forms of material culture had fairly clear associations with kingship, even if we cannot demonstrate that each example was itself a royal project. If the indexical value of kingly things on its own can constitute hegemony (through emulation or metonymy), then kingship does not just appropriate cultural resources; it also creates them—reinscribing itself into the lived experience of its subjects. It is to this topic of the state as the maker of experience that we now turn in our penultimate chapter.

Chapter 9

Local Space in a Global State

> *I am king, I am lord, I am praiseworthy, I am exalted, I am important,*
> *I am magnificent, I am foremost, I am a hero, I am a warrior, I am a lion,*
> *and I am virile; Ashurnasirpal, strong king, king of Assyria.*
>
> —*Ashurnasirpal II "Annals" col. i ll. 31b-33 (trans. Grayson 1991:*
> *195–96)*

Thus far, we have focused on the constitution of Moab as a state identity by means of cultural resources already available in local forms of social life. Such a focus is artificially narrow as it implies that states exist in isolation and that state formation simply alters, rather than generates, the social contexts in which it occurs. The assumption of isolation is always problematic, and for Iron II Moab it is particularly so. As we have already seen, the local political context was embedded in a regional one of competing polities that was in turn embedded in the global context of an expanding Neo-Assyrian empire. Hence, state formation in Moab was in continual dialogue with shifting local, regional and global contexts. The need to account for the regional and global scales in Iron Age state formation is clear and largely without controversy. In contrast, the question of the state's creative role in transforming local contexts is the subject of considerable debate.

As we saw in our discussion of "tribal states," recent scholarship has put heavy emphasis on the limited, decentralized, and largely unintrusive nature of the Iron Age state in Transjordan (e.g., Bienkowski and van der Steen 2001; Knauf 1992a). This position is drawn in contrast to an earlier, and still prevalent, view in the study of Israel and Judah that presents Iron Age state formation as a classic rupture of traditional kin-based society, a *communitas* to *civitas* or *gemeinschaft* to *gesellschaft* transformation (Frick 1985; Gottwald 2001). However, both characterizations limit the activity of the state in society primarily to formal administrative practices. In effect, the question becomes one of the degree to which the state is (or is not) the author of society. From this perspective, our evidence for the direct assertion of institutionalized control over resources and political decision making at the local level is limited; although so too (in the case of Moab) are excavated contexts that represent this local level.

Our discussion of state formation suggests that there is more involved than the simple question of the presence or absence of state policy and state directives. In particular, in arguing against the "thingness" of the state we suggested that one effect of state formation was the articulation and subtending of smaller sites of power. As in Bourdieu's image of "statesque capital," such smaller sites are effectively coupled together under state hegemony but nonetheless retain a certain autonomy. It is this strategic coupling that enables the claim for centralized power to be positively asserted and affirmed without requiring that it actually be realized in each local instance. Hence, the question of the impact of state formation is not limited to the question of state authorship but must also include the question of what state formation enables, constrains, and influences.

To put the matter simply, one could approach this question in a new way by asking, "What difference did Moab make?" In other words, what ways of being did the process of state formation make possible or impossible in relation to Moab, regardless of the direct role of state agents? The remaking of people's lives may not have been the explicit goal of state agents in the Iron Age, as it was for their twentieth-century counterparts (see Scott 1998). However, any project framed as the desire of king or kingdom directed toward a body of subjects has both intended and unintended consequences for those involved. Similarly, the creation of new pathways for authority also creates new paths that certain people pursue. Obviously, the scale, priorities, operative logic, and potential success of such state projects varies with the historical bloc in which given polities are embedded. However, this does not mean that one can assign state formation an epiphenomenal status in Moab (Knauf's "thin veneer of central administration") simply because it does not engage in space-time restructuring to the same degree as the modern state. In fact, if we grant a significant role to the global or regional level in shaping Iron Age Moab, then we must also consider the transformation of the local context, as the division between these putative levels is largely an artifice of analysis.

State Agencies

Within the Syro-Palestinian archaeological literature, one finds two foci in discussions that portray the state as active in society during the Iron II period. The first is empirical, concerned with reconstructing specific administrative practices on a case-by-case basis. The second is idealist and links the state to a "national culture" witnessed by patterns in the distribution of material culture. In both cases, the concern is overwhelmingly with Judah and (secondarily) Israel, reflecting the dominant biblical focus of the field. However, either directly or by implication, one can also find both foci in discussions of relevance to Moab.

The administrative approach has focused in particular on (1) reconstructing tax/tribute collection and delivery systems, (2) royal supply systems, (3) "frontier" policies marked by fortresses and fortifications, (4) "public works" projects, (5) "national" systems of weights and measures, (6) judiciary procedures, (7) scribal schools and documentary practices, and (8) the administrative functions attached to specific titles witnessed in biblical and epigraphic material.[1]

Of the categories of evidence employed in these administrative studies, several are directly attested from (or ascribed to) Iron Age Moab. These include inscribed weights (Daviau 2002),[2] a royally sanctioned legal document (Bordreuil and Pardee 1990; 2000; Cross 1996),[3] stamp seals bearing personal titles (Avigad and Sass 1997: 372–386; Timm 1989: 159–264; 1993),[4] a relatively large-scale water reservoir (Ray 2001: 99–107),[5] and frontier fortifications (see below). On its own, this material remains rather scanty. However, given the minimal excavation thus far conducted in Iron II contexts within the territory of Moab, the presence of categories of material already well known from Palestine suggests that administrative practices were largely paralleled in neighboring southern Levantine polities.

While material traces of administrative practices are certainly attested, the scale and interpretation of these activities remains an open question. For example, of the 1,189 West Semitic stamp seals and seal impressions inscribed with personal names in Avigad and Sass' (1997) corpus, approximately 7 percent ($n = 78$) bear titles.[6] These titles (see Avigad and Sass 1997: 466–68) include those that seem specific to state/royal agents,[7] and to temple and other religious personnel[8], as well as a number that do not directly imply royal administration[9], perhaps facilitating some conception of a division between "private" and "public" occupations. However, biblical evidence, such as it is, suggests that royal administrative positions were frequently distributed within families, beginning with the family of the king (see Avishur and Heltzer 2000: 62–74; Fox 1996, 2000: 72–77). While priests show clear lineal descent of the same title[10], it is less clear that other titles descended within families, so much as specific families formed a limited pool of those likely to hold titles.

Here we encounter directly the scholarly divide noted above. On one hand, one could imagine a centralized court in which specific officials were responsible for specific tasks that were directly reflected in the titles that they held (cf. Avishur and Heltzer 2000; Fox 2000). On the other hand, one could imagine a network of personal links based on patronage and marriage spinning outward from the king to incorporate important families who held de facto authority in specific regions through their position within local kin-based hierarchies (cf. Lemche 1994, 1996; Niemann 1993). In this latter context, titles would have operated largely as honorifics marking necessary concessions on the part of the king, as claims to central authority were propagated by means of traditional decentralized networks of power.

In truth, the apparent necessity of choosing within these dichotomies ("personal" versus "bureaucratic," "institutions" versus "kinship," "legal" versus "traditional") is largely a by-product of the analytical categories used to study the state.[11] As we saw in Chapter 1, this is the language of classic nineteenth-century social theory and is closely tied to the specific historical process of state formation in modern (and early modern) Europe. On reflection, it hardly seems surprising that both status and class distinctions should be constituted within the idiom of family and descent or that state hegemony should operate by means of such familiar cultural resources. If it is hegemony that defines the state (or at least state formation), rather than archetypal content or form, then the problem of fitting evidence to universal models ultimately derived from a particular historical context (i.e., modern Europe) suddenly dissolves. Instead, we might get further by pursuing the question of how various smaller sites of power were articulated within specific state hegemonies.

Here, Bourdieu's (1977: 185–97) concept of social "fields" becomes relevant. As defined in Chapter 1, fields are domains of specific social practice constituted by interrelated sites, embodied skills, and culturally transmitted information. For example, writing in the Iron Age could be considered one such field, as it involved specific technologies, knowledge, and textual genres that were learned and hence transmitted over time. The problem is conceptualizing where this field "resided" and how it was reproduced, especially in relation to the state. Typically, this has been taken as a question of scribes, scribal schools, and royal sponsorship of literary specialists. Yet, here we enter something of a "Catch-22" argument. On one hand, the evidence for formal education in the Iron Age southern Levant is very limited (Crenshaw 1998), especially in comparison to Egypt or Mesopotamia. On the other hand, epigraphic evidence witnesses both the title "scribe" (*spr*—Avishur and Heltzer 2000: 54–62; Fox 2000: 96–110) and well-defined genres of practice, form, and content in the creation of texts (Lemaire 1981). Hence, scholars tend either to assume "schools" as institutions necessary to produce the epigraphic evidence (Lemaire 1981; Mettinger 1971) or to downplay the regularity of the epigraphic material in light of the lack of evidence for formal institutions (Davies 1998).[12] Similarly, the question of schools comes to stand for the field of writing itself, such that it becomes difficult to conceptualize attested scribal traditions when the presumption of institutionalized state sponsorship is questioned (e.g., Jamieson-Drake 1991).

The problem is that Iron Age writing systems have their own histories that are not contained within any particular state, or indeed within the Iron Age (see Naveh 1987; Sass 1988). In particular, the "systems theoretic" assumption of a strict functional relationship between the state as a mechanism, and writing as a tool, for managing information ignores the embodied practice of writing. That is to say, one does not simply learn to write; rather, certain people learn to write in a particular mode, according to particular conventions and in relation to particular contexts. This field of writing is therefore a "tradition," but it also constitutes a point in a specific social space that differentiates, for example, between those who can and cannot write and between contexts and instances in which writing is used (cf. Bourdieu 1989). In the case of the Iron Age, state formation entrains rather than creates this field of writing. For example, the Mesha Inscription was produced by a rather skilled scribe (or scribes), well versed both in the techniques of inscribing letters on basalt and in contemporary genres of royal inscriptions. My argument has been that this act of inscription occurred very early in the history of Moabite state formation. Indeed, one would be hard-pressed to build an argument for a developed administrative infrastructure in need of scribes in ninth-century Moab on the basis of the available evidence. Hence, scribal knowledge suited to state purposes seems already to have been in circulation in some form prior to the emergence of the state's administrative needs in the Iron Age. This fact is witnessed in an admittedly spotty manner by epigraphic finds from the Iron I–Iron IIA periods (Renz 1995) and is hardy surprising, given the long history of state sponsored writing in the Bronze Age Near East.

At the same time, once articulated within various state hegemonies, the field of writing took on new forms that were increasingly intertwined with the practices of state agents. To use the convenient example of Renz's (1995) corpus of Hebrew inscriptions, one sees a dramatic increase in both the number and the diversity of epigraphic finds from Palestine in the last 150–200 years of the Iron II period (Figure 9.1), corresponding with the unequivocal presence of "classic" archaeological correlates of the state.[13] Although the raw number of texts remains limited even at its peak, epigraphic finds from the mid-eighth through mid-sixth centuries B.C.E. indicate a greater variety of textual practices being performed than at the beginning of the Iron II period. Furthermore, as many of these practices involve marking or recording personal names, the intersection of royal administrative initiatives and the field of writing raises the possibility that new subject positions were being formed. For example, one finds seal impressions with a name in the standard formula "X *ben* Y" (X son of Y) on clay bullae that most likely sealed papyrus documents. One also finds lists of names in the same patronymic formula written on ostraca, sometimes accompanied by numerals (e.g., Aufrecht 1989: 137), presumably the result of remittances or disbursements. At a simple semantic level, the two instances are virtually identical in being composed of interchangeable patronymic names. Yet, the deployment of writing in each case suggests a rather significant distinction. Clearly, a difference exists between sealing

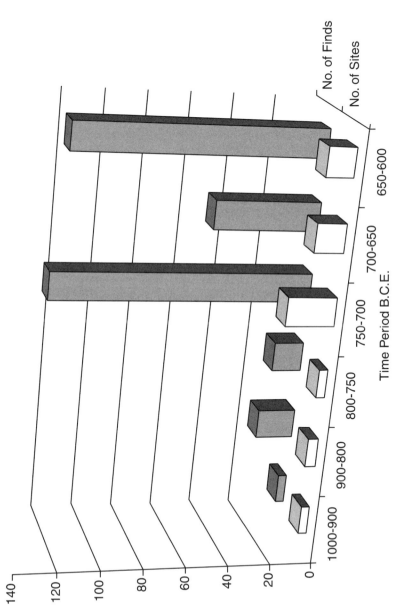

Figure 9.1. Frequency of provenanced Iron Age Hebrew inscriptions by half-century. Based on data published in Renz (1995).

a document and having one's name listed on a document, that is to say between accounting for and being counted. These are different positions occupied within the same social space, divided by one's relation to a particular administrative technology.

My argument is not that somehow "bureaucratization" dissolved, or even weakened, kinship and personal patronage ties, replacing them whole cloth with status roles and class relations. Rather, I am arguing that as the uses of writing expanded in a manner complementary to royal projects, the field of writing itself was not only coupled to state hegemony, it actually mediated (and hence made possible) particular social relations central to that hegemony (e.g., collecting taxes, fulfilling corvée labor obligations, seeking sanctioned legal decisions, etc.). Such written interventions may well have been discontinuous and infrequent events in the lives of most people. Nonetheless, these sorts of links whereby specific fields of action come to imply state hegemony by association (e.g., record keeping, military activity, religious festivals, etc.) is precisely how state formation could encapsulate and transform social relations without requiring that the state form a "master intelligence," pulling all strings and hatching every plot.

Along these lines we may also be able to make sense of the otherwise suspect idea of "national cultures" in the Iron II period. Numerous scholars have, with differing degrees of thoroughness, argued that the distribution of particular forms of material culture was in some way coincident with the historically attested territory of particular Iron Age polities (e.g., Herr 1997; Kletter 1999; Worschech 2000). This is particularly relevant to the question of writing, as "nationality"[14] (along with "date") has become the primary taxonomic category in the paleographic analysis of Iron Age texts. For example, most of our evidence for personal titles from Moab, as well as the lone "legal" papyri, are unprovenanced and ascribed to Moab on the basis of personal names containing the theophoric element "Kemosh," the morphology of the letters used, and the iconography that sometimes accompanies inscriptions on seals and seal impressions (Israel 1987; Timm 1989: 159–302; 1993). The single excavated "Moabite" seal ("Palty son of Ma'aš the memorist/herald") was found in a tomb containing eighth–fifth century B.C.E. material at Umm Uḍaynah, northwest of Amman (Abu-Taleb 1985; Hadad 1984; Hadidi 1987), that is to say, well outside the historically attested territory of Moab.

As in the case of "Ammonite" pottery (see Chapter 3), very little serious work has been done to explicate exactly why we should have "national" scripts or iconographic repertoires in the Iron II period. Material contexts for the production of seals in the form of workshops have been hypothesized on the basis of repetition of design elements (Lemaire 1995; Parayre 1993), yet diversity within "national" categories usually leads to the conclusion that multiple workshops existed within any one polity. The closest we come to an explanation is Christoph Uehlinger's (1993: xxiii) appeal to a Geertzian common "symbolic system," but again the question arises "why should this adhere at the level of nationality."[15] Similarly, Raz Kletter's (1999) thorough study of seventh–century "Judaean" material culture claims to be concerned specifically with political boundaries as a means of avoiding the pitfalls of ethnicity. Kletter develops Liverani's (1990: 79–86) suggestion that borders would be significant under the "pluralistic" ideology of peer polities who must acknowledge the territorial claims of their neighbors and seek such acknowledgment in return. However, we are offered no reason as to why a range of artifacts of diverse materials and uses should correlate with such political boundaries, except for the implied "ethnic" (and primordialist) reference to the political domination of "Judaeans" within "traditional" Judah (Kletter 1999: 27–28, cf. 42–43). Hence, even if the distributional argument holds,[16] one needs to account for how the boundary effects of state formation might have entrained distinct fields of social practice (e.g., pottery making, domestic ritual, economic exchange, etc.), constraining their development in a locally homogeneous and globally distinct manner. Until this is done, the concept of national cultures will mystify rather than explain distributional patterns in the archaeological record. One might add that, as a discipline, Biblical Archaeology is hardly in need of any further mystification.

Domesticating the Landscape

Perhaps the most notable change within the territory of Moab coincident with the process of state formation lies in the density, distribution, and form of settlement. In all areas surveyed, there is a marked increase in the number of sites occupied during the Iron II period (see Table 4.2). This general trend, however, masks very significant distinctions by chronological subphase, geographical subregion, and settlement form that we can draw only incompletely from the available data.

As we noted already in Chapters 5 and 7, settlement is very sparsely attested in the period immediately before and during the expansion and consolidation of Mesha's hegemony (i.e., tenth through ninth centuries B.C.E.; see Table 5.1). Most of our current evidence for building projects,[17] site foundation, and settlement growth within the territory of Moab during the Iron II period dates after the events depicted in the MI. Where we can distinguish subdivisions within the Iron II period, we find settlement in the Iron IIB period (ca. 900–700 B.C.E.) concentrated on the western side of the plateau,[18] although a few sites are (re)founded along the eastern margins, foreshadowing dramatic changes that follow in the Iron IIC period (ca. 700–550 B.C.E.).

Despite our fragmentary evidence, we can suggest that a number of regional centers grew considerably in size during the late ninth or (more likely) the eighth century B.C.E. The mound of Dhiban was artificially expanded on the southeast by about three quarters of a hectare, reaching a total of at least three hectares in area. Other sites grew to be considerably larger. Balu'a reached almost ten hectares in area, more than doubling the extent of the early Iron Age settlement (Worschech 1990b, 1995). Similarly, stratified eighth-century pottery has been discovered on at least three sides of the *tall* at Madaba, suggesting that its entire sixteen hectares may have been occupied in the second half of the Iron IIB period (Harrison et al. 2000; and pers. comm.).

While we lack the necessary site size information to analyze regional settlement patterns with any rigor, one can again see how this evidence could be used to argue opposed positions on the question of the pervasiveness of the Iron Age state. On one hand, upswings in building projects, sedentarization, site pioneering, and population all seem to follow on state formation in Moab, suggesting a causal link between the two. On the other hand, in terms of site size and distribution, regional centers such as Dhiban, Madaba, Jalul, and Balu'a (and probably also al-Karak and ar-Rabba) are not clearly integrated into a single regional system of exchange and central administration. The impression one gains from the available settlement data is an ensemble of local centers with an immediate catchment area of attached communities, little different from that suggested for prestate Moab in the MI. While Dibon (Dhiban) was significant to Mesha and prominent among Moabite settlements mentioned in the Bible, we have no direct evidence that it was in any meaningful sense the exclusive capital of Moab.[19]

Not atypically for Iron Age political centers (cf. London 1992), much of the mound at Dhiban (Dibon) appears to have been taken up by so-called public buildings.[20] Barring significant Iron Age settlement on the southern mound (beneath the modern town), it is doubtful that Dibon constituted much of a national "center" during the Iron Age in terms of population, production, or distribution. If anything, Dibon may have represented a "regal-ritual" center, in Fox's terminology (Fox 1977: 39–43), defined primarily by its central position in an ideologically defined spatial hierarchy.

While this decentralization is problematic if the state is viewed as a central intelligence directing social life, we have already seen that hegemony facilitates the entrainment of social fields to state interests without requiring the direct oversight of those fields. This can be illustrated in a fairly direct manner by the reemergence of Iron Age settlement on the arid "frontiers" of the eastern plateau of Moab.

Forts and Farmsteads

The ninth century saw the building of a "fort" on top of the abandoned Iron I site at Ara'ir (Olávarri 1965, 1969: Pl. 1).[21] The structure is a single unit, approximately 50 m square (Olávarri 1965: 80; 1969: Pl. 1), constituted by a casemate wall.[22] Its identification as a fort comes from its parallels with similar structures from the Negev Desert of Palestine (Beit-Arieh and Cresson 1991; Cohen 1983, 1994, 1995: 110–18; Cohen and Yisrael 1995a, b; Herzog 2001). The Negev examples are, in turn, tied directly to royal administration (in the case of Arad) by letters from the king, among other figures, directing the commander of the fort (Eliashab ben 'Ashyahu) to carry out specific tasks (Aharoni 1981).

Much as in the Negev, Ara'ir eventually constituted one of a series of possible forts founded within the territory of Moab, especially along its eastern margins (Figure 9.2). Excavated examples include Lahun (Homès-Fredericq 1992: 191–98; 1997: 68–78) and Ḥ. al-Mudaybi' (Mattingly et al. 1999), the latter, as we saw in Chapter 8 possessing the "royal" architectural feature of "Proto-Aeolic" capitals. Many of the sites recorded by Nelson Glueck (1934, 1939) in this same region include massively built "towers" ranging from about four to twenty meters on a side. These are difficult to interpret due to post-Iron Age occupation, and because they seem to be found in at least three different kinds of sites: (1) forts marked by large, usually rectangular fortified enclosures forming a single integrated architectural unit, (2) settlements marked by agglomerations of houses and other architectural features, and (3) isolated structures (towers, small enclosures, single buildings). The best candidates for forts among Glueck's sites include the large (75 × 50 m) rectangular complex at Ḥ. al-Hiri (Glueck 1934: 112), and perhaps the oval enclosure at Ḥ. ar-Rumayl (Glueck 1939: 118–23; Ji and 'Attiyat 1997: 121–22; Montlivault-Villeneuve 1989) rebuilt from the Iron I period. On the west side of the plateau such forts are less well-know, although clear examples are found on the north mound at Tall Iktanu (Prag 1989) and just north of the territory of Moab on the southern bank of Wadi Kafrayn (Mallon 1933: 405–07; Prag and Barnes 1996: 41–48). Furthermore, as at Ara'ir, Lahun, and perhaps Ḥ. ar-Rumayl, several sites occupied in the Iron I period appear to have been rebuilt with large towers, if not full-scale forts in the Iron II period (e.g., Boz al-Mishala—Strobel 1990: 83–85,1997: 273–74; Zwickel 1990: 151; 'Ayn Musa/al-Mašhad—Benedettucci 1998: 125–27; Glueck 1935: 110, Pl. 22).

In truth, it is quite difficult to maintain a strict dividing line between the smallest forts and the largest isolated structures (cf. Figures 9.3 and 9.5) on the basis of surface remains alone. However, there are several interpretive reasons for maintaining this distinction. Most obvious are the fully developed defensive technologies (corner towers, buttresses, offset/inset walls, gateways) witnessed in the architecture of the largest of these forts (e.g., Ḥ. al-Mudaybi') and shared in part by the smaller forts (esp. gateways and corner towers). Furthermore, the forts investigated thus far seem to have been founded earlier than the isolated towers and small enclosures found in the same area, although both are occupied contemporaneously during the late seventh–sixth centuries B.C.E.[23] Finally, the density and distribution

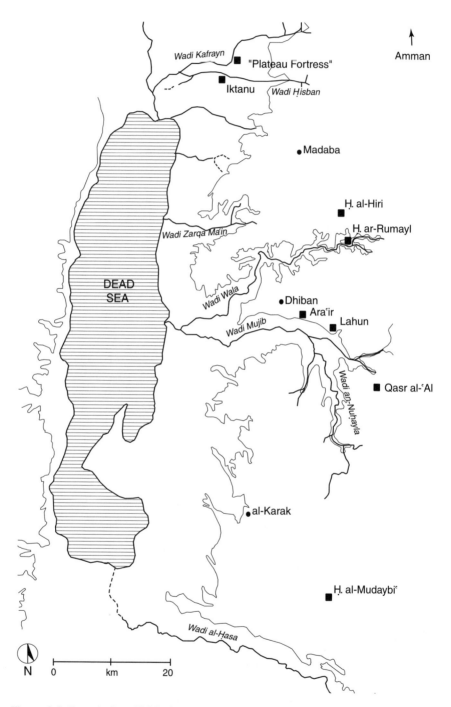

Figure 9.2. Forts in Iron II Moab.

of the isolated structures makes it difficult to interpret them in strictly military terms.

Our best evidence in this regard comes from the overlapping surveys along the eastern edge of the Karak Plateau (Koucky 1987; Miller 1991; Routledge 1995, 1996a). In contrast to the three nucleated villages of the late Iron I (ḤMM, ḤMA and Ḥ. Abu al-Ḥaraqa—see Chapter 5) at least 61 late Iron II sites are known from this approximately 15 × 50 km area (Figure 9.4).[24] Including Ḥ. al-Mudaybiʿ, four of these sites possess large rectangular enclosures of more than 50 meters on a side,[25] suggesting that they were built as forts. Two other sites are probably villages (Miller 1991: nos. 316, 355). However, the majority of these sites (74%, $n = 45$) can be characterized as isolated structures, especially towers, rectangular enclosures, or a combination of the two.[26]

Dispersed single units or compounds are characteristic of rural settlement in the southern Levant and elsewhere in the eastern Mediterranean from the Iron II period through to the early Middle Ages. In the southern Levant, up through the 1980s, such sites were consistently referred to as "watchtowers" or "border forts" and ascribed a military function.[27] Such work regularly emphasized the monolithic construction of these sites and the inter-visibility of their sight lines (e.g., Petrie and Pape 1952).

Recently, scholarly opinion has shifted and a new consensus has emerged around the concept that these sites were in some way associated with agricultural (or agropastoral) activities.[28] The arguments in favor of this position revolve around three points: (1) physical location of the sites, (2) associated installations, and (3) analogous structures from the recent past.

Recent survey work south of Amman has shown that "tower" sites tend to be located on hillsides, rather than hilltops, overlooking arable wadis (Geraty et al. 1989: 195–96; Hopkins n.d.). As such, they have poor strategic locations but good agricultural ones.[29] Both Dornemann (1983: 123) and Kletter (1991: 39) note that tower sites tend to be poorly distributed across the landscape, showing a tendency to cluster in groups. In the vicinity of Amman, towers frequently occur in conjunction with agricultural installations such as wine presses, olive presses, and terraces (Herr et al. 1991: 338; Najjar 1992). Such clusters of features (towers, presses, and terraces) are extremely common discoveries in archaeological surveys in the Mediterranean region (Applebaum et al. 1978; Cherry et al. 1991; Dar 1986: 88–125; Lohmann 1992), lending strong support to the agricultural, as opposed to military, interpretation (Figure 9.5).

Banning presents further arguments for multiple, but primarily agricultural, uses for stone-built towers on analogy with Mediterranean and Middle Eastern practices of the recent past. In particular, Banning (1992: 622–23) notes the common use of stone-built towers for field shelter and storage, particularly during harvest, and the use of similar structures by pastoralists as seasonal storage for nonportable items. Furthermore,

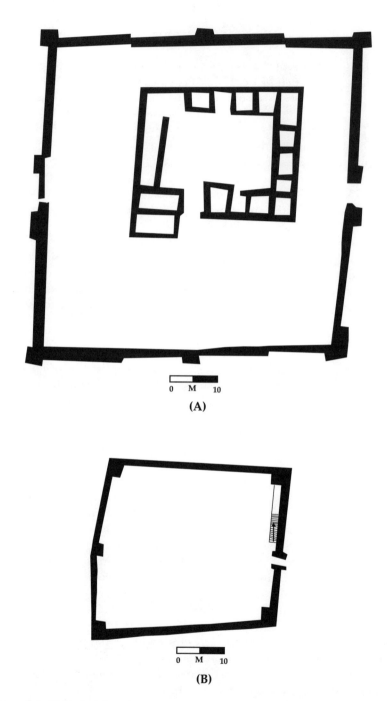

(A)

(B)

Figure 9.3. Al-Mudaybiʿ and Lahun Forts. (A) Ḥirbat al-Mudaybiʿ (after Mattingly et al. 1997: Fig. 1); (B) Lahun (after Homès-Fredericq 1997: Fig. 46).

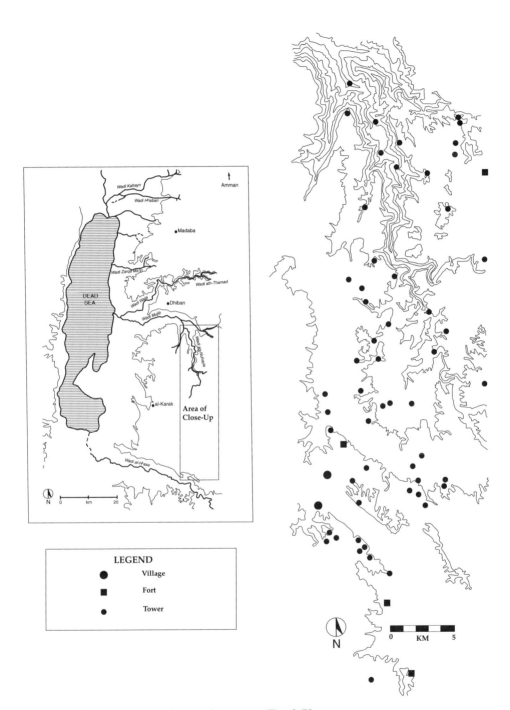

Figure 9.4. Late Iron II sites on the eastern Karak Plateau

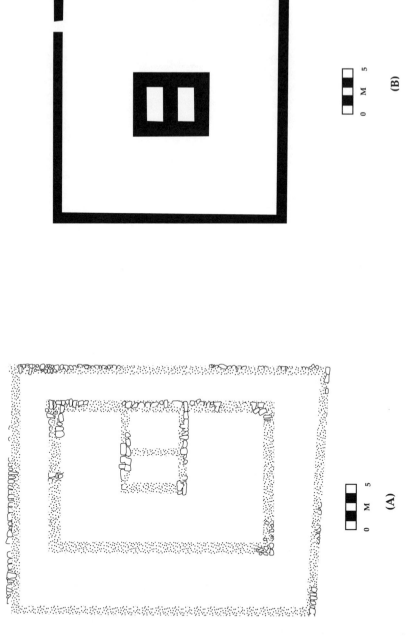

Figure 9.5. Late Iron II towers from the eastern Karak Plateau. (A) Ḥirbat ath-Thamayil (surface remains); (B) Ḥirbat ad-Dabba (schematic).

Banning (1992: 623) notes that the massive stones used in the construction of many of these towers can be accounted for, not by a desire for thick defensive walls, but more simply by the fact that the builders have made ready use of naturally fragmented blocks without further dressing (see also Glueck 1939: 167).

In Biblical Hebrew, Akkadian, and Greek the word for "tower" (*migdal*, *dimtu*, *pyrgos*) includes within its semantic field an agricultural building adjacent to cultivated land.[30] Several Greek texts are particularly interesting in this regard. In a fourth-century law-court speech recorded by (pseudo) Demosthenes (Orations 47. 52), the plaintiff recounts a raid on his estate, during which his wife and children were accosted in their courtyard, to which a house was attached, while the servant girls locked themselves in the family's *pyrgos*. On another occasion, Xenophon (Anabasis 8.8: 12–15) records the unsuccessful raid on the fortified *pyrgos* of a wealthy Persian farmer near Pergammon by Greek soldiers. In both accounts a picture is presented of towers as integral parts of farms, serving the further purpose of providing a refuge against brigandry and warfare.

Actual towers in the Greek landscape are the subject of considerable discussion. Robin Osborne (1985, 1986, 1987, 1992) goes to great lengths to emphasize the diversity of possible uses for particular towers (agriculture, personal memorials, lighthouses, watch posts—Osborne 1986, 1987: 63–69) and the diverse ways in which buildings "on the land" might be occupied, given the importance of wealthy absentee landlords and various leasing arrangements in Greek agriculture (Osborne 1985, 1987: 53–74; 1992). At the same time, it is clear that in ancient Greece a particular kind of rural settlement existed, characterized by the existence of a tower, agricultural installations, and an enclosed courtyard. Such settlements are best characterized as residential agricultural estates (Cherry et al. 1991; Lohmann 1992; Young 1956). The striking parallels between such settlements and those from Iron Age Transjordan can be seen in the corpus collected by Young (1956: Fig. 7).

For the eastern Karak Plateau, the arguments for an agricultural interpretation of the Amman area towers do not all apply equally well. The two sites discovered in 2000 on colluvial terraces in the Wadi an-Nuḥayla are associated with agricultural check dams and have very poor lines of sight. Tower sites on the plateau and steppe, however, tend to be located on high ground with relatively good visibility of the surrounding region. Even when views are obscured by higher ridges, one can usually see at least one other tower nearby. Except for cisterns, agricultural installations are not common at these sites.

At the same time, these isolated structures are numerous, closely spaced, and unevenly distributed across the landscape (see Routledge 1996a: 278–79). Current evidence indicates strong clusterings of sites along the south ridge of the Fajj al-'Usaykir, and in the vicinity of Khirbat ath-Thamayil.

Both of these areas provide good access to shallow tributary wadis that contain the remains of check dams of indeterminate age. Furthermore, a functional study of artifact assemblages from three of these tower enclosures suggested that a full range of grain and food preparation activities were being carried out on site (Routledge 1996a: 214–46). Certainly, if all of the sites under consideration were to be considered defensive in nature, one would have to wonder at both the unbridled enthusiasm and the poor planning skills of the Moabite military authorities.

Within the limits of the available data, we can suggest that at the end of the ninth and through the eighth century B.C.E. putative forts and small nucleated settlements were founded in the territory abandoned at the end of the Iron I period. At some point in the seventh century, it appears that large numbers of isolated structures began to be built in the interstices created by these forts and nucleated settlements. Ceramic evidence from intensely investigated tower sites suggests that they were abandoned toward the end of Iron IIC (ca. 550 B.C.E.—Routledge 1996a: 207–13). Fairly massive destruction layers at both Ḥ. al-Mudayna ath-Thamad (Chadwick et al. 2000: 262) and Ḥ. al-Mudaybiʿ (McMurray 2002) contain trilobate projectile points, indicating a similar sixth-century abandonment date.

The initial strategy of this settlement expansion would seem to be one of laying claim to, and pacifying, the eastern transitional zone from plateau to steppe. Some indication of this concern can be seen in a Neo-Assyrian account of a Moabite campaign against Qedarite nomads, evidently conducted in the steppe east of Moab (see below). Furthermore, Ezekiel 25: 9 states that Yahweh will "open up the sides" of Moab and allow its frontier settlements to be destroyed by "men of the east," implying again that the eastern margins of sedentary occupation were highly contested zones. At the same time, imagining a massive resettlement campaign in the Iron IIC period stretches the available evidence. It also fails to explain the dramatic change in the social form of settlement as represented by isolated sites that could not have housed much more than a single domestic group.

Again, the historical impact of state hegemony lies not in an overall directing will of the state but rather in the entrainment of divergent social fields along complementary paths marked out by state hegemony. The contrast between the nucleated settlement pattern of the Iron IB period and the dispersed settlement pattern of the Iron IIC period implies a number of significant social and economic changes in life on the eastern Karak Plateau. In the Iron IB period, nucleation provided for personal security and risk abatement (through direct patronage and on-site storage) at the probable cost of some land and travel stress in agropastoral production. Dispersed settlements would have allowed for more intensive land use by being "on the land" but would also have individualized, and hence heightened, risk. Furthermore, given the low yield potentials of the eastern Karak Plateau outside of the wadi bottoms (especially east of Wadi an-Nuḥayla), a significant proportion of these tower sites are likely to have been pastoral feed stations, providing secure storage for supplemental livestock feed (see Routledge 1996a: 272–338).[31] Such an intense concentration on livestock in a context where both communal and mobile risk-buffering strategies have been limited suggests very strongly that these isolated sites were dependent on exchange. Hence, economically we see the emergence of an exchange-dependent system of agropastoral production. Politically, we see personal security abrogated to state sponsored initiatives (forts, military campaigns). Socially, we see a world where, for at least some people, direct attachment to a community is no longer a fundamental necessity of social existence.

All these changes are linked to ongoing state formation in Moab, although none can be simplistically explained by the state alone. Furthermore, none of these changes can be said to be inevitable outcomes of state hegemony, as if they were already implied in the discursive structure of state formation. Hegemony as state formation is profoundly historical, as it is continually reconstituted by discursive strategies that select from and seek to contain the discordant elements of a given historical bloc. Hegemony is, therefore, a target in motion. It can, of course, be overthrown and displaced in the maelstrom of historical change. But hegemony is also a frame of reference that specific agents (so empowered) can creatively adapt to new circumstances by giving new meanings to old signs, perpetuating a tradition of political domination even as that tradition is transformed. In fact, we see both the transformation and the collapse of Moabite hegemony in this last phase of the Iron Age. Overwhelmingly, the historical context for these developments is the emergence of world empires, first in the form of Neo-Assyria (ca. 934–609 B.C.E.) and subsequently in Neo-Babylonia (ca. 609–539 B.C.E.) and Achaemenid Persia (539–333 B.C.E.). We must, therefore, link the local and global contexts of Moabite state formation if we are to understand the relationship between hegemony, history, and social change.

Incorporation into the Assyrian Empire

Moab does not figure in the earliest encounters between Assyria and the Levant, overlapping as they do with Mesha's own state building activities (see Chap. 7). Moab first appears in a building inscription of Tiglath-Pileser III dating to 728 B.C.E. Here the Moabite king Salamanu is listed as a giver of tribute (*madattu*), along with kings from Ammon, Edom, and Judah, among others (Tadmor 1994: 170–71). Since *madattu* was the annual obligation of polities who had already submitted themselves to the Assyrian king as clients (Elat 1982: 244–45; Postgate 1974: 129–20; 1992: 254), it is reasonable to presume that Moab had submitted to Tiglath-Pileser III in the course of his 734 B.C.E. campaign to aid Ahaz of Judah (see Cogan and

Tadmor 1988: 190–94; Na'aman 1991: 91–94; Oded 1974, 1993; Weippert 1982; among others). Between 728 B.C.E. and approximately 652 B.C.E., the toponym Moab appears in 14 published Neo-Assyrian documents.[32] In most cases, these inscriptions mention Moab in relation to the delivery of tribute. In only one case, under Sargon II in 713 B.C.E., is there any suggestion that Moab resisted the Assyrian Empire. Moab is listed in Sargon II's Prism A (Luckenbill 1926: no.195; Pritchard 1969: 287) as among those client states who were convinced to join an alliance against Assyria by the king of Ashdod. However, the inclusion of Moab among a list (ND 2765)[33] of tribute bearers immediately following Sargon II's campaign against Ashdod in 712 B.C.E. indicates that Moab's resistance to Assyria was short-lived. Hence, it seems that until Assyria's withdrawal from the west after circa 640 B.C.E. Moab remained within the Assyrian Empire as a relatively docile client state.

Structure of the Assyrian Empire

Neo-Assyrian imperial ideology was universal and monolithic in its assertion of dominance (cf. Liverani 1979b; Tadmor 1997). In common with many instances of empire (cf. Cooper and Stoler 1989), this ideology was embedded in a complex relationship of creating, expropriating, and denying objects of conquest (cf. Cifarelli 1995; Fales 1982; Zaccagnini 1982). Hence the paradoxical dynamic of discourse constantly distinguishing Assyrians from others (cf. Cifarelli 1995; Machinist 1993), even as Assyria absorbed and was transformed by those it conquered, becoming virtually bilingual in its use of Aramaic (see Tadmor 1991).

These "tensions of empire," to use Cooper and Stoler's (1989) term, require careful attention to the interplay of representation and practice. Assyrian domination could be interpreted in different ways, depending upon the position and context of the interpreter. Hence, for example, one finds Moab portrayed geographically as a point on the western edge of the known universe, which in being known is by definition ruled by the king of Assyria (Horowitz 1993). Yet, on closer examination such monolithic visions of rule fall apart, as it is clear that the Assyrians were, to a large measure, dependent on the cooptation of local rulers.

Here an important division should be made within the Assyrian Empire between those lands directly incorporated into Assyria proper and those polities standing in a patron-client relationship with the king of Assyria (Cogan 1974: 42–61; Postgate 1974: 119–30, 1992: 251–55). Using the Assyrian's own terms, Nicholas Postgate (1992) has aptly distinguished between the "Land of Assur" and the "Yoke of Assur." In the former case, polities were subsumed into Assyria proper as provinces with their leadership disembedded from local cultural and political traditions.[34] These new provinces were subject to the same taxation and corvée responsibilities (*ilku*) as other parts of Assyria (Cogan 1974: 50–51; Postgate 1979: 202–5).

In the latter case, polities were only subordinated by Assyrian imperialism. Local institutions of kingship could be maintained, provided rulers submitted to Assyrian dominion, presented regular tribute (*biltu/madattu*) and appropriate gifts (*tamartu/namurtu*), and supported the policies of the Assyrian king (Bar 1996; Cogan 1974: 55–56; Elat 1982; Lamprichs 1995: 121–29; Postgate 1992: 252–55).

After 734 B.C.E., Moab was under the "Yoke of Assur," and their relationship might be best described as that of patron and client (Postgate 1992: 252). That Moab was never incorporated directly into the Land of Assur is evident in the role given to Moab and Moabites in Neo-Assyrian documents (cf. Bienkowski 2000b). Moab, or the king of Moab, is listed as a bringer of tribute (*madattu*) in two inscriptions, of special gifts of loyalty (*tamartu*) in two inscriptions, and of building materials for the royal palace in one inscription. Moabite tribute bearing officials (*serani*) are mentioned in a further two inscriptions, while two inscriptions mention Moab in conjunction with the delivery of precious metals and hence are likely references to tribute or gift delivery. [35] The institution of *madattu* and the *serani* officials who deliver it were an integral part of patron and client relations in the Neo-Assyrian Empire.

The *serani* officials were required to travel to the capital and to deliver their nation's tribute in an elaborate state ritual that served to reinforce the asymmetrical relationship between patron and client (Postgate 1974: 123–27).[36] At the same time, these *serani* officials were hosted by the Assyrian court and given food rations, clothes, and small precious gifts (Postgate 1974: 127–28). Note for example that Padû-il of Ammon (Bit-amman) is recorded as having been given two gold rings and each of his two servants one silver ring in a lengthy list of such disbursements to *serani* officials (Johns 1898: no. 1110; Postgate 1974: 337–42). Hence, client rulers and their agents were not merely overwhelmed by the Assyrian court's grandeur, they were also bonded to the court by the precepts of gift exchange. To quote Nicholas Postgate (1992: 260): "we should not see the client rulers as cowering in their citadels, waiting to be irradiated with Assyrian influence, but absorbing the scene in Nineveh, fingering the tapestries and envying the silverware."

Both *madattu* and *serani* were terms used only with reference to foreigners from Assyrian client states, never with reference to the Assyrian provinces (Postgate 1974: 120, 124). Indeed, there is only one reference to Moab that might be construed as indicating a status other than that of a semi–independent client state. In a fragmentary text from Fort Shalmaneser (Dalley and Postgate 1984: no. 143 = ND 10025), dating to either Tiglath-Pileser III or Sargon II, an official from Moab is referred to as *šaknu*. The title *šaknu* was frequently used to refer to an official charged with administering an Assyrian province (Pečirková 1977: 212–13).

However, this evidence alone cannot support an argument for any further integration of Moab into Assyria proper. As Henshaw (1967: 519–20) has noted, the term *šaknu* was also used as a scribal analogy to describe foreign rulers. It is likely, therefore, that ND 10025 refers to a high Moabite official, and indeed Dalley and Postgate (1984: 253) suggest that perhaps this term is used interchangeably with *serani* when applied to foreign dignitaries.

Further evidence for Moab's status in the Assyrian Empire might be taken from the various prism accounts of Assurbanipal's campaigns against the Qedarite Arab leaders Yauta and Ammuladi (see Eph'al 1982: 142–69 for a discussion of these texts). In Cylinder B, Kamashaltu King of Moab is credited with defeating the Qedarite leader Ammuladi and delivering him to Assurbanipal in Nineveh (Borger 1996: BVIII43, pp. 115, 244). The language used to describe Kamashaltu specifically and the "kings of the Westland" more generally is that of the loyalty oath (*adê*) (see Cogan 1974: 42–49; Oded 1993; Parpola and Watanabe 1988).[37] While not limited to patron-client relations, such oaths are particularly characteristic of these relations, capturing as they do the underlying imperial ideology of Assyrian domination (see Liverani 1979b).

Such examples of these treaties and loyalty oaths as have survived are largely unilateral in nature, emphasizing the duties of the client to the Assyrian king (Parpola and Watanabe 1988: xv–xvi). This included the provision of troops for Assyrian military operations and the promise of nonaggression against Assyrian interests (Parpola and Watanabe 1988: xxxviii).[38] The absence, in many cases, of corresponding duties for the king of Assyria emphasizes the imbalance of power represented by these documents. However, the degree of inequality expressed in these agreements varied directly with the importance of the client state in terms of Assyrian political and economic interests (Parpola and Watanabe 1988: xvi).

Assyrian royal inscriptions, if not the *adê* texts themselves, do stress the role of the Assyrian king as the protector of his clients (Oded 1993: 68–70). As such, Assyrian military and political support was linked to the *adê* oath and provided a client ruler with some degree of internal and external security. For example, the pretext for Sennacherib's famous campaign against Judah and Phoenicia in 701 B.C.E. is the deposition of Padi from the throne of Ekron by his own people and his subsequent imprisonment by Hezekiah (Pritchard 1969: 287–88). With regard to Moab itself, some evidence of an Assyrian concern for the security of Moab's eastern borders might be seen in two different documents. ND 2773 (Donner 1957: 156–58; Saggs 1955: 131–33) reports the slaughter of the inhabitants of a Moabite city by the men of GIDIR land as an issue of which the Assyrian king should be aware, and one which a senior Assyrian provincial official must address.[39] In the Rassam Cylinder (Borger 1996: AVII112, pp. 61, 245), Assurbanipal records a string of military victories against Yaite the Qedarite stretching from Damascus to Edom and including Moab (with a city determinative).

The motivation for this campaign is Yaite's raiding of Assyria's western clients. Such responses were not, however, duties or responsibilities of the Assyrian king (Oded 1993: 70–71). Instead, they were favors, geared to furthering Assyrian interests (Parpola and Watanabe 1988: xxiii-xxiv). Therefore, Assyrian aid was not magnanimous. Entering an *adê* relationship with Assyria turned out to be irreversible until at least the middle of the seventh century B.C.E. Hence, clients were locked into a dangerous bind of compliance or retribution. As Parpola and Watanabe (1988: xvi) state: "These 'favours' had a price tag attached to them . . . (namely) the loss of the 'beneficiary's' political independence."

Here a central issue (from the client ruler's point of view) in the political structure of the Assyrian Empire has been touched on. Assyrian patronage brought a certain degree of stability, including protection from one's neighbors, one's own citizens, and ultimately from Assyria itself. With this the client ruler was given something of a free hand in administering internal political and economic affairs.[40] At the same time, Assyrian patronage put strict limits upon the power-building strategies open to client rulers. Territorial expansion, greater control over trade, and particularly trade alliances[41] were denied to these rulers. Furthermore, although not oppressive (Elat 1982), the annual tribute and occasional special gifts that Assyrian patronage required were a further limit on the ability of client leaders to accumulate power and wealth locally.

This situation was inherently unstable. Obviously, the ideal situation for the client ruler would be to accrue the benefits of Assyrian patronage without any of the costs. Primarily this would have been manifest in the temptation, once integrated into the Assyrian Empire, to divert the course of tribute and trade, attempting to keep a larger share at home. To do so was to court disaster, as both biblical and Assyrian inscriptional accounts attest. However, as Eph'al (1983: 96–97) has pointed out, there were logistical limits on the Assyrians' ability to maintain a significant military presence for any length of time at distant points such as the southern Levant. Hence, the evident policy for ambitious client rulers was to retreat behind fortifications and hope that the Assyrian army could not afford to conduct a long series of sieges (Eph'al 1983: 96–97; 1997), as would appear to have been the strategy of Hezekiah in 701 B.C.E. (2 Kings 18: 13–19: 37).

From the perspective of the Mesopotamian core, local client rulers represented something of a paradox. The relative independence of these leaders provided an efficient means of converting local agricultural surplus into portable luxury goods (through local exchange), articulating long-distance trade, and buffering the boundaries of the empire. On the other hand, this same independence made the Mesopotamian core subject to the power-building strategies of these local rulers. For the Mesopotamian core there must have been a constant balancing of policy between incorporation and independence, notable perhaps in the differential treatment afforded different polities (especially Phoenicia and Philistia) after rebellion (see Allen 1997; Elat 1991: 21–23).

Neither Cause Nor Effect

Returning to the question of the impact of state hegemony, and particularly the relationship between global and local social change, we must begin by looking beyond the collective actors through whom our historical narratives have been conveyed. We cannot take either Assyria or Moab for granted. Both are hegemonic identities that, on one hand, were inherited as a frame of reference and, on the other hand, had to be reproduced. In this sense, client and patron were mutually implicated in the form and reproduction of each other's rule within the limits set by the vastly superior power of the Mesopotamian core. Within the Neo-Assyrian Empire, the rulers of client states such as Moab, and their agents, occupied a precarious but important position. Such figures mediated between a global political economy of preciosities and grand alliances and a local political economy of primary production and kin– and community–based loyalties. Hence, while the rulers and officials of client kingdoms encountered their Assyrian counterparts in the personalized terms of submission and service, such relations affirmed their local hegemony by assuming that clients represented their subjects *in toto*.

Whatever the historical merit of the actual speech (see Cogan and Tadmor 1988: 240–44), the author of 2 Kings 18: 26–29 very insightfully captures the dynamics of this mediatory role in an encounter between Judean and Assyrian officials during Sennacherib's seige of Jerusalem:

Eliakim son of Hilkiah, Shebna, and Joah then said to the Rab-Shakeh, "Please speak Aramaic with your servants; we understand it. Do not speak Judean with us within earshot of the people on the wall." But the Rab-Shakeh answered them, "Was it to your master and to you that my master has sent me to speak these words? Was it not rather to the men sitting on the wall, who, together with you, will have to eat their own excrement and drink their own urine?" Then the Rab-Shakeh stepped forward and called out loudly in Judean, "Hear the message of the Great King, the king of Assyria. Thus said the king, "Do not let Hezekiah deceive you, for he cannot save you from me." (2 Kings 18: 26–29)

This precarious relationship suggests significant incentives on the part of client rulers to lay claim to territory more thoroughly and exclusively. The obligation of tribute and forced military alliance, as well as the opportunity of trade routes and military resistance, hinged on the generation of disposable resources. Records of actual tribute from Moab are limited, but they suggest the delivery of the same categories of precious goods as other Levantine polities (especially horses, precious metal, and textiles).[42] As these goods were not necessarily indigenous to Moab, rulers had to involve themselves in interregional exchange in order to possess such items.[43] Hence, from a top-down perspective, trade, agricultural intensification, and militarization stand out as possible catalysts for social change in the late Iron Age.

It is precisely these same historical conditions that some scholars have credited with a significant reordering of social life in the neighboring state of Judah, one which eventually gave rise to the dominant ideological perspectives of the Tanak (Old Testament) itself (Finkelstein and Silberman 2001; Halpern 1991, 1996). In particular, Baruch Halpern (1991, 1996) has argued that in preparing to resist Assyria, Judah began under Hezekiah to militarize its countryside, centralize its administration, and seek to generate and control economic production to a greater degree. For Halpern, the devastation wrought in the countryside by Sennacherib spurred these trends along, as Jerusalem emerged as a primate center in a depopulated territory. Traditional landholding elites and corporate kin groups were disenfranchised in favor of court members. What in the eighth century had been a radical critique of traditional place- and ancestor-oriented religious practices became in the seventh century the official religious policy of a state–sponsored monotheism centralized in Jerusalem. Furthermore, Halpern argues that in the face of a globalized culture under Assyrian hegemony and extensive trade, these homogenizing transformations of traditional life were themselves cast as the recovery of an "authentic" Yahwistic identity.

As the breathtaking leaps of faith and logic that underlie Halpern's arguments might lead one to suspect, there are many problems with the specific details of his explanation.[44] However, he does provide us with a compelling picture of how pervasive and profound social change might follow on state mediation between global and local contexts. In particular, Halpern conveys a sense of how specific projects (fortification building) and specific events (Sennacherib's campaign in 701 B.C.E.) could have had cumulative effects that reordered human experience in dramatic ways. Furthermore, Halpern raises (but does not resolve) the important issue of change within hegemony where meanings fixed to cultural resources by state formation are radically changed, often against violent resistance, without the dissolution of the state itself.[45]

Halpern's observations are, however, limited by the "total" role he gives to the state as an agent in his explanation. For Halpern, the state is both pervasive and all-powerful. Indeed, he explicitly argues (not without some cause) that the late Iron II state of Judah under Josiah was totalitarian in its efforts to centralize and homogenize Judean society (Halpern 1996: 330–38). Yet, the impossibility of a "total state" is precisely Gramsci's sober message of hope. I say sober, because it highlights the necessity of tacit consent by some in even the most dictatorial regime and the degree to which state hegemonies carry divergent social fields along in their wake. As in the example of writing, social (and settlement) changes in Iron IIC Moab and its neighbors were constituted by the coupling of distinct social fields to state hegemony, rather than by the state itself as a singular directive will.

Trade and the Taste for Luxury

The southern Levant proved to be the convergence point of several important trade routes. These were; the overland route for aromatics and minerals from Arabia, the overland and maritime route for precious natural and manufactured goods from Egypt, and the point of entry for goods from the Mediterranean world (Astour 1995; Eph'al 1982: 12–17). By the eighth century we have clear, if somewhat unevenly distributed, evidence for the revival of international trade along these routes on a significant scale (see Aubet 1993; Avitz-Singer 1999; Cavigneaux and Ismail 1990: no. 2; Edens and Bawden 1989; Sherratt and Sheratt 1993).

Scholars have debated the degree of Assyrian involvement in such trade over and against their extraction of such goods by coercive means (Diakonoff 1969: 28–29; Elat 1991; Jankowska 1969: 274–76; Oppenheim 1967, 1969; Postgate 1979: 207). What is clear is that Assyrian policy showed a marked interest in controlling the access points to the main trade routes (Briant 1982: 150–61; Brinkman 1979: 229; Edens and Bawden 1989: 79–81; Eph'al 1982: 15–16; Na'aman 1979) and in maintaining the trading activities of particular subject peoples (Frankenstein 1979: 286–91; Oded 1974; Allen 1997; see ND 2715, Saggs 1955: 127–30).

Interestingly, Lin Foxhall (1998) has argued that early Greek poetry and the biblical prophets suggest the parallel development of elite identities constructed around the sensuous consumption of trade goods (especially select wine and scented oils) in the eighth to the sixth centuries B.C.E. Furthermore, in both biblical and Greek literature, this sensuous consumption is opposed within elite circles by an alternative ascetic orientation stressing the moral "authenticity" of local practices in contrast to foreign excess, even as "local practices" are recast in the process (cf. Halpern 1996; Morris 2000).

For Transjordan, archaeological evidence for distinct elite identities, perhaps partially disembedded from kinship and locality, is clearest in the late sixth and fifth centuries B.C.E., after the dissolution of the Iron Age monarchies. Here we find individuated burials (Yassine 1984) and funerary assemblages that closely parallel those from elsewhere in the Persian Empire (Routledge 1997b; cf. Nunn 2000). From the late eighth through the early sixth centuries B.C.E., archaeological evidence from the southern Levant points to the widespread intensification of agropastoral production, particularly viticulture (Gitin 1997; Herr 1995; Routledge 1996a). Some scholars (Chaney 1989, 1999; Hopkins 1996) have taken prophetic indictments against those "who add field to field until there is room for no one" (Isa. 5: 8) as evidence for land consolidation and the disenfranchise-ment of subsistence farmers in the face of intensified "cash crop" (olive oil and wine) production for export.

The possible emergence of elite identities disconnected from kin- and locality-based loyalties seems to have been an important factor in the forms taken by social and political life from the late eighth century B.C.E. through to the dissolution of Iron states in the sixth century B.C.E. Here we see clearly the intertwining of state initiatives with various social fields. On one hand, the military infrastructure of the state and its international relations made possible a secure social space outside of kin and locality networks in which landowning and administrative classes could emerge and be demar-cated more clearly as a structure of relations.[46] This social space was latent to some extent in the monopoly logic of state hegemony, yet, as shown by Halpern, it developed under the specific historical conditions of Assyrian imperialism. On the other hand, alienable resources and people were of central importance to state projects. Indeed, both the intensification of agricultural production and the creation of "detached" people (on both ends of the economic spectrum) were necessary for Moab and its neigh-boring polities to develop the kind of "statesque capital" evidenced in the independent directive power of the state that emerges in the eighth century B.C.E. State administrative expansion, agricultural intensification, increased production for trade, and "detached" elite identities were all, in this sense, strategically coupled developments.

Moab and Babylon

The last two decades of Assurbanipal's long reign (668–627 B.C.E.) seem to have been taken up by the suppression of revolt in Babylonia, ending in something of a Pyrrhic victory (see Frame 1989). Between 627–609 B.C.E., four successive kings see out the eventual collapse of Neo-Assyria in the face of an ascendant Babylon and its Median allies. After circa 605 B.C.E. Egypt and Babylon pursued strategies in the southern Levant that were similar to those pursued by Assyria. However, neither power seems to have dedicated the same attention as Assyria to documenting their military tri-umphs, or to building an administrative infrastructure (see Vanderhooft 1999). As a result, our knowledge of late seventh- and sixth-century impe-rialism is much sparser than that for the previous two centuries.

We do know that both a resurgent Egypt (under Psammetichus I, Necho II, and Psammetichus II) and Babylon actively sought hegemony over the Philistine and Phoenician coast (especially Gaza and Tyre), hence showing a typical concern for controlling the nodal points of international trade (Stager 1996). At the same time, while both powers actively manipulated local dynastic successions (Egypt—installation of Jehoiakim [2 Kings 23: 34]; Babylon—installation of Zedekiah 2 Kings 24: 17) and extracted tribute from clients, neither disembedded the local political system via direct incorporation. Indeed, both Egypt and Babylon appear to have initially continued common Neo-Assyrian practices of binding client states by treaty.[47] Common client obligations would seem to have continued, as is witnessed by Nebuchadnezzar's use of Moabite and Ammonite troops to raid Judah, according to 2 Kings 24: 2.

The primary structural distinction between the period of Neo-Assyrian hegemony in the west and the period of Egyptian/Neo-Babylonian competition in the west was the very existence of this competition. Fundamentally, the existence of a viable second power was destabilizing for the imperial structure inherited from Assyria by the Babylonians (Malamat 1988). Mesopotamian empires had rather limited means of securing unequal control over trade networks with external point n except by the political cooptation of point n minus 1. In other words, unlike modern world systems, economic imperialism beyond the scope of political imperialism was seldom achieved by the Mesopotamian empires. The semiperipheral client states on the outer edges of the imperial core played the important role of articulators in the commercial links formed between external or semi-external polities and the imperial core. With a relatively weak Egypt, the barriers to rebellion among such client states were proportionately high. However, with the emergence of a strong Saite Egypt, rebellion becomes a much more obvious strategic option. Playing one power off against another was a short-term strategy on the part of small states necessitated by uncertainty over who would ultimately hold dominion.

Under these circumstances, independence of the client states in the southern Levant became an impediment to, rather than an articulator of, surplus flow. Furthermore, Egyptian ambitions to form an alternate imperial core in the west meant that there could be no simple agreement between the two powers without a significant shrinkage and reordering of Mesopotamian imperial control (as in the loss of access to land and sea trade focused on Tyre and Gaza). As such, it seems clear that the necessary counter (from a Mesopotamian perspective) to an active Egypt was the expansion of the pacified borders of the empire and the subjugation of Egypt itself. This indeed marks the policy of both Babylon and Achaemenid Persia from sometime after Nebuchadnezzar's transformation of Judah from a client state under Zedekiah into a province under Gedaliah in 586 B.C.E., down to Cambyses' invasion of Egypt in 526 B.C.E. This strategy is marked by a second element as well, which includes the extension of the semiperipheral portion of the empire into northern Arabia, culminating in the famous sojourn of Nabonidus in Tayma.

The End of Moab

Josephus (Antiquities 10.9.7) preserves a tradition that in the twenty-third year of Nebuchadnezzar's reign (582 B.C.E.) he conducted a campaign against Ammon and Moab. As John Lindsay (1976: 27–29) notes, this tradition parallels a small deportation of Judahites in Nebuchadnezzar's twenty-third year, as recorded in Jeremiah 52: 30. Furthermore, it casts Moab and Ammon into the rebellious roles suggested by their participation in Zedekiah's anti-Babylon summit (Jer. 27: 3–7) and more particularly the sponsorship of Gedaliah's assassination by the Ammonite king Ba'alis (Jer. 40:14). Hence a 582 date for a military conquest of Moab has been accepted by many scholars on the basis of Josephus (Lemaire 1994c; Lindsay 1976; Miller 1989b: 26).

Alternatively, Nabonidus, the last king of Babylon, campaigned to, and then stationed himself permanently in, the northwest Arabian (Hejazi) oasis city of Tayma for the decade between circa 553 and 543 B.C.E. (see Beaulieu 1989: 149–65). A large-scale, badly eroded rock relief found near Sela' in northern Edom in 1994 (Dalley and Goguel 1997) is Neo-Babylonian and ascribable to Nabonidus on typological grounds.[48] Such reliefs are usually memorials of military campaigns (see Dalley and Goguel 1997). Furthermore, it is now recognized that the fragmentary Verse Account of his campaign to Tayma in 552 B.C.E. records the conquest of a city in Edom (Beaulieu 1989: 171–74; Eph'al 1982: 185–88; Lindsay 1976: 34–36). If one supposes that Nabonidus campaigned against Moab as well as Edom, then this strategy can be seen as an attempt to incorporate and extend what were the limits of his empire. Indirectly disembedding the political economy of Moab would contribute to a larger policy directed at Egypt. More directly, it provided Babylon with direct control over the routes of passage (both for trade and logistics) to Arabia. As Eph'al (1982: 191) notes, Babylonians as well as Arabs were engaged in the caravan trade between Uruk and Tayma during Nabonidus' reign. Therefore, it is likely that the preferred trade route would have been north of the Nafud Desert through Jauf (Dumah/Adummatu) to southern Mesopotamia, rather than through the Levant (Potts 1988: 129–31). Certainly, trade taking this route could also travel northwest from Jauf up Wadi Sirhan to Amman.

Archaeologically, material from the eastern Karak Plateau would seem to favor a mid-sixth century date for site abandonment (hence under Nabonidus), although this remains somewhat uncertain (see Routledge 1996a: 207–13). Why, however, should Nabonidus' sojourn in Arabia have been so devastating to Moab in particular? Ammon continues to prosper into the fifth century, as indicated by rich tomb groups such at Umm Uḍaynah (Hadad 1984; cf. Herr 1999b), while both Busayra and Tawilan in Edom show evidence for rather vibrant and continuous occupation into at least the fourth century B.C.E. (Bennett and Bienkowski 1995; Bienkowski 2001b). Simple slaughter or deportation of Moabites may have been involved, but a better explanation lies in the geography of international trade. If the preferred northern trade route from Tayma had shifted to Jauf and away from Ma'an under Nabonidus, then Moab would be bypassed completely. Under these conditions, Amman would become the gateway from Damascus to Wadi Sirhan (and hence Jauf), while southern Edom would remain on the western route to Gaza (cf. Avitz-Singer 1999). Hence, events in the Hejaz could potentially affect Moab in a relatively singular manner.

We do not know if the state apparatus of Moab was violently dissasembled by mass deportations, as it was in the case of the Neo-Babylonian conquest of Judah, although some similar event seems likely. We can, however, suggest that the coupling of state initiatives with "detached" elite identities, agropastoral intensification, and a focus on production for trade facilitated a hegemonic crisis in Moab, when both state security and the flow of luxury commodities were destabilized. We have no direct evidence regarding this crisis, in terms either of settlements or of the ordering of social life. A similar collapse of state hegemony in the case of Judah almost certainly underlies the singular universalized vision of Yahweh that is placed at the center of the Tanak (Old Testament). In other words, this was a period when the stable referents of Iron Age polities (e.g., Kemosh, king, and the land of Moab) were radically destabilized. In the course of the sixth century we can say with some certainty that life did not simply "decompose" into the constitutent communities of the state. In making itself out of the cultural resources of communal life, state hegemony had in turn remade those communities.

Moab as a state identity seems to dissolve rather rapidly following the sixth century. In contrast with Ammon (Herr 1992a), there is no evidence for its continued use as an administrative designation under Persian or Hellenistic rule. Similarly, as already noted, Moab contrasts with both Ammon and Edom in its lack of evidence for settlement and external trade contacts in the fifth and fourth centuries B.C.E. By the time of Josephus, Moab can still be used as an ethnoym designating a subdivision of the "Arabian peoples" (*Antiquities* xiii.xiii 5). However, it is most commonly used in its original role as a territorial designation (e.g., Ptolemy *Geography*: 5: 16: 4; Eusebius *Onomastica* 124: 15–17). We return, therefore, to the striking facts suggested by the semantic history of Moab, namely that its very solidity as a state identity involved forgetting that it had not, and would not, always be so.

Chapter 10
Once Again, the State

*If the French Revolution were to recur eternally, French historians would be
less proud of Robespierre. But because they deal with something that will not
return, the bloody years of the Revolution have turned into mere words, theories, and discussions, have become lighter than feathers, frightening no one.
There is an infinite difference between a Robespierre who occurs only once in
history and a Robespierre who eternally returns, chopping off French heads.*

—*Milan Kundera,* The Unbearable Lightness of Being

Having reached the conventional end of Moab's eventful history, it is fitting
to ask just what we have learned from the detailed analysis of the preceding
pages. From the beginning, we defined the project at hand in terms of
the state as a concept, an effect, and a problem. So perhaps we should
begin here; asking what Moab might contribute to cross-cultural and cross-
temporal discussions of the state and, in return, asking what such discussions offer for our understanding of Moab.

The state has experienced something of an academic revival in recent
years, spurred on, it seems, by events that have outpaced the terms and concepts available for their description. Anthropologists, for example, have
increasingly confronted the paradox of postcolonial states which "fail" to
meet the universal criteria of traditional state discourse (e.g., territorial
sovereignty, monopoly on violence) while continuing to perpetuate themselves, often in relation to a constellation of private interests, NGOs, and
international organizations (e.g., IMF, World Bank). These realities have
rendered problematic the boundedness and coherence of the state, highlighting the degree to which it is performative in nature, arising as a
historical effect of specific practices conducted in relation to specific discursive formations.

As I argued in the opening chapter, these very modern concerns highlight a distinct set of problems for those who would study complex polities
of the distant past, while at the same time providing a method and a vocabulary that makes possible a distinctly new understanding of the premodern
state. The problems arise because, from at least the eighteenth century on,

explicit reflection on what the state is, or ought to be, has been intimately linked to the historical process of state formation itself, first in Europe, then globally through colonialism and the subsequent Euro-American domination of international political discourse. Hence, the terms and concepts we have inherited as neutral descriptors of a universal phenomenon are themselves constitutive of that phenomenon.

For this reason, the very idea of the state existing before such state discourse is highly problematic, suggesting that premodern polities should be discussed in rather different terms. At the same time, a focus on the performative nature of the modern state highlights a conceptual domain with significant potential for the understanding of premodern polities. As noted in Chapter 1, polities have a named presence that depends on practices and discourses that render them concrete. It is precisely this process of concretization, of giving material substance and political agency to a nominal term, that I suggested was central to the comparative study of state formation and that I attempted to illustrate with the case of Iron Age Moab.

Whether, in the absence of state discourse, one should continue to employ the term "state" as I have in this book is a legitimate question, but one with limited substantive import for the larger issues at hand. These larger issues include the question of whether specific instances of complex polity formation can have a general theoretical, cross-cultural, and cross-temporal relevance once we have acknowledged that the state is something other than a structural *Bauplan* to which "society" conforms under specific circumstances. In its historical specificity, our study of Moab has sought to answer this question affirmatively, showing that this general relevance can be obtained by shifting from a taxonomic orientation focused on trait definition to a performative orientation focused on practices and intellectual products. The result is not a common form for the state (which is historically variable) but rather the recognition of common problems relating to collective power and its instantiation in people's lives.

Here, the writings of Antonio Gramsci have proven particularly relevant. In Gramsci's concept of hegemony we found a means of conceiving of state formation as a moral order, or frame of reference, orienting action through the binding of force and consent. In particular, his characterization of the relationship between hegemony and "common sense" (Gramsci 2000: 324–49) proved vital in highlighting hegemony as the interested and selective transformation of "inarticulate" cultural resources embedded in practical experience. This realization freed us from the false choice of volunteerism and state determinism. It also overcame the inadequacies of "micropower" approaches, such as those of Foucault and Bourdieu, which fail to account for the relative coherence and intentionality of state projects and state agents as well as the agency of those who resist such projects, often on a case-by-case basis. Importantly, Gramsci's state is limited in that its hegemony is never complete and alternative orders are always latent in the very "common sense" from whence the state's own cultural resonance derives. At the same time, state hegemony seeks to set limits and to define the possibilities of existence within its domain. It is this struggle over domination, meaning, and consent, what Gramsci termed a "war of position," that stands at the heart of state formation as a process.

In the case of Moab, we followed this process of fixing, contesting and dissolving hegemony through several distinct historical moments. In the Late Bronze Age, the hegemony of an "urban" elite sought to articulate traditions of ancestor veneration and gift giving in order both to distinguish elite lineages and to encompass the community, attaching distinct identities to a simple class division of tribute givers and receivers. The state hegemony of Iron Age Moab was constituted in quite a different manner, with the land of Moab sacralized as the property of the god Kemosh, who laid claim to this land in toto (people, resources, etc.) through the agency of his chief representative, the king. Hence, despite the use of Moab as a geographic term in the Late Bronze Age, we were able to show that political hegemony in this region was discontinuous across the traumatic divide of the Late Bronze-Iron Age transition.

In the later Iron Age, assertions of political dominance resonated because they were structured by and through forms of identification already well established in early Iron Age communities (i.e., segmentation, genealogy, and domestic autonomy). Indeed, we were able to note the parallel manifestation of these cultural resources in community organization (e.g., the spatial relations of house and village) during the Iron I period and in the intellectual products (e.g., royal inscriptions and building projects) of the state during the Iron II period. Hence, the kingdom of Moab appeared not as a rival, seeking to dissolve kinship and community loyalties, but rather as their necessary extension, encompassing kin and community in a segmentary manner. At the same time, the construct of Moab as a territory to which the king laid claim made possible the imagining of new kinds of relations and identities that cut across kinship and community and that played on, or ran parallel to, royal institutions. This emerged most acutely as the Neo-Assyrian Empire began to systematically impose itself on the horizons of the small states of the Iron Age Levant. Militarization, agricultural intensification, and the cosmopolitan possibilities of trade within the threatening stability of a *pax Assyrica* were the outward signs of elite identities and royal institutions increasingly disembedded from locality and kinship.

However, before we slip away completely into a historical narrative of hypostatized actors (Moab, Assyria, elites, etc.), we need to be clear on what we envision when we talk about state hegemony. As Jessop suggested (1990: 242–43), the state is not a "global calculating subject." State hegemony is an effect of specific projects carried out by specific actors. In the case of Moab, it involved on one hand the assertion that such a totality existed (i.e., a uniform sacralized land entrusted to the king) and on the other hand a series of practices and dispositions that were predicated on this existence (e.g., state building programs, military expeditions, tax collection, gestures of allegiance, "legitimate" use of force). The complementary dynamic of asserting that, and acting as if, Moab existed generated Moabite state hegemony. Agents encountered these state effects historically and culturally, initially as something suddenly made relevant by the military successes of Mesha against Israel and subsequently as an inherited historical reality. Hence, those living in Moab encountered the "Land of Moab" as a frame of reference that structured lives in very specific ways by differentially empowering people to act. At the same time, as the eventual dissolution of Moab makes clear, this frame of reference was subject to interpretation, evaluation, and rejection.

It is in this sense that the abstract form of the state basic to taxonomic definitions is insufficient for understanding state formation. In many ways, the position I have laid out holds much in common with classic social theory. I have recognized state formation as a specific moment, not found in all human collectives. I have suggested that it involves a monopoly logic, most particularly with regard to legitimate violence, even if never fully realized. Finally, I have recognized the generality of this process, in the sense that state formations can be compared and explained along broadly similar lines. However, a fundamental distinction lies in the "thingness" granted to the state in both neoevolutionism and traditional political philosophy. While classic social theory has focused on the phylogeny of the state as a species of political organization, often through the ontogeny of its specific instantiations, I have argued that no such "thing" exists.

What does exist is a process that constitutes hegemony as an effect. Hence, the study of the state cannot be limited to initial conditions (e.g., warfare, population growth), nor can it treat as singular, holistic, or systemic the named identity by which hegemony is signified. At the same time, it is insufficient to stop with the recognition that the state is an effect, as its greatest mystery is that this effect also has effects. As people engage hegemony historically as a frame of reference, they are both constrained and enabled differentially according to who they are and what they are trying to do (see Jessop 1996). These effects entail both the "force" and the "consent" of Gramsci's hegemony, as state formation not only concentrates the means of violence and coercion, it also makes possible new creative powers resident in the directing and coordinating possibilities of the coupling of diverse social fields. In this manner, the impact of state formation is felt not only in the direct assertion of state authority (e.g., taxation, military service) but also in the ways of being made possible by these new creative powers (e.g., administrative/military positions, land grants, suppression of "brigandry," securing of property rights). It should be added that the most immediate effect of these new paths that not everyone can follow is to extend the possibilities for social and economic difference.

In the specific case of Moab, we have already argued that this need not mean that the state existed as a centralized control mechanism. By coupling diverse social fields (e.g., writing, agricultural production, military activity), state hegemony in Moab created new possibilities that were marked in particular by the intensification of agropastoral production on its eastern margins. Even if we were to accept a very limited view of the Iron Age state as little more than a vehicle for occasional acts of violence, we cannot dismiss it as a "thin veneer of administration." Indeed, it was by means of such occasional acts of violence that the "Land of Moab" promised to constitute a space where encroaching neighbors could be held at bay, where Assyria could be appeased (and occasionally resisted), where the cosmological order of Kemosh could be properly maintained, and where those positioned to do so could find new ways to expand their wealth and influence.

The distinct theoretical advantages of this neo-Gramscian approach lie in its ability to reunite archaeological investigation of premodern polities with current critical discourse on the modern state. This reunion comes both from highlighting the historical, rather than epochal, nature of the state's social form and by illustrating performative and strategic hegemony as common ground in the critical analysis of political domination. Neo-evolutionism, in its commitment to form over process, could never frame the question in these terms. Hence, the singular self-image of modern state discourse could only be perpetuated as a universal form and never interrogated as the product of a cultural and historical context. Similarly, the mainstream of postprocessual archaeology has fled from the specter of totality with a determination and haste that has left it unprepared to confront political issues on anything but a personal and present-minded scale. Hence, the modern/premodern divide remains untranscended, and the large-scale cultural and social effects of political domination are explored principally through the construction of genealogies of the present. Ironically, while such macroeffects are central to postprocessual archaeology's critical engagement with the present (e.g., colonialism, nationalism, capitalism, gender), they have taken a backseat to the subjective, the experiential, and the personal in postprocessual archaeology's critical engagement with the past.

So, What About Moab?

The case of Iron Age Moab, in its contextual detail and historical specificity, has allowed us to illustrate the efficacy of a neo-Gramscian approach to the problem of state formation in nonmodern contexts. Yet, what about our understanding of Iron Age Moab itself? What substantive gains have come from the theoretically informed and at times abstract approach within which this study has been framed?

Even as I write, the question of how one should conceptualize Iron Age Levantine states exists as a problem of practical and pressing importance for regional specialists. In the first instance, this question arose not from abstract reflection on the nature of the state but from traditional concerns with chronological attribution and the correlation of archaeological and textual evidence, especially the Bible. Most prominent has been Israel Finkelstein's sustained attack on what has traditionally been understood as the archaeological correlates of the biblical "United Monarchy" (Saul, David, Solomon—see Finkelstein 1996b, 1998b, 1999; Finkelstein and Silberman 2001). However, what began as a typical historicist debate, radical only from a limited internal perspective, soon raised problems of much wider import. Finkelstein's assertion that there is no archaeological evidence in Palestine datable to the period of the United Monarchy (tenth century B.C.E) indicative of the existence of a centralized state automatically raised the question of what was meant by the word "state."

Finkelstein's arguments find a place alongside earlier work by so-called minimalist biblical scholars (e.g., Jamieson-Drake 1991; Thompson 1992). Hence, his arguments must be understood in relation to long-running, highly divisive debates over issues, such as the historicity of the Bible, whose political and religious stakes are very high for many parties. At the same time, while it is unclear that Finkelstein's understanding of tenth century chronology will prevail (Bruins, van Plicht, and Mazar 2003; Finkelstein and Piasetsky 2003), even those opposed to his position admit that the biblical narratives cannot be read at face value and that our common-sense understanding of terms like "king," "kingdom," or "state" is insufficient for clarifying the nature of Iron Age polities. In other words, with or without the tenth century as traditionally understood, Iron Age monarchy is conceptually problematic, resistant to our own common-sense understandings of politics, rule, and polity. These conclusions overlap with an already established suspicion of the scale, age, and authority of Iron Age kingdoms in Transjordan (see Chapter 6) and are contemporary with somewhat similar concerns regarding the Aramean kingdoms of Iron Age Syria (Massetti-Rouault 2001; Sader 2000). Hence, recent scholarship has been notable for its exploration of a diverse range of alternative, often decentralized state models, such as the "patrimonial" and "tribal" states discussed in Chapter 6, the "patronage society" (Lemche 1996), the "segmentary state" (Routledge 2000b), and the "ethnic state" (Joffe 2002).

Our discussion of Moab contributes to these intradisciplinary discussions on two distinct levels. In terms of concepts for framing research, it should be clear that the imposition of exotic state models, with their concomitant list of diagnostic traits, will not resolve the problems we face in interpreting Iron Age political life. Instead, in adopting a neo-Gramscian perspective, we have shown the value (indeed, the necessity) of the detailed contextual study of local cultural resources and their historically specific deployment within given intellectual projects and products. While this approach eliminates the possibility of an easy answer to the question of why and how state formation occurred, it also highlights several practical strategies of relevance to the study of Iron Age polities. For example, as illustrated by our focus on segmentary forms of identification in the constitution of Moab, there is considerable potential in tracing the genealogy of the symbols, metaphors, and organizing principles of particular states back to the social context from whence they were strategically appropriated. Hence, one can and should consider issues like the use of the term "Israel" in the Merneptah Stele or the history of the phrase "Bêt David" (House of David) without first positing (or denying) continuity and unity in the social referent of these terms. To do otherwise is to ignore a central moment in the process of state formation, namely the strategic appropriation of resonant cultural resources such as collective terms and symbols.

In terms of a focus for the empirical analysis of Iron Age polities, we have mapped out a detailed narrative of state formation in Moab that situates this process firmly within a broader Levantine context, without subsuming local developments to a single regional model. Such a shift in orientation is long overdue in discussions of the Iron Age within Israel/Palestine, where the political and ideological burden of affirming or rejecting the historicity of the biblical text has often stifled creative engagement with the available evidence. Situating local developments within a Levantine, rather than biblical, context as an initial strategy would radically change the form taken by syntheses of the Iron Age. For example, in Chapter 6 we noted the strategic deployment of kinship, and especially the "house," as a political metaphor across the Iron Age Levant. In Chapter 8, we identified the use of common material indices of kingship (e.g., inscriptions, built environment, art), while in Chapter 9 we identified the local implications of Neo-Assyrian imperialism, which was after all a general regional phenomenon. In each case, the juxtaposition of local and regional evidence would open the door to new ways of understanding local historical and archaeological sequences. For example, new insights into Jerusalem's apparent status as a small stronghold in the tenth century B.C.E (Steiner 2001) and its relation to subsequent understandings of Judah as the "House of David" are more likely to be derived from comparisons with Mesha in Dibon, the career of Gush the Yahanean (see Chapter 6), or even from Late Bronze Age Jerusalem (see Na'aman 1996), than from revisiting (yet again) the question of biblical historicity. Indeed, biblical historicism limited to the narrow question of "did this actually happen" ultimately retards the possibilities for historical understanding of the Iron Age.

Why in the End Should We Study the State?

While we have emphasized throughout this book the analytical necessity of historical specificity in understanding state formation, it is not the perpetual uniqueness of such political dominance that renders it immediately relevant but rather its "eternal recurrence." It is a minimum condition of interpretation that the past be rendered at least partially intelligible, and hence past politics always afford the opportunity for reflection on the present. However, recognizing commonality in the process and strategy of state formation over time carries with it two opposed dangers that threaten to undermine the reflexive potential of the past.

On one hand, it is rather easy, from the distance that archaeology provides, to approach state hegemony as a discursive formative to be characterized and cleverly deconstructed, as if, in Kundera's words, it was something "lighter than feathers." Yet, these academic games of playful engagement, of "seeing the lie" and then going for tea, fail to penetrate the paradox of violence at the heart of the state. They fail because the very ideological "lightness" they expose tells us nothing of the human experiences of fear, hope, hatred, loyalty, resignation, and resistance that bear down heavily on particular people situated in relation to particular state hegemonies. I have argued repeatedly throughout this book that the state is a construct. Yet, it is a construct with powerful effects capable of causing and preventing violent death and human suffering; in other words, it is a construct whose specificity makes all the difference.

On the other hand, analyzing Moab in general and comparative terms that might be applied to state formation at any time or place lends this process a sense of inevitability. The state's six-thousand-year history of consistent violence and monopoly logic suggests a Faustian bargain that people must make to realize the creative potential of living in large-scale social groups and to do so with a modicum of security. This was certainly the conclusion of neoevolutionists, and it continues to haunt our discussions today. Indeed, the fear of such implied determinism goes a long way toward explaining the absence of a significant postprocessual engagement with the state.

Yet, the point of a neo-Gramscian analysis is not to document the inevitability of the state, but rather its contingency. Viewed from the long-term perspective of archaeology, state formation is striking in its inconstancy. We lose sight of this when, on one hand, our taxonomic categories make one state the same as the next, and on the other hand, we accept hegemony's own teleology and treat contingent transformations as moments in the internal evolution of a single state. Both the dissolution of, and radical change within, state hegemony can and does happen all the time.

Our analysis of Moab has emphasized that state formation took historically and culturally contingent forms. However, we have also seen that something contingent is not thereby insubstantial, nor without profound effects. States articulate our most potent cultural resources and embed them in a structure of violence that at once attracts and demands our attention. The point of studying the state is not, therefore, to indulge in mere theories but to recognize the heavy human cost that surrounds the formation and dissolution of particular state hegemonies. It is also to recognize that the tools and resources for constituting political orders are embedded in the specificity of our own cultural and historical experiences. Indeed, it is to see that the potential for new forms of governance, even for an end to the structured violence of the state, is not drifting in utopian dreams; it is here, before our eyes, in our very own lives.

Notes

Chapter 1. The "Thingness" of the State

1. In this book Transjordan refers to the territory encompassed by the post-1991 boundaries of the Hashemite Kingdom of Jordan, which is entirely east of the Jordan Rift Valley. I use Palestine to refer to the territory west of the Rift Valley currently constituted by the state of Israel and the Palestinian territories. I use the phrases Jordan, state of Israel and Palestinian territories when referring to modern polities. The southern Levant refers to all of the territory south of the headwaters of the Orontes River and west of the Syrian Desert. In transcribing place names in Transjordan I have attempted to follow the Department of Antiquities of Jordan's system for the transcription of Arabic. For well-known sites from elsewhere I have tended to follow the transcriptions most frequently found in the literature.

2. The Middle Assyrian Empire represented an important third Late Bronze Age empire that reached the eastern edge of the northern Levant in the Orontes Valley. The political and ideological dynamics of the Late Bronze Age international system formed by these competing empires has been discussed in an insightful and sophisticated manner by Mario Liverani (1990).

3. Neo-Hittite states in particular were not linguistically homogeneous.

4. This evidence is more ambiguous for the southern Levant, which, as in most periods after the Chalcolithic, is marked by smaller-scale settlements and lower degrees of social differentiation than the north. The monumental EB III palace of Tel Yarmuth (Miroschedji 1999), the less coherent EB III palace 3177 at Megiddo (Kempinski 1989), and the immense storage capacity of the "bee-hive granary" complex at Khirbat Karak (Esse 1991) stand in sharp contrast to the more usual southern Levantine EB II–III pattern of small fortified sites constituted by houses and small temples.

5. In this book I employ the low Egyptian chronology of Kenneth Kitchen (1996a). For the Iron Age I presume the traditional "high" chronology in assigning dates to the subdivisions of the relative chronology. For the current controversy see the exchange between Finkelstein and Mazar (Finkelstein 1996b; 1998b; Mazar 1997; Bruins, van Plicht, and Mazar 2003).

6. Flannery (1972) did allow for internal structural "pathologies" ("meddling," "hyper-cohesion," "usurption") that could result in change, especially system collapse. However, as the analogy with disease implies, such maladaptations are not viewed as integral to the system itself, in contrast to a concept like "contradiction" in Structural Marxism.

224 Notes to Pages 11–29

7. Foucault himself recognized this, stating in a 1978 interview, "In the last few years society has changed and individuals have changed too; they are more and more diverse, different, and independent. There are ever more categories of people who are not compelled by discipline, so that we are obliged to imagine the development of society without discipline. The ruling class is still impregnated with the old technique. But it is clear that in the future we must separate ourselves from the society of discipline of today" (Foucault 1994: 533, as translated in Hardt 1995: 41). The notion of a transition from "disciplinary societies" to "societies of control" has been exposued most particularly by Gilles Deleuze (1992).

8. Jessop (1996: 124) usefully defines structure as that which a given agent cannot change pursuing a given strategy in a given context over a given period of time.

9. In another recent paper, Barrett clearly distinguishes "structural conditions" from "structuring principles," defining the former as the "accumulated mass, the debris of history, which confronts the living" and the latter as the "means of inhabiting certain structural conditions" (Barrett 2000: 65). He also states that structural conditions can be studied in the abstract, divorced from the practices that brought them into being (like signs in semiotics), provided one recognizes that these conditions do not do anything (they have no agency). This is a rather excellent statement of the principles of analytical dualism. It is, however, only a description of Giddens' position insofar as he is inconsistent in utilizing this structure-agent dualism methodologically, but denying it theoretically (see Mouzelis 1992, 2000). Unfortunately, Barrett's paper is unreferenced, except to say that he relied on "the usual suspects," i.e., Giddens, Bourdieu, Foucault and Baumann (Barrett 2000: 68). Hence, it is unclear as to how he understands these tensions in Giddens' work.

10. Although one could selectively cite Kuhn (1970) to this effect.

11. See Chapter 2 for a discussion of Bourdieu's concept of doxa.

12. For example, in his illustrative review of French state formation from the twelfth to the twentieth centuries, Bourdieu (1999) does not mention the revolution and treats l'ancien régime and the First Republic as continuous moments in the state's long-term consolidation of "the various species of capital"

13. For example, modern standing armies and police forces (repositories of physical force capital) are dependent on an efficient fiscal system (economic capital), which in turn is dependent both on physical force capital and on an effective judicial system (judiciary capital), which is itself dependent on both economic and physical force capital.

Chapter 2. Hegemony, Polity, Identity

In the plans of a king, as in those of the heavens, faithful subjects must close their eyes, and subjugating their sense to the power of the crowns, whatever the laws, believe that they are good. Text as quoted in Ranum (1968: 145).

1. As a number of scholars have shown (Anderson 1976–77: 15–18; Laclau and Mouffe 2001: 7–65), Gramsci borrowed this term from Russian Social Democracy, where it referred to the ideological leadership of the proletariat over other aligned groups (e.g., the peasantry). Yet in Gramsci's hands the concept was greatly expanded as a tool for the analysis of the state/culture relationship. To quote Perry Anderson (1976–77: 20): "Gramsci extended the notion of hegemony from its original application to the perspectives of the working class in a bourgeois revolution against a feudal order, to the mechanisms of bourgeois rule over the working class in a stabilized capitalist society."

2. In Bourdieu's own infinitely parenthetical terms: "The structures constitutive of a particular type of environment (e.g., the material conditions of existence characteristic of a class condition) produce *habitus*, systems of durable transposable *dispositions*, structured structures predisposed to function as structuring principles, that is as principles of the generation and structuring of practices and representations which can be objectively 'regulated' and 'regular' without in any way being the product of obedience to rules, objectively adapted goals without presupposing a conscious aiming at ends or an express mastery of the operations necessary to attain them and, being all this, collectively orchestrated without being the product of the orchestrating action of a conductor" (Bourdieu 1977: 72).

3. Again to quote Bourdieu (1977: 164): "Every established order tends to produce (to very different degrees and with very different mechanisms) the naturalization of its own arbitrariness."

4. For example, the portion of the house given over to adult male activities such as prayer and the entertainment of guests is associated with cleanliness and light, and is spatially and conceptual distinguished from the portion of the house given over to female and child-related activities, which are associated with darkness and impurity.

5. Bourdieu states: "It is when the social world loses its character as a natural phenomenon that the questions of the natural or conventional character (*phusei* or *nomo*) of social facts can be raised" (1977: 169).

6. Bourdieu (1977: 164) states that "when there is a quasi-perfect correspondence between the objective order and the subjective principles of organization (as in ancient societies) the natural and social world appears as self-evident."

7. Compare the prescient views of Gramsci in relation to colloquial language: "Besides the 'immanent grammar' in every language there is also . . . a 'normative' grammar (or more than one). This is made up of the reciprocal monitoring, reciprocal teaching, and reciprocal 'censorship' expressed in such questions as 'What did you mean to say?,' 'What do you mean?,' 'Make yourself clearer,' etc. and in mimicry and teasing. This whole complex of actions and reactions come together to create a grammatical conformism, to establish 'norms' or judgements of correctness or incorrectness. But this 'spontaneous' expression of grammatical conformity is necessarily disconnected, discontinuous and limited to local social strata or local centers" (Gramsci 2000: 354).

8. Without using the poststructuralist framework of Laclau and Mouffe, Femia (1981) provides a comparable reading of Gramsci, especially on the relationship of hegemony to "common sense."

9. While Laclau and Mouffe (2001: 105) define "elements" rather minimally as "any difference that is not discursively articulated," I find it more productive to merge "elements" with so-called practice or structuration theory as the dually structured cultural resources of a habitus. This helps combat the slippage Jessop (1990: 302) notes in Laclau and Mouffe's work, whereby discourse comes to mean ideological discourse without reference to its (material) conditions of acceptance. At the same time, it does not require that one treat cultural resources as ahistorical core values or basic irreducible realities, something Laclau (2000: 71) cogently argues against with the example of the concept of "black" in South Africa.

10. These comments are made within the context of Gramsci's notes on the Risorgimento and the Italian state; hence, as with much of Gramsci's work, they could be read as a specific historical analysis of political developments within the Italian Peninsula, rather than a generalization about all premodern states.

11. For a detailed critique, especially of Giddens's characterization of premodern states, see Routledge (2003).

Chapter 3. Land and Story

1. In what follows I use the word "Bible" to refer specifically to the Tanak ("Old Testament").

2. Scholars have debated the priority and hence chronology of these accounts (Bartlett 1978; Van Seters 1972, 1980).

3. Deut 2: 28–29 suggests that Israel passed peacefully through Moab, with the permission of the Moabites. See Miller 1989a.

4. For example, black-burnished bowls, crow-step decorated wares, double ring-based bowls, offset rim bowls, and a written script strongly influenced by Aramaic scripts.

5. The existence of strike-slip faulting, driving apart the Arabian and Sinai Peninsulas, is debated. Ne'ev and Emery (1995: 11–20) present a simplified standard view that explains the Rift Valley in terms of a subsidence between two subplates (Arabian and Sinai) moving apart in a north-south as well as an east-west direction. Horowitz (2001: 497–508) adamantly argues a minority position that only standard faulting with no lateral offset is involved.

6. Mitchel (in Labianca and Lacelle1986: 47–48) suggests updated equivalents for these soil classifications in terms of USDA and FAO soil classification systems. Moormann's system remains the most widely used in Jordan and for this reason is retained here.

Chapter 4. Beginnings I: The Late Bronze Age

1. Ellen Morris (2001: 1081–84) notes that *dmi* was also used to refer to Egyptian centers in Canaan, and in several instances for very large fortresses with attached populations.

2. Following Darnell and Jasnow (1993: 266) and Kitchen (1996b: 50) in reading this as singular rather than plural, as does Kitchen (1964: 50).

3. I do not here include the topographic list of Thutmose III at Karnak and the literature surrounding its interpretation as an itinerary through Transjordan (e.g., Kitchen 1992: 25; Redford 1982; Timm 1989: 34–60), as this list does not actually use the term "Moab."

4. It is relatively certain that this last list is one of two Ramses II copies of an earlier list from the reign of Amenhotep III on his temple at Soleb in Nubia. Moab is one of the toponyms found only at Amara-west. This raises the insoluable question of whether Moab was originally a toponym during the reign of Amenhotep III that was deleted or damaged in the extant reliefs from Soleb, or whether it was one of a relatively small group of new toponyms introduced by Ramses II (see Timm 1989: 9–14).

5. The Amarna Letters are an archive of 382 clay tablets dating to the fourteenth century B.C.E. and originating at the site of Tell al-Amarna in Egypt. These tablets are mostly international correspondence, written in cuneiform Akkadian, from both Egyptian vassal city-states in the Levant and contemporary "superpowers" (e.g., Hatti, Babylon, Assyria, Mittani).

6. Bourke et al. (1994: 104–9, 1998: 196–201) refer to this as a "Governor's Residency" (Oren 1984; 1992), due to its central court design, while recognizing that this category has little specific cultural meaning in its current broad usage. I would tend to reserve this descriptor for dwellings showing relatively direct evidence for occupation by Egyptian officials (e.g., Beth Shean 1500, 1700; Tall ash-Shari'a; Aphek) and recognize that these overlap in form with structures occupied by local rulers.

7. Two found at Beth Shean (Rowe 1930: 24–30) and one at Tell ash-Shihab in southern Syria (Müller 1904; Smith 1901).

8. One found at Beth Shean (Černý 1958; Rowe 1930: 33–36), one at Shayk Sa'id in southern Syria (Erman 1893; Kitchen 1964: 68–70), and one at Tura in the extreme north of Transjordan that may also have originated in Shayk Sa'id (Wimmer 2002). Two further unattributable royal stele fragments were also found at Beth Shean (Rowe 1930: 36).

9. However, the pottery illustrated by Tubb from the main horizon of the residency (Area AA, stratum 12) clearly includes Iron Ib (i.e., post-Egyptian empire) material (Tubb 1988: Fig. 19: 4–7, 9, 12–13, 17; Fig. 20: 2–3, 5–6).

10. For example, Irbid (Dajani 1964), Quwayliba/Abila (Kafafi 1984), Pella (Bourke and Sparks 1995), Qatarat as-Samra (Leonard 1979, 1981, 1985), Saḥem (Fischer 1997), Baq'ah (McGovern 1986), Jabal Nuzha—Amman (Dajani 1966), Sahab (Dajani 1970), Madaba Tomb A (Harding 1953; prob. Iron IA).

11. Most of these finds are reported in preliminary reports that do not provide complete quantitative or contextual descriptions.

12. Pella (Bourke and Sparks 1995), T. as-Sa'idiyya (Leonard 1994; Pritchard 1980; Tubb 1988), Qatarat as-Samra (Leonard 1979, 1981, 1985), Baq'ah (McGovern 1986), Amman—Jabal Nuzha (Dajani 1966) Amman Airport (Hennessy 1966, 1985, 1989; Hankey 1974a, b, 1995; Herr 1983a, b), Sahab (Dajani 1970), Madaba Tomb A (Harding 1953; Prob. Iron IA).

13. Pella (Bourke 2002), Abu Kharaz (Fischer 1991a, b: 79–80, 1993: 282–83), Dayr 'Alla (Franken 1992), Amman Airport (Hennessy 1966, 1985, 1989, Hankey 1974a, b, 1995; Herr 1983a, b).

14. Pella (Bourke et al. 1994: 104–9; Bourke1997: 196–201), T. al-Fukhar (McGovern 1997; Strange 1997), T. as-Sa'idiyya (Tubb 1995: 140, Fig. 2), Sahab (Ibrahim 1987), T. al-'Umayri (Herr, Clark, and Geraty 2002).

15. So-called cult stands are a category of presentation vessel found in temples but not tombs after the Chalcolithic period. Elaborate bichrome goblets and pedestaled kraters also seem to be primarily associated with temple contexts (e.g., Abu Kharaz—Fischer 1991a: Figs 5a: 10 and 5b: 1–3; Dayr 'Alla—Franken 1992: Figs. 7–2: 17–18; 7–6: 12–13; cf. Beth Shean/ Tell Husn—Rowe and Fitzgerald 1940: Pl. 70A: 1–4; James and McGovern 1993: Figs.13: 5; 18: 1; Lachish Fosse Temple—Tufnell 1940: Pl. 47; Tel Mevorakh (Tell Murbarak)—Stern 1984: Figs. 6: 1–2 and 7: 1–2).

16. Lev-Tov and Maher (2001: 99–105) discuss discrepancies between species sacrificed according to Ugaritic ritual texts and those represented in excavated temple and tomb faunal assemblages.

17. Within the Emar calendar (Fleming 2000: 165–67), the month of Abî shares a very specific ritual (the hunt of Aštart) on the sixteenth day with the month of Marzḫāni. The name Marzḫāni derives from marzaḫū, which at Ugarit is the name of a feasting association and is equivalent to the Biblical Hebrew word marzeah (e.g., Jeremiah 16:5). Scholars are deeply divided as to whether these feasts were in fact intended for the dead as a form of ancestor veneration (Lewis 1989; Pardee 1996; Pope 1981; Schmidt 1994).

18. See Lewis 1989; Pitard 1996; Schmidt 1994; van der Toorn 1996.

19. See Coale and Demeny 1983. The lower figures are based on Coale and Demeny's Model West Level 6 Female stable population model (death rate = 30.77/ 1000), the higher on their Model West Level 2 Female stable population model (death rate = 44.44/1000). Both cases presume a growth rate of r = 0.0. For detailed arguments supporting such high-pressure mortality regimes in the Roman Empire, see Bagnall and Frier 1994; Parkin 1992; and Saller 1994. For the relevance of this Roman evidence for the Levant see Routledge 1996b and Schloen 2001: 122–33.

20. This does not include the 280 pit burials Gonen (1992: 88–90) lists from Tall as-Sa'idiyya in order to match the geographic boundaries of Finkelstein's population study. As of 1996, the figure for the Tall as-Sa'idiyya cemetery stood at 482, with about 450 dating to the LB II–Iron IA period (Tubb 1997).

21. Poor preservation and poor reporting practices mean that we cannot determine with any certainty the total number of bodies buried in the currently known tombs.

22. Claims for a possible site (Harding 1958: 10) and a sherd concentration (Hennessy 1985: 90) under the runway about 300 meters east and northeast of the Amman Airport "Temple" cannot be substantiated (Hennessy 1985: 90).

23. This included 465 sherds of Mycenaean IIA–IIIB and 11 sherds of Late Minoan III pottery (Hankey 1974a; Herr 1983a: 20), representing 50–60 vessels. There were fewer than 50 sherds of Cypriot Base Ring I and II and White Slip I and II (Hankey 1974a: 142), inverting the usual quantitative relationship between Cypriot and Mycenaean pottery in the Late Bronze Age Levant. One largely complete Qurraya Ware ("Midianite") bowl and at least 5 other sherds were also found (Hankey 1995: 182; Pl. 14: 4). These appear to have originated in the northern Hejaz region of what is now Saudi Arabia.

24. These include a so-called *khepesh* sword (Hankey 1995: Fig. 6; Hennessy 1985: Fig. 6), at least four daggers (Hankey 1995: 179; Hennessy 1985: Fig. 9) and more than forty projectile points (Hankey 1995: 179–81; Hennessy 1985: Figs. 7, 9).

25. Hankey (1974b) reports 8 whole stone vessels and 280–90 fragments from the 1955 and 1966 excavations, representing at least 62 original vessels.

26. Deposition is framed by Late Mycenaean IIIB1 sherds (post-1340 B.C.E.—see Warren and Hankey 1989: 138, 169) from the foundation trenches on one end, and the homogeneous LB IIB-IR IA local pottery assemblage on the other.

27. The earliest Aegean pottery is Mycenaean IIB (post-1450) and the latest is Mycenaean IIIB1 (post-1340). The Cypriot pottery ranges from Base Ring I and Red Lustrous ware (post-1500) to Base Ring II and White Slip II (post-1400). The cylinder seals and scarabs range from the fifteenth to the thirteenth centuries in date (Ward 1964; Tournay 1967). The Egyptian stone bowls date from the Late Predynastic period (aproximately 3500–3200 B.C.E.) to the Nineteenth Dynasty (1295–1186 B.C.E.).

28. The human bone at the site was very fragmentary, representing an estimated minimum of eight persons (Hennessy 1985: 97–99).

29. A stone platform adjacent to the structure showed signs of burning and a high concentration of bones, leading Herr to label it an incinerator. For other suggestions that do not take full account of the finds (esp. the human bone), see Wright (1966); Fritz (1971); Ottoson (1980: 101–4).

30. McGovern (1989: 134) suggests that Rujm al-Henu east (McGovern 1983) was a Quadratbau structure when originally constructed in LB I.

31. At Mabrak, some four km southeast of the Amman Airport "Temple," a Quadratbau building was discovered exposed on the surface. According to Yassine (1988: 61), the only finds were "several nondescript body sherds . . . which can be broadly dated to the Late Bronze-Iron Age." Subsequent investigation of the site by Mohammed Waheeb (1992) revealed several associated structures and installations, leading him to label the site an agricultural complex.

32. Besides its form, the presumed central room of the structure included a central pillar formed by two stacked stone drums embedded in the floor, much as was found at the Amman Airport "Temple" (Hennessy 1966: Pl. 33; McGovern 1989: 130).

33. This included a variety of domesticates, as well as a wild carnivore and a herbivore, many of which were represented by whole body parts (McGovern 1989: 128).

34. This included whole vessels placed into the buildings foundation trenches (McGovern 1989: 130).

35. The presence of these early sarcophagi in Transjordan makes it that much more difficult to disconnect the Iron II examples from Transjordan (Yassine 1988: 33–40 with references) from the better-known LB II–Iron I examples from Beth Shean, Dayr al-Balaḥ, Tall al-Farah (south), and Lachish (Tell ed-Duweir) in Palestine. Hence, the ethnic designations often given to these sarcophagi (Egyptian, Philistine, etc.) should be rethought (cf. Yassine 1988: 33–40).

36. The five surviving examples are all relatively rare Furumark shapes in southern Levant (FS 45. 166, 220), otherwise attested in Transjordan only at the Amman Airport "Temple" (Leonard 1994). Notes suggest that the original assemblage also included pilgrim's flasks (FS 189 and 192), a straight-sided alabastron (FS 93), and squat stirrup jars (Bourke and Sparks 1995: 151–53).

37. Bourke (1997: 110) reports that the fourth and fifth cervical vertebrae appear to have been severed at an oblique angle by a sharp object.

38. The surviving notes suggest that the bulk of the Mycenaean pottery was Myc. IIIA2 in date (post-1370 B.C.E.—Hankey and Warren 1989: 169, Table 3.1), although some IIIB1 is also noted (Bourke and Sparks 1995: 152–153). Stephen Bourke and Rachel Sparks seem to favor dating at least the DAJ Tomb 1 and 2 complex to the fourteenth century, as this promises a connection with the Amarna period and named historical figures like Mut-Ba'al (Bourke and Sparks 1995: 166–67).

39. In an Amarna letter from the Egyptian pharaoh to Aziru, the ruler of Amurru (EA 162), a list of "the king's enemies" is given with the order that these people be are to be delivered to the king with copper shackles on, what Moran (1992: 249) translates as their "ankles." It is therefore possible, though speculative, that the Pella victim was a captive rather than a retainer/servant.

40. Graeber's (2001: 33) characterization of Appadurai's essay as "anthropology as it might be written by Milton Friedman" overstates the neoclassical orthodoxy of Appaduai's approach and understates its semiotic focus. At the same time, Graeber shows clearly the unresolved tension in this essay between value as a product of individual demand and "regimes of value" (Appadurai's term) as structures of cultural meaning.

41. Rib-Adda's constant use of the proverb "For the lack of a cultivator, my field is like a woman without a husband" in the context of his alarm over defecting peasantry suggests a dependence on *ḫupšu* labor in one form or another.

42. While all these possibilities are refracted for us through the lens of what might be Rib-Adda's paranoia or a more general political posturing (Liverani 1979a, 1983), such events were at least conceivable for Late Bronze Age *ḫazannu*

43. A minority position questions the presumed noble status of *maryanu* altogether (Beal 1992: 178–83).

44. Attempts to connect *'apiru* to *'ibrîm*, the biblical Hebrew word for "Hebrew," persist despite the many linguistic problems this entails (Loretz 1984; Rainey 1995: 482–83). More serious is the question of the appropriate sociological referent of the term in the Amarna letters (Astour 1999; Gottwald 1979: 394–409; Moran 1987; Na'aman 1986; Rainey 1995; Rowton 1976).

45. E.g., "Why do you love the *'apiru* but hate the mayors (*ḫazannu*)?" (EA 286: 20; Moran 1992: 326); "Now he is l[ike] the *'apiru*, a runaway dog" (EA 67: 17; Moran 1992: 137).

46. Vassals in the Amarna letters often complain of other rulers "buying off" people when fomenting revolt and encouraging the land to "go over" to the *'apiru* (see EA 246; EA 280).

47. On the complexity of "bedouin" as a signifier in both social scientific and Jordanian nationalist discourse see Layne 1994: 12–17.

48. This is contested by William Ward (1972: 50–56), who considers *shasu* to be a social category with military connections not unlike that ascribed to *'apiru* (i.e., mercenaries, brigands, raiders).

49. The Hesban Regional Survey (Ibach 1987) recorded 148 sites in an area of about 250 km², of which 6 (ca. 4%) yielded at least one LB or MB/LB sherd. The Wadi al-Ḥasa survey (MacDonald 1988) recorded 409 sites dating from the Chalcolithic period or later in an area of about 250 km² of which only 1 (ca. 0.25%) yielded sherds dated to the LB period. Notably even this identification has been called into question by subsequent excavation (see Bienkowski 1995a; Bienkowski et al. 1997; Bienkowski and Adams 1999). The *Limes Arabicus* Survey (Koucky 1987) recorded 404 sites in an area of about 550 km², none of which yielded LB sherds. The Dhiban Plateau Survey (Ji and Lee 2000) has thus far recorded 421 sites in an area of about 200 km², of which 10 (ca. 2.38%) yielded at least one LB sherd.

50. Note, for example, that the forty-two sherds illustrated as examples of Iron I pottery in the final report (Miller 1991: 255–57, 274) come from nineteen sites, six of which (sites 52, 60, 88, 289, 366, 391) have no Iron I pottery assigned to them in the site description section and hence do not appear on the summary list of Iron I sites (Miller 1991: 309). Four of these sites do have Late Bronze Age pottery ascribed to them, suggesting that perhaps the same sherd was assigned to two different time periods (LB and IR I) at different stages of processing and analysis.

51. This procedure was carried out using Program K-Means, a shareware program written and distributed by Pierre Legendre of the Département de sciences biologiques, Université de Montréal.

52. The membership of this cluster remains constant through iterations of K = 6, 7, 8, and 9.

53. This cluster includes the "suspect" site of Ḥ. Dubab (Bienkowski and Adams 1999).

54. Irregular sites, especially those associated with pastoralism, such as caves and open camps, are to my mind the most likely source for new Late Bronze Age sites in south central Transjordan.

55. The Hesban Regional Survey recorded only two Late Bronze Age sites (Iktanu and Jalul) south of Wadi Ḥisban (Ibach 1987: 157–58). Of these, excavations do not seem to confirm a Late Bronze occupation at Tall Iktanu (Prag 1989). Tall Jalul has yielded significant quantities of Late Bronze Age pottery (Groves et al. 1995; Ibach 1978), but no occupational contexts have been found thus far in excavation (Herr et al. 1996: 71–75, 1997: 154–57). At Madaba, Tomb A spans the end of Late Bronze II and the beginning of Iron I and contains sherds of Late Mycenaean IIIB pottery (Harding 1953; Leonard 1994), suggesting as yet unconfirmed occupation on the *tall* (see Harrison et al. 2000). As Kenneth Kitchen (1964: 55; 1992: 28–29) has argued repeatedly, the place name of Tbniw (Tabunu/Tibunu) mentioned in the register beneath the "Moab relief" from Luxor discussed above, transfers rather straightforwardly into Moabite (and Hebrew) as Dayban/Dibon. Unfortunately, six seasons of excavation at the site have failed to reveal any clear Late Bronze Age remains (Morton 1989; Routledge n.d.; Tushingham 1972; Winnett and Reed 1964). Chang-Ho Ji (Ji and Lee 2000: Table 1) reports ten sites with Late Bronze Age pottery between Wadi Wala and Wadi Mujib. Four of these sites are described in preliminary reports (Ji and Lee 1998: 561–64; 2000: 500–501), all of which are said to contain pottery from the Late Bronze II and Iron I periods. This may reflect settlement at the very end of the Late Bronze Age, or the difficulties of distinguishing between LB IIB and Iron IA wares in a survey context.

56. As a cautionary tale, we might consider recent research on the Karak Plateau in the seventeenth to nineteenth centuries C.E. (Johns 1994; Lancaster and

Lancaster 1995). This work has questioned the emphasis on tribal disorder and agrarian decline under Ottoman misrule common in earlier literature (e.g., Lewis 1987). In particular, despite the abandonment of most villages besides al-Karak itself, it is clear that this town served as a regional center for the seasonally mobile populations of the plateau engaged in pastoralism and mixed farming.

57. In these depictions, however, there are usually also streamers hanging down from the band behind the god's back.

58. Horsfield and Vincent (1932) show a gazelle head between the horns of the left-hand male figure, a detail that identifies the Canaanite god Reshef on Egyptian reliefs. However, both Ward and Martin's (1964) drawing and my own examination of the stele reveal only a small rectangular "blob" at this point, allowing the head-dress to be not only that of Reshef, but also a standard Pharaonic double crown or the headdress of Ba'al.

59. Routledge reemphasizes Ward and Martin's own observations that the hier-atic signs in their proposed transcriptions include many irregularities in form and positioning that they aptly describe as "a grotesque caricature of Egyptian writing" (Ward and Martin 1964: 13). Routledge goes on to note that it is extremely rare to have baselines for texts in graffito hieratic, although these are commonly found on hieroglyphic inscriptions. Furthermore, graffito hieratic has a distinct preference for signs that trail into other lines of text, often below the line. This style is not evi-dent in the transcription proposed by Ward and Martin and is not visible in the traces that can be seen today on the Balu'a Stele. Finally, Egyptian hieratic is in-variably written from right to left, while Ward and Martin's transcription proposes hieratic that is written from left to right. Even in the case of Egyptian hieroglyphic texts, right to left is the preferred direction for texts. This direction is occasionally altered, but only in the case of a clear graphic need such as in paired inscriptions or when accompanying a scene that is oriented left to right.

60. Ward (1972: 51 n. 4) himself says that his reading "met with little success."

61. Warembol (1983: 70 n.52), for example, uses Ward and Martin's transcrip-tion to propose reading the throne name of Amenhotep II in the third register.

62. Helga Weippert (1988: 666–67) argues that the stele's "nonEgyptian" lunar and solar symbols suggest a date in the ninth century B.C.E. on analogy with stele and wall panels from north Syria. This ignores Bronze Age examples of such motifs (e.g., Bernett and Keel 1998: 34–40).

63. Here I have presumed local artists. The impossibility of the central figure in "legitimate" Egyptian art rules out official Egyptian artists as one sees at Serabit al-Khadem in the Sinai and Beth Shean in Israel. The distinction between local and expatriate Egyptian artists seems in this case unknowable and not particularly significant.

64. I have discovered two cooking pot sherds from the otherwise unattested Middle Bronze I period (Albright's MB IIA) in unpublished material from Willam Morton's 1955, 1956, and 1965 excavation seasons. This reminds us again that the absence of Late Bronze Age sherds may well reflect rarity and sampling bias, rather than site abandonment.

Chapter 5. Beginnings II: The Early Iron Age

1. The paucity of Iron I remains in southern Transjordan (i.e., Edom) is a point of some controversy (Bienkowski 1992a, b, 2001a; Finkelstein 1995b: 127–37). However, the absence of any viable Late Bronze Age sites in Edom means that the Iron I period is still better represented than the LB.

2. The Migdal temple at Pella is the lone exception, continuing in an attenuated

form well into the Iron IIB period (ca. 800 B.C.E.). Ritual caches and possible small shrines begin to be found again in the late Iron IB period (Herr, Clark, and Geraty 2002; Yassine 1988: 115–35).

3. This is clearest at Tall al-'Umayri (Herr 1998, 1999a, 2000; Herr and Clark 2001, Herr, Clark and Geraty 2002), where late in LB IIB a substantial Late Bronze Age "palace" was intentionally filled to the tops of its walls (3 m high) and used as a platform for a well-defined pillared (a.k.a. "Four-Room") house attached to a casemate wall in classic Iron Age style. Other probable examples include Tall al-Fuḥar (Strange 1997; 2000); Dayr 'Alla (Franken 1969, 1992; van der Steen 1997); and Sahab (Ibrahim 1987, 1989).

4. E.g., the so-called Four-Room and Three-Room patterns (Braemer 1982; Holladay 1992, 1997).

5. Marked by its mention in Merneptah's victory stele of 1207 B.C.E. (Lichtheim 1976). I should add that the exegetical question of whether the Israel of Merneptah has anything to do with biblical accounts of the settlement period is secondary to the fact that a collective named Israel (whatever that may have been) is attested.

6. The "conquest" theory (Albright 1939; Wright 1940) largely paraphrased Joshua 1–11 by associating the destruction and disruption of settlements at the end of the Late Bronze Age with the entry of the Israelites into Canaan. However, some sites explicitly named in Joshua as being captured show no occupation in the Late Bronze Age ('Ai, Jericho), while at other sites the destruction and disruption of settlement are spread out over as much as a century (see Finkelstein 1988; Stager 1998).

7. The "peaceful infiltration" theory (Alt 1966) argues that Israel was a tribal confederation resulting from a long process of peaceful settlement in the under-populated highlands of Palestine by pastoral nomads originating in the Syrian desert and eastern Transjordan. The most pointed critiques of this position have noted the dependence of pastoral nomads on exchange relations with agricultural-ists and the probable lack of "deep desert" nomads before large-scale camel herd-ing (de Geus 1976; Lemche 1985).

8. The "peasant revolt" theory (Gottwald 1979; Mendenhall 1962, 1973) argues that the traditions of a small group of escaped Egyptian slaves provided a unifying egal-itarian identity for otherwise indigenous 'apiru who had revolted against the "feu-dal system" of the lowland Late Bronze Age, withdrawn to highland Palestine, and "retribalized." Criticism has focused on Gottwald's treatment of the Amarna Letters (Rainey 1995) and archaeological evidence (Finkelstein 1988), his large-scale and unified view of "tribal" systems (Lemche 1985), and the Israel-specific nature of the theory given the large-scale change evident in Transjordan (Stager 1998).

9. Here I disagree with McNutt (1999: 216) in that social structural models can only serve as tools to raise questions about ancient information if the models them-selves are open to question, that is to say dialectically engaged with evidence.

10. North of Wadi Zarqa, Iron I settlement on the plateau increases more rapidly than in the Jordan Valley (see Braemer 1992). However, (1) the number of Iron I sites in the Ghawr (Jordan Valley) increases as well; (2) site density remains higher in the Jordan Valley; (3) the majority of Late Bronze Age sites in both the Ghawr and the highlands continue to be occupied in the Iron I period. Hence, there do not appear to be wholly distinct settlement processes under way in each of these geographic zones.

11. Interestingly, some scholars have credited highland settlement in Transjordan to the displacement of lowland populations in Palestine (Knauf 1992a: 48; Stager 1998: 90–91), while others credit highland settlement in Palestine to the movement of populations from the highlands of Transjordan (van der Steen 1999; Zertal 1994: 66–69). While both scenarios are possible (even simultaneously), neither ef-fectively addresses the Late Bronze and early Iron Age evidence from Transjordan.

12. In fact, the early dating of Tall al-'Umayri Area A Phase 13 suggests that an "Iron Age" community was already established while the Dayr 'Alla temple and perhaps also the Amman Airport "Temple" were still in use.

13. By this I mean that most current explanations look to a division in Late Bronze Age society and draw their highland settlers from that segment of the population. Hence, even when questioning the historicity of the biblical account of an Israelite conquest and settlement and suggesting that the ethnogenesis of Israel was a gradual, in situ development, these explanations still imply that "proto-Israelites" shared a common background that distinguished them from "mainstream" Canaanite society.

14. On the southern end of the Karak Plateau, overlooking Wadi al-Ḥasa, Glueck included Ḥ. al-Mudaynat ar-Ras, Ḥ. al-Mudayna on the Wadi al-Ḥasa and Ḥ. al-'Akkuzah in his list of Iron I fortresses, but Iron I occupation has only been confirmed at Ḥ. al-'Akkuzah (MacDonald 2000; Mattingly 1996: 363–64; Miller 1991: 149–50), and even this is not unequivocal (cf. Miller 1991: 158–60). Excavations at Ḥ. al-Mudaybi', Glueck's lone fort on the southeastern side of the Karak Plateau (between Wadi al-Ḥasa and Wadi al-Lajjun), have shown that it was not founded the first half of the eighth century B.C.E. (see Chaps. 8 and 9). As we saw already in Chapter 4, soundings at Ḥ. Dubab on the south-western side of the Karak Plateau have questioned the presence of either a Late Bronze or an Iron I occupation at this site (Bienkowski and Adams 1999: 168–70), eliminating another of Glueck's early fortresses. North of the Wadi Mujib, excavations at Ḥirbat al-Mudayna on the Wadi ath-Thamad (henceforth ḤMTh), one of Glueck's key fortresses for the north-eastern frontier of Moab (Glueck 1939: 121–22), have shown that the fortifications of this site were not built until the end of the ninth or beginning of the eighth century B.C.E. (Chadwick et al. 2000; Daviau 2002). Better candidates for fortified Iron I sites might be found among Glueck's other fortresses on the east side of the Dhiban Plateau, although surface collections at each site contain substantial later material that could easily explain the visible architectural remains (see Ji and 'Attiyat 1997; Ji and Lee 1998).

15. The possibility of single storage towers and/or farm buildings adjacent to fields in the wadi bottoms seems probable. None have yet been found, although in an initial season of survey in the Wadi an-Nuḥayla we did identify two isolated buildings devoid of artifacts that appear from their construction techniques to date to the early Iron Age.

16. Given the different estimated house densities noted for ḤMA (max ≈ 20.5/ha), ḤMM (max ≈ 30/ha), and Lahun (max ≈ 37.5/ha), I am reluctant to ascribe much significance to this small absolute range in site size.

17. Initial radiocarbon assays yielded what appear to be anomalous results (Routledge 2000a: 47–48). Further assays were not available at the time of writing.

18. Homès-Fredericq (1997: 65) suggests that the site was comprised of " 60 à 80 maisons, peut-être même 100 maisons." However, the relatively constant width of the casemates (e.g., Homès-Fredericq 1997: Fig. 32) when extrapolated would seem to support the lower figure given here.

19. These calculations are taken from Tushingham and Pedrette (1995).

20. Thus far nine houses have been drawn in detail from surface remains, eight of which are essentially complete. Four of these houses have been partially excavated.

21. House area is inclusive of walls. House plans are derived from surface remains, hence they represent only the most coherent and accessible houses at the site. These tend also to be the largest houses. More indicative of the probable size of the remaining houses at ḤMA is building 900 (71.5 m²), which is 34 m² smaller than the next smallest house (building 600). We have relatively clear archaeological evidence for single story dwellings from two burned rooms (504b, 106—see

Routledge 2000a: 53–54). Hence, figures represent ground floor area only, recognizing that some houses may have had whole or partial second stories.

22. The presence of culm bases and twining weeds suggests that the grain was harvested by uprooting or low cutting, rather than by more rapid high cutting. This strategy is usually aimed at maximizing straw recovery, as more of the stalk is retained and stored (Hillman 1981). This storage assemblage is also characterized by a relatively high proportion of weed seeds as well as culm nodes, suggesting that the barley was stored after a coarse sorting but before sieving. In both cases this evidence favors interpreting this assemblage as grain stored for animal fodder, with an emphasis on supplementing the barley with straw, culm fragments, and weeds.

23. As is typical of Iron Age sites in arid to semiarid zones, sheep and goats constitute the majority of our faunal sample (77%). However, the size of our identifiable bone sample (n = 212) is too small at present to be taken as representative (Lev-Tov n.d.).

24. Based on a sustainable annual grazing rate of 5–8 ha per sheep (Assawi) or large goat (Maaz Jabali). See Routledge (1996a: 312–317) for model.

25. On the social significance of Iron Age gates see Chapter 8.

26. Of the house plans from Lahun published in Werner van Hoof's Licentiaat dissertation (van Hoof 1997: 21–45, Figs. 16–47), six (houses 1, 2, 3, 8, 9, 11) are complete enough to estimate overall area, which like HMA ranges widely from 63.50–160.00 m². Hence, at approximately 108 m² House 1 is not the largest house on the site. Direct evidence for control of storage is not obvious at Lahun. Indeed, one of the more striking features of the houses at Lahun is the consistent size and location of small, often doorless stone-paved rooms, reasonably interpreted as storage bins/silos (Homès-Fredericq 2000: 190).

27. Despite recent excavation, the Early Iron Age at Balu'a remains ambiguous and the degree of continuity between Iron I and Iron IIB settlement unclear (see Worschech 1990b, 1995; Worschech and Ninow 1999: 169).

28. Homès-Fredericq (2000: 182) states that blocked doorways are concentrated in houses in the northern section of Lahun. This might prove a worthwhile starting point for future studies of the site's abandonment.

29. The exact contemporaneity of these silos cannot be established, hence their total capacity is likely to be a misleading figure.

30. See Faust 2000 for a thorough recent study of Iron II villages in Palestine from this perspective.

31. The "African Frontier" model has been applied directly to Hopi communities by Schlegel (1992). Perhaps coincidentally, McGuire and Saitta (1996: 211) provide a nearly identical description of late Prehispanic Western Pueblo communities, but without reference to either Kopytoff or Schlegel.

32. Hisban Str. 21; and mixed LB IIB–Iron I contexts from Tall Jalul contain pottery equivalent to Tall al-'Umayri Field A Phase 13 (Herr 1998; Ray 2001: 43–45). Madaba Tomb A suggests a similarly early settlement (Harding 1953), while early twelfth-century material appears in subfloor fills at Dhiban (Routledge n.d.). Lahun (Homès-Fredericq 1992: 193–94; 1997: Figs. 33–34) is thus far the lone exception of an early Iron I settlement on the eastern plateau, insofar as the illustrated pottery from Ara'ir (Olávarri 1965: Figs. 1–2) does not necessitate the excavator's early dating of the site.

33. Excavated examples include Dhiban, Madaba, Hisban, and Jalul.

Chapter 6. Structures and Metaphors

1. Namely ecological adaptation in the case of tribalism, and an epochal *mentalité* in the case of "patrimonialism."

2. Knauf distinguishes between tribal states and "Bedouin states," the latter being a very specific social formation that appears first in the late eighth century B.C.E. and is dependent on the military use of camels and long-distance trade (esp. Knauf 1992b). For a critique of Knauf's application of this model to the Nabataean kingdom, see Macdonald 1991.

3. See Cavigneaux and Ismail (1990: no. 2) for textual attestation of a trade caravan from Tayma in the northern Hejaz (western Saudi Arabia) in the Middle Euphrates Valley in the eighth century B.C.E.

4. "Tribe," particularly in Africa, is seen largely as a classificatory tool of colonial governments using linguistic and cultural criteria to define an exotic category that in a Western context would be considered a form of ethnicity (Fried 1975). Yet, in a Middle Eastern context, the social formations in question are much more specific and could, at least in the case of Arabic speakers, be encompassed by a word like *qabila* and embedded in an intellectual tradition of analysis going back at least to Ibn Khaldun. Furthermore, the conceptual frameworks for understanding the tribes of both anthropology and biblical studies (if not archaeology per se) are not easily teased apart. They have passed through the same channels, from medieval authors such as Ibn Khaldun to those nineteenth-century Orientalists (e.g., Robertson-Smith and Wellhausen) who analyzed both biblical and Bedouin cultural practices as a single "Semitic" system (see Bonte and Conte 1991). None of this means that the term tribe is automatically acceptable as a specific characteristic of the Middle East. It only means that tribe is a term that invites dissection rather than dismissal, fusing as it does local, comparative, and Orientalist images of social relations in the history and culture of the Middle East.

5. For Emmanuel Marx (1977), a tribe existed as that network of relations by which individuals could meet their subsistence needs in a sustainable manner. This included both rights in sufficient land (principally grazing land) and access to sufficient men to defend that land in the case of conflicting claims to its use. Marx claims that these two factors (territory and allies) balance themselves in that the seasonal, geographical, and annual variation in available pasture in arid lands means that large territories are needed regardless of the number of people using those territories. The idiom of patrilineal descent, used flexibly to mark shared economic and political interests rather than genetic relation, is the vehicle through which tribe-as-subsistence-unit is realized. Salzman (1979) notes that the lack of congruence in many cases between tribal territory and pasture undermines the "strong" version of Marx's formulation, something Marx himself accepts with qualifications (Marx 1979).

6. The Wazir family of Tibne acted as the dominant clan in the al-Kura district of Jordan, particularly under Kulab al-Shrayda (Wazir), who successfully resisted Emir Abdullah's attempt to incorporate al-Kura into Hashemite Transjordan until Tibne was bombed by the R.A.F. in 1922. The Wazir family's dominance was based on 8 villages (out of 25 in al-Kura) comprised of clans that considered themselves to be "people of Tibne." The majority of the population of these villages belonged to clans said to descend from the same individual ("Hammad"), but these clans bore no common name (e.g., Bani Hammad or Awlad Hammad) and were never referred to collectively as *qabila* (tribe) or *ashira* ("clan"). The only collective names ("people of Tibne," or the "clans of Tibne") included clans with no genealogical link to Hammad, although at least one clan was considered an affine through a strategic marriage, while another was named for an eponymous ancestor said to have accompanied Hammad when he migrated from Wadi Hammad near Karak to Tibne in the fifteenth century (see Antoun 1972: 16–19, 36–46). While this is a flexible use of kinship for political purposes, it is not a unilineal descent system, nor is it a "generative genealogy." Lemche's (1985) suggestion that this is a tribe in formation confuses history with social typology.

7. Dresch (1989: 24) terms them confederacies for the purpose of exposition, even though no distinction is made in the naming of these confederacies and their constituent tribes (i.e., both are called *qabila*). These tribes include only about half of all inhabitants of northern Yemen. *Qabili* ("tribe member") functions much like a status group in the Weberian sense (see Mundy 1995: 39–49).

8. Similarly, the contention (LaBianca and Younker 1995: 404) that the specificity and rigidity of intra-tribal genealogical organization is a function of investment in plow agriculture ("land-tied" versus "range-tied" tribalism) is countered, to give one example, by Caroline Humphrey's study of Central Asian Burayt tribes. Humphrey states, "In using genealogies and ancestral myths to attach groups to particular bits of territory, the sedentarized Ekhirit-Bulagat made certain that their genealogies would be both contradictory and internally inconsistent. This example demonstrates that the holding of communal property does not necessarily cause "kinship" relations to be unambiguously defined, but may have the reverse effect: when property becomes scarce, this leads to a confusion in the genealogy because people are motivated to put forward conflicting claims. Unilineal genealogies become internally inconsistent when they are required simultaneously to fulfill two functions: legitimizing claims to property . . . and defending the interests of junior lineage segments against the claims of senior groups" (Humphrey 1979: 258).

9. These links are all the more significant in the case of polygamous marriage. Note that in the story of Abimelech's abortive attempt to set himself up as king over Israel (Judg. 9:1–3), he uses the support of "the whole clan of his mother's family" against his sixty-nine brothers (the offspring of his father Jeruba'al/Gideon's "many wives").

10. As Mundy (1995: 123–26) points out, this cannot be reduced to a structural pattern, as class, wealth, and family circumstances play a significant role in the explicit emphasis placed on affinal alliance in any individual marriage.

11. As Talal Asad (1979: 424) aptly notes, "Does one have to spell out the implication of a logic which holds that, in the final analysis, the rich are proportionately no better off than the poor, because their greater power to spend is more than matched by their greater need?"

12. This counts among the principal legitimizing claims of the Zaydi Imams, who ruled Yemen from ca. 897 until 1962; the Alawite dynasty of Morocco, and the Hashemite dynasty of Jordan. Others, such as the House of Ibn Saud in Saudi Arabia and the Imamate of Oman, claim descent from significant sectarian reformers. Islam also provides for a tradition of power grounded in the textual authority of religious and legal learning (see Messick 1993).

13. Dresch (1986: 309) compares the two positions as follows: "Lineage theory and segmentation are not at all the same thing; indeed they represent two different types of anthropology. The first deals with sequences of events at the level of observation (and in particular with the appearance of groups), while the second deals with formal relations that characterize the types of events possible."

14. Maynard (1988) has shown that the Protestants he studied in Portillo, Ecuador, classified themselves in segmentary terms—the principle of differentiation being doctrine, the cultural idiom of expression being denominations, and the practices where these differences were realized (or sometimes ignored) being everything from joint worship services to acceptable marriage partners to the businesses one frequented.

15. Though this applies also to Herzfeld (1992).

16. Or perhaps more accurately, the private domain of the god who grants dominion to the king.

17. Sader (1987: 272–73) makes the rather strained argument that *bît*-X and *mār*-X have distinct referents (territory and dynasty). As Table 6.1 shows, this cannot be maintained if one considers Aramaic and Assyrian evidence together.

18. E.g., "There was a long war between the house of Saul and the house of David; David grew stronger and the house of Saul became weaker and weaker" (2 Sam. 3: 1).

19. Composed in theory of a conjugal couple, their successive male descendants and families, and unmarried female descendants.

20. Stager (1985: Table 4) underestimates the impact of high mortality rates, as he mistakenly adds two to the average family sizes estimated by Burch (1972: Table 2.1).

21. Interestingly, the stems themselves have an uncertain genealogical relation to one another (Mundy 1995: 93, 187)

22. It is perhaps more nearly correct to say that Weber downplays the differences between household and polity, suggesting that over time political authorities tend to usurp coercive powers to themselves until they acquire the autocratic power over the polity that he ascribes to the patriarch within his household (see Weber 1978: 1013–14).

Chapter 7. Mesha and the Naming of Names

1. The MI is written in a variant of the Phoenician alphabetic script (arguably to be termed Moabite) and is very close to biblical Hebrew in its grammar, syntax, and vocabulary. The events narrated in the MI should probably be dated to 855–830 B.C.E. (Dearman 1989: 163). However, the actual inscription of the stele and at least some of the events it relates could date as much as several decades later, depending upon the length of Mesha's reign (see Lemaire 1991a).

2. *bm[t.y]š*. Lipiński (1971: 327–28) reconstructs *bn[th.n]š*' in this lacuna, meaning "As a victor I built it."

3. Reading *mlkn* for *šlkn*. This reading may not require an emendation of the text, since the small size and slight angle of the initial *š* (see Dussaud 1912) means that it could in fact be the head of a *mem* with an obscured tail.

4. Lipiński (1971: 329) suggests reading *k[mš]* at the end of line 6, but there does not appear to be sufficient room for two letters.

5. This rather awkward translation follows Niccacci (1994: 236) in reading lines 7b and 7c–8a as coordinate clauses, rather than seeing 7b as dependent on line 7a. To its credit, this solution allows for a consistent use of the "noun phrase + finite verb" construction to initiate paragraphs, hence introducing the events connected with "the land of Madaba" (line 8–10a) in a manner that is syntactically equivalent to the paragraphs concerned with the other cities. Furthermore, this solution takes account of the sentence divider that separates 7b from 6b/7a, but not from 7c/8a. However, as noted below, the role of sentence dividers is ambiguous at several points in the MI, and is not therefore compelling as evidence. Irsigler (1993: 114–15) recognizes the syntactic divide at line 7b but suggests that this is simply a case where contextually defined meaning takes precedence over syntactical patterns.

6. This translation follows the syntactical reading recently suggested by Rainey (1998).

7. Read *hyt* rather than *ryt* with Lemaire (1987: 206–7).

8. Beeston (1985: 144–45); Lipiński (1971: 332–34); Na'aman (1997: 83–84); and Rainey (1998: 246–51) all provide extended reviews and bibliographies regarding the main proposals for translating these words. All such proposals remain speculative. What does seem certain is that the *'ryl dwdh* of line 12 is in parallelism with the *'[..]ly yhwh* of line 17. However, the use of two different verbs and the use of a plural noun in line 17 show that the lines are not identical. This is important since Lemaire (1987: 209) cites Lidzbarski's (1902: 7) reading of the lower part of

a vertical stroke in the lacuna at the end of line 17 to justify reconstructing '[*ry*] *ly*. However, since it seems necessary to reconstruct an object marker here (Na'aman 1997: n. 20; Cooke 1903: 12), there is insufficient room for two additional letters. As a result, the traditional reconstruction [*k*] *ly.yhwh* "the vessels of Yahweh" is still to be preferred. On analogy with line 17, the *'ryl* of its *dwd* should be some sort of cultic object, favoring the translation "the altar-hearth of its beloved [i.e., city-god]" (Segert 1961: 240) or "the lion-statue of its beloved [i.e., city-god]" (Gibson 1971: 80).

9. From *r's* ("head"—see Segert 1971: 219 n. 81; Gibson 1971: 81). Alternatively, "all of its best" (Niccacci 1994: 230). Less likely is a plural form "all of its chiefs/ leaders" (e.g., Cross and Freedman 1952: 41), as this noun is referenced with a third masculine singular pronominal suffix in the subsequent verb.

10. The reading [*lm'*]*yn* "for the spring" fits the lacuna and the context (Cross and Freedman 1952: 41). Note, however, that Lemaire (1994a: 35) reads *lmyn* in his correction of Lidzbarski's facsimile of the MI and translates it as " water." Unfortunately, Lemaire does not comment on this reading.

11. Line 28 is a syntactical crux in the MI. Smelik (1992: 71) and Lipiński (1971: 339) both note that the traditional reconstruction [*b*] *'š* near the beginning of 28 implies that this clause is dependent on *'nk.bnty* of 27b, despite the fact that a nominal *ky* clause comes in between them. Furthermore, Andersen (1966: 85) notes that a "sentence divider" should probably be restored just before the word in question, since this occurs after all *ky* clauses in the MI. Hence the traditional reconstruction rests on a kind of poetic parallelism not found elsewhere in the text. As a result, Lipiński (1971: 339), followed by Smelik (1992: 71), proposed reading [*w*] *'š*. At the same time, 27b begins as "*'nk* + *qatal*," while 28b continues the very strong paragraph structure of this section with "*w'anak* + *qatal*." Therefore, while the arguments of Lipiński and Smelik make sense, it is difficult to see 28a as anything but a minor break in the larger paragraph sequence. Oddly enough, Lemaire (1987: 209) supports Clermont-Ganneau's (1875: 172) original reading of [*b*] *'š* on the basis of a direct examination of the stele, but then translates the line as [w] *'š* in a later publication (Lemaire 1994a: 33). Whichever reconstruction is preferred, and despite the problems involved, it seems best to see syntactical continuity from line 21b through line 31a.

12. Following the proposed reading of Lemaire (1994a, b). Within the MI one might expect the construction *bēt* - X to be either a toponym or "the temple of X." However, the use of "Israel" for the northern kingdom but "House of David" for Judah in the Tel Dan Inscription (Biran and Naveh 1995) provides a good parallel for this reading.

13. This translation follows Lemaire's (1987: 210) suggested reading of the end of line 33 as *wl[t]y.mšm.'š[r . . .]*. The stroke visible in Dussaud's (1912) photograph at the end of the lacuna in question could belong to either a *yod* or a *he* (contra Na'aman 1997: n. 13). No matter which of the current readings one prefers, 33b remains syntactically problematic, as one would expect it to begin with a *wayyiqtol* or a 'noun phrase+ finite verb' construction.

14. See 2 Samuel 8 and 1 Chronicles 18. The Euphrates is named in 1 Chronicles 18: 3 and in the *Qere* of 2 Samuel 8: 3. The *Kethib* merely writes "river" (*nahar*).

15. 2 Kings 1: 1 and 3: 5 claim that Moab, under Mesha, "revolted" on the death of Ahab son of Omri. The Mesha Inscription (ll. 7–8) states that Omri took possession of the "Land of Madaba" all of his days and half the days of his son, forty years in total.

16. The Karak fragment preserves portions of three lines of text, the first of which replicates in part line1 of the MI: [. . .]mšyt.mlk.m'b.h[d...]; (. . .moshyat king of Moab the [D . . .]). Because naming conventions would lead one to expect a patronym as the last element in the king's personal name, Freedman (1964)

reasonably suggests that the Karak fragment was also an inscription of Mesha, beginning "I am Mesha son of Chemoshyat, king of Moab, the Dayboni." However, we should also use due caution, as the "yat" portion of Mesha's father's name often used in transcribing the MI is a reconstruction based on the Karak fragment. Furthermore, as Timm (1989: 277) points out, including word dividers less than half (12/27) of the proposed common characters are actually attested in both the MI and the Karak fragment.

17. A basalt stele fragment found on the surface at Dhiban preserves parts of six letters and a word divider but is too incomplete to read (Murphy 1952; Timm 1989: 266–69). A curved basalt fragment excavated at Balu'a (Worschech, Rosenthal, and Zayadine 1986: 302–3) appears to be an inscribed object, rather than a stele. It contains the letters *tmlk*, which could be a royal reference written without word dividers ("[. . .]t. mlk" = "[. . .]t. king"), or it could be a name or a word fragment. The inscribed incense altar recently discovered at Kh. al-Mudayna ath-Thamad appears to be a private, rather than royal, dedication to an otherwise unknown goddess (Dion and Daviau 2000).

18. Most notably in both the MI and biblical Hebrew, this is achieved by alterations in the placement and aspect of the verb. Put simply, Verb-Subject-Object (VSO) is the dominant word order in the MI and in biblical Hebrew narratives. Narrative continuity is achieved by continuity in verbal aspect (perfect/imperfect) coupled with the use of the conjunction *waw* ("and" or "but"). Discontinuity is achieved by variation in verbal aspect, the shifting of word order, or the deletion of the *waw*. In other words, discontinuity is achieved by breaking the flow of the narrative. Such direct syntactical marking is the primary means used in the MI and biblical Hebrew to provide internal structure to narratives.

19. This includes both cases with SVO word order and cases beginning with *casus pendens* constructions.

20. In what follows, *qatal* and *yiqtol* are used as a conventional means of representing paradigmatic verb forms in Hebrew grammar. These are otherwise known as the perfect and imperfect aspects or, inaccurately, as the past and future tenses. *Wayyiqtol* (*waw + yiqtol*) is the distinct narrative form of the Hebrew verb, sometimes known as the *waw*-consecutive. *'anāk* is simply the pronoun "I," while *ky* is a conjunction ("that," "for," "when") that here introduces subordinate clauses. A lower case "x" designates the intervening presence of any elements besides the verb forms, pronouns and conjunctions specified above.

21. Recognition of the macrostructuring role of these two verbal constructions is not unique to Niccacci. For example, Müller (1994: 383–85) distinguishes between what he calls the "*votiveinschriftlichen Teil*" (marked by the use of the *wayyiqtol*) and the "*bauinschriftlichen Teil*" (marked by the use of *w'anāk*) of the MI. Similarly, Irsigler (1993: 112–13) distinguishes between what he calls "*besprechende Erzählung*" (marked by the use of the *wayyiqtol*) and "*erzählender Diskurs*" (marked by *'anāk + qatal* in 1.m.s.).

22. The first section (ll. 1–4) is characterized as biographical due to the dominance of *'anāk* and the use of *w'anāk + qatal* to continue the narrative. However, the use of a *wayyiqtol* construction in line 3 is atypical. Section 4, although fragmentary, is clearly of the narrative type (introduced, by a *casus pendens* construction). Section 5, on the other hand, is more fragmentary and much less certain. Basically, it is the appearance of *w'anāk* in line 34 that suggests a shift to the biographical form, since *'anāk* is not used in the narrative sections of the MI.

23. These divisions match those of Niccacci (1994), except for section 4, which I begin at line 31b, rather than 30b. Niccacci reads 30b–31a as *casus pendens + wayyiqtol* because of the sentence divider after *bt dbltn* in line 30a. However, as Andersen (1966: 86–87) notes, in lines 3 and 16 the "sentence dividers" clearly come in the

middle of single sentences—so their use is a little ambiguous. For this reason I have chosen to see *beth ba'alma'on* in 30b as continuing the list of sites at which Mesha built temples begun in line 29. A wide range of other schemes exists for identifying major units within the MI. De Moor's (1988) "tricolon" poetic rendering pays so little attention to syntax that it cannot be integrated with most other approaches. Auffret (1980) maintains very similar paragraph divisions to those used here but proposes different section divisions (ll. 1–10a; 10b–21a; 21b–31a) based on word repetition. The division of the first two sections seems unconvincing in light of the text-level syntax. Both Smelik (1992) and Irsigler (1993) offer divisions, the former based on content and the latter on syntax, that are similar to mine except for their partitioning off of lines 28–31a. Finally, Parker (1997: 44–58) offers a scheme for division based on content that is identical to mine, with the exception of the fifth section, which he does not recognize.

24. A location for Ḥawronen on the west side of the Karak Plateau seems well established (see Dearman 1990; Mittmann 1982; Na'aman 1994a; Schottroff 1966; Worschech and Knauf 1986).

25. More than one scholar (Parker 1997: 54; Smelik 1992: 72) has suggested that the closure provided by 30–31a indicates that lines 31b–34 are a later addition to the MI. Instead, I would point to this as evidence that the north-south division of Moab was the principal one in the MI. Further evidence for the existence of a "mental map" in the MI, predicated on a north-south division of Moab lies in word choice. In particular, the contrast between lines 14 and 32 is rather striking. Line 14 reads *wy'mr.ly.kms.lk.'hz.'t.nbh.* (and Kemosh said to me "Go, seize Nebo. . ."). Line 32 is very similar, reading *[wy]'mr.ly.kms.rd.hlthm.bhrwrnn.* (and Kemosh said to me "Go down, fight against Ḥawronen"). The choice of *hlk* ("to go") for the order to attack Nebo and *yrd* ("to go down, descend") for the order to attack Ḥawronen seems to be based on a spatial distinction in the location of the two sites. Certainly one would have to descend some 800 meters in crossing Wadi Mujib on the way from Dibon to Ḥawronen, but this fact is likely not inconsequential to the logic by which Moab was partitioned in the MI. Against giving too great a role to this north-south distinction is the absence of distinct names for each unit in the MI (though note the use of *mišor* as a designation for northern Moab in the Hebrew Bible).

26. It is significant that the *wayyiqtol* at the beginning of 14b that links the two campaigns is *wy'mr.ly.kms* "and Kemosh said."

27. On "all GN" as a polity designation see Grosby 1997.

28. The noun *mišma'at* is used (from *šema'* = "hear"/"obey"). While this has the limited sense of a select group of attendants or a bodyguard in 1 Samuel 22: 14 and 2 Samuel 23: 23, it is used to refer to the Ammonites as subjects of a restored Israel in Isaiah 11: 4. Even if one prefers the translation "bodyguard," it is clear that the reference to "all of Dibon" makes its use metaphorical. Therefore, it is clearly a hierarchical relationship of subjugation or obedience that is of importance in the use of *mišma'at* in line 28.

29. See Ahlström 1982: 16 for etymological evidence linking *qrḥ* to Akkadian *kirhu* = "acropolis" or "walled area."

30. See Parry 1986 and Weiner 1992 for critiques of the long tradition of reading Mauss strictly in terms of a "social calculus" of reciprocity. Asymmetrical exchange (e.g., tribute) is not reciprocal, but it structures a relationship nonetheless—note that the events of 1 Kings 20 are precipitated by Ben-Hadad's impolite methods in extracting tribute from his client Ahab.

31. This assumes the traditional, and I think more parsimonious, position of associating Gad with Israel, against Knauf (1988: 162, n. 689) and Na'aman (1997: 87), who see the men of Gad as Moabites (cf. Rainey 1998: 244–246).

32. See Routledge (2000b: 239–44) for an extended review of this literature. Note

that the critique of the segmentary state model's essentialism presented here is not clearly developed in my earlier article.

Chapter 8. Replicative Kinship

1. Although these could perhaps have been read aloud for the illiterate, as is at least claimed in the epilogue of Hammurabi's law code (Hallo and Younger 2000: 351).

2. The Amman Citadel Inscription (Aufrecht 1989: 154–63; Hübner 1992: 17–21) does not mention a king in the preserved portion of the inscription, but rather seems to record the direct speech of the god Milkom. However, in common with royal inscriptions it seems to focus on a construction program. The direct speech of a deity is recorded in the MI (ll. 14 and 32) and the Zakkur Inscription (ll. A11–17), hence one cannot discount the royal character of the inscription on this grounds alone. The very fragmentary Amman Theatre Inscription (Aufrecht 1989: 151–54; Hübner 1992: 21–23) may contain the phrase *bn'm[wn]* or "Son(s) of 'Amm[on]," which as a polity designation would also suggest a royal inscription. Cf. the inscribed metal bottle from Tell Siran, which contains the phrase "king of the Son(s) of 'Ammon" (Aufrecht 1989: 203–11; Hübner 1992: 26–30). One small stele fragment was discovered in fill within the Iron Age east gate of the citadel at Samaria (Sukenik 1936). Its context would seem to support its possible royal association. Two Iron Age stele fragments have been discovered in Jerusalem, one in the City of David excavations (Ariel 2000: 1–2) and one in the Ophel excavations (Ben-Dov 1994). This does not, of course, include the recently forged Yehoash Inscription. The Tel Dan Inscription (Biran and Naveh 1993, 1995) would appear to have been erected by a king of Aram-Damascus on the (re)capture of the city of Dan (Tall al-Qadi). The Tel Miqne inscription is a classic dedicatory inscription, featuring an object (a temple), royal donor, a deity, and a request for blessings (Gitin et al. 1997). The putative author, Ikausu son of Padi, names himself as *sr 'qrn* ("ruler of Ekron") rather than *mlk 'qrn* ("King of Ekron"), however, both he and Padi are given the title of king in Assyrian records.

3. Major, specifically kingly, examples include the nine Phoenician and Aramaic royal stele (Kilamuwa, Panamuwa I, Panamuwa II, and six by Bar-Rakib) from the site of Zincirli, Turkey (Tropper 1993), the Aramaic Zakkur Inscription from Tall Afis, Syria (Gibson 1975: 6–17; Hallo and Younger 2000: 155), the Phoenician Azatiwada inscription from Karatepe, Turkey (Bron 1979; Rollig in Çambel 1999; Hallo and Younger 2000: 148–50). See Çambel (1999) and Hawkins 2000: 44–68 for the Hieroglyphic Luwian version of this bilingual inscription), the Aramaic treaties from Sefire, Syria (Hallo and Younger 2000: 213–17; Lemaire and Durand 1984), and from Byblos, Lebanon, the Phoenician Ahiram sarcophagus inscription (Gibson 1982: 12–16; Hallo and Younger 2000: 181) and the Phoenician dedicatory inscriptions of Yaḥimilik and Yeḥawmilk (Gibson 1982: 17–19, 93–99; Hallo and Younger 2000: 146–47, 151–52). Major, as yet unpublished, Phoenician royal inscriptions have been announced from Incirli (Carter et al. 1998) and Ivriz (Dinçol 1994), both in southern Turkey. The recent publication of J. D. Hawkins's monumental *Corpus of Hieroglyphic Luwian Inscriptions* (Hawkins 2000) provides convenient critical editions of upward of forty well-preserved royal (i.e., kingly) inscriptions (along with numerous nonkingly and fragmentary royal inscriptions). Due to the limits of my linguistic competency, I have relied primarily on Phoenician and Aramaic examples in the discussion that follows. Nonetheless, it is difficult to overstress the richness and relevance of these Neo-Hittite examples, which include inscriptions by queens/princesses and state officials as well as kings.

4. The Zakkur Inscription seems to have two introductions. Line 1 begins with a dedicatory-style introduction, identifying the object before the king, but this is followed immediately by the memorial-style introduction "I am Zakkur, king of Hamath and Lu'ash . . ."

5. Indeed, a direct contrast is drawn as Omri is said to have dwelt in the land of Madaba "in his days" in line 8.

6. For example, in the recently discovered Tel Dan Inscription the author contrasts the loss of territory either during or at the end of his father's life, with its reclamation on his ascent to the throne (see Parker 1997: 58–60).

7. E.g., "Whoever of my sons seizes the scepter in Y'DY and sits on my throne and reig[ns in my place, may he not] stretch out his hand with the sword against [the sons of?] my Houses, [either out of anger or out of] violence; may he not commit murder, either out of wrath or [. . .]; and may he not be an avenger? [who executes?], whether with his bow or with his words . . ." (Tropper 1993: 86–87; Hallo and Younger 2000: 157).

8. E.g., Judges 2: 14; 1 Kings 16: 1–4; 2 Kings 13: 3, etc.

9. The identity of this otherwise unattested state remains unclear; for literature, see Dion 1997: 131 n. 87.

10. Yehawmilk of Byblos, Zakkur of Hamath, Panamuwa I, and the author of the Tel Dan inscription state that specific deities made them king. Azatiwada credits the king of the Danunians with empowering him; Bar-Rakib credits the Assyrian king Tiglath-Pileser III with making both his father (Panamuwa II) and him king of Sam'al/Y'DY.

11. Although, interestingly, the use of seers and diviners as mediums is explicitly stated.

12. Panamuwa II's rival is in fact Panamuwa I, apparently in keeping with Y'DY/Sam'al's tradition of usurpation.

13. The Tel Miqne Inscription lacks the relative pronoun but still conveys this meaning syntactically (see Rainey 1998: 242).

14. Probably best translated as "temple" in the first two cases and "palace" in the third.

15. I owe this observation to an unpublished paper by D. Bruce MacKay, read at the University of Toronto in April 1989.

16. Clermont-Ganneau published a plan in 1870 (see Clermont-Ganneau 1870–71), but this was schematic and not the result of systematic surveying.

17. It appears that in the years 1950–53, directing the Dhiban excavations went hand in hand with what were then one-year interim appointments as director of the American School in Jerusalem. Hence, Winnett, Reed, and Tushingham only directed the Dhiban excavations while in residence in Jerusalem.

18. In 1991, with the help of Larry McKinney, then of Midwestern Baptist Seminary, I was able to examine many of the notes and artifacts from Dr. Morton's excavations still stored at the seminary. These eventually passed to his widow, Mrs. Thelma Morton, who in 1997 graciously donated both notes and artifacts to the University of Pennsylvania Museum, where they are now archived. Work on this unpublished material from Dhiban has been generously supported by the White-Levy Program for Archaeological Publication.

19. I would like to thank Robert Miller for informing me of further Dhiban documents in the archive of the American School in Jerusalem (now the Albright Institute for Archaeological Research). These were examined and copied in 1999 by Benjamin Porter, a Ph.D. candidate at the University of Pennsylvania. While helpful, these additional documents (such as a lone surveyor's notebook from one of the three seasons) also confirmed that a significant proportion of the original excavation documentation remained unaccounted for.

20. Not surprisingly, given that the sections seem to have been drawn independent of the area supervisor, there are a number of logical inconsistencies in the stratigraphic sequence as described in fieldnotes and as drawn in the balk sections.

21. Foundation trenches are noted in a very unsystematic, indeed idiosyncratic, manner in the fieldnotes for Field L. It appears that the primary north/south wall on the eastern side of Field L (wall 16) was founded directly on its associated floor level in the south, had fill containing mixed EB and Iron I pottery heaped against it in the area of wall 16a, and cut through preexisting EB deposits in the north.

22. In keeping with the approach of Kathleen Kenyon at Samaria and Jericho (where Morton worked), Morton and his team appear to have assigned material on surfaces, floor makeup and fills immediately below the floor interface to the same locus. This makes living surfaces very difficult to both identify and/or critically evaluate from the fieldnotes. It also tends to make it difficult to draw fine distinctions in the relative chronology of these deposits.

23. This cannot be clearly demonstrated from the surviving fieldnotes.

24. Morton (1989: 244) reads the third letter as š (*shin*); however, the faint but definite tail of a *mem* can be seen on visual inspection of the sherd.

25. For exceptions see below.

26. Ussishkin (1989b) suggests that the Megiddo building is a shrine, an identification which Stern (1990) contests.

27. Cf. the negative affirmation of this in Psalm 69: 12: "I am the subject of gossip for those who sit in the gate and drunkards make songs about me."

28. To my mind, the gate stratigraphy as described does not eliminate the possibility of two construction phases, it only means that the second phase had to be rather extensive, including the building of the benches and a replastering of the roadway. Indeed, the fact that the southern rooms appear to be constricted by the available space would seem to favor their secondary construction.

29. This statement goes beyond the available ^{14}C data, which only indicate that one cannot discount the contemporaneity of these gates. In Chapter 9 we will consider circumstantial evidence for the systematic construction of fortifications on Moab's eastern frontier at this time.

30. Both excavations report trilobate, or so-called Scythian, bronze projectile points in destruction debris. At Kh. al-Mudayna ath-Thamad the point was discovered in the gate complex (Chadwick et al. 2000: 262), while at Kh. al-Mudaybi' it was discovered within the fort, adjacent to the outer wall (Area A, Sq. I3— McMurray 2002). These projectile points are generally dated to the sixth century. Mattingly et al. (1999: Fig. 19: 2, 5, 12–15) have published a small number of sherds from the gate area at al-Mudaybi'. Typologically, these fall generally in the eighth–early sixth century B.C.E. (in contrast with Fig 19: 10 from Area A, which is specifically late seventhsixth century B.C.E. in date). Although not from the gate complex itself, pottery published from the immediately adjacent shrine 149 at al-Mudayna (Daviau and Steiner 2000: Figs. 12–13) should be dated typologically to the seventh–early sixth century B.C.E. (esp. Daviau and Steiner 2000: Fig. 12: 1–3, 8, Fig. 13: 5), indicating at the very least that the site (and probably also the gate) was in use at this time.

31. Warembol's criteria for an Iron II date (the *sndty* kilt and the Ba'al streamer) are not specific enough to support his argument (see Cornelius 1994 for L.B. examples of both). However, the figure's body position is close to Phoenician transformations of the winged Seth as "serpent-slayer" motif, where the wings are transferred from the anthropomorphic figure to the creature. Usually, Phoenician figures on ivory are beardless with an Egyptian coiffure, or bearded with Ba'al curls. However, a good example, with a cap and streamer (though admittedly bearded), comes from an eighth century "Phoenician" bronze bowl discovered at

Olympia in Greece (Markoe 1985: 316–18). Compare also the ninth–eighth century Qadbun/Tall Kazael Stele now in the Tartus museum (Matthiae 1997: 234).

32. What is usually identified as "Phoenician" art in the Iron Age is characterized by the repeated employment of a limited range of scenes and motifs selected from within the canon of Egyptian art. One such scene is Seth-Ba'al slaying a serpent or a griffin with a serpentine body.

33. This does not include the four female-headed capitals (Abou-Assaf 1980: Taf. 12–16) already mentioned above in relation to the Amman Citadel "Palace."

34. On the second statute this object, while clearly floral, is less certainly a lotus blossom.

35. E.g., Ahiram, Kilamuwa, Panamuwa I, Bar-Rakib, and several uninscribed examples from Zincirli. See van Loon (1986), who argues that the drooping lotus indicates that the figure depicted is dead. This cannot be demonstrated from the Yarḥ'azar statue alone.

36. Indeed, even reaching Phoenician colonies in the West. See Falsone (1989).

Chapter 9. Local Space in a Global State

1. Evidence for tax/tribute collection systems includes the Samaria Ostraca, see Kaufman (1982); Rainey (1979). Possible evidence for a royal supply system includes the "*lmlk*" ["belonging to the king"] storage jars, see Vaughn (1999) with bibliography. On fortified frontiers see Cohen (1995) and Meshel (1992). For "public works" projects such as subterranean water systems, see Shiloh (1992). For weights and measures see Kletter (1998). The Mešad Hašavyahu and Moussaïeff ostraca provide evidence for judicial procedures, see Bordreuil et al. (1998); Lemaire (1971). For scribal schools and documentary practices see Crenshaw (1998); Lemaire (1981); cf. Davies (1998); Jamieson-Drake (1991). For administrative titles see Avishur and Heltzer (2000); Fox (2000); Mettinger (1971); Rüterswörden (1985).

2. Recent excavations at Kh. al-Mudayna ath-Thamad have discovered two inscribed weights. One appears to match in form, weight, and inscription the 10 *gerah* weight of the so-called "Judean Inscribed weight" system (Kletter 1998). The other bears the inscription *šlšn* ("thirty") and fits comfortably by weight (16.31 gr) within the *gera* sequence, although neither the unit (30) nor the use of writing rather than hieratic numbers is attested in Palestine.

3. If authentic, and correctly ascribed as originating in Moab (see below), this sixth-century papyrus document from an unidentified private collection represents a divine recognition of property transfer between individuals, sealed with a bullae stamped *lmlk 'k(t/n/)* ("belonging to the King"—GN).

4. "son of the king" (Avigad and Sass: 1997 no. 1006; Timm 1989: no. 18), "the memorist/herald" (Avigad and Sass 1997 no. 1011; Timm 1989: no. 22), "the scribe" (Avigad and Sass 1997: nos. 1007–10; Timm 1989: nos. 3, 11).

5. The Str. 18/17 reservoir from Tall Ḥisban measures ca. 17.5 x 17.5 x 7.0 m (2143.75 m³), with one of its walls built of ashlar masonry laid as "headers and stretchers" (Ray 2001: 99–108).

6. This figure does not include four examples that either certainly, or probably, bear the title "king" (Avigad and Sass 1997: nos. 400, 712, 1048–49). Nor does it include the estimated 21 seals (Lemaire 1981) used to produce the more than 1,716 (Vaughn 1999) *lmlk* seal impressions on jar handles.

7. *bn hmlk* ("son of the king"), *'bd* RN/ *'abd hmlk* ("servant of the king"), PN *'šr 'l hbyt* ("PN who is over the house") PN *'šr 'l hms* ("PN who is over the corvée"), *šr* ("govenor/ commander") *šr h'r* ("governor of the city"), *šr hmsgr* ("porter of the prison"), *hmzkr* ("the memorist/herald"), *hnss* ("the standard-bearer?"), *hspr* ("the scribe").

8. *'bd* DN ("Servant of DN"), *khn* ("Priest"), *hrp'* ("healer").

9. *hṣrp* ("the goldsmith"), *'mt* ("maidservant"), *n'r* ("steward").

10. Here I do not refer to the tribe of Levi, which may well represent a "retrofitting" of priesthood to a unified genealogy (see Ahlström 1982: 50–51). Rather, I refer to the specific representation of individual priests as descendants of priests. For example, one can trace five generations of priests within the "House of Eli," linking Yahweh's curse against Eli in 1 Samuel 2: 27–36 with its final realization in Abiathar's banishment from the priesthood in 1 Kings 2: 27.

11. As well as the polemic divide within one branch of biblical studies, which requires every statement on the Iron Age to somehow reflect on the hermeneutic question of biblical historicity.

12. Behind this looms the larger question of the composition of biblical texts, and particularly whether or not a social context existed within Iron Age Judah that could account for the writing, editing and collection of what eventually became the Rabbinic and early Christian "canon."

13. Here one must also account for local historical variation which saw extensive eighth-century B.C.E. occupation in both Judah and Israel, followed by an Assyrian-induced decline in the seventh century (with Israel no longer existing as an independent polity). In terms of textual production, this "decline" is balanced in the case of Judah by the dramatic growth of Jerusalem as a primate administrative center (see Ofer 2001, Steiner 2001 and Zertal 2001).

14. In fact, the categories employed (Hebrew, Aramean, Phoenician, Ammonite, Moabite, and Edomite) are an odd blend of "nation," "ethnicity," and "cultural/linguistic area." Furthermore, the categories are largely dependent on perspectives inherited from biblical and Greco-Roman literature, notable for example in the fact that Aramaean and Phoenician remain undivided despite incorporating many diverse polities, and despite the fact that "Phoenician" is a Greek, rather than an indigenous or even a Near Eastern category.

15. Or, more correctly, the amalgam of nationality, ethnicity and language/dialect that forms the most commonly deployed categories in epigraphic analysis.

16. In the case of epigraphy I have significant reservations with regards to the "national" character of the so-called Moabite script. Note, for example, that the small corpus of provenanced inscriptions is very diverse. The ostracon from Morton's excavations at Dhiban (Morton 1989: Fig. 12) includes a vertical *mem* and a three-bar *ḥet* like those of the Amman Citadel Inscription, as opposed to the two-bar *ḥet* and large horizontal *mem* of the MI. Also, the incense altar inscription from Ḥ al-Mudayna ath-Thamad (Dion and Daviau 2000) contains a large-headed, as opposed to the expected "star-shaped," *'aleph*. On the other hand, the "Edomite" seal excavated at 'Ein Ḥazeva (Cohen and Yisrael 1995a: 24 [Hebrew]) in the Negev would almost certainly have been labeled "Moabite" if acquired on the antiquities market (large-headed *mem*, 2–bar *ḥet*, two worshipers, and a cult-stand). To my mind, an endeavor that requires discounting our few provenanced inscriptions as "imports" or "idiosyncratic" in order to preserve the hypothetical construct of a national script is suspect.

17. The lone possible exception is the reservoir at Ḥisban, which the excavators have recently suggested could be Iron IIA (tenth century) rather than early Iron IIB (ninth century) in date (Ray 2001: 99–108; Sauer 1994: 240–44). However, the dating criteria are both meager and ambiguous.

18. Ḥisban (Ray 2001: 53–57, 121–26), Madaba (Piccirillo 1975; Thompson 1986), Jalul (Herr et al. 1996: 71–75, 1997: 154–57), and Dhiban (Morton 1989; Tushingham 1972; see Chapter 8 above).

19. On the tricky issue of biblical Kir-Hareseth as a second capital of Moab (not) located at modern al-Karak see Jones 1991.

20. Neither of Morton's major areas (L and H) contained domestic structures (Morton 1989; Routledge n.d.), while Tushingham's artificial "podium" covered over domestic architecture, and its scale suggests that it was intended for large-scale structures now removed.

21. Olávarri argues for continuous settlement through the tenth century. This is a possible, but not necessary, conclusion from the published pottery.

22. From Olávarri's plans and sections it is evident that the site's stratigraphic complexity is not fully conveyed in his preliminary reports. This is particularly evident in terms of the multiple walls depicted on the the west side of the site and by the remains exposed on the interior of the fort, all of which appear to predate the fort's construction.

23. For Iron IIC pottery from the last Iron Age phase of each site, see Mattingly et al. 1999: 139 and Daviau and Steiner 2000: Figs. 12–13 (Fig. 13: 1–2 are earlier). The Lahun "fort" is clearly occupied in the Iron IIC period, as witnessed by the discovery of an Egyptian Twenty-Sixth Dynasty "New Year's" bottle (Homès-Fredericq 1982) and less precisely by an Iron IIC cosmetic palette (Homès-Fredericq 1995). At the same time, at least one published vessel (Homès-Fredericq 1992: Fig. 16.8c) from the "fort" belongs typologically in the Iron IIB period. In contrast with the other forts, the published evidence from Ara'ir does not necessitate its continued occupation in the Iron IIC period. For evidence supporting the Iron IIC date of intensively investigated "towers" on the eastern Karak Plateau, see Routledge 1996a: 133–213.

24. This list represents only highly probable Iron II sites, as the attribution of numerous small sites and pastoral camps to the Iron Age by the Limes Arabicus Project (Koucky 1987) proved problematic on reinvestigation by the author in 1992 (site selection criteria are presented in Routledge 1996a: 61–69). Sixty is certainly a conservative figure, as two of these sites were discovered in an initial, abbreviated survey of the alluvial and colluvial terraces of the Wadi an-Nuhayla in 2000, which had not been covered in either the CMS (Miller 1991) or LAP (Koucky 1987) surveys.

25. Mudaybi', Mhai (CMS 238), ash-Sharif (CMS 436), and Qasr al-'Al (LAP 117)

26. Of the remaining sites, six appear to be related to pastoralism (LAP 253, 229, 607, 679b, 693, 695), two are unquestionably covered by buildings postdating the Iron Age (LAP 665, CMS 154), and two are completely obscured by collapsed stone (CMS 228, 330).

27. E.g., Conder (1889: 193); Gese (1958); Graf-Reventlow (1963); Hentschke (1960); Mackenzie (1911: 25–40); Parker (1987: 797–98); Petrie and Pape (1952); Thompson (1989); for early doubts but no alternative, see Dornemann (1983: 123–24).

28. See Banning (1992); Bikai (1993: 524–27); Herr et al. (1989: 195–98; 1991: 335–42); Hopkins (n.d.); Kletter (1991); Najjar (1992); Zayadine (1986). See McGovern (1983: 112–13) for an intermediate position.

29. Additionally, a significant number of the small round towers found in the MPP survey area turned out to be lime kilns (Herr et al. 1991: 343–52).

30. For lexical information, see Brown et al. (1979: 153); Gelb (1956: 144–45 [2]); and Liddell and Scott (1940: 1556). For discussions see Heltzer (1979); Jankowska (1982); Osbourne (1985, 1986, 198); Preisigke (1919); Routledge (1996a: 263–69); and Zacagninni (1979: 50–51).

31. This would also account for the paucity of associated agricultural/viticultural installations (presses, vats, etc.).

32. To the examples published by Parpola (1970: 230) one may now add those in Dalley and Postgate (1984: 252–53, no.143) and Horowitz (1993). Borger and Tadmor (1982: 250) note that the Mu-u,/'u-na-a-a of ND 400 (Wiseman 1951: 23–24) cannot be emended to Mu-u'-ba-a-a = Moab, although I have not found anyone inclined to do so in the first place, so the point may be moot.

33. For editions of the text, see Cogan (1974: 118); Donner (1957: 159–61); and Saggs (1955: 134–35).

34. Postgate (1992: 252) notes: "While the provincial capitals were often the traditional local centers, the governors were usually (if not always) 're-deployed' members of old families of Assur rather than re-employed local dynasts."

35. For Moab sending tribute see Tadmor (1994: 170–71) and Luckenbill (1926: §195). For gifts of loyalty see Borger (1996: CIII41, pp. 19, 2112) and Luckenbill (1926: §239). For building materials see Borger (1956: AV56, p. 58). For Moabite tribute-bearing officials, see Saggs (1955: 134–35 [24 ND 2765], 1959: 159–60 [ND 2762]). For the delivery of precious metals, see Waterman (1930: no. 632) (= Pritchard 1969: 301) and Johns (1898: 928). For a newer edition, see Postgate (1974: 309–11).

36. Note in this regard the strong visual support this message would have received from the military conquest and tribute presentation scenes found on the wall reliefs of reception halls of Neo-Assyrian palaces (see Reade 1979; Russell 1991).

37. Cylinder B = "Kamshaltu King of Moab, a servant belonging to me" (Borger 1996: BVIII43, pp.115, 244); Cylinder C = "kings of the Westland whom [DNs] have given me as my property" (Pritchard 1969: 298).

38. Note, for example, that Musuri king of Moab is required (after delivering *tamartu*) to participate in Assurbanipal's campaign against Taharqa (Rassam Cylinder and Cylinder C—Borger 1996: AVII112, pp. 61, 245).

39. If the Qurdi-Assur of ND 2773 is to be connected with the Qurdi-Assur-lamur of ND 2686 and ND 2715, then the issue would seem to have been taken up by the Assyrian consul (*qepu*) in Tyre (who is perhaps also responsible for Sidon—see ND 2715). However, this identification cannot be made with any certainty (Donner 1957: 170; Saggs 1955: 152). For ND 2686 and ND 2715, see Saggs (1955: 127–31).

40. Oded (1979: 182–85; cf. Eph'al 1982: 149 n. 514), arguing primarily from the cylinder accounts of Assurbanipal's campaign against the Qedarite Arabs, has claimed that Assyrian troops were stationed in garrisons from Damascus south to the Hejaz. As Bienkowski (1992c: 3–5; 2000: 48–52) points out, the permanent stationing of troops in Ammon, Moab, and Edom is not at all clear from these texts. Indeed, given that Kamashaltu of Moab is credited with defeating Ammuladi the Qedarite leader in Cylinder B, while Assurbanipal takes credit for the victory in his "Letter to Assur," it is possible that references to "My troops" in these texts could be a reference to the troops of client kingdoms (Bienkowski 1992c: 4). In any case, there is little to indicate direct or extensive involvement on the part of Assyria in the day-to-day affairs of Moab. ND 2773 (Saggs 1955: 131–33) is problematic as evidence for such involvement, since it is not clear if the person reporting the slaughter of Moabite citizens is a Dibonite (hence local), a Tabalite (hence from a presumed Assyrian province), or a Tafilaite (and hence an Edomite); and only the final correspondent (Qurdi-Assur) is clearly either an Assyrian or an official. All it does show is a possible regional hierarchy for communication between Assyria and Moab (i.e., Moab-Tab'al-Tyre-Nimrud; or alternately Moab-Tyre-Nimrud). On the interpretation of ND 2773, see Donner (1957: 171–72); Mazar (1957: 237–38); Mittmann (1973); Oded (1970: 180); Saggs (1955: 132); Timm (1989: 324–26).

41. Note, for example, that in ND 2715 (Saggs 1955: 127–30) the people of Sidon (?) were free to cut wood in Mt. Lebanon, but they were not allowed to sell it to the Egyptians or Philistines.

42. ND2765 (Saggs 1955: 134–35; Cogan 1974: 118) records the Moabite *serani* delivering horses. BrM K 1295 (Waterman 1930: no. 632; Pritchard 1969: 301) records the delivery of one mina of gold from Moab. ADD 928 (Johns 1898: no.928; Postgate 1974: 309–11) records what context would suggest is the delivery of silver (objects?) from Moab.

43. This conclusion contrasts with that of Jankowska (1969: 275), who argues that Assyrian tribute lists point to regional specialization in production.

44. Halpern's use of archaeological data to demonstrate the decline of extended families and a new focus on the individual is particularly problematic. Late Iron II cooking pots do not simply get smaller as a reflection of family size (Halpern 1991: 71). Through the length of the Iron Age one finds both large, wide-mouthed cooking pots and small, narrow-mouthed cooking pots. The large form becomes uncommon during the seventh–sixth centuries, while the small form (in many cases) shows evidence of a technological shift from thick, calcite-tempered wares aimed at dissipating thermal-induced cracking through the proliferation of voids, to thin, silicate-tempered wares aimed at resisting thermal-induced cracking at its onset. These paired changes seem to reflect cooking practices or cuisine, rather than simply the volume of food prepared. As for the spread of bench tombs, with their apparently individuating features (Halpern 1991: 71–73), one should remember that those for which in situ skeletal remains are reported still tend to contain dozens of bodies (see Bloch-Smith 1992).

45. In the case of Judah, this is a rather complex issue as the Bible in its anti-monarchic moments also presents a counterhegemony to that of the Iron Age state (e.g., YHWH is king, Israel is a nation of priests, etc.), one which makes sense in the aftermath of exile and state collapse. Hence, Halpern folds into the seventh century some aspects of biblical thought that are traditionally seen as responses to exile and/or the theocratic organization of the province of Yehud within the Persian Empire.

46. Here it is important to recognize with Bourdieu (1989) that "class" is not a group of people per se; rather, it is a relational structure that people constitute and inhabit through common dispositions and repeated practices.

47. For Egypt and Ekron (?) this is witnessed in the Adon letter (Porten 1981), while for Babylonia and Judah one might cite 2 Kings 24:1.

48. As the cuneiform text has proven itself too eroded to be successfully read.

Chapter 10. Once Again, the State

Milan Kundera, *The Unbearable Lightness of Being,* trans. Michael Henry Heim (New York: Harper and Row, 1984), 2.

Abbreviations

AAA	American Anthropological Association.
AA	*American Anthropologist.*
AASOR	*Annual of the American Schools of Oriental Research.*
ÄAT	Ägypten und Altes Testament.
ABD	*The Anchor Bible Dictionary.* 7 vols. Ed. David Noel Freedman. Garden City, N.Y.: Doubleday.
ADAJ	*Annual of the Department of Antiquities of Jordan.*
AfO	*Archiv für Orientforschung.*
AJ	*The Archaeology of Jordan.* Ed. Burton MacDonald, Russell Adams, and Piotr Bienkowski. Sheffield: Sheffield Academic Press, 2001.
AJ II 1	*Archaeology of Jordan II1. Field Reports: Surveys and Sites A-K.* Ed. Denyse Homès-Fredericq and J.Basil Hennessy. Leuven: Peeters, 1989.
AJ II 2	*Archaeology of Jordan II 2. Field Reports: Sites L-Z,.* Ed. Denyse Homès-Fredericq and J. Basil Hennessy. Leuven: Peeters, 1989.
AJB	*The Archaeology of Jordan and Beyond: Essays in Honor of James A. Sauer.* Ed. Lawrence E. Stager, Joseph A. Greene, and Michael D. Coogan. SAHL 1. Winona Lake, Ind.: Eisenbrauns, 2000.
Al-Ansâb	*Al-Ansâb: La Quête des origines: Anthropologie historique de la société tribale arabe.* Ed. Pierre Bonte, Édouard Conte, Constant Hamès, and Abdel Ould Cheikh. Paris: Éditions de la Maison des Sciences de l'Homme, 1991.
Ammon	*Ancient Ammon,* Ed. Burton MacDonald and Randall Younker. SHCANE 17. Leiden: Brill, 1999.
AOAT	Alter Orient und Altes Testament.
ARA	*Annual Review of Anthropology.*
Architecture	*The Architecture of Ancient Israel.* Ed. Aharon Kempinski and Ronny Reich. Jerusalem: IES, 1992.
AS	*Archaic States.* Ed. Gary M. Feinman and Joyce Marcus. Santa Fe, N.M.: School of American Research Press, 1998.
ASHL	*The Archaeology of Society in the Holy Land.* Ed. Thomas Levy. New York: Facts on File, 1995.
Assyria	*1995 Assyria 1995: Proceedings of the Tenth Anniversary Symposium.* Ed. Simo Parpola and Robert M. Whiting. Helsinki: Neo-Assyrian Text Corpus Project.
AUSS	*Andrews University Seminary Studies.*
BA	*Biblical Archaeologist.*

BAR	*Biblical Archaeology Review.*
BASOR	*Bulletin of the American Schools of Oriental Research.*
BN	*Biblische Notizen.*
CA	*Current Anthropology.*
CANE	*Civilizations of the Ancient Near East.* 3 vols. Ed. Jack M. Sasson. New York: Scribner's, 1995.
CHANE	Culture and History of the Ancient Near East.
CMAO	Contributi e Materiali di Archeologia Orientale.
EEM	*Early Edom and Moab: The Beginning of the Iron Age in Southern Jordan.* Ed. Piotr Bienkowski. Sheffield: J. R. Collis, 1992.
EI	*Eretz-Israel.*
FNM	*From Nomadism to Monarchy: Archaeological and Historical Aspects of Early Israel.* Ed. Israel Finkelstein and Nadav Na'aman. Jerusalem: IES/Yad Izhak Ben-Zvi, 1994.
HANES	History of the Ancient Near East Studies.
HSM	Harvard Semitic Monographs.
IEJ	*Israel Exploration Journal.*
IES	*Israel Exploration Society.*
IFAO	Institut Français d'Archéologie Orientale.
JAA	*Journal of Anthropological Archaeology.*
JAOS	*Journal of the American Oriental Society.*
JBL	*Journal of Biblical Literature.*
JEA	*Journal of Egyptian Archaeology.*
JESHO	*Journal of the Economic and Social History of the Orient.*
JFA	*Journal of Field Archaeology.*
JNES	*Journal of Near Eastern Studies.*
JRAI	*Journal of the Royal Anthropological Institute.*
JRAS	*Journal of the Royal Asiatic Society.*
JSOT	*Journal for the Study of the Old Testament.*
JSOT Suppl.	Supplement to the *Journal for the Study of the Old Testament.*
JSSEA	*Journal of the Society for the Study of Egyptian Antiquities.*
MANE	Monographs on the Ancient Near East.
MMA	Monographs in Mediterranean Archaeology.
NEA	*Near Eastern Archaeology.*
OBO	Orbis Biblicus Orientalis.
OEANE	*The Oxford Encyclopedia of Archaeology in the Near East.* 5 vols. Ed. Eric Meyers. New York: Oxford University Press, 1997.
OIP	Oriental Institute Publications.
Origins	*Origins of the State: The Anthropology of Political Evolution,* ed. Ronald Cohen and Elman Service. Philadelphia: Institute for the Study of Human Issues, 1978.
PEFA	*Palestine Exploration Fund Annual.*
PEFQS	*Palestine Exploration Fund Quarterly Statement.*
PEQ	*Palestine Exploration Quarterly.*
PP	*Power and Propaganda: A Symposium on Ancient Empires.* Ed. Mogens Larsen. Mesopotamia 7. Copenhagen: Akademisk Forlag.
PRSF	*Power Relations and State Formation.* Ed. Thomas Patterson and Christine Gailey Washington, D.C.: AAA, 1987
RA	*Revue d'assyriologie et d'archéologie oriental.*
RB	*Revue Biblique.*
RLA	*Reallexicon der Assyriologie und Vorderasiatischen Archäologie.*
SAHL	Harvard Semitic Museum Publications—Studies in the Archaeology and History of the Levant.

SAIAIJ	*Studies in the Archaeology of the Iron Age in Israel and Jordan.* Ed. Amihai Mazar. *JSOT* Suppl. 331. Sheffield: Sheffield Academic Press, 2001.
SHAJ	*Studies in the History and Archaeology of Jordan.*
SHCANE	Studies in the History and Culture of the Ancient Near East.
SIMA	Studies in Mediterranean Archaeology.
SMIM	*Studies in the Mesha Inscription and Moab.* Ed. A. Dearman. Atlanta: Scholars Press, 1989.
State/Culture	*State/Culture: State Formation after the Cultural Turn.* Ed. George Steinmetz. Ithaca, N.Y.: Cornell University Press, 1999.
TA	*Tel Aviv.*
TCMP	*Trade, Contact, and the Movement of Peoples in the Eastern Mediterranean: Essays in Honor of J. Basil Hennessy.* Ed. Stephen Bourke and Jean-Paul Descoeudres. Mediterranean Archaeology Suppl. 3. Sydney: MEDITARCH, 1995.
UF	*Ugarit-Forschungen.*
UMM	University Museum Monographs.
VT	*Vetus Testamentum.*
WA	*World Archaeology.*
ZAW	*Zeitschrift für die alttestamentliche Wissenschaft.*
ZDPV	*Zeitschrift des Deutschen Palästina-Vereins.*

References

Abou-Assaf, Ali
1980 Unterschungen zur Ammonitischen Rundbildkunst. *UF* 12: 7–102.
Abou-Assaf, Ali, Pierre Bordreuil, and Alan R. Millard
1982 *La Statue de Tell Fekherye et sa bilingue assyro-araméenne.* Paris: Éditions Recherche sur les Civilisations.
Abrams, Philip
1988 (1977) Notes on the Difficulty of Studying the State. *Journal of Historical Sociology* 1 (1): 58–89.
Abu-Lughod, Lila
1986 *Veiled Sentiments: Honor and Poetry in a Bedouin Society.* Berkeley: University of California Press.
1989 Zones of Theory in the Anthropology of the Arab World. *ARA* 18: 267–306.
Abu-Taleb, Mohammed
1985 The Seal of *plty ben m's* the Mazkîr. *ZDPV* 101: 21–29.
Adams, Robert McCormick
1978 Strategies of Maximization, Stability, and Resilience in Mesopotamian Society, Settlement, and Agriculture. *Proceedings of the American Philosophical Society* 22: 329–35.
2001 Complexity in Archaic States. *Journal of Anthropological Archaeology* 20: 345–60.
Agar-und Hydrotechnik GMBH
1977 *National Water Master Plan of Jordan.* Vol 3. Amman: Natural Resources Authority.
Aharoni, Yohanan
1979 *The Land of the Bible: A Historical Geography.* 2nd ed. Trans. Anson Rainey. Philadelphia: Westminster.
1981 *Arad Inscriptions.* Ed. Anson Rainey. Jerusalem: IES.
Ahlström, Ghösta
1982 *Royal Administration and National Religion in Ancient Palestine.* SHCANE 1. Leiden: Brill.
Albright, William Foxwell
1939 The Israelite Conquest in the Light of Archaeology. *BASOR* 74: 11–22.
1943 Two Little Understood Amarna Letters from the Middle Jordan Valley. *BASOR* 89: 7–17.
1949 *The Archaeology of Palestine.* London: Penguin Books.
Allen, Mitchell
1997 Contested Peripheries: Philistia in the Neo-Assyrian World-System. Ph.D. dissertation, UCLA.

Alonso, Ana
  1994 The Politics of Space, Time, and Substance: State Formation, Nationalism, and Ethnicity. *ARA* 23: 379–405.
Alt, Albrecht
  1940 Emiter und Moabiter. *Palästina Jahrbuch* 36: 29–43.
  1966 (1930) The Settlement of the Israelites in Palestine. Pp. 135–69 in *Essays on Old Testament History and Religion.* Oxford: Blackwell.
Amiran, Ruth and Immanuel Dunyavesky
  1958 The Assyrian Open-Court Building and its Palestinian Derivatives. *BASOR* 149: 25–32.
'Amr, Abdel-Jalil
  1990 Four Ammonite Sculptures from Jordan. *ZDPV* 107: 158–67.
van Andel, Tjeerd, Eberhard Zangger, and Anne Demitack
  1990 Land Use and Soil Erosion in Prehistoric and Historical Greece. *JFA* 17 (4): 379–96.
Andersen, Francis
  1966 Moabite Syntax. *Orientalia* 35: 81–120.
Anderson, Perry
  1974 *Passages from Antiquity to Feudalism.* London: New Left Books.
  1976–77 The Antinomies of Antonio Gramsci. *New Left Review* 100: 5–78.
Antoun, Richard
  1972 *Arab Village: A Social Structural Study of a Transjordnian Peasant Community* . Bloomington: Indiana University Press.
Appadurai, Arjun
  1986 Introduction: Commodities and the Politics of Value. Pp. 3–63 in *The Social Life of Things: Commodities in Cultural Perspective.* Ed. Arjun Appadurai. Philadelphia: University of Pennsylvania Press.
Applebaum, Shimon, Shimon Dar, and Ze'ev Safrai
  1978 The Towers of Samaria. *PEQ* 110: 91–100.
Arav, Rami and Monika Bernett
  2000 The *bît-ḫilani* at Bethsaida: Its Place in Aramean/Neo-Hittite and Israelite Palace Architecture in the Iron Age II. *IEJ* 50 (1–2): 47–81.
Archer, Margaret
  1996 Social Integration and System Integration: Developing the Distinction. *Sociology* 30 (4): 679–99.
Ariel, Donald, ed.
  2000 *Excavations at the City of David 1978–1985, Directed by Yigal Shiloh.* Vol. 6, *Inscriptions.* Qedem 41. Jeusalem: Hebrew University.
Arnon, Itzhak
  1972 *Crop Production in Dry Regions.* Volume II, *Systematic Treatment of the Principal Crops.* London: Leonard Hill.
Asad, Talal
  1975 Anthropological Texts and Ideological Problems: An Analysis of Cohen on Arab Villages in Israel. *Economy and Society* 4 (3): 251–82.
  1979 Equality in Nomadic Social Systems? Notes Towards the Dissolution of an Anthropological Category. Pp. 419–28 in *Pastoral Production and Society,* ed. Équipe écologie et anthropologie des sociétés pastorales. Cambridge: Cambridge University Press.
  1992 Conscripts of Western Civilization. Pp. 333–52 in *Dialectical Anthropology: Essays in Honor of Stanley Diamond,* vol. 1, ed. Christine Gailey. Gainesville: University Press of Florida.

Astour, Michael
    1995 Overland Trade Routes in Western Asia. Pp. 1401–20 in *CANE* Vol. 3.
    1999 The Ḫapiru in the Amarna Texts. *UF* 31: 31–50.
Atran, Scott
    1986 Hamula Organisation and Masha'a Tenure in Palestine. *Man* 21 (2): 271–95.
Aubet, Maria
    1993 *The Phoenicians and the West.* Cambridge: Cambridge University Press.
Auffret, Pierre
    1980 Essai sur la structure littéraire de la stèle de Mésha. *UF* 12: 109–124.
Aufrecht, Walter
    1989 *A Corpus of Ammonite Inscriptions.* Lewiston, N.Y.: Edwin Mellen Press.
Avigad, Nahman and Benjamin Sass
    1997 *Corpus of West Semitic Stamp Seals.* Jerusalem: IES.
Avishur, Yitshak and Michael Heltzer
    2000 *Studies on the Royal Administration in Ancient Israel in the Light of Epigraphic Sources.* Tel Aviv: Archaeological Center Publications.
Avitz-Singer, Lily
    1999 Beersheba—A Gateway Community in Southern Arabian Long-Distance Trade in the Eighth Century B.C.E. *TA* 26: 3–74.
Badawy, Alexander
    1954 *A History of Egyptian Architecture.* Cairo: Imprimérie Urwand.
Bagnall, Roger and Bruce Frier
    1994 *The Demography of Roman Egypt.* Cambridge: Cambridge University Press.
Baines, John
    1996 Contextualizing Egyptian Representations of Society and Ethnicity. Pp. 339–84 in *The Study of the Ancient Near East in the 21st Century*, ed. Jerrold Cooper and Glenn Schwartz. Winona Lake, Ind.: Eisenbrauns.
Banning, Edward
    1985 Peasants, Pastoralists, and *Pax Romana*: Mutualism in the Southern Highlands of Jordan. *BASOR* 261: 25–50.
    1992 Towers. Pp. 622–24 in *ABD,* vol. 6.
Bär, Jürgen
    1996 *Der assyrische Tribut und seine Darstellung.* AOAT Band 243. Vluyn: Butzon & Bercker Kevelaer.
Bartlett, John
    1978 The Conquest of Sihon's Kingdom: A Literary Re-Examination. *JBL* 97: 347–51.
Baruch, Uzi
    1986 The Late Holocene Vegetational History of Lake Kinneret (Sea of Galilee), Israel. *Paléorient* 12 (2): 37–48.
    1990 Palynological Evidence of Human Impact on the Vegetation as Recorded in Late Holocene Lake Sediments in Israel. Pp. 283–93 in *Man's Role in the Shaping of the Eastern Mediterranean Landscape*, ed. Sytze Bottema, G. Entjes Nieborg, and Willem van Zeist. Rotterdam: Balkema.
    2000 A Thesis on Agency. Pp. 61–68 in *Agency in Archaeology*, ed. Marcia-Anne Dobres and John Robb. New York: Routledge.
    2001 Agency, the Duality of Structure, and the Problem of the Archaeological Record. Pp. 141–64 in *Archaeological Theory Today*, ed. Ian Hodder. Cambridge: Polity Press.
Bawden, Garth
    1989 The Andean State as a State of Mind. *Journal of Anthropological Research* 45: 327–32.

Beal, Richard
1992 *The Organization of the Hittite Military*. Texte der Hethiter 20. Heidelburg: Winter.
Beaulieu, Paul-Alain
1989 *The Reign of Nabonidus King of Babylon, 556–539 B.C.E.* New Haven, Conn.:
Yale University Press.
Beeston, Alfred
1985 Mesha and Ataroth. *JRAS* (2): 143–48.
Beetham, David
1991 *The Legitimation of Power*. Atlantic Highlands, N.J.: Humanities Press
International.
Beidelman, Thomas
1989 Agnostic Exchange: Homeric Reciprocity and the Heritage of Simmel and
Mauss. *Cultural Anthropology* 4 (3): 227–59.
Beit-Arieh, Itzak and Bruce Cresson
1991 Horvat Uza: A Fortified Outpost on the Eastern Negev Border. *BA* 54: 126–35.
Bellamy, Richard and Darrow Schecter
1993 *Gramsci and the Italian State*. Manchester: Manchester University Press.
Ben-David, Chaim
2003 The "Ascent to Luhith" and the "Road to Horonaim": New Evidence for
Their Identification. *PEQ* 133 (2): 136–44.
Bender, Friedrich
1974 *Geology of Jordan*. Trans. Moh'd Kamal Khdeir, David H. Parker, and U.
Wilkening. Berlin: Gebrüder Borntraeger.
Bendor, Shunia
1996 *The Social Structure of Ancient Israel*. Jerusalem: Simor.
Ben Dov, Meir
1994 A Fragmentary First Temple Period Hebrew Inscription from the Ophel.
Pp. 73–75 in *Ancient Jerusalem Revealed*, ed. Hillel Geva. Jerusalem: IES.
Benedettucci, Francesco
1998 The Iron Age. Pp. 110–27 in *Mount Nebo: New Archaeological Excavation,
1967–1997*, ed. Michèle Piccirillo and Eugenio Alliata. Jerusalem: Studium
Biblicum Franciscanum.
Bennett, Crystal
1974 Excavations at Buseirah, Southern Jordan, 1972: Preliminary Report.
Levant 6: 1–24.
1975 Excavations at Buseirah, Southern Jordan, 1973: Third Preliminary Report.
Levant 7: 1–19.
1977 Excavations at Buseirah, Southern Jordan, 1974: Fourth Preliminary
Report. *Levant* 9: 1–10.
1983 Excavations at Buseirah (Biblical Bozrah). Pp. 9–17 in *Midian, Moab and
Edom: The History and Archaeology of Late Bronze Age and Iron Age Jordan and
North-West Arabia*, ed. John Sawyer and David Clines. *JSOT* Suppl. 24. Sheffield:
JSOT Press.
Bennett, Crystal and Piotr Bienkowski
1995 *Excavations at Tawilan in Southern Jordan*. British Academy Monographs in
Archaeology 8. Oxford: Oxford University Press.
Bernett, Monika and Othmar Keel
1998 *Mond, Stier und Kult am Stadttor*. OBO 161. Fribourg/Göttigen: University
Press/Vandenhoeck and Ruprecht.
Betancourt, Philip
1977 *Aeolic Style in Architecture: A Survey of Its Development in Palestine, the
Halikarnassos Peninsula, and Greece, 1000–500 B.C.* Princeton, N.J.: Princeton
University Press.

Bienkowski, Piotr
1990 Umm al-Biyara, Tawilan, and Buseirah in Retrospect. *Levant* 22: 91–109.
1992a The Beginning of the Iron Age in Edom: A Reply to Finkelstein. *Levant* 24: 167–69.
1992b The Date of Sedentary occupation in Edom: Evidence from Umm el-Biyara, Tawilan and Buseirah. Pp. 99–112 in *EEM*.
1992c The Beginning of the Iron Age in Southern Jordan: A Framework. Pp. 1–12 in *EEM*.
1995a Observations on Late Bronze-Iron Age Sites in the Wadi Hasa, Jordan. *Levant* 27: 29–37.
1995b The Architecture of Edom. *SHAJ* 5: 135–43.
2000 Transjordan and Assyria. Pp. 44–58 in *AJB*.
2001a The Iron Age and Persian Periods in Jordan. *SHAJ* 7: 265–74.
2001b The Persian Period. Pp. 347–65 in *AJ*.
Bienkowski, Piotr and Russell Adams
1999 Soundings at Ash-Shorabat and Khirbet Dubab in the Wadi Hasa, Jordan: The Pottery. *Levant* 31: 149–72.
Bienkowski, Piotr, Russell Adams, R.A. Philpott, and Leonie Sedman
1997 Soundings at Ash-Shorabat and Khirbet Dubab in the Wadi Hasa, Jordan: The Stratigraphy. *Levant* 29: 41–70.
Bienkowski, Piotr, Crystal Bennett and Marta Balla
2002 *Busayra: Excavations by Crystal-M. Bennett 1971–1980.* British Academy Monographs in Archaeology 13. Oxford: Oxford University Press
Bienkowski, Piotr and Eveline van der Steen
2001 Tribes, Trade, and Towns: A New Framework for the Late Iron Age in Southern Jordan and the Negev. *BASOR* 323: 21–47.
Bikai, Pierre
1993 Excavations at Khirbet Salameh. *ADAJ* 37: 521–32.
Bintliff, John
1992 Erosion in the Mediterranean Lands. Pp. 125–31 in *Past and Present Soil Erosion: Archaeological and Geographical Perspectives*, ed. Martin Bell and John Boardman. Oxford: Oxbow Monographs.
Biran, Avraham
1994 *Biblical Dan.* Jerusalem: IES.
Biran, Avraham and Joseph Naveh
1993 An Aramaic Stele Frament from Tel Dan. *IEJ* 43(2–3): 81–98.
1995 The Tel Dan Inscription: A New Fragment. *IEJ* 45: 1–18.
Blanton, Richard
1998 Beyond Centralization: Steps Toward a Theory of Egalitarian Behavior in Archaic States. Pp. 135–72 in *AS*.
Blanton, Richard, Gary M. Feinman, Stephen Kowalewski, and Peter Peregrine
1996 A Dual-Processual Theory for the Evolution of Mesoamerican Civilization. *CA* 37 (1): 1–14.
Bleiberg, Edward
1996 *The Official Gift in Ancient Egypt.* Norman: University of Oklahoma Press.
Bloch-Smith, Elizabeth
1992 *Judahite Burial Practices and Beliefs about the Dead. JSOT* Suppl. 123. Sheffield: Sheffield Academic Press.
Bodine, Walter, ed.
1995 *Discourse Analysis of Biblical Literature.* Atlanta: Scholars Press.
Bonte, Pierre
1991 Égalité et hiérarchie dans une tribu maure: Les Awlâd Qaylân de l'Adrar mauritanien. Pp. 145–99 in *Al-Ansâb*.

1994 Manière de dire ou manière de faire: Peut-on parler d'un mariage "arabe"? Pp. 371–98 in *Épouser au plus proche: Inceste, prohibitions, et stratégies matrimoniales autour de la Méditerranée*, ed. Pierre Bonte. Paris: Éditions de l'École des Hautes Études en Sciences Sociales.

2000 L'Échange est-il un universel? *L'Homme* 154–55: 39–66.

Bonte, Pierre and Édouard Conte
1991 Le Tribu arabe: Approches anthropologiques et orientalistes. Pp. 13–50 in *Al-Ansâb*. Bonte, Pierre, Édouard Conte, and Paul Dresch

2001 Introduction. Pp. 17–51 in *Émirs et présidents: Figures de la parenté et du politique dans le monde arabe*, ed. Pierree Bonte, Édouard Conte and Paul Dresch. Paris: Éditions du CNRS.

Bordreuil, Pierre and Dennis Pardee
1990 Le Papyrus du Marzeah. *Semitica* 38: 49–68.

2000 Épigraphie moabitique—Nouvel examen du "Papyrus du Marzeah." *Semitica* 50: 224–26.

Bordreuil, Pierre, Felice Israel, and Dennis Pardee
1998 King's Command and Widow's Plea: Two New Hebrew Ostraca of the Biblical Period. *NEA* 61: 2–13.

Borger, Rykle
1956 *Die Inschriften Asarhaddons Königs von Assyrien*. AfO Beiheft 9. Graz: Self-Published.

1996 *Beiträge zum Inschriftenwerk Assurbanipals*. Wiesbaden: Harrassowitz.

Borger, Rykle and Hayim Tadmor
1982 Zwei Beiträge zur Alttestamentlichen Wissenschaft Aufgrund der Inschriften Tiglathpilesers III. *ZAW* 94: 244–51.

Bottéro, Jean
1954 *Le Problème des Ḫabiru*. Cahiers de la Société Asiatique 12. Paris: Imprimérie Internationale.

1972 Ḫabiru. *RLA* 4 (1): 14–27.

Bourdieu, Pierre
1970 The Berber House or the World Reversed. *Social Science Information* 9: 151–70.

1977 *Outline of a Theory of Practice*. Trans. Richard Nice. Cambridge: Cambridge University Press.

1989 Social Space and Symbolic Power. *Sociological Theory* 7 (1): 14–25.

1999 Rethinking the State: Genesis and Structure of the Bureaucratic Field. Pp. 53–75 in *State/Culture*.

Bourke, Stephen
1997 Pre-Classical Pella in Jordan: A Conspectus of Ten Years' Work (1985–1995). *PEQ* 129: 94–115.

2002 Excavating Pella in Jordan's Migdal Temple: The 2001 Field Season. Paper read at the Third International Congress on the Archaeology of the Ancient Near East, Paris.

Bourke, Stephen and Rachael Sparks
1995 The DAJ Excavations at Pella in Jordan 1963/64. Pp. 149–67 in *TCMP*.

Bourke, Stephen, Rachel Sparks, Karen N. Sowada, and L. D. Mairs
1994 Preliminary Report on the University of Sydney's Fourteenth Season of Excavations at Pella (Tabaqat Fahl) in 1992. *ADAJ* 38: 81–126.

Bourke, Stephen, Rachel Sparks, Karen N. Sowada, P. Bruce McLaren, and L. D. Mairs
1998 Preliminary Report on the University of Sydney's Sixteenth and Seventeenth Season of Excavations at Pella (Tabaqat Fahl) in 1994/95. *ADAJ* 42: 179–211.

Bradburd, Daniel
1987 Tribe, State, and History in Southwest Asia: A Review. *Nomadic Peoples* 23: 57–71.
Braemer, Frank
1982 *L'Architecture domestique du Levant a l'Âge du Fer*. Paris: Éditions Recherche sur les Civilisations.
1992 Occupation de sol dans la région de Jérash aux périodes de Bronze Récent et du Fer. *SHAJ* 4: 191–98.
Brandl, Baruch
1985 A Proto-Aeolic Capital from Gezer. *IEJ* 34: 173–76.
Briant, Pierre
1982 *État et pasteurs au moyen-orient ancien*. Cambridge: Cambridge University Press.
Brichto, Herbert
1973 Kin, Cult, Land, and Afterlife: A Biblical Complex. *Hebrew Union College Annual* 44: 1–54.
Brinkman, John
1979 Babylonia Under the Assyrian Empire, 745–627 B.C. Pp. 223–50 in *PP*.
1980 Kassiten. *RLA* 5: 464–73.
Bron, François
1979 *Recherches sur les inscriptions phéniciennes de Karatepe*. Geneva: Droz.
Brown, Francis, Samuel Driver, and Charles A. Briggs
1979 *The New Brown-Driver-Briggs-Gesenius Hebrew and English Lexicon*. Peabody, Mass.: Hendrickson.
Brown, Robin
1992 Late Islamic Ceramic Production and Distribution in the Southern Levant: A Socio-Economic and Political Interpretation. Ph.D. Dissertation, State University of New York at Binghamton.
Bruins, Hendrik
1986 *Desert Environment and Agriculture in the Central Negev and Kadesh-Barnea During Historical Times*. Nijkerk: MIDBAR Foundation.
Bruins, Hendrik, Johannes van Plicht and Amihai Mazar
2003 [14]C Dates from Tel Rehov: Iron-Age Chronology, Pharaohs and Hebrew Kings. *Science* 300: 315–18.
Brunner-Traut, Emma
1980 Lotos. Pp. 1091–95 in *Lexicon der Ägyptologie*. Band 3. Wiesbaden: Harrassowitz.
Buci-Glucksmann, Christine
1980 *Gramsci and the State*. Trans. David Fernbach. London: Lawrence and Wishart.
Buddenhagen, Ivan
1990 Legumes in Farming Systems in Mediterranean Climates. Pp. 3–29 in *The Role of Legumes in the Farming Systems of the Mediterranean Areas*, ed. Ahmed Osman, M. M. Ibrahim, and Michael Jones. Dordrecht: Kluwer.
Bunimovitz, Shlomo
1994 The Problem of Human Resources in Late Bronze Age Palestine and Its Socioeconomic Implications. *UF* 26:1–20.
1995 On the Edge of Empires—Late Bronze Age (1500–1200 B.C.E.). Pp. 320–31 in *ASHL*.
Bunnens, Guy, ed.
2000 *Essays on Syria in the Iron Age*. Ancient Near Eastern Studies Suppl. 7. Louvain: Peeters.
Burch, Thomas
1972 Some Demographic Determinants of Average Household Size: An

Analytical Approach. Pp. 91–102 in *Household and Family in Past Time*, ed. Peter Laslett and Richard Wall. Cambridge: Cambridge University Press.

Calhoun, Craig, Edward LiPuma, and Moishe Postone, eds.
1993 *Bourdieu: Critical Perspectives*. Chicago: University of Chicago Press.

Çambel, Halet
1999 *Corpus of Hieroglyphic Luwian Inscriptions*. Vol. 2. New York: Walter de Gruyter.

Canova, Reginetta
1954 *Iscrizioni e monumenti protocristiani del paese di Moab*. Rome: Pontifico Instituto di Archeologia Cristiana.

Carneiro, Robert
1978 Political Expansion as an Expression of the Principle of Competitive Exclusion. Pp. 205–23 in *Origins*.

Carrier, James, ed.
1995 *Occidentalism: Images of the West*. Oxford: Clarendon Press.

Carter, Elizabeth, Bruce Zuckerman, and Stephen Kaufman
1998 The Incirli Stela. *www.humnet.ucla.edu/humnet/nelc/stelasite/stelainfo.html*.

Cassin, Elena
1987 *Le Semblable et le différent: Symbolismes du pouvoir dans le Proche-Orient ancien*. Paris: Dècouverte.

Caton, Steven
1987 Power, Persuasion, and Language: A Critique of the Segmentary Model in the Middle East. *International Journal of Middle Eastern Studies* 19: 77–102.
1990 *"Peaks of Yemen I Summon": Poetry as Cultural Practice in a North Yemeni Tribe*. Berkeley: University of California Press.

Cavigneaux, Antoine and Bahija Ismail
1990 Die Statthalter von Suhu und Mari im 8 Jhr. v. Chr. *Baghdader Mitteilungen* 21: 321–411.

Černý, Jaroslav
1956 *Graffiti hiéroglyphiques et hiératiques de la nécropole thébaine*. Cairo: IFAO.
1958 Stela of Ramses II from Beisan. *EI* 5: 72–82.

Chadwick, Robert, P. M. Michèle Daviau, and Margreet Steiner
2000 Four Seasons of Excavations at Khirbat al-Mudayna on Wadi ath-Thamad, 1996–1999. *ADAJ* 44: 257–70.

Chaney, Marvin
1989 Bitter Bounty: The Dynamics of Political Economy Critiqued by the Eighth-Century Prophets. Pp. 15–30 in *Reformed Faith and Economics*, ed. Robert Stivers. Lanham, Md.: University Press of America.
1999 Whose Sour Grapes? The Addressees of Isaiah 5: 1–7 in the Light of Political Economy. *Semeia* 87: 105–22.

Chatterjee, Partha
1990 A Response to Taylor's "Modes of Civil Society." *Public Culture* 3 (1): 119.

Cherry, John, Jack Davis and Eva Mantzourani
1991 The Towers of Northwest Keos. Pp. 285–298 in *Landscape Archaeology as Long-term History: Northern Keos in the Cycladic Islands from Earliest Settlement Until Modern Times*, ed. John Cherry, Jack Davis, and Eva Mantzourani. Los Angeles: UCLA Institute of Archaeology.

Chesson, Meredith
1999 Libraries of the Dead: Early Bronze Age Charnel Houses and Social Identity at Urban Bab edh-Dhra', Jordan. *JAA* 18: 137–64.

Christopherson, Gary
2000 In Pursuit of the Longue Durée: Using a Geographic Information System to Model Archaeological Settlement Patterns in the Region of Tell el-'Umeiri, Jordan. Ph.D. Dissertation, University of Arizona.

Christopherson, Gary and D. Philip Guertin
  1995 Soil Erosion, Agricultural Intensification, and Iron Age Settlement in the
  Region of Tall al-'Umayri, Jordan. Paper read at the ASOR Annual Meeting,
  Philadelphia. www.casa.arizona.edu/MPP/Um_erosion/erosion_pap.html
Cifarelli, Megan
  1995 Enmity, Alienation, and Assyrianization: The Role of Cultural Difference
  in the Visual and Verbal Expression of Assyrian Ideology in the Reign of
  Ashurnasirpal II (883–859 B.C.). Ph.D. Dissertation, Columbia University.
Claessen, Henri, and Peter Skalnik
  1978 *The Early State.* The Hague: Mouton.
Clark, Geoffrey, Michael Neely, Burton MacDonald, Joseph Schuldenrein, and
  Khairieh 'Amr
  1992 The Wādî al-Ḥasa Paleolithic Project—1992: Preliminary Report. *ADAJ* 36:
  13–23.
Clark, Geoffrey, Deborah Olszewski, Joseph Schuldenrein, Nazmieh Rida, and
  James Eighmey.
  1994 Survey and Excavation in Wādî al-Ḥasa: A Preliminary Report of the 1993
  Field Season. *ADAJ* 38: 41–55.
Clastres, Pierre
  1977 *Society Against the State: Essays in Political Anthropology.* Trans. Robert Hurley.
  New York: Urizen Books.
Clemens, David
  2001 *Sources for Ugaritic Ritual and Sacrifices.* AOAT 284. Münster: Ugarit-Verlag.
Clermont-Ganneau, Charles
  1871 Un plan de la Ville de Diban. *Revue archéologie* n.s., 22: 159–60.
  1875 La Stèle de Mésha. *Revue Critique* September 11: 166–74.
Cline, Eric
  1994 *Sailing the Wine-Dark Sea: International Trade and the Late Bronze Aegean.*
  British Archaeological Reports International Series 591. Oxford: Tempus
  Reparatum.
Clines, David
  1972 X, X ben Y, ben Y: Personal Names in Hebrew Narrative Style. *VT* 22: 266–87.
Coale, Ansley and Paul Demeny
  1983 *Regional Model Life Tables and Stable Populations.* 2nd ed. New York: Academic
  Press.
Cogan, Mordechai
  1974 *Imperialism and Religion: Assyria, Judah, and Israel in the Eighth and Seventh
  Centuries B.C.E..* Missoula, Mont.: Scholars Press.
Cogan, Mordechai and Hayim Tadmor
  1988 *II Kings: A New Translation with Introduction and Commentary.* Anchor Bible.
  Garden City, N.Y.: Doubleday.
Cohen, Abner
  1965 *Arab Border-Villages in Israel: A Study of Continuity and Change in Social
  Organization.* Manchester: Manchester University Press.
Cohen, Mark
  1993 *The Cultic Calendars of the Ancient Near East.* Bethesda, Md.: CDL Press.
Cohen, Rudolph
  1983 *Kadesh-Barnea: A Fortress from the Time of the United Monarchy.* Jerusalem:
  Israel Museum.
  1994 The Fortress at 'En Ḥaṣeva. *BA* 57 (4): 203–14.
  1995 Fortresses and Roads in the Negev During the First Temple Period. Pp.
  80–126 in *Eilat: Studies in the Archaeology, History, and Geography of Eilat and the
  Aravah.* Jerusalem: IES (in Hebrew).

Cohen, Rudolph and Yigael Yisrael
  1995a *On the Road to Edom: Discoveries from 'En Ḥazeva.* Jerusalem: The Israel Museum.
  1995b The Iron Age Fortress at 'En Ḥaṣeva. *BA* 58: 223–35.
Comaroff, Jean and John Comaroff
  1991 *Of Revelation and Revolution: Christianity, Colonialism, and Consciousness in South Africa.* Vol.1. Chicago: University of Chicago Press.
  1992 *Ethnography and the Historical Imagination.* Boulder, Colo.: Westview Press.
Conder, Charles
  1889 *Survey of Eastern Palestine.* London: Palestine Exploration Fund.
Cooke, George
  1903 *A Textbook of North-Semitic Inscriptions.* Oxford: Clarendon Press.
Cooper, Frederick and Ann Stoler
  1989 Tensions of Empire: Colonial Control and Visions of Rule. *American Ethnologist* 16(4): 609–21.
Coote, Robert and Keith Whitelam
  1987 *The Emergence of Israel in Historical Perspective.* Sheffield: Almond Press.
Copeland, Lorraine and Claudio Vita-Finzi
  1978 Archaeological Dating of Geological Deposits in Jordan. *Levant* 10: 10–25.
Cordova, Carlos
  1999 Landscape Transformation in the Mediterranean-Steppe Transition Zone of Jordan: A Geoarchaeological Approach. *Arab World Geographer* 2 (3): 182–201.
  2000 Geomorphological Evidence of Intense Prehistoric Soil Erosion in the Highlands of Central Jordan. *Physical Geography* 21 (6): 538–67.
Cornelius, Izak
  1994 *The Iconography of the Canaanite Gods Reshef and Ba'al: Late Bronze and Iron Age I Periods (c. 1500–1000 BCE).* OBO 140. Fribourg: University Press/Vandenhoeck and Ruprecht.
Corrigan, Philip and Derek Sayer
  1985 *The Great Arch.* Oxford: Blackwell.
Crenshaw, James
  1998 *Education in Ancient Israel: Across the Deadening Silence.* Garden City, N.Y.: Doubleday.
Cribb, Roger
  1991 *Nomads in Archaeology.* Cambridge: Cambridge University Press.
Cross, Frank
  1988 Reuben, First-Born of Jacob. *ZAW* 100, Suppl.: 46–66.
  1996 A Papyrus Recording a Divine Legal Decision and the Root *rhq* in Biblical and Near Eastern Legal Usage. Pp. 311–20 in *Texts, Temples and Traditions: A Tribute to Menahem Haran,* ed. Michael V. Fox. Winona Lake, Ind.: Eisenbrauns
Cross, Frank and David Freedman
  1952 *Early Hebrew Orthography: A Study of the Epigraphic Evidence.* New Haven, Conn.: American Oriental Society.
Crowfoot, John
  1934 An Expedition to Balu'ah. *PEFQS:* 76–84.
Crumley, Carole
  1987 A Dialectical Critique of Hierarchy. Pp. 35–56 in *PRSF.*
Crüsemann, Frank
  1996 Human Solidarity and Ethnic Identity: Israel's Self-Definition in the Genealogical System of Genesis. Pp. 57–76 in *Ethnicity and the Bible,* ed. Mark G. Brett. Leiden: Brill.
Currid, John and Avi Navon
  1989 Iron Age Pits and the Lahav (Tell Halif) Grain Storage Project. *BASOR* 273: 67–78.

Dahl, Gudrum and Anders Hjort
   1976 *Having Herds: Pastoral Herd Growth and Household Economy*. Stockholm
      Studies in Social Anthropology 2. Stockholm: Department of Anthropology,
      University of Stockholm.
Dajani, Rafiq
   1964 Iron Age Tombs from Irbed. *ADAJ* 8–9: 99–101.
   1966 Jabal Nuzha Tomb at Amman. *ADAJ* 11: 48–51.
   1970 A Late Bronze -Iron Age Tomb Excavated at Sahab, 1968. *ADAJ* 15: 29–34.
Dalfes, H. Nüzhet, Georges Kukla, and Harvey Weiss, eds.
   1997 *Third Millennium B.C. Climate Change and Old World Collapse*. New York: Springer.
Dalley, Stephanie and Anne Goguel
   1997 The Sela Sculpture: A Neo-Babylonian Rock Relief in Southern Jordan.
      ADAJ 41: 169–76.
Dalley, Stephanie and Nicholas Postgate
   1984 *The Tablets from Fort Shalmaneser*. London: British School of Archaeology in
      Iraq.
Dar, Shimon
   1986 *Landscape and Pattern: An Archaeological Survey of Samaria 800 B.C.E.–636
      C.E.* 2 vols. British Archaeological Reports International Series 308 (i–ii).
      Oxford: British Archaeological Reports.
Darnell, John and Richard Jasnow
   1993 On the Moabite Inscriptions of Ramses II at Luxor Temple. *JNES* 52:
      263–74.
von Dassow, Eva
   1997 Social Stratification of Alalah under the Mittani Empire. Ph.D. Disser-
      tation, New York University.
Daviau, P. M. Michèle
   1997 Moab's Northern Border: Khirbet al-Mudayna on the Wadi ath-Thamad. *BA*
      60 (4): 222–28.
Daviau, P. M. Michèle and Paul-Eugène Dion
   1994 El the God of the Ammonites? The *atef*-Crowned Head from Tell Jawa,
      Jordan. *ZDPV* 110: 158–67.
   2002a Moab Comes to Life. *BAR* 28 (1): 38–49, 63.
   2002b Economy-Related Finds from Khirbat al-Mudayna (Wadi ath-Thamad,
      Jordan). *BASOR* 328: 31–48.
Daviau, P. M. Michèle and Margreet Steiner
   2000 A Moabite Sanctuary at Khirbat al-Mudayna. *BASOR* 320: 1–21.
Davies, Norman de G.
   1903–1908 *The Rock Tombs at Amarna*. 6 vols. London: Egypt Exploration Society.
Davies, Philip
   1998 *Scribes and Schools: The Canonization of the Hebrew Scriptures*. Louisville, Ky.:
      Westminister/John Knox.
Dearman, J. Andrew
   1989 Historical Reconstruction and the Mesha‘ Inscription. Pp.155–210 in *SMIM*.
   1990 The Moabite Sites of Horonaim and Luhith. *PEQ* 122: 41–6.
   1992 Settlement Patterns and the Beginning of the Iron Age in Moab. Pp. 65–75
      in *EEM*.
   1997 Roads and Settlements in Moab. *BA* 60 (4): 205–13.
Deleuze, Gilles
   1992 Postscript on the Socieities of Control. *October* 59: 3–7.
Dever, William
   1991 Archaeological Data on the Israelite Settlement: A Review of Two Recent
      Works. *BASOR* 284: 77–90.

2001 *What Did the Biblical Writers Know and When Did They Know It?* Grand Rapids, Mich.: Eerdmans.

Diakonoff, Igor
1969 Main Features of the Economy in the Monarchies of Ancient Western Asia. Pp. 13–32 in *Third International Conference of Economic History*. Paris: Mouton.

Diamond, Stanley
1974 *In Search of the Primitive: A Critique of Civilization.* New Brunswick, N.J.: Transaction Books.

Diehl, Michael
2000 Some Thoughts on the Study of Hierarchies. Pp. 11– 30 in *Hierarchies in Action: Cui Bono?*, ed. Michael Diehl. Carbondale, Ill.: Center for Archaeological Investigations, Southern Illinois University.

Dietrich, Manfred and Oswald Loretz
1969 Die Soziale Struktur von Alalakh und Ugarit, II. Die Sozialen Gruppen *hupše-namē*, *haniahne-ekū*, und *marjanne* nache Texten aus Alalah IV. *Die Welt des Orient* 5: 57–93.

Digard, Jean-Pierre
1987 Jeux de structures: Segmentarité et pouvoir chez les nomades baxtyâri d'Iran. *L'Homme* 102: 112–53.

Dinçol, Belkis
1994 New Archaeological and Epigraphic Finds from Ivriz: A Preliminary Report. *TA* 21: 117–118.

Dion, Paul-Eugène
1997 *Les Araméens à l'âge du Fer: Histoire politique et structures sociales.* Paris: Gabalda.

Dion, Paul-Eugène and P. M. Michèle Daviau
2000 An Inscribed Incense Altar of Iron Age II at Ḥirbet el-Mudēyine (Jordan). *ZPDV* 116 (1): 1–13, Taf. 1–2.

Dirks, Nicholas
1993 *The Hollow Crown: Ethnohistory of an Indian Kingdom.* 2nd ed. Cambridge: Cambridge University Press.

Dobres, Marcia-Anne and John E. Robb
2000 Agency in Archaeology: Paradigm or Platitude? Pp. 3–18 in *Agency in Archaeology*, ed. Marcia-Anne Dobres and John E. Robb. New York: Routledge.

Domingues, José
2000 Social Integration, System Integration, and Collective Subjectivity. *Sociology* 34 (2): 225–41.

Donahue, Jack
1985 Hydrologic and Topographic Change During and After Early Bronze Occupation at Bab edh-Dhra and Numeira. *SHAJ* 2: 131–40.

Donahue, Jack, Brian Peer, and R. Thomas Schaub
1997 The Southeastern Dead Sea Plain: Changing Shorelines and Their Impact on Settlement Patterns Through Historical Periods. *SHAJ* 6: 127–36.

Donner, Herbert
1957 Neue Quellen zur Geschicte des Staates Moab in der Zweiten Hälfte des 8. Jahrh. v. Chr. *Mitteilungen des Instituts für Orientforschung* 5: 155–84.

Donner, Herbert and Ernst Axel Knauf
1986 Gor es-Safi-Wadi al-Karak. *AfO* 33: 266–67.

Dornemann, Rudolph
1983 *The Archaeology of the Transjordan.* Milwaukee: Milwaukee Public Museum.

Dothan, Trude
1979 *Excavations at the Cemetery of Deir el-Balah.* Qedem 10. Jerusalem: Institute of Archaeology, Hebrew University.

1982 *Philistines and Their Material Culture.* New Haven, Conn.: Yale University Press.

Doughty, Charles
1888 *Travels in Arabia Deserta.* Cambridge: Cambridge University Press.

Drennan, Robert
1996 One for All and All for One: Accounting for Variability Without Losing Sight of Regularities in the Development of Complex Society. Pp. 25–34 in *Emergent Complexity: The Evolution of Intermediate Societies,* ed. Jeanne E. Arnold. Archaeology Series 9. Ann Arbour, Mich.: International Monographs in Prehistory.
2000 Games, Players, Rules, and Circumstances. Pp. 177–96 in *Cultural Evolution: Contemporary Viewpoints,* ed. Gary M. Feinman and Linda Manzanilla. New York: Kluwer/Plenum.

Dresch, Paul
1986 The Significance of the Course Events Take in Segmentary Systems. *American Ethnologist* 13 (2): 309–24.
1988 Segmentation: Its Roots in Arabia and its Flowering Elsewhere. *Cultural Anthropology* 3 (1): 50–67.
1989 *Tribes, Government, and History in Yemen.* Oxford: Clarendon.
2000 Wilderness of Mirrors: Truth and Vulnerability in Middle Eastern Fieldwork. Pp. 109–27 in *Anthropologists in a Wider World,* ed. Paul Dresch, Wendy James, and David Parkin. New York: Berghahn.

Drews, Robert
1993 *The End of the Bronze Age.* Princeton, N.J.: Princeton University Press.

Drinkard, Joel
1989 The Literary Genre of the Mesha' Inscription. Pp. 131–54 in *SMIM.*
2002 The Volute Capitals of Israel and Jordan: A New Look at an Ancient Architectural Feature. *Virtual Karak Resources Project,* www/vkrp/.org/studies/historical/capitals/.

Drioton, Etienne
1933 A Propos de stèle du Balou'a. *RB* 42: 353–65.

Dunnell, Robert
1980 Evolutionary Theory and Archaeology. Pp. 38–99 in *Advances in Archaeological Method and Theory,* ed. Michael Schiffer. New York: Academic Press.

Dussaud, Rene
1912 *Les Monuments palestiniens et judaiques (Musée du Louvre).* Paris: E. Leroux.

Earle, Timothy
2000 Archaeology, Property, and Prehistory. *ARA* 29: 39–60.

Edelman, Diane
1996 Ethnicity and Early Israel. Pp. 25–55 in *Ethnicity and the Bible,* ed. Mark G. Brett. Leiden: Brill

Edens, Christopher and Garth Bawden
1989 History of Taymā' and Hejazi Trade During the First Millennium B.C. *JESHO* 32: 48–103.

Ehrenreich, Robert, Carole Crumley, and Janet Levy, eds.
1995 *Heterarchy and the Analysis of Complex Societies.* Archaeological Papers of the AAA 6. Arlington, Va.: AAA.

Eickelman, Dale
1989 *The Middle East: An Anthropological Approach.* 2nd ed. Englewood Cliffs, N.J.: Prentice-Hall.

al-Eisawi, Daoud
1985 Vegetation in Jordan. *SHAJ* 2: 45–57.

Elat, Moshe
    1982 The Impact of Tribute and Booty on Countries and People Within the
        Assyrian Empire. *AfO* 19: 245–51.
    1991 Phoenician Overland Trade Within the Mesopotamian Empires. Pp. 21–35
        in *Ah, Assyria . . . Studies in Assyrian History and Ancient Near Eastern
        Historiography Presented to Hayim Tadmor*, ed. Mordechai Cogan and Israel
        Eph'al. Jerusalem: Magnes Press.
Elias, Norbert
    1978 *The Civilizing Process*. Vol. 1. *The History of Manners*. Trans. Edmund Jephcott.
        New York: Pantheon Books.
    1982 *The Civilizing Process*. Vol. 2. *State Formation and Civilizations*. Trans. Edmund
        Jephcott. New York: Pantheon Books.
Eph'al, Israel
    1982 *The Ancient Arabs: Nomads on the Borders of the Fertile Crescent Ninth—Fifth
        Centuries B.C.* Jerusalem: Magnes Press.
    1983 On Warfare and Military Control in the Ancient Near Eastern Empires:
        A Research Outline. Pp. 88–106 in *History, Historiography and Interpretation:
        Studies in Biblical and Cuneiform Literature*, ed. Hayim Tadmor and Moshe
        Weinfeld. Jerusalem: Magnes Press.
    1997 Ways and Means to Conquer a City. Pp. 49–53 in *Assyria 1995*.
Eph'al, Israel and Joseph Naveh
    1993 The Jar of the Gate. *BASOR* 289: 59–65.
Erman, Adolf
    1893 Die Denkmal Ramses II in Ostjordanland. *Zeitschrift für Ägyptische Sprache un
        Alterumswissenschaft* 31: 100–101.
Erman, Adolf and Hermann Grapow
    1926 *Wörterbuch de Aegyptischen Sprache*. 6 vols. Leipzig: J. C. Hinrichs.
Esse, Douglas
    1991 *Subsistence, Trade, and Social Change in Early Bronze Age Palestine*. Chicago:
        Oriental Institute.
Evans-Pritchard, Edward E.
    1940 *The Nuer*. Oxford: Clarendon Press.
Fabian, Johannes
    1983 *Time and the Other: How Anthropology Makes Its Object*. New York: Columbia
        University Press.
Falconer, Steven
    1994 Development and Decline of Bronze Age Civilization in the Southern
        Levant: A Reassessment of Urbanism and Ruralism. Pp. 305–33 in *Development
        and Decline in the Mediterranean Bronze Age*, ed. Sturt W. Manning. Sheffield:
        J. R. Collis.
Fales, F. Mario
    1982 The Enemy in Assyrian Royal Inscriptions: "The Moral Judgement." Pp.
        425–35 in *Mesopotamien und seine Nachbarn*, ed. Hans Nissen and Johannes
        Renger. Berlin: Dietrich Reimer.
    1996 An Aramaic Tablet from Tell Shioukh Fawqani, Syria: The Text. *Semitica* 46:
        89–121.
Falsone, Gioacchino
    1989 Da Nimrud a Mozia: Un tipo statuario di stile fenicio egittizzante. *UF* 21:
        153–93.
Fardon, Richard
    1987 "African Ethnogenesis": Limits to the Comparability of Ethnic Phenomena.
        Pp. 168–88 in *Comparative Anthropology*, ed. Ladislav Holy. Oxford: Blackwell.

Faust, Avraham
1999 Differences in Family Structure between Cities and Villages in Iron Age II. *TA* 26: 233–52.
2000 The Rural Community in Ancient Israel During the Iron Age II. *BASOR* 317: 17–39.
Feinman, Gary M.
1998 Scale and Social Organization: Perspectives on the Archaic State. Pp. 95–133 in *AS*.
2000 Cultural Evolutionary Approaches and Archaeology. Pp. 3–14 in *Cultural Evolution: Contemporary Viewpoints*, ed. Gary M. Feinman and Linda Manzanilla. New York: Kluwer/Plenum.
Feinman, Gary M. and Joyce Marcus, eds.
1998 *Archaic States*. Santa Fe: School of American Research Press.
Feldman, Marian
1998 Luxury Goods from Ras-Shamra-Ugarit and their Role in the International Relations of the Eastern Mediterranean and Near East During the Late Bronze Age. Ph.D. Dissertation, Harvard University.
Femia, Joseph
1981 *Gramsci's Political Thought*. Oxford: Clarendon Press.
Field, John
1999 Geoarchaeological Reconnaissance of Wadi Mujib, Jordan. *Geological Society of America Abstracts with Programs* 31.
Finkelstein, Israel
1986 '*Izbet Ṣarṭah: An Early Iron Age Site near Rosh Ha'ayin, Israel.* British Archaeological Reports International Series 299. Oxford: British Archaeological Reports.
1988 *The Archaeology of the Israelite Settlement.* Jerusalem: IES.
1995a The Great Transformation: The "Conquest" of the Highlands Frontiers and the Rise of the Territorial States. Pp. 349–65 in *ASHL*.
1995b *Living on the Fringe*. MMA 6. Sheffield: Sheffield Academic Press.
1996a The Territorial-Political System of Canaan in the Late Bronze Age. *UF* 28: 221–55.
1996b The Archaeology of the United Monarchy. *Levant* 28: 177–87.
1997 Pots and People Revisted: Ethnic Boundaries in the Iron Age. Pp. 216–237 in *The Archaeology of Israel : Constructing the Past, Interpreting the Present*, ed. Neil A. Silberman and David Small. Sheffield: Sheffield Academic Press
1998a From Sherds to History: A Review Article. *IEJ* 48 (1–2): 120–31.
1998b Bible Archaeology or Archaeology of Palestine in the Iron Age? A Rejoinder. *Levant* 30: 167–74.
1999 State Formation in Israel and Judah: A Contrast in Context, a Contrast in Trajectory. *NEA* 62: 35–52.
2000 Omride Architecture. *ZDPV* 116 (2): 114–38.
2001 The Rise of Jerusalem and Judah: The Missing Link. *Levant* 33: 105–15.
Finkelstein, Israel and Nadav Na'aman, eds.
1994 *FNM*.
Finkelstein, Israel and Amos Perevolotsky
1990 Processes of Sedentarization and Nomadization in the History of Sinai and the Negev. *BASOR* 279: 67–88.
Finkelstein, Israel and Eli Piasetsky
2003 Comment on "¹⁴C Dates from Tel Rehov: Iron Age Chronology, Pharaohs and Hebrew Kings." *Science* 302: 586b.
Finkelstein, Israel and Neil A. Silberman
2001 *The Bible Unearthed*. New York: Simon and Schuster.

Fischer, Peter
  1991a A Possible Late Bronze Age Sanctuary at Tell Abu al-Kharaz, Transjordan. *Journal of Prehistoric Religion* 5: 42–47.
  1991b Tell Abu al-Kharaz. The Swedish Jordan Expedition 1989. First Season Preliminary Report from Trial Soundings. *ADAJ* 35: 67–104.
  1993 Tell Abū al-Kharaz. The Swedish Jordan Expedition 191991. Second Season Preliminary Excavation Report. *ADAJ* 37: 279–306.
  1997 *A Late Bronze to Early Iron Age Tomb at Saḥem, Jordan.* Wiesbaden: Harrassowitz.
  1999 Chocolate-on-White Ware: Typology, Chronology, and Provenance: The Evidence from Tell Abu al-Kharaz, Jordan Valley. *BASOR* 313 (1999): 1–29.
Flannery, Kent
  1972 The Cultural Evolution of Civilizations. *Annual Review of Ecology and Systematics* 3: 399–426.
  1998 The Ground Plans of Archaic States. Pp. 15–57 in *AS.*
  1999 Process and Agency in Early State Formation. *Cambridge Archaeological Journal* 9 (1): 3–21.
  2002 Prehistoric Social Evolution. Pp. 225–44 in *Archaeology: Original Readings in Method and Practice,* ed. Peter Peregrine, Carol Ember, and Melvin Ember. Upper Saddle River, N.J.: Prentice-Hall.
Fleming, Daniel
  2000 *Time at Emar: The Cultic Calendar and the Rituals from the Diviner's Archive .* Winona Lake, Ind.: Eisenbrauns.
Fontana, Benedetto
  1993 *Hegemony and Power.* Minneapolis: University of Minnesota Press.
Fortes, Meyer
  1953 The Structure of Unilinear Descent Groups. *AA* 55: 17–41.
Fortes, Meyer and Edward E. Evans-Pritchard, eds.
  1940 *African Political Systems.* Oxford: Oxford University Press
Foucault, Michel
  1977 *Discipline and Punish: The Birth of the Prison.* Trans. Alan Sheridan. New York: Pantheon Books.
  1980 *Power/Knowledge: Selected Interviews and Other Writings.* Ed. Colin Gordon. New York: Pantheon.
  1988 Technologies of the Self. Pp. 16–49 in *Technologies of the Self,* ed. Luther Martin, Huck Gutman, and Patrick Hutton. London: Tavistock.
  1991 Governmentality. Pp. 87–104 in *The Foucault Effect,* ed. Graham Burchell, Colin Gordon, and Peter Miller. Chicago: University of Chicago Press.
  1994 La société disciplinaire en crise. Pp. 532–34 in *Dits et écrits,* vol. 3. Paris: Gallimard.
Fox, Nili
  1996 Royal Officials and Court Families: A New Look at the YLDYM (yeladîm) in 1 Kings 12. *BA* 59: 225–32.
  2000 *In the Service of the King: Officialdom in Ancient Israel and Judah.* Cincinnati: Hebrew Union College.
Fox, Richard G.
  1977 *Urban Anthropology: Cities in Their Cultural Settings.* Englewood Cliffs, N.J.: Prentice-Hall.
Foxhall, Lin
  1998 Cargoes of the Heart's Desire: The Character of Trade in the Archaic Mediterranean World. Pp. 295–310 in *Archaic Greece: New Approaches and New Evidence,* ed. Nick Fisher and Hans van Wees. London: Duckworth.

Frame, Grant
  1989 *Babylonia 689–627 BC: A Political History*. Leiden: Nederlands Institute Istanbul.
Franken, Henrikus J.
  1969 *Excavations at Tell Deir 'Alla I: A Stratigraphical and Analytical Study of the Early Iron Age Pottery*. Documenta et Monumenta Orientis Antiqui 16. Leiden: Brill.
  1992 *Excavations at Tell Deir 'Alla: The Late Bronze Age Sanctuary*. Louvain: Peeters Press.
Frankenstein, Susan
  1979 The Phoenicians in the Far West: A Function of Neo-Assyrian Imperialism. Pp. 263–94 in *PP*.
Frankfort, Henri
  1952 The Origin of the Bît Hilani. *Iraq* 14: 120–31.
Freedman, David
  1964 A Second Mesha Inscription. *BASOR* 175: 50–51.
Frick, Frank
  1985 *The Formation of the State in Ancient Israel: A Survey of Models and Theories*. Social World of Biblical Antiquity Series 4. Sheffield: Almond Press.
Fried, Morton
  1975 *The Notion of Tribe*. Menlo Park, Calif.: Cummings.
Fritz, Volkmar
  1971 Erwagungen zu dem Spatbronzezeitlichen Quadratbau bei Amman. *ZDPV* 87: 140–52.
  1979 Die Pälaste während der assyrischen, babylonischen, und persischen Vorherrschaft in Pälastina. *Mitteilungen der Deutschen Orient-Gesellschaft* 111: 63–74.
  1983a Päläste Während der Bronze-und Eisenzeit in Pälästina. *ZDPV* 99: 1–42.
  1983b Die Syrische Bauform des Hilani und die Frage seiner Verbreitung. *Damaszener Mitteilungen* 1: 43–58.
Frumkin, Amos, Israel Carmi, Israel Zak, and Mordechai Margitz
  1991 The Holocene Climate Record of the Salt Caves of Mount Sedom, Israel. *The Holocene* 1 (3): 191–200.
  1994 Middle Holocene Environmental Change Determined from the Salt Caves of Mount Sedom, Israel. Pp. 315–32 in *Late Quaternary Chronology and Paleoclimates of the Eastern Mediterranean*, ed. Ofer Bar-Yosef and Renee Kra, RADIO-CARBON. Tucson: Department of Anthropology, University of Arizona.
Furumark, Arne
  1941 *The Mycenaean Pottery: Analysis and Classification*. Stockholm: Kungl. Vitterhets.
Gaballa, Gaballa Ali
  1976 *Narrative in Egyptian Art*. Mainz: Philipp von Zabern.
Gailey, Christine
  1987 *Kinship to Kingship: Gender Hierarchy and State formation in the Tongan Islands*. Austin: University of Texas Press.
Gailey, Christine and Thomas Patterson
  1987 Power Relations and State Formation. Pp. 1–26 in *PRSF*.
Gardiner, Alan
  1947 *Ancient Egyptian Onomastica*. 2 vols. Oxford: Oxford University Press.
  1957 *Egyptian Grammar*. 3rd ed. Oxford: Griffith Institute.
Gelb, Ignatius, ed.
  1956 *Chicago Assyrian Dictionary*. vol. 6. Chicago: University of Chicago Press.
Gellner, Ernst
  1969 *Saints of the Atlas*. Chicago: University of Chicago Press.

Genge, Heinz
    1979 *Nordsyrisch-Südanatolische Reliefs.* 2 vols. Copenhagen: Royal Danish Academy of Sciences and Letters.
van Gennep, Arnold
    1960 (1909) *The Rites of Passage.* Trans. M. Vizedom and G. Caffee. Chicago: University of Chicago Press.
Geraty, Lawrence, Larry Herr, Øystein LaBianca, and Randall Younker
    1989 *Madaba Plains Project 1: The 1984 Season at Tell el-'Umeri and Vicinity and Subsequent Studies.* Berrien Springs, Mich.: Andrews University Press.
Germer-Durand, Eugène
    1907 *Un Musée palestinien: Notice sur le Musée Archéologie de Notre-Dame de France à Jérusalem.* Paris: Maison de la Bonne Presse.
Gese, Hartmut
    1958 Ammonitische Grenzfestungen Zwischen Wadi es-Sir und Na'ur. *ZPDV* 74: 55–64.
de Geus, Cornelius .H. J.
    1976 *The Tribes of Israel.* Studia Semitica Neerlandica 18. Assen: Van Gorcum.
Geuss, Raymond
    2001 *History and Illusion in Politics.* Cambridge: Cambridge University Press.
Gibson, John
    1971 *Textbook of Syrian Semitic Inscriptions.* Vol 1, *Hebrew and Moabite Inscriptions.* Oxford: Clarendon.
    1975 *Textbook of Syrian Semitic Inscriptions.* Vol. 2, *Aramaic Inscriptions.* Oxford: Clarendon.
    1982 *Textbook of Syrian Semitic Inscriptions.* Vol. 3, *Phoenician Inscriptions.* Oxford: Clarendon.
Giddens, Anthony
    1979 *Central Problems in Social Theory.* Berkeley: University of California Press.
    1984 *The Constitution of Society.* Berkeley: University of California Press.
    1985 *The Nation-State and Violence.* Berkeley: University of California Press.
Gillespie, Susan
    2000 Lévi-Strauss: Maison and société à maisons. Pp. 22–52 in *Beyond Kinship: Social and Material Reproduction in House Societies,* ed. Rosemary Joyce and Susan Gillespie. Philadelphia: University of Pennsylvania Press.
Gingrich, André
    1995 The Prophet's Smile and Other Puzzles: Studying Arab Tribes and Comparing Close Marriages. *Social Anthropology* 3 (2): 147–70.
Gitin, Seymour
    1997 The Neo-Assyrian Empire and its Western Periphery: The Levant with a Focus on Philistine Ekron. Pp. 77–103 in *Assyria 1995.*
Gitin, Seymour, Trude Dothan, and Joseph Naveh
    1997 A Royal Dedicatory Inscription from Ekron. *IEJ* 47 (1–2): 1–16.
Gitin, Seymour, Amihai Mazar, and Ephraim Stern
    1998 *Mediterranean Peoples in Transition: Thirteenth to Early Tenth Centuries B.C.E.* Jerusalem: IES.
Giveon, Raphael
    1971 *Les Bédouins shosou des documents égyptiens.* Leiden: Brill.
Gledhill, John
    1989 The Imperial Form and Universal History: Some Reflections on Relativism and Generalization. Pp. 108–26 in *Domination and Resistance,* ed. Daniel Miller, Michael Rowlands, and Christopher Tilley. New York: Routledge.
    2000 *Power and Its Disguises: Anthropological Perspectives on Politics.* 2nd ed. London: Pluto Press.

Glueck, Nelson
1934 Explorations in Eastern Palestine 1. *AASOR* 14. New Haven, Conn.: ASOR.
1935 Explorations in Eastern Palestine 2. *AASOR* 15. New haven, Conn.: ASOR.
1939 Exploration in Eastern Palestine 3. *AASOR* 18–19. New Haven, Conn.: ASOR.
1970 *The Other Side of the Jordan.* Rev. ed. Cambridge, Mass.: ASOR.
Godelier, Maurice
1999 *The Enigma of the Gift.* Trans. Nora Scott. Chicago: University of Chicago Press.
Goldberg, Paul
1986 Late Quaternary Environmental History of the Southern Levant. *Geoarchaeology* 1 (3): 225–44.
Gonen, Rivka
1984 Urban Canaan in the Late Bronze Age. *BASOR* 253: 61–73.
1992 *Burial Patterns and Cultural Diversity in Late Bronze Age Canaan.* ASOR Dissertation Series. Winona Lake, Ind.: Eisenbrauns.
Goodfriend, Glenn
1987 Chronostratigraphic Studies of Sediments in the Negev Desert, Using Amino Acid Epimerization Analysis of Land Snail Shells. *Quaternary Research* 28: 374–92.
1999 Terrestrial Stable Isotope Records of Late Quaternary Paleoclimates in the Eastern Mediterranean Region. *Quaternary Science Review* 18: 501–13.
Gordon, Colin
1991 Governmental Rationality: An Introduction. Pp. 1–51 in *The Foucault Effect,* ed. Graham Burchell, Colin Gordon, and Peter Miller. Chicago: University of Chicago Press.
Görg, Manfred
1989 *Beiträge zur Zeitgeschichte der Anfänge Israels.* Wiesbaden: Harrassowitz.
Gottwald, Norman
1979 *The Tribes of Yahweh.* Maryknoll, N.Y.: Orbis.
2001 *The Politics of Ancient Israel.* Library of Ancient Israel. Louisville, Ky.: Westminster John Knox.
Graeber, David
2001 *Toward an Anthropological Theory of Value: The False Coin of Our Own Dreams.* New York: Palgrave.
Graf-Reventlow, Henning G.
1963 Das Ende der Ammonitischen Grenzfestungskette? *ZDPV* 79: 127–37.
Graham, M. Patrick
1989 The Discovery and Reconstruction of the Mesha Inscription. Pp. 41–92 in *SMIM.*
Gramsci, Antonio
1971 *Selections from the Prison Notebooks of Antonio Gramsci.* Ed. and trans. Quintin Hoare and Geoffrey Nowell Smith. New York: International Publishers.
2000 *The Antonio Gramsci Reader: Selected Writings 1916–1935.* Ed. David Forgacs. New York: NYU Press.
Grayson, A. Kirk
1991 *The Royal Inscriptions of Mesopotamia: Assyrian Periods.* Vol. 2. *Assyrian Rulers of the Early First Millennium B.C. 1 (1114–859 B.C.).* Toronto: University of Toronto Press.
1996 *The Royal Inscriptions of Mesopotamia: Assyrian Periods* Vol. 3. *Assyrian Rulers of the Early First Millennium BC 2 (858–745 B.C.).* Toronto: University of Toronto Press.
Greenberg, Moshe
1955 *The Ḫab/piru.* American Oriental Series 39. New Haven, Conn.: American Oriental Society.

Grimal, Nicolas-Christophe
1986 *Les Termes de la propegande royale égyptienne.* Paris: Imprimérie Nationale.
Grosby, Steven
1997 Borders, Territory and Nationality in the Ancient Near East and Armenia. *JESHO* 40 (1): 1–29.
Groves, Jennifer, Karen A. Borstad, and Gary Christopherson
1995 A Preliminary Report on the Tall Jalul Surface Sherding Project. Paper read at the ASOR Annual Meeting, Philadelphia. www.casa.arizona.edu/MPP/ tjsurf_surv/tjsspap.html.
Haas, Jonathan
1982 *The Evolution of the Prehistoric State.* New York: Columbia University Press.
Habermas, Jürgen
1987 *The Theory of Communicative Action.* Vol. 2. *Lifeworld and System: A Critique of Functionalist Reason.* Trans. Thomas McCarthy. Cambridge: Polity Press.
Hadad, Hufsi
1984 Umm-Uthainah Tomb. *ADAJ* 28: 7–14, 50–58 (in Arabic).
Hadidi, Adnan
1987 An Ammonite Tomb at Amman. *Levant* 19: 101–20.
Haider, Peter
1987 Zum Moab-Feldzung Ramses II. *Studien zur Altägyptischen Kultur* 14: 107–23.
Hall, John A.
1985 *Powers and Liberties: the Causes and Consequences of the Rise of the West.* Oxford: Blackwell.
Hallo, Willian and K. Lawson Younger, eds.
2000 *The Context of Scripture* Vol. 2. Leiden: Brill.
Halpern, Baruch
1991 Jerusalem and the Lineages in the Seventh Century BCE: Kinship and the Rise of the Individual Moral Liability. Pp. 11–107 in *Law and Ideology in Monarchic Israel,* ed. Baruch Halpern and Deborah Hobson. *JSOT* Suppl. 124. Sheffield: Sheffield Academic Press.
1996 Sybil, or Two Nations? Archaism, Kinship, Alienation, and the Elite Redefinition of Traditional Culture in Judah in the Eighth-Seventh Centuries B.C.E. Pp. 291–338 in *The Study of the Ancient Near East in the 21st Century,* ed. Jerrold Cooper and Glenn Schwartz. Winona Lake, Ind.: Eisenbrauns.
Halstead, Paul
1987 Traditional and Ancient Rural Economy in Mediterranean Europe. Plus Ça Change? *Journal of Hellenic Studies* 107: 77–87.
Hamès, Constant
1991 De la chefférie tribale à la dynastie étatique: généalogie et pouvoir à la époque almohado-ḥafṣide (XII–XIVe siècles). Pp. 101–40 in *Al-Ansâb.*
Hankey, Vronwy
1974a A Late Bronze Age Temple at Amman I. The Aegean Pottery. *Levant* 6: 131–59.
1974b A Late Bronze Age Temple at Amman II. Vases and Objects Made of Stone. *Levant* 6: 160–78.
1981 Imported Vessels of the Late Bronze Age at High Places. Pp. 108–17 in *Temples and High Places in Biblical Times,* ed. Avraham Biran. Jerusalem: Keter Press.
1995 A Late Bronze Age Temple at Amman Airport: Small Finds and Pottery Discovered in 1955. Pp. 169–85 in *TCMP.*
Hansen, Mogens
1998 *Polis and City-State: An Ancient Concept and its Modern Equivalent.* Copenhagen: Royal Danish Academy of Sciences and Letters.

Hansen, Thomas and Finn Stepputat
  2001 *States of Imagination: Ethnographic Explorations of the Postcolonial State.*
     Durham, N.C.: Duke University Press.
Harding, G. Lancaster
  1953 An Early Iron Age Tomb at Madaba. *PEFA* 4: 27–33.
  1958 Recent Discoveries in Jordan. *PEQ* 90: 7–18.
Hardt, Michael
  1995 The Withering of Civil Society. *Social Text* 45: 27–44.
Harlan, Jack
  1985 The Early Bronze Age Environment of the Southern Ghor and the Moab
     Plateau. *SHAJ* 2: 125–29.
Harrison, Timothy, Brian Hesse, Stephen Savage, and Douglas Schnurrenberger
  2000 Urban Life in the Highlands of Central Jordan: A Preliminary Report of the
     1996 Tall Mādābā Excavations. *ADAJ* 44: 211–29.
Hasel, Michael
  1998 *Domination and Resistance: Egyptian Military Activity in the Southern Levant, ca.
     1300–1185 B.C.* Leiden: Brill.
Hawkins, John
  2000 *Corpus of Hieroglyphic Luwian Inscriptions.* Vol. 1. New York: Walter de
     Gruyter.
Hayden, Brian and Aubrey Cannon
  1982 The Corporate Group as an Archaeological Unit. *JAA* 1 (2): 132–58.
Healy, Kieran
  1998 Conceptualizing Constraint: Mouzelis, Archer and the Concept of Social
     Structure. *Sociology* 32 (3): 509–22.
Heltzer, Michael
  1979 *Dimtu-gt-pyrgos*: An Essay About the Non-Etymological Sense of These
     Terms. *Journal of Northwest Semitic Languages* 7: 31–35.
Hennessy, J. Basil
  1966 Excavations at a Late Bronze Temple at Amman. *PEQ* 98: 155–62.
  1985 Thirteenth Century B.C. Temple of Human Sacrifice at Amman. *Studia
     Phoenicia* 3: 85–104.
  1989 'Amman Airport. Pp. 167–78 in *AJ II 1*.
Henry, Donald
  1992 Seasonal Movements of Fourth Millennium Pastoral Nomads in Wadi
     Ḥisma. *SHAJ* 4: 137–41.
Henshaw, Richard
  1967 The Office of Šaknu in Neo-Assyrian Times. I. *JAOS* 87: 517–25.
Hentschke, Richard
  1960 Ammonitische Grenzfestungen Südwestlich von Amman. *ZPDV* 76: 103–23.
Herr, Larry
  1983a *The Amman Airport Excavations, 1976.* AASOR 48. Winona Lake, Ind.:
     Eisenbrauns.
  1983b The Amman Airport Structure and the Geopolitics of Ancient Trans-
     jordan. *BA* 46 (4): 223–29.
  1992a Two Stamped Jar Impressions of the Persian Province of Ammon from Tell
     el-'Umeiri. *ADAJ* 36: 163–66.
  1992b Shifts in Settlement Patterns of Late Bronze and Iron Age Ammon. *SHAJ*
     4: 175–78.
  1995 Wine Production in the Hills of Southern Ammon and the Founding of Tall
     al-'Umayri in the Sixth Century B.C. *ADAJ* 39: 121–25.
  1997 The Iron Age II Period: Emerging Nations. *BA* 60 (3): 114–83.
  1998 Tell el-'Umayri and the Madaba Plains Region During the Late Bronze-Iron

Age I Transition. Pp. 251–64 in *Mediterranean Peoples in Transition: Thirteenth to Early Tenth Centuries BCE*, ed. Seymour Gitin, Amihai Mazar, and Ephraim Stern. Jerusalem: IES.

1999a Tall al-'Umayri and the Reubenite Hypothesis. *EI* 26: 64*–77*.

1999b The Ammonites in The Late Iron Age and Persian Period. Pp. 219–37 in *Ammon*.

2000 The Settlement and Fortification of Tell al-'Umayri in Jordan during the LB/Iron I Transition. Pp. 167–79 in *AJB*.

Herr, Larry and Douglas Clark
2001 Excavating the Tribe of Reuben. *BAR* 27 (2): 43–47, 64–72.

Herr, Larry and Muhammad Najjar
2001 The Iron Age. Pp. 323–45 in *AJ*.

Herr, Larry, Douglas Clark, and Lawrence Geraty
2002 *2002 Season of Excavation at Tall al-'Umayri: A Summary.* www.wwc.edu/academics/theology/mpp/umayri/index.

Herr, Larry, Lawrence Geraty, Øystein LaBianca, and Randall Younker
1991 *Madaba Plains Project 2: The 1987 Season at Tell el-'Umeri and Vicinity and Subsequent Studies.* Berrien Springs, Mich.: Andrews University Press.

Herr, Larry, Lawrence Geraty, Øystein LaBianca, Randall Younker, and Douglas Clark.
1996 Mādabā Plains Project 1994: Excavations at Tall al-'Umayrî, Tall Jalūl, and Vicinity. *ADAJ* 40: 63–81.

1997 Mādabā Plains Project 1996: Excavations at Tall al-'Umayrî, Tall Jalūl, and Vicinity. *ADAJ* 41: 145–67.

Herzfeld, Michael
1987 *Anthropology Through the Looking-Glass: Critical Ethnography in the Margins of Europe.* Cambridge: Cambridge University Press.

1992 Metapatterns. Pp. 66–86 in *Representations in Archaeology*, ed. Jean-Claude Gardin and Christopher Peebles. Bloomington: Indiana University Press.

1997 *Cultural Intimacy: Social Poetics in the Nation-State.* New York: Routledge.

Herzog, Ze'ev
1984 *Beer-Sheba II: The Early Iron Age Settlements.* Tel Aviv: Tel Aviv University, Institute of Archaeology.

1992 Settlement and Fortification Planning in the Iron Age. Pp. 231–74 in *Architecture*.

1994 The Beer-sheba Valley: From Nomadism to Monarchy. Pp. 122–49 in *FNM*.

2001 The Date of the Temple at Arad: Reassessment of the Stratigraphy and the Implications for the History of Religion in Judah. Pp. 156–78 in *SAIAJ*.

Hesse, Brian and Paula Wapnish
1997 Can Pig Remains Be Used for Ethnic Diagnosis in the Ancient Near East? Pp. 238–70 in *The Archaeology of Israel: Constructing the Past, Interpreting the Present*, ed. Neil A. Silberman and David Small. Sheffield: Sheffield Academic Press.

Higginbotham, Carol
2000 *Egyptianization and Elite Emulation in Ramesside Palestine: Governance and Accommodation on the Imperial Periphery.* CHANE 2. Leiden: Brill.

Hill, J. Brett
2000 Geoarchaeological Research of Holocene Occupations in Wādî al-Ḥasa: A Preliminary Report on the 1999 Season. *ADAJ* 44: 11–17.

Hillman, Gordon
1981 Reconstructing Crop Husbandry Practices from Charred Remains of Crops. Pp. 123–162 in *Farming Practice in British Prehistory*, ed. Roger Mercer. Edinburgh: Edinburgh University Press.

Hodder, Ian
2000 Agency and Individuals in Long-Term Processes. Pp. 21–33 in *Agency in Archaeology*, ed. Marcia-Anne Dobres and John Robb. New York: Routledge.
Hoffman, John
1995 *Beyond the State: An Introductory Critique*. Cambridge: Polity Press.
Holladay, John
1987 Religion in Israel and Judah under the Monarchy: An Explicitly Archaeological Approach. Pp. 249–99 in *Ancient Israelite Religion: Essays in Honor of Frank Moore Cross*, ed. Patrick Miller, Paul Hanson and Steven McBride. Philadelphia: Fortress.
1992 House, Israelite. Pp. 308–18 in *ABD*, vol. 3.
1995 The Kingdoms of Israel and Judah: Political and Economic Centralization in the Iron IIA-B (ca. 1000–750 BCE). Pp. 368–98 in *ASHL*.
1997 Four-Room House. Pp. 337–42 in *OEANE*. Vol 2.
Homès-Fredericq, Denyse
1982 Un Goulot de bouteille de nouvel an, trouvé à Lehun (en Jordanie). Pp. 79–90 in *Studia Paulo Naster Oblata*, ed. Jan Quagebauer. Leuven: Peters.
1992 Late Bronze and Iron Age Evidence from Lehun in Moab. Pp. 187–202 in *EEM*.
1995 A Cosmetic Palette from Lehun, Jordan. Pp. 265–70 in *TCMP*.
1997 *Lehun et la Voie Royale/en de Koningsweg*. Brussels: Comité Belge de Fouilles en Jordanie/Belgisch Comité voor Opgravingen in Jordanië.
2000 Excavating the First Pillar House at Lehun (Jordan). Pp. 180–195 in *AJB*.
van Hoof, Werner
1997 De Private Architectuur in het Moab-gebied (Jordanië) Tijdens de Late Bronstijd en Vroege Ijertijd (ca. 1550–1000 v.Chr.). Licentiaat Dissetation, Free University of Brussels.
Hopkins, David
1985 *The Highlands of Canaan: Agricultural Life in the Early Iron Age*. Social World of Biblical Antiquity Series 3. Sheffield: Almond Press.
1996 Bare Bones: Putting Flesh on the Economics of Ancient Israel. Pp.121–39 in *The Origins of the Ancient Israelite States*, ed. Volkmar Fritz and Philip Davies. Sheffield: Sheffield Academic Press.
n.d. Hinterland Probes and the Excavation of Site 84. Unpublished Report for the Madaba Plains Project.
Horn, Siegfried
1973 The Crown of the King of the Ammonites. *AUSS* 11: 170–80.
1986 Why the Moabite Stone was Blown to Pieces. *BAR* 12 (3): 50–61.
Horowitz, Aharon
1979 *The Quaternary of Israel*. New York: Academic Press.
2001 *The Jordan Rift Valley*. Exton: A. A. Balkema.
Horowitz, Wayne
1993 Moab and Edom in the Sargon Geography. *IEJ* 43(2–3): 151–6.
Horsfield, George and Hugues Vincent
1932 Un Stèle Egypto-Moabite au Balou'a. *RB* 41: 417–25.
Hübner, Ulrich
1988 Die ersten moabitischen Ostraka. *ZDPV* 104: 68–73.
1990 Die erste gross formatige Rundplastik aus den Eisenzeitlichen Moab. *UF* 21: 227–31.
1992 *Die Ammoniter: Unterschungen zur Geschichte, Kultur und Religion einer transjordanischen Volkes im 1. Jahrtausend v. Chr.* Abhandlungen des Deutschen Palästinavereins 16. Wiesbaden: Harrassowitz.

Humann, Karl and Otto Puchstein
  1890 *Reisen in Kleinasien und Nord-Syrien.* Berlin: Dietrich Reimer.
Humbert, Jean-Baptiste, and Fawzi Zayadine
  1992 Trois campagnes de fouilles à Ammân (1988–1991), troisième terrasse de la Citadelle. *RB* 99 (1): 214–60.
Humphrey, Caroline
  1979 The Uses of Genealogy: A Historical Study of the Nomadic and Sedentarised Buryat. Pp. 235–60 in *Pastoral Production and Society,* ed. Equipe écologie et anthropologie des sociétés pastorales. Cambridge: Cambridge University Press.
al-Hunjul, Nasfat
  1995 *The Geology of the Madaba Area: Map Sheet 3153 II.* Amman: Geology Directorate.
el-Hurani, M. H., and Mahmud Duwayri
  1986 Policies Affecting Field Crop Production in the Rain-Fed Sector. Pp. 55–72 in *Agricultural Policy in Jordan,* ed. Alison Burrel. London: Ithaca Press/ Shoman Foundation.
Ibach, Robert, Jr.
  1978 An Intensive Surface Survey at Jalul. *AUSS* 16: 215–22.
  1987 *Archaeological Survey of the Hesban Region.* Hesban 5. Berrien Springs, Mich.: Andrews University Press.
Ibrahim, Moawiyah
  1987 Saḥāb and Its Foreign Relations. *SHAJ* 3: 73–81.
  1989 Sahab. Pp. 516–20 in *AJ II 2.*
Irsigler, Hubert
  1993 Großsatzformen in Althebraischen und die Syntaktische Struktur der Inschrift des Konigs Mescha von Moab. Pp. 81–121 in *Syntax und Text,* ed. Hubert Irsigler. St. Ottilien: EOS.
Israel, Felice
  1987 Studi Moabiti I: Rassgna di Epigrafia Moabita e i Sigilli. Pp. 101–38 in *Atti della 4a giornata di Studia Camito-Semitici e Indo-europei,* ed. Giuliano Bernini and Vermondo Brugnatelli. Milan: Unicopli.
Issar, Arie and Dan Yakir
  1997 The Roman Period's Colder Climate—Isotopes from Wood Buried in the Roman Siege-Ramp of Masada. *BA* 60 (2): 101–6.
Jacobs, Linda
  1983 Survey of the south Ridge of Wadi 'Isal, 1981. *ADAJ* 27: 245–74.
James, Frances
  1966 *The Iron Age at Beth Shan.* Philadelphia: University Museum.
James, Frances and Patrick McGovern
  1993 *The Late Bronze Egyptian Garrison at Beth Shan: A Study of Levels VII and VIII.* University Museum Monograph 85. Philadelphia: University Museum.
Jamieson-Drake, David
  1991 *Scribes and Schools in Monarchic Judah.* Social World of Biblical Antiquity Series 9. Sheffield: Sheffield Academic Press.
Jankowska, Ninel
  1969 Some Problems in the Economy of the Assyrian Empire. Pp. 253–76 in *Ancient Mesopotamia: Socio-Economic History,* ed. Igor Diakonoff. Moscow: Nauka.
  1982 Extended Family and Its Specialization in Araphe. Pp. 8–20 in *Economy of the Nuclear or Extended Family in Oriental Antiquity. Proceedings of the Eighth International Economic History Congress (Section B11).* Budapest: Akademiai Kiado.

Jessop, Bob
  1982 *The Capitalist State: Marxist Theories and Methods.* New York: New York University Press.
  1990 *State Theory: Putting the Capitalist State in Its Place.* Cambridge: Polity Press.
  1996 Interpretive Sociology and the Dialectic of Structure and Agency. *Theory, Culture and Society* 13 (1): 119–28.
Ji, Chang-Ho and Taysir ʻAttiyat
  1997 Archaeological Survey of the Dhîbān Plateau, 1996: A Preliminary Report. *ADAJ* 41: 115–44.
Ji, Chang-Ho and Jong Keun Lee
  1998 Preliminary Report of the Survey on the Dhîbān Plateau, 1997. *ADAJ* 42: 549–71.
  2000 A Preliminary Report on the Dhîbān Plateau Survey Project, 1999: The Versacare Expedition. *ADAJ* 44: 493–506.
Joffe, Alexander
  1993 *Settlement and Society in the Early Bronze Age I and II, Southern Levant: Complexity and Contradiction in a Small-Scale Society.* MMA 4. Sheffield: J.R. Collis.
  2002 The Rise of Secondary States in the Southern Levant. *JESHO* 45 (4): 425–67.
Johns, Claude
  1898 *Assyrian Deeds and Documents.* Cambridge: Deighton, Bell.
Johns, Jeremy
  1994 The Long Durée: State and Settlement Strategies in Southern Transjordan Across the Islamic Centuries. Pp. 1–31 in *Village, Steppe, and State: The Social Origins of Modern Jordan*, ed. Eugene Rogan and Tariq Tell. London: British Academic Press.
Jones, Brian
  1991 In Search of Kir Hareseth: A Case Study in Site Identification. *JSOT* 52: 3–24.
Jones, Siân
  1997 *The Archaeology of Ethnicity.* London: Routledge.
Kafafi, Zeidan
  1984 Late Bronze Age Pottery from Qwēlbe (Jordan). *ZPDV* 100: 12–29.
Kamlah, Jens
  2000 *Der Zeraqōn-Survey, 1989–1994.* Abhanlungen des Deutschen Palästina-Vereins 27,1. Wiesbaden: Harrassowitz
Kapferer, Bruce
  1988 *Legends of People, Myths of State.* Washington, D.C.: Smithsonian University Press.
Karp, Ivan and Keith Maynard
  1983 Reading The Nuer. *CA* 24 (4): 481–503.
Kaufman, Ivan
  1982 The Samaria Ostraca: An Early Witness to Hebrew Writing. *BA* 45: 229–39.
Keel, Othmar, Menahem Shuval, and Christoph Uehlinger
  1990 *Studien zu den Stempelsiegeln aus Palästina/Israel III.* OBO 100. Fribourg/Göttigen: University Press/Vandenhoeck and Ruprecht.
Kempinski, Aharon
  1989 *Megiddo: A Royal City-State and Royal Center in North Israel.* Munich: C.H. Beck.
Kenyon, Kathleen
  1979 *Archaeology in the Holy Land.* 4th ed. London: Ernest Benn.
Kertzer, David
  1996 *Politics and Symbols: The Italian Communist Party and the Fall of Communism.* New Haven, Conn.: Yale University Press.

Khresat, Sa'eb A., Zakir Rawajfih, and M. Mohammed
    1998 Land Degradation in North-western Jordan: Causes and Processes. *Journal of Arid Environments* 39: 623–29.
Kitchen, Kenneth
    1964 Some New Light on the Asiatic Wars of Ramesses II. *JEA* 50: 47–70.
    1969 *Ramesside Inscriptions: Historical and Biographical.* Vol 2. Oxford: Blackwell.
    1976 Two Notes on Ramesside History. *Oriens Antiquus* 15: 313–14.
    1992 The Egyptian Evidence on Ancient Jordan. Pp. 21–34 in *EEM.*
    1996a The Historical Chronology of Ancient Egypt: A Current Assessment. *Acta Archaeologica* 67: 1–13.
    1996b *Ramesside Inscriptions: Notes and Comments* Vol. II. Oxford: Blackwell.
Kletter, Raz
    1991 The Rujm al-Malfuf Buildings and the Assyrian Vassal State of Ammon. *BASOR* 284: 33–50.
    1998 *Economic Keystones: The Weight System of the Kingdom of Judah. JSOT* Suppl. 276. Sheffield: Sheffield Academic Press.
    1999 Pots and Polities: Material Remains of Late Iron Age Judah in Relation to Its Political Borders. *BASOR* 314: 19–54.
Knapp, A. Bernard
    1993 *Society and Polity at Bronze Age Pella: An Annales Perspective.* Sheffield: Sheffield Academic Press.
Knapp, A. Bernard and John Cherry
    1994 *Provenience Studies and Bronze Age Cyprus: Production, Exchange, and Politico-Economic Change.* Monographs in World Archaeology 21. Madison, Wis.: Prehistory Press.
Knauf, Ernst Axel
    1985 *Bwtrt* und Batora. *Göttinger Miszellen* 87: 45–48.
    1988 *Midian. Untersuchungen zur Geschicte Palästinas und Nordarabiens am Ende des 2. Jahrtausends v. Chr.* Wiesbaden: Harrassowitz.
    1992a The Cultural Impact of Secondary State Formation: The Cases of the Edomites and the Moabites. Pp. 47–54 in *EEM.*
    1992b Bedouin and Bedouin States. Pp. 634–38 in *ABD,* vol. 1.
    1992c Jeremia XLIX 1–5: Ein Zweires Moab-Orakel im Jeremia-Buch. *VT* 42: 124–28.
    2000 Jerusalem in the Late Bronze Age and Early Iron Ages: A Proposal. *TA* 27: 75–90.
Knauf-Belleri, Ernst Axel
    1995 Edom: The Social and Economic History. Pp. 93–117 in *You Shall Not Abhor an Edomite For He is Your Brother: Edom and Seir in History and Tradition,* ed. Diane Edelman. Atlanta: Scholars Press.
Kohl, Philip
    1984 Force, History, and the Evolutionist Paradigm. Pp. 127–34 in *Marxist Perspectives in Archaeology,* ed. Matthew Spriggs. Cambridge: Cambridge University Press.
    1987 State Formation: Useful Concept or Idée Fixe? Pp. 27–34 in *PRSF.*
Kopytoff, Igor
    1987 The Internal African Frontier: The Making of African Political Culture. Pp. 3–84 in *The African Frontier: The Reproduction of Traditional African Societies,* ed. Igor Kopytoff. Bloomington: Indiana University Press.
Koucky, Frank
    1987 Survey of the Limes Zone. Pp. 41–105 in *The Roman Frontier in Central Jordan: Interim Report on the Limes Arabicus Project, 1980–1985.* British Archaeological Reports International Series 340. Oxford: British Archaeological Reports.

1992 The Environs of Pella: Roads, Fords, amd Occupational Sites. Pp. 199–204 in *Pella in Jordan 2*, ed. Anthony McNicoll, Philip Edwards, Jack Hanbury-Tenison, J. Basil Hennessy, Timothy Potts, Robert Smith, A. Walmsley, and Pamela Watson. Sydney: Department of Archaeology, University of Sydney.

Kraus, Wolfgang
1998 Contestable Identitites: Tribal Structures in the Moroccan High Atlas. *JRAI* n.s. 4: 1–22.

Kristiansen, Kristian and Michael Rowlands
1998 *Social Transformations in Archaeology*. New York: Routledge.

Kuhn, Thomas
1970 *The Structure of Scientific Revolutions*. 2nd ed. Chicago: University of Chicago Press.

Kuhrt, Amélie
1995 *The Ancient Near East: c. 3000–300 B.C.* 2 vols. London: Routledge.

Kulke, Hermann
1995 Introduction: The Study of the State in Pre-modern India. Pp. 1–47 in *The State in India: 1000–1700*, ed. H. Kulke. Oxford: Delhi.

Kunin, Seth
1995 *The Logic of Incest: A Structuralist Analysis of Hebrew Mythology*. *JSOT* Suppl.185. Sheffield: Sheffield Academic Press.
1999 Israel and the Nations: A Structuralist Survey. *JSOT* 82: 19–43.

Kuper, Adam.
1982 Lineage Theory: A Critical Retrospect. *ARA* 11: 71–95.
1988 *The Invention of Primitive Society: Transformations of an Illusion*. New York: Routledge.

Kürschner, Harald, ed.
1986 *Contributions to the Vegetation of Southwest Asia*. Wiesbaden: Ludwig Reichert.

Kurtz, Donald
1996 Hegemony and Anthropology: Gramsci, Exegeses, Reinterpretations. *Critique of Anthropology* 16 (2): 103–35.

LaBianca, Øystein
1990 *Sedentarization and Nomadization: Food System Cycles at Hesban and Vicinity in Trans-Jordan*. Hesban I. Berrien Springs, Mich.: Andrews University Press.
1999 Excursus: The Salient Features of Iron Age Tribal Kingdoms. Pp. 19–23 in *Ammon*.
n.d. *A Forest That Refuses to Disappear: Cycles of Environmental Degeneration and Regeneration in Jordan*. Report to the National Geographic Society. http://www.casa.arizona.edu/MPP/ngs_report/ngs_rep.html

LaBianca, Øystein and Larry Lacelle, eds.
1986 *Environmental Foundations*. Hesban 2. Berrien Springs, Mich.: Andrews University Press.

LaBianca, Øystein and Randall Younker
1995 The Kingdoms of Ammon, Moab, and Edom: The Archaeology of Society in Late Bronze/Iron Age Transjordan (ca. 1400–500 B.C.E.). Pp. 399–415 in *ASHL*.

Laclau, Ernesto
2000 Identity and Hegemony: The Role of Universality in the Constitution of Political Logics. Pp. 44–89 in *Contingency, Hegemony, Universality*, ed. Judith Butler, Ernesto Laclau, and Slavoj Žižek. London: Verso.

Laclau, Ernesto and Chantal Mouffe
1987 Post-Marxism Without Apologies. *New Left Review* 166 (November/December): 79–106.
2001 *Hegemony and Socialist Strategy: Towards a Radical Democratic Politics*. 2nd ed. London: Verso.

Lamon, Robert and Geoffrey Shipton
    1939 *Megiddo I: Seasons of 1925–1934. Strata I–V.* OIP 42. Chicago: University of
        Chicago Press.
Lamprichs, Roland
    1995 *Die Westexpansion des Neuassyrischen Reiches.* AOAT 239. Vluyn: Butzon and
        Bercker Kevelaer.
Lancaster, William
    1981 *The Rwala Bedouin Today.* Cambridge: Cambridge University Press.
Lancaster, William and Felicity Lancaster
    1995 Land Use and Population in the Area North of Karak. *Levant* 27: 103–24.
Layne, Linda
    1994 *Home and Homeland: The Dialogics of Tribal and National Identities in Jordan.*
        Princeton, N.J.: Princeton University Press.
Leach, Edmund
    1969 *Genesis as Myth and Other Essays.* London: Cape.
Leahy, Anthony
    1995 Ethnic Diversity in Ancient Egypt. Pp. 225–234 in *CANE*, vol. 1.
van der Leeuw, Sander, and James McGlade, eds.
    1997 *Time, Process, and Structured Transformation in Archaeology.* New York:
        Routledge.
Legendre, Pierre
    2001 *Program K-Means Users Guide.* Montréal: Département de Sciences Biolo-
        giques, Université de Montréal.
Lemaire, André
    1971 L'Ostracon de Mesad Hashavyahu (Yavneh-Yam) replacé dans son con-
        texte. *Semitica* 21: 57–71.
    1981 *Les Écoles et la formation de la Bible dans l'ancien Israël.* OBO 39.
        Fribourg/Göttingen: University Press/Vandenhoeck and Ruprecht.
    1987 Notes d'épigraphie nord-ouest sémitique. *Syria* 64: 205–16.
    1991a La Stèle de Mésha et l'histoire d'Israël. Pp.143–169 in *Storia e tradizioni di
        Israele*, ed. Daniele Garrone and Felice Israel. Brescia: Paideia.
    1991b Hazaël de Damas, Roi d'Aram. Pp. 91–108 in *Marchands, diplomates et
        empereurs: Études sur la civilization mésopotamienne offertes à Paul Garelli*, ed.
        Domminique Charpin and Francis Joannès. Paris: Éditions Recherche sur les
        civilisations.
    1994a House of David Restored in Moabite Inscription. *BAR* 20 (3): 31–37.
    1994b La Dynastie davidique (BYT DWD) dans deux inscriptions ouest-
        sémitiques du IXe S. AV. J.-C. *Studi Epigrafici e Linguistici sul Vicino Oriente Antico*
        11: 17–19.
    1994c Les Transformations politiques et culturelles de la Transjordanie au VIe
        Siècle av. J-C. *Transeuphratène* 8: 9–27.
    1995 Recherches sur les ateliers sigillaires Jordaniens au Fer II. *SHAJ* 5: 479–88.
Lemaire, André, and Jean-Marie Durand
    1984 *Les Inscriptions araméennes de Sfiré et l'Assyrie de Shamshi-ilu.* Geneva: Librairie
        Droz.
Lemche, Niels
    1985 *Early Israel: Anthropological and Historical Studies on the Israelite Society Before the
        Monarchy. VT* Suppl. 37. Leiden: E. J. Brill.
    1994 Kings and Clients: On Loyalty Between the Ruler and Ruled in Ancient
        "Israel." *Semeia* 66: 119–32.
    1996 From Patronage Society to Patronage Society. Pp. 106–20 in *The Origins of
        the Ancient Israelite States*, ed. Volkmar Fritz and Philip Davies. Sheffield:
        Sheffield Academic Press.

Lemke, Thomas
    2001 "The Birth of Bio-politics": Michel Foucault's Lecture at the Collège de
        France on Neo-liberal Governmentality. *Economy and Society* 30 (2): 190–207.
Lenski, Gerhard and Jean Lenski
    1978 *Human Societies: An Introduction to Macro-Sociology.* New York: McGraw-Hill.
Lenzen, Cherie
    1988 Tell Irbid and Its Context: A Problem in Archaeological Interpretation. *BN*
        42: 27–35.
    1989 Irbid. Pp. 298–300 in *AJI 1.*
Lenzen, Cherie, Robert Gordon, and Alison McQuitty
    1985 Excavations at Tell Irbid and Beit Ras. *ADAJ* 29: 151–159.
Leonard, Albert
    1979 Kataret es-Samra: A Late Bronze Age Cemetery in Transjordan? *BASOR*
        234: 53–65.
    1981 Kataret es-Samra: A Late Bronze Age Cemetery in Transjordan. *ADAJ* 25:
        179–95.
    1985 The Kataret es-Samra Project. *ADAJ* 29: 289–90.
    1987 The Significance of the Mycenaean Pottery Found East of the Jordan River.
        SHAJ 3: 261–66.
    1994 *An Index to the Late Bronze Age Aegean Pottery from Syria-Palestine. SIMA* 114.
        Jonsered: Paul Åströms.
Leonard, Albert and Eric Cline
    1998 The Aegean Pottery at Megiddo: An Appraisal and Analysis. *BASOR* 309:
        3–39.
Lev-Tov, Justin
    n.d. *Faunal Remains from Ḥirbat al-Mudayna al-'Aliya: The 1998 and 2000 Seasons.*
        Report for the Ḥirbat al-Mudayna al-'Aliya Archaeological Project, University
        of Liverpool.
Lev-Tov, Justin and Edward Maher
    2001 Food in Late Bronze Age Funerary Offerings: Faunal Evidence from Tomb
        1 at Tell Dothan. *PEQ* 133: 91–110.
Lewis, Norman
    1987 *Nomads and Settlers in Syria and Transjordan, 1800–1980.* Cambridge:
        Cambridge University Press.
Lewis, Theodore
    1989 *Cults of the the Dead in Ancient Israel and Ugarit.* HSM 39. Atlanta: Scholars
        Press.
    1991 The Ancestral Estate (naḥalat 'elohîm) in 2 Samuel 14: 16. *JBL* 110: 597–612.
Lichtheim, Miriam
    1976 *Ancient Egyptian Literature*, vol. II. *The New Kingdom.* Berkeley: University of
        California Press.
Liddell, Henry and Robert Scott
    1940 *A Greek-English Lexicon.* 9th Ed. Oxford: Clarendon Press.
Lidzbarski, Mark
    1902 Eine Nachprüfung der Mesainschrift. Pp. 1–10 in *Ephemeris für Semitische
        Epigraphik I.* Giessen: J. Ricker.
Lindsay, John
    1976 The Babylonian Kings and Edom, 605–550 B.C. *PEQ* 108: 23–39.
Lipiński, Edouard
    1971 Etymological and Exegetical Notes on the Mesha' Inscription. *Orientalia* 40:
        325–40.
Lipschitz, Oded
    1990 The Date of the "Assyrian" Residence at Ayyelet ha-Shahar. *TA* 17: 96–99.

Liver, Jacob
1967 The Wars of Mesha, King of Moab. *PEQ* 99: 14–31.
Liverani, Mario
1979a *Three Amarna Letters.* MANE 1/5. Malibu: Undena.
1979b The Ideology of the Assyrian Empire. Pp. 297–317 in *PP.*
1983 Political Lexicon and Political Ideologies in the Amarna Letters. *Berytus* 31: 41–56.
1987 The Collapse of the Near Eastern Regional System at the End of the Bronze Age: The Case of Syria. Pp. 66–73 in *Centre and Periphery in the Ancient World,* ed. Michael Rowlands, Mogens Larsen and Kristian Kristiansen. Cambridge: Cambridge University Press.
1988 The Growth of the Assyrian Empire in the Habur / Middle Euphrates Area: A New Paradigm. *State Archives of Assyria Bulletin* 2 (2): 81–98.
1990 *Prestige and Interest: International Relations in the Near East ca. 1600–1100 B.C.* HANES 1. Padua: Sargon.
Lockwood, David
1964 Social Integration and System Integration. Pp. 244–265 in *Explorations in Social Change,* ed. George Zollschan and Walter Hirsch. London: Routledge and Kegan Paul.
Lohmann, Hans
1992 Agriculture and Country Life in Classical Attica. Pp. 29–60 in *Agriculture in Ancient Greece,* ed. Beri Wells. Stockholm, Swedish Institute in Athens.
London, Gloria
1992 Tells: City Center or Home? *EI* 23: 71*-79*.
van Loon, Maurits
1986 The Drooping Lotus Flower. Pp. 245–52, pls. 59–61 in *Insight Through Images: Studies in Honor of Edith Porada,* ed. Marilyn Kelly-Buccellati. Malibu, Calif: Undena.
Loprieno, Antonio
1988 *Topos und Mimesis: zum Auslander in der Ägyptischen Literatur.* Ägyptologische Abhandlungen 48. Wiesbaden: Harrassowitz.
Loretz, Oswald
1984 *Ḫabiru-Hebräer: eine sozio-linguistiche studie über die herkunft des gentiliziums ʿibri vom appellativum ḫabiru.* Beiheft zur ZAW 160. Berlin: Walter de Gruyter.
Loud, Gordon
1936 An Architectural Formula for Assyrian Planning. *RA* 33: 153–60.
1939 *The Megiddo Ivories.* OIP 52. Chicago: University of Chicago Press.
Luckenbill, Daniel
1926 *Ancient Records of Assyria and Babylonia,* Vol. 2. Chicago: University of Chicago Press.
de Luynes, H. d'Albert duc
1874 *Voyage d'exploration à la Mer Morte à Pétra et sur la rive gauche de Jordain,* vol. 2. Paris: Arthur Bertrand.
MacDonald, Burton
1988 *The Wadi al-Hasa Survey 1979–1983.* Waterloo, Ont.: Wilfrid Laurier University Press.
2000 *East of the Jordan: Territories and Sites in the Hebrew Scriptures.* Boston: ASOR
MacDonald, Michael C.
1991 Was the Nabataean Kingdom a "Bedouin State?" *ZDPV* 107: 102–19.
Machinist, Peter
1993 Assyrians on Assyria in the First Millennium B.C. Pp. 77–104 in *Anfänge politischen Denkens in der Antike. Die nahöstlichen Kulturen und die Griechen,* ed. Kurt Raaflaub. Munich: Oldenbourg.

Mackenzie, Duncan
1911 Megalithic Monuments of Rabbath-Ammon at Amman. *PEFA* 1: 23–24, 33–35.
1913 Dibon: The City of King Mesa and of the Moabite Stone. *PEFQS*: 57–79.

Malamat, Avraham
1988 The Kingdom of Judah Between Egypt and Babylon: A Small State Within a Great Power Confrontation. Pp. 117–29 in *Text and Context: Old Testament and Semitic Studies for F.C. Fensham*, ed. Walter T. Claassen. *JSOT* Suppl. 48. Sheffield: Sheffield Academic Press.

Malinowski, Bronislaw
1922 *Argonauts of the Western Pacific*. London: Routledge and Kegan Paul.

Mallon, Alexis
1933 Deux Fortresses au Pied des Monts de Moab. *Biblica* 14: 400–407.

Mann, Michael
1986 *The Sources of Social Power*. Vol 1. Cambridge: Cambridge University Press.

Marcus, Joyce and Kent Flannery
1996 *Zapotec Civilization: How Urban Society Evolved in Mexico's Oaxaca Valley*. New York: Thames and Hudson.

Marfoe, Leon
1979 The Integrative Transformation: Patterns of Sociopolitical Organization in Southern Syria. *BASOR* 234: 1–42.

Markoe, Glenn
1985 *Phoenician Bronze and Silver Bowls from Cyprus and the Mediterranean*. Berkeley: University of California Press.

Marx, Emmanuel
1977 The Tribe as a Unit of Subsistence: Nomadic Pastoralism in the Middle East. *AA* 79: 343–66.
1979 Back to the Problem of the Tribe. *AA* 81: 124–25.

Massetti-Rouault, Maria Grazia
2001 *Cultures locales du Moyen-Euphrate modeles et evenements II–I mill. av. J-C.* Subartu 8. Turnhout: Brepols.

Masson, Emilia
1976 Un nouvel examen des tablettes de Deir 'Alla (Jordanie). *Minos: Revista de Filologia Egea* 15: 7–33.

Master, Daniel
2001 State Formation Theory and the Kingdom of Israel. *JNES* 60 (2): 117–131.

Matthiae, Paolo
1997 *I Primi Imperi e I Principati del Ferro., 1600–700 A.C.* Rome: Electra.

Mattingly, Gerald
1983 The Exodus-Conquest and the Archaeology of Transjordan: New Light on an Old Problem. *Grace Theological Journal* 4 (2): 245–62.
1989 Moabite Religion and the Mesha' Inscription. Pp. 211–38 in *SMIM*.
1996 Al-Karak Resources Project 1995: A Preliminary Report on the Pilot Season. *ADAJ* 40: 349–67.
1997 A New Agenda for Resarch on Ancient Moab. *BA* 60: 214–21.

Mattingly, Gerald, John Lawlor, John Wineland, James Pace, Amy Bogaard and Michael Charles
1999 Al-Karak Resources Project 1997: Excavations at Khirbat al-Muḍaybi'. *ADAJ* 43: 127–44.

Mauss, Marcel
1990 (1925) *The Gift: The Form and Reason for Exchange in Archaic Societies*. Trans. W. D. Halls. New York: Norton.

Maynard, Kent
    1988 On Protestants and Pastoralists: The Segmentary Nature of Socio-Cultural
        Organisation. *Man* n.s. 23: 101–17.
Mazar, Amihai
    1997 Iron Age Chronology: A Reply to I. Finkelstein. *Levant* 29: 157–74.
Mazar, Benjamin
    1957 The Tobiads. *IEJ* 7: 137–45, 229–38.
Mazzoni, Stefania
    1997 The Gate and the City: Change and Continuity in Syro-Hittite Urban
        Ideology. Pp. 307–38 in *Die Orientalische Stadt: Kontinuität, Wandel, Bruch*, ed.
        Gernot Wilhelm. Saarbrücken: Saarbrücker Verlag.
Mazzoni, Stefania, ed.
    1994 *Nuove fondazioni nel Vicino Orient antico: realta e ideologia.* Pisa: Giardini.
Mbembe, Achille
    1992 Provisional Notes on the Postcolony. *Africa* 62: 3–37.
McGovern, Patrick
    1983 Test Soundings of Archaeological and Resistivity Survey Results at Rujm al-
        Ḥenu. *ADAJ* 27: 105–41.
    1986 *The Late Bronze and Early Iron Ages of Central Tranjordan: The Baqʿah Valley
        Project, 1977–1981.* Philadelphia: University Museum of the University of
        Pennsylvania.
    1989 The Baqʿah Valley Project 1987, Khirbet Umm ad-Dananir and al-Qeṣir.
        ADAJ 32: 123–36.
    1992 Settlement Patterns of the Late Bronze and Iron Ages in the Greater
        Amman Area. *SHAJ* 4: 179–83.
    1997 A Ceramic Sequence for Northern Jordan: An Archaeological and
        Chemical Perspective. *SHAJ* 6: 421–25.
McGuire, Randall
    1992 *A Marxist Archaeology.* New York: Academic Press.
McGuire, Randall and Robert Paynter, eds.
    1991 *The Archaeology of Inequality.* Oxford: Blackwell.
McGuire, Randall, and Dean Saitta
    1996 "Although They Have Petty Captains, They Obey Them Badly": The
        Dialectics of Prehispanic Western Pueblo Social Organization. *American
        Antiquity* 61 (2): 197–216.
McIntosh, Susan
    1999 Pathways to Complexity: An African Perspective. Pp. 1–30 in *Beyond
        Chiefdoms: Pathways to Complexity in Africa*, ed. Susan McIntosh. Cambridge:
        Cambridge University Press.
McLennan, Gregor
    1995 After Postmodernism—Back to Sociological Theory? *Sociology* 29 (1):
        117–32.
McMurray, Heather
    2002 An Iron II Scythian Point from Khirbat al-Mudaybiʿ. *Virtual Karak Resources
        Project.* www.vkrp.org/studies/historical/scythian-point/.
McNutt, Paula
    1999 *Reconstructing the Society of Ancient Israel.* Louisville, Ky.: Westminster John
        Knox Press.
Meeker, Michael
    1979 *Literature and Violence in North Arabia.* Cambridge: Cambridge University
        Press.
Mendenhall, George
    1962 The Hebrew Conquest of Palestine. *BA* 25: 66–87.

1973 *The Tenth Generation: The Origins of the Biblical Tradition.* Baltimore: Johns Hopkins University Press.

Meshel, Ze'ev
1992 The Architecture of the Israelite Fortresses in the Negev. Pp. 294–301 in *Architecture.*

Meskell, Lynn
1999 *Archaeologies of Social Life: Age, Sex, Class, Etc, in Ancient Egypt.* Oxford: Blackwell.
2001 Archaeologies of Identity. Pp. 187–213 in *Archaeological Theory Today,* ed. Ian Hodder. Cambridge: Polity Press.

Messick, Brinkley
1993 *The Calligraphic State: Textual Domination and History in a Muslim Society.* Berkeley: University of California Press.

Mettinger, Tryggve
1971 *Solomonic State Officials* Coniectanea Biblica Old Testament Series 5. Lund: C. W. K. Gleerup.

Meyer, John
1999 The Changing Cultural Content of the Nation-State: A World Society Perspective. Pp. 123–43 in *State/Culture.*

Miller, Daniel
1995 Consumption and Commodities. *ARA* 24: 141–61.

Miller, J. Maxwell
1974 The Moabite Stone as a Memorial Stele. *PEQ* 106: 9–18.
1989a The Israelite Journey Through (Around) Moab and Moabite Toponymy. *JBL* 108 (4): 577–95.
1989b Moab and the Moabites. Pp. 1–40 in *SMIM.*
1991 *Archaeological Survey of the Kerak Plateau.* ASOR Archaeological Reports 1. Atlanta: Scholars Press.
1992 Early Monarchy in Moab? Pp. 77–91 in *EEM.*

Miroschedji, Pierre de
1999 Yarmuth: The Dawn of City-States in Southern Canaan. *NEA* 62: 2–19.

Mitchell, Timothy
1999 Society, Economy, and the State Effect. Pp. 76–97 in *State/Culture.*

Mittmann, Siegfried
1973 Das Südliche Ostjordanland im Lichte eines Neu-Assyrischen Keilschrift-briefes aus Nimrud. *ZPDV* 89: 15–25.
1982 The Ascent of Luhith. *SHAJ* 1: 175–80.

Montlivault-Villeneuve, Estelle de
1989 Rumeil. Pp. 491–94 in *AJ II 2.*

de Moor, Johannes
1988 Narrative Poetry in Canaan. *UF* 20: 149–71.

Moormann, Frank
1959 *Report to the Government of Jordan on the Soils of East Jordan.* Rome: Food and Agriculture Organization of the United Nations.

Moran, William
1987 Join the 'Apiru or Become One? Pp. 209–12 in *"Working With No Data": Semitic and Egyptian Studies Presented to Thomas O. Lambdin,* ed. David Golomb and Susan Tower Hollis. Winona Lake, Ind.: Eisenbrauns.
1992 *The Amarna Letters.* Baltimore: Johns Hopkins University Press.

Morris, Ellen
2001 The Architecture of Imperialism: An Investigation into the Role of Fortresses and Administrative Headquarters in New Kingdom Foreign Policy. Ph.D. Dissertation, University of Pennsylvania.

Morris, Ian
  1986 Gift and Commodity in Archaic Greece. *Man* n.s. 21 (1): 1–17.
  2000 *Archaeology as Cultural History: Words and Things in Iron Age Greece.* Oxford:
    Blackwell.
Morton, William
  1955 Report of the Director of the School in Jerusalem. *BASOR* 140: 4–7.
  1957 Dhiban. *RB* 64: 221–23.
  1989 A Summary of the 1955, 1956, and 1965 Excavations at Dhiban. Pp. 239–46
    in *SMIM.*
Mountjoy, Penelope
  1986 *Mycenaean Decorated Pottery: A Guide to Identification.* Göteborg: Paul Ästroms.
Mouzelis, Nicos
  1991 *Back to Sociological Theory: The Construction of Social Orders.* New York: St.
    Martin's Press.
  1992 The Interaction Order and the Micro-Macro Distinction. *Sociological Theory*
    10 (1): 122–28.
  1995 *Sociological Theory: What Went Wrong? Diagnosis and Remedies.* New York:
    Routledge.
  1997 Social and System Integration: Lockwood, Habermas, Giddens. *Sociology* 31
    (1): 111–19.
  2000 The Subjectivist-Objectivist Divide: Against Transcendence. *Sociology* 34 (4):
    741–62.
Müller, Hans-Peter
  1994 König Mêša' von Moab und der Gott der Geschichte. *UF* 26: 373–95.
Müller, W. Max
  1904 The Egyptian Monument of Tell esh-Shihab. *PEFQS:* 78–80.
Mundy, Martha
  1995 *Domestic Government: Kinship, Community, and Polity in North Yemen.* New York:
    St Martin's Press.
Munson, Henry, Jr.
  1989 On the Irrelevance of the Segmentary Lineage Model in the Moroccan Rif.
    AA 91: 386–400.
Murphy, Roland E.
  1953 Israel and Moab in the Ninth Century B.C. *Catholic Biblical Quarterly* 15:
    409–17.
Murphy, William and Carol Bledsoe
  1987 Kinship and Territory in the History of a Kpelle Chiefdom (Liberia). Pp.
    123–147 in *The African Frontier: The Reproduction of Traditional African Societies,*
    ed. Igor Kopytoff. Bloomington: Indiana University Press.
Na'aman, Nadav
  1979 The Brook of Egypt and the Assyrian Policy on the Border of Egypt. *TA* 6:
    68–90.
  1986 Ḥapiru and Hebrews: The Transfer of a Social Term to the Literary Sphere.
    JNES 45 (4): 271–88.
  1991 Forced Participation in Alliances in the Course of the Assyrian Campaigns
    to the West. Pp. 80–98 in *Ah, Assyria . . . Studies in Assyrian History and Ancient
    Near Eastern Historiography Presented to Hayim Tadmor,* ed. Mordechai Cogan and
    Israel Eph'al. Jerusalem: Magnes Press.
  1994a The Campaign of Mesha Against Horonaim. *BN* 73: 27–30.
  1994b The "Conquest of Canaan" in the Book of Joshua and in History. Pp.
    218–81 in *FNM.*
  1996 The Contribution of the Amarna Letters to the Debate on Jerusalem's
    Position in the Tenth Century B.C.E. *BASOR* 304: 17–27.

1997 King Mesha and the Foundation of the Moabite Monarchy. *IEJ* 47 (1–2): 83–92.

Najjar, Mohammed
1992 Salvage Excavations at Khilda. *ADAJ* 36: 420–29 (in Arabic).
1999 "Ammonite" Monumental Architecture. Pp. 103–12 in *Ammon*.

Naroll, Raoul
1962 Floor Area and Settlement Population. *American Antiquity* 27: 587–89.

Naveh, Joseph
1987 *Early History of the Alphabet*. 2nd ed. Jerusalem: Magnes Press.

Negueruela, Ivan
1982 The Proto-Aeolic Capitals from Mudeibi'a, in Moab. *ADAJ* 26: 395–401.

Neev, David and Kenneth O. Emery
1995 The Destruction of Sodom, Gomorrah, and Jericho. New York: Oxford University Press.

Nevo, Yehuda
1991 *Pagans and Herders : A Re-Examination of the Negev Runoff Cultivation Systems in the Byzantine and Early Arab Periods*. Negev: IPS.

Niccacci, Alverio
1994 The Stele of Mesha and the Bible: Verbal System and Narrativity. *Orientalia* 63 (3): 226–48.

Niemann, Hermann
1993 *Herrschaft, königtum und staat: skizzen zur Soziokulterellen Entwicklung im monarchischen Israel*. Forschungen zum Alten Testament 6. Tübingen: J. C. B. Mohr.

Nietzsche, Friedrich
1969 *On the Genealogy of Morals/ Ecce Homo*. Ed. Walter Kaufmann. New York: Vintage Books.

Nigro, Lorenzo
1994 *Richerche sull'Architettura Palaziale della Palestina nelle età del Bronzo e del Ferro*. CMAO 5. Rome: Università Degli Studi Di Roma "La Sapienza."

Nougayrol, Jean
1955 *Le Palais royal d'Ugarit*. Vol. 3. *Textes accadiens et hurrites des Archives est, ouest, et centrales*. Mission de Ras Shamra 6. Paris: Imprimérie Nationale.

Nunn, Astrid
2000 Nekropolen und Gräber in Phönizien, Syrien und Jordanien zur Achämenidenzeit. *UF* 32: 389–463.

Nyerges, A. Endre
1992 The Ecology of Wealth-in-People: Agriculture, Settlement, and Society on the Perpetual Frontier. *AA* 94 (4): 860–81.

Oded, Bustany
1970 Observation on Methods of Assyrian Rule in Transjordania in the Time of Tiglath-Pileser III. *JNES* 29: 177–86.
1974 The Phoenician Cities and the Assyrian Empire in the Time of Tiglath-Pileser III. *ZPDV* 90: 38–49.
1979 *Mass Deportations and Deportees in the Neo-Assyrian Empire*. Wiesbaden: Harrassowitz.
1986 The Table of Nations (Genesis 10)—A Socio-Cultural Approach. *ZAW* 98: 14–31.
1993 Ahaz's Appeal to Tiglath-Pileser III in the Context of the Assyrian Policy of Expansion. Pp. 63–71 in *Studies in the Achaeology and History of Ancient Israel in Honour of Moshe Dothan*, ed. Michael Heltzer, Arthur Segal, and Daniel Kaufman. Haifa: Haifa University Press.

Ofer, Avi
2001 The Monarchic Period in the Judean Highland: A Spatial Overview. Pp. 14–37 in *SAIAIJ*.

Olàvarri, Emilio

1965 Sondages à Arô'er sur l'Arnon. *RB* 72: 77–94.

1969 Fouilles à Arô'er sur l'Arnon. *RB* 76: 230–59.

1977–78 Sondeo Arqueologico en Khirbet Medeineh junto a Smakieh (Jordania). *ADAJ* 22: 136–49.

1983 La Campagne de Fouilles 1982 à Khirbet Medeinet al-Mu`arradjeh près de Smakieh (Kerak). *ADAJ* 27: 165–78.

Olmo, Gregorio del

1999 *Canaanite Religion: According to the Liturgical Texts of Ugarit.* 2nd ed. Trans. Wilfred G. Watson. Betheseda: CDL Press.

Oppenheim, A. Leo

1967 Essay on Overland Trade in the First Millennium B.C. *Journal of Cuneiform Studies* 21: 236–54.

1969 Comment on Diakonoff. Pp. 33–40 in *Third International Conference of Economic History.* Paris: Mouton.

Oren, Eliezer

1984 Governor's Residencies in Canaan Under the New Kingdom: A Case Study of Egyptian Administration. *JSSEA* 14 (2): 36–56.

1992 Palaces and Patrician Houses in the Middle and Late Bronze Ages. Pp. 105–20 in *Architecture.*

Ornan, Tallay

1986 *A Man and His Land: Highlights from the Moshe Dayan Collection.* Jerusalem: Israel Museum.

Orthmann, Winfried

1971 *Unterschungen zur späthethitischen kunst.* Bonn: Rudolf Habelt.

Osbourne, Robin

1985 Buildings and Residence on the Land in Classical and Hellenistic Greece: The Contribution of Epigraphy. *Annual of the British School at Athens* 80: 119–28.

1986 Island Towers: The Case of Thasos. *Annual of the British School at Athens* 81: 166–78.

1987 *Classical Landscape with Figures: The Ancient Greek City and Its Countryside.* London: Georg Philip.

1992 Is It a Farm? The Definition of Agricultural Sites and Settlements in Ancient Greece. Pp. 21–27 in *Agriculture in Ancient Greece,* ed. Berit Wells. Stockholm: Swedish Institute in Athens.

Ottoson, Magnus

1980 *Temples and Cult Places in Palestine.* Boreas 12. Uppsala: Almqvist and Wiksell.

Palmer, Edward Henry

1881 The Desert of Tih and the Country of Moab. Pp, 1–70 in *The Survey of Western Palestine.* London: Palestine Exploration Fund.

Palumbo, Gaetano

1990 *The Early Bronze Age IV in the Southern Levant: Settlement Patterns, Economy, and Material Culture of a "Dark Age".* CMAO 3. Rome: University of Rome.

1994 *Jordan Antiquities Database and Information System.* Amman: Department of Antiquities/American Center for Oriental Research.

Parayre, Dominique

1993 À propos des sceaux ouest-sémitiques: Le Rôle de l'iconographie dans l'attribution d'un sceau à une aire culturelle et à un atelier. Pp. 27–51 in *Studies in the Iconography of Northwest Semitic Inscribed Seals,* ed. Benjamin Sass and Christoph Uehlinger. OBO 125. Fribourg/ Göttigen: University Press/ Vandenhoeck and Ruprecht.

Pardee, Denis
  1996 *Marziḥu, Kispu,* and the Ugaritic Funerary Cult: A Minamalist View. Pp. 273–87 in *Ugarit, Religion and Culture,* ed. Nicholas Wyatt and Wilfred G. Watson. Münster: Ugarit-Verlag.
Parker, S. Thomas
  1987 *The Roman Frontier in Central Jordan. Interim Report on the Limes Arabicus Project, 1980–1985.* 2 vols. British Archaeological Reports International Series 340. Oxford: British Archaeological Reports.
Parker, Simon
  1997 *Stories in Scripture and Inscriptions: Comparative Studies on Narratives in Northwest Semitic Inscriptions and the Hebrew Bible.* New York: Oxford University Press.
Parkin, Tim
  1992 *Demography and Roman Society.* Baltimore: Johns Hopkins University Press.
Parpola, Simo
  1970 *Neo-Assyrian Toponyms.* Neukirchen-Vluyn: Butzon and Bercker Kevelaer.
Parpola, Simo and Kazuko Watanabe, eds.
  1988 *Neo-Assyrian Treaties and Loyalty Oaths.* State Archives of Assyria. Helsinki: Helsinki University Press.
Parry, Jonathan
  1986 The Gift, the Indian Gift, and the "Indian Gift." *Man* n.s. 21: 453–73.
Pauketat, Timothy
  2001 Practice and History in Archaeology. *Anthropological Theory* 1: 73–98.
Pauketat, Timothy and Thomas Emerson
  1999 Representations of Hegemony as Community at Cahokia. Pp. 302–17 in *Material Symbols: Culture and Economy in Prehistory,* ed. John Robb. Carbondale: Center for Archaeological Investigations, Southern Illinois University.
Paynter, Robert
  1989 The Archaeology of Equality and Inequality. *ARA* 18: 369–99.
Pečirková, Jana
  1977 The Administrative Organization of the Neo-Assyrian Empire. *Archív Orientlání* 45: 211–28.
Peirce, Charles Sanders
  1931 *Collected Papers of Charles Sanders Peirce.* 8 vols. Ed. Charles Hartshorne and Paul Weiss. Cambridge, Mass.: Harvard University Press.
Perkmann, Markus
  1998 Social Integration and System Integration: Reconsidering the Classical Distinction. *Sociology* 32 (3): 491–507.
Peters, Emrys
  1967 Some Structural Aspects of the Feud Among the Camel-Herding Bedouin of Cyrenaica. *Africa* 37: 261–82.
  1972 Shifts in Power in a Lebanese Village. Pp. 165–97 in *Rural Politics and Social Change in the Middle East,* ed. Richard Antoun and Iliya Harik. Bloomington: Indiana University Press.
Petrie, William Flinders and C. Pape
  1952 Malfuf Near 'Amman. Pp. 38–42 in *Ancient Gaza,* vol. 5, ed. Ernest MacKay and Margaret Murray. British School of Egyptian Archaeology Publication 64. London: British School of Egyptian Archaeology.
Piccirillo, Michele
  1975 Una Tomba del Ferro I a Madaba. *Liber Annuus* 25: 199–224.
Piccirillo, Michele and Eugenio Alliata
  1999 *Madaba Map Centenary, 1897–1997: Travelling Through the Byzantine-Umayyad Period, Proceedings of the International Conference Held in Amman, 7–9 April 1997.* Jerusalem: Studium Biblicum Franciscanum.

Pintore, Franco
  1978 *Il Matrimonio Interdinastico nel Vicino Oriente Durante i Secoli XV–XIII.* Rome: Instituto per l'Oriente, Università di Roma.
Pitard, Wayne
  1987 *Ancient Damascus: A Historical Study of the Syrian City-State from Earliest Times until Its Fall to the Assyrians in 732 B.C.E.* Winona Lake, Ind.: Eisenbrauns.
  1996 Care of the Dead at Emar. Pp. 123–40 in *Emar: The History, Religion, and Culture of a Syrian Town in the Late Bronze Age,* ed. Mark Chavalas. Bethesda, Md.: CDL Press.
Pitt-Rivers, Julian
  1977 *The Fate of Shechem, or, The Politics of Sex : Essays in the Anthropology of the Mediterranean.* Cambridge: Cambridge University Press.
Polanyi, Karl, ed.
  1957 *Trade and Market in the Early Empires: Economies in History and Theory.* Chicago: Henry Regnery.
Pope, Marvin
  1981 The Cult of the Dead at Ugarit. Pp. 159–79 in *Ugarit in Retrospect: Fifty Years of Ugarit and Ugaritic,* ed. Gordon Young. Winona Lake, Ind.: Eisenbrauns.
Porten, Bezeal
  1981 The Identity of King Adon. *BA* 44: 41–45.
Portugali, Juval
  1994 Theoretical Speculations on the Transition from Nomadism to Monarchy. Pp. 203–17 in *FNM.*
Postgate, Nicholas
  1974 *Taxation and Conscription in the Assyrian Empire.* Studia Pohl, Series Major 3. Rome: Biblical Institute Press.
  1974b Remarks on Conditions in the Assyrian Countryside. *JESHO* 17: 244–71.
  1979 The Economic Structure of the Assyrian Empire. Pp. 193–221 in *PP.*
  1992 The Land of Assur and the Yoke of Assur. *WA* 23 (3): 247–63.
Potts, Daniel
  1988 Trans-Arabian Routes of the Pre-Islamic Period. Pp. 127–62 in *L'Arabie et ses mers bordieres,* vol. I, ed. Jean-François Salles Lyon: Maison de l'Orient Méditerranéen.
Potts, Timothy
  1987 A Bronze Age Ivory-Decorated Box from Pella (Paḥel) and its Foreign Relations. *SHAJ* 3: 59–71.
Powell, John H.
  1988. *The Geology of The Karak Area.* Amman: Hashemite Kingdom of Jordan, Geological Mapping Division, Ministry of Energy And Mineral Resources.
Prag, Kay
  1989 Preliminary Report on the Excavations at Tell Iktanu, Jordan, 1987. *Levant* 21: 33–45.
Prag, Kay and Hugh Barnes
  1996 Three Fortresses on the Wadi Kafrain, Jordan. *Levant* 28: 41–61.
Preisigke, Friedrich
  1919 Die Begriff PYRGOS und STEGH bei der Hausanlage. *Hermes* 54: 423–32.
Prewitt, Terry
  1981 Kinship Structures and the Genesis Genealogies. *JNES* 40 (2): 87–98.
  1990 *The Elusive Covenant.* Bloomington: Indiana University Press.
Price, Barbara
  1978 Secondary State Formation: An Explanatory Model. Pp. 161–86 in *Origins.*
Price, T. Douglas and Gary M. Feinman
  1995 *Foundations of Social Inequality.* New York: Plenum Press.

Pritchard, James
1980 *The Cemetery at Tell es-Sa'idiyeh.* UMM 41. Philadelphia: University Museum of the University of Philadelphia.
Pritchard, James, ed.
1969 *Ancient Near Eastern Texts Relating to the Old Testament.* 3rd ed. Princeton, N.J.: Princeton University Press.
Puech, Emile
1978 Un ivoire de Bît-Gusî (Arpad) à Nimrud. *Syria* 55: 163–69.
Pulak, Çemal
1998 The Uluburin Shipwreck: An Overview. *International Journal of Nautical Archaeology* 27 (3): 188–224.
Radcliffe-Brown, Alfred Reginald
1940 Preface. Pp. xi–xxiii in *African Political Systems,* ed. Meyer Fortes and Edward E. Evans-Pritchard. Oxford: Oxford University Press.
Rainey, Anson
1965 The Military Personnel of Ugarit. *JNES* 24: 17–27.
1979 The *Sitz im Leben* of the Samaria Ostraca. *TA* 6: 91–94.
1995 Unruly Elements in Late Bronze Canaanite Society. Pp. 481–96 in *Pomegranates and Golden Bells: Studies in Biblical, Jewish, and Near Eastern Ritual, Law, and Literature in Honor of Jacob Milgrom,* ed. David Wright, David Noel Freedman and Avi Hurvitz. Winona Lake, Ind.: Eisenbrauns.
1998 Syntax, Hermeneutics and History. *IEJ* 48 (3–4): 239–51.
Ranum, Orest
1968 *Paris in the Age of Absolutism: An Essay.* New York: Wiley.
Ray, Paul
2001 *Tell Hesban and Vicinity in the Iron Age.* Hesban 6. Berrien Springs, Mich.: Andrews University Press.
Reade, Julian
1979 Ideology and Propaganda in Assyrian Art. Pp. 329–43 in *PP.*
Redford, Donald
1982 Bronze Age Itinerary in Transjordan (Nos. 89–101 of Thutmose III's List of Asiatic Toponyms). *JSSEA* 12: 55–74.
1990 *Egypt and Canaan in the New Kingdom.* Beer-Sheva 4. Beer-Sheba: Ben-Gurion University of the Negev.
1992 *Egypt, Canaan, and Israel in Ancient Times.* Princeton, N.J.: Princeton University Press.
1997 The Ancient Egyptian "City": Figment or Reality? Pp. 210–20 in *Aspects of Urbanism in Antiquity: From Mesopotamia to Crete,* ed. Walter Aufrecht, Neil Mirau, and Steven Gauley. *JSOT* Suppl. 244. Sheffield: Sheffield Academic Press.
Reed, William and Fredrick Winnett.
1963 A Fragment of an Early Moabite Inscription from Kerak. *BASOR* 172: 1–9.
Reich, Ronny
1975 The Persian Building at Ayyelet ha-Shaḥar: The Assyrian Palace of Hazor? *IEJ* 25: 233–37.
1992 Palaces and Residences in the Iron Age. Pp. 214–22 in *Architecture.*
Reisner, George, Clarence Fisher, and David Gordon
1924 *Harvard Excavations at Samaria, 1908–1910.* Cambridge, Mass.: Harvard University Press.
Renz, Johannes
1995 *Die Althebräischen Inschriften.* 5 vols. Darmstadt: Wissenschaftliche Buchgesellschaft.

Rendsburg, Gary
   1981 A Reconstruction of Moabite-Israelite History. *Journal of the Ancient Near East Society* 13: 67–73.
Reviv, Hanoch
   1989 *Elders in Ancient Israel: A Study of a Biblical Institution.* Jerusalem: Magnes Press.
Riklin, Shmuel
   1997 Bet Ayré. *'Atiqot* 32: 7–20 (in Hebrew).
Roseberry, William
   1994 Hegemony and the Language of Contention. Pp. 355–66 in *Everyday Forms of State Formation,* ed. Gil Joseph and Daniel Nugent. Durham: Duke University Press.
Rosen, Arlene
   1986 Environmental Change and Settlement at Tel Lachish. *BASOR* 263: 55–60.
   1991 Early Bronze Age Tel Erani: An Environmental Perspective. *TA* 18 (2): 192–204.
   1995 The Social Response to Environmental Change in Early Bronze Age Canaan. *JAA* 14: 26–44.
Rosen, Lawrence
   1979 Social Identity and Points of Attachment: Approaches to Social Organization. Pp. 19–122 in *Meaning and Order in Morroccan Society,* ed. Clifford Geertz, Hilda Geertz, and Lawrence Rosen. Cambridge: Cambridge University Press.
Roth, Martha
   1987 Age at Marriage and the Household: A Study of Neo-Babylonian and Neo-Assyrian Forms. *Comparative Studies in Society and History* 29 (4): 715–47.
Routledge, Bruce
   1995 Archaeological Explorations in the Vicinity of Khirbet ath-Thamayil— 1992. *ADAJ* 39: 127–47.
   1996a Intermittent Agriculture and the Political Economy of Iron Age Moab. Ph.D. Dissertation, University of Toronto.
   1996b Structural Constraints on Family Size in Iron Age Palestine. Paper read at the ASOR Annual Meeting. New Orleans, LA.
   1996c State, Empire and Identity in Iron Age Jordan. Pp. 519–25 in *Debating Complexity: Proceedings of the 26th Annual Chacmool Conference,* ed. Daniel Meyer, Peter Dawson, and Donald Hanna. Calgary: Archaeological Association of the University of Calgary.
   1997a Learning to Love the King: Urbanism and the State in Iron Age Moab. Pp. 130–44 in *Aspects of Urbanism in Antiquity: From Mesopotamia to Crete,* ed. Walter Aufrecht, Neil Mirau, and Steven Gauley. *JSOT* Suppl. 244. Sheffield: Sheffield Academic Press.
   1997b Mesopotamian "Influence" in Iron Age Jordan: Issues of Power, Identity and Value. *Bulletin of the Canadian Society for Mesopotamian Studies* 32: 33–41.
   2000a Seeing Through Walls: Interpreting Iron I Architecture at Khirbat al-Mudayna al-'Aliya, Jordan. *BASOR* 319: 37–70.
   2000b The Politics of Mesha: Segmented Identities and State Formation in Iron Age Moab. *JESHO* 43 (3): 221–56.
   2003 The Antiquity of the Nation? Critical Reflections from the Ancient Near East. *Nations and Nationalism* 9 (2): 213–33.
   n.d. *William Morton's Excavations at Dhiban.* Manuscript in preparation.
Routledge, Carolyn
   2000 The Balu'a Stele Revisited. Paper read at the ASOR Annual Meeting, Nashville, Tenn.

Rowe, Alan
1930 *The Topography and History of Beth-Shan, with Details of the Egyptian and Other Inscriptions Found on the Site*. Publications of the Palestine Section I, University of Pennsylvania Museum. Philadelphia: University of Pennsylvania Press.

Rowe, Alan and Gerald Fitzgerald
1940 *The Four Canaanite Temples of Beth-Shan*. Publications of the Palestine Section II, University of Pennsylvania Museum. Philadelphia: University of Pennsylvania Press.

Rowton, Michael
1974 Enclosed Nomadism. *JESHO* 17: 1–30.
1976 Dimorphic Structure and the Problem of the 'Apirû-'Ibrîm. *JNES* 35 (1): 13–20.

Russell, John
1991 *Senacherib's Palace Without Rival at Nineveh*. Chicago: University of Chicago Press.

Rüterswörden, Udo
1985 *Die Beamten der Israelitischen Königszeit: Eine Studie zu šr und vergleichbaren Begriffen*. Stuttgart: Kohlhammer.

Sader, Hélène
1987 *Les États araméens de Syrie depuis leur fondation jusqu'à leur transformation en provinces assyriennes*. Beiruter Texte und Studien 36. Beirut: Deutschen Morgenländischen Gesellschaft.
2000 The Aramaean Kingdoms of Syria: Origin and Formation Processes. Pp. 61–76 in *Essays on Syria in the Iron Age*, ed. Guy Bunnens. Ancient Near Eastern Studies Supplement 7. Louvain: Peeters.

Saggs, Harold W. F.
1955 The Nimrud Letters, 1952—Part 2. *Iraq* 17: 126–54, Pl. 30–35.
1959 The Nimrud Letters, 1952—Part 5. *Iraq* 21: 158–79, Pl.43–49.

Sahlins, Marshall
1963 Poor Man, Rich Man, Big Man, Chief: Political Types in Melanesia and Polynesia. *Comparative Studies in Society and History* 3: 285–303.

Saller, Richard
1994 *Patriarchy, Property, and Death in the Roman Family*. Cambridge: Cambridge University Press.

Salles, Jean-François
1995 Ritual mortuaire et ritual social à Ras Shamra/Ougarit. Pp. 171–84 in *The Archaeology of Death in the Ancient Near East*, ed. Stuart Campbell and Anthony Green. Oxford: Oxbow.

Salzman, Philip
1978 Does Complementary Opposition Exist? *AA* 80: 53–70.
1979 Tribal Organization and Subsistence: A Response to Emmanuel Marx. *AA* 81: 121–24.
2000 Hierarchical Image and Reality: The Construction of a Tribal Chiefship. *Comparative Studies in Society and History* 42: 49–66.

Sass, Benjamin
1988 *The Genesis of the Alphabet and Its Development in the Second Millennium B.C.* ÄAT 13. Wiesbaden: Harrassowitz.

Sassoon, Anne
1980 *Gramsci's Politics*. Surrey: Biddles.

Sauer, James
1986 Transjordan in the Bronze and Iron Ages: A Critique of Glueck's Synthesis. *BASOR* 263: 1–26.
1994 The Pottery at Hesban and Its Relationship to the History of Jordan: An

Interim Hesban Pottery Report, 1993. Pp. 225–81 in *Hesban After 25 Years*, ed. David Merling and Lawrence Geraty. Berrien Springs, Mich.: Institute of Archaeology/ Horn Archaeological Museum, Andrews University.

de Saulcy, Louis Félicien
1854 *Narrative of a Journey Round the Dead Sea and in the Bible Lands, 1850 and 1851, Including an Account of the Sites of Sodom and Gomorrah.* Ed. Edward de Warren. London: Richard Bentley.

Sayer, Derek
1994 Everyday Forms of State Formation: Some Dissident Remarks on "Hegemony." Pp. 367– 77 in *Everyday Forms of State Formation*, ed. Gil Joseph and Daniel Nugent. Durham, N.C.: Duke University Press.

Schlegel, Alice
1992 African Political Models in the American Southwest: Hopi as an Internal Frontier Society. *AA* 94: 377–97.

Schloen, David
2001 *The House of the Father as Fact and Symbol: Patrimonialism in Ugarit and the Ancient Near East.* SAHL 2. Winona Lake: Eisenbrauns.

Schmidt, Brian
1994 *Israel's Beneficent Dead: Ancestor Cult and Necromancy in Ancient Israelite Religion and Tradition.* Tübingen: J. C. Mohr.

Schneider, David
1984 *A Critique of the Study of Kinship.* Ann Arbor: University of Michigan Press.

Schottroff, Willy
1966 Horonaim, Nimrim, Luhith, und der Westrand des "Landes Ataroth." *ZDPV* 82: 163–208.

Schuldenrein, Joseph and Geoffrey Clark
1994 Landscape and Prehistoric Chronology of West-Central Jordan. *Geoarchaeology* 9 (1): 31–55.

Scott, James C.
1985 *Weapons of the Weak: Everyday Forms of Peasant Resistance.* New Haven, Conn.: Yale University Press.
1990 *Domination and the Arts of Resistance.* New Haven, Conn.: Yale University Press.
1998 *Seeing Like a State.* New Haven, Conn.: Yale University Press.

Segert, Stanislav
1961 Die Sprache der Moabitischen Königsinschrift. *Archív Orientální* 29: 197–267.

Shanks, Michael and Christopher Tilley
1988 *Social Theory and Archaeology.* Albuquerque: University of New Mexico Press.

Shawabkeh, Khalid
1991 *The Geology of the Adir Area: Map Sheet.* Amman: Geology Directorate.

el-Sherbini, Abdel-Aziz
1979 *Food Security Issues in the Arab Near East.* Oxford: Pergamon Press.

Sherratt, Susan and Andrew Sherratt
1991 From Luxuries to Commodities: The Nature of Mediterranean Bronze Age Trading Systems. Pp. 351–86 in *Bronze Age Trade in the Mediterranean. Papers Presented at the Conference Held at Rewley House, Oxford, December 1989*, ed. Noel Gale. *SIMA* 90. Jonsered: Paul Åströms.
1993 The Growth of the Mediterranean Economy in the Early First Millenium BC. *WA* 24 (3): 361–78.

Shilling, Chris
1997 The Undersocialised Conception of the Embodied Agent in Modern Sociology. *Sociology* 31 (4): 737–54.

Shiloh, Yigal
  1979 *The Proto-Aeolic Capital and Israelite Ashlar Masonry.* Qedem 11. Jerusalem: Institute of Archaeology, Hebrew University.
  1980 Solomon's Gate at Megiddo as Recorded by Its Excavator. *Levant* 12: 69–76.
  1992 Underground Water Systems in the Land of Israel in the Iron Age. Pp. 275–93 in *Architecture.*
Shryock, Andrew
  1997 *Nationalism and the Genealogical Imagination: Oral History and Textual Authority in Tribal Jordan.* Berkeley: University of California Press.
Silberman, Neil
  1982 *Digging for God and Country.* Garden City, N.Y.: Anchor Books.
Simmons, Ellen
  2000 Subsistence in Transition: Analysis of an Archaeobotanical Assemblage from Khirbet al-Mudayna al-'Aliya. M.Sc. dissertation, University of Sheffield.
  n.d. A Preliminary Analysis of Archaeobotanical Remains from Khirbat al-Mudayna al-'Aliya: The 2000 Season. Manuscript.
Singer, Michael
  1991 Physical Properties of Arid Region Soils. Pp. 81–109 in *Semiarid Lands and Deserts: Soil Resources and Reclamation,* ed. John J. Skujins. New York: Marcel Dekker.
Singer-Avitz, Lily
  1999 Beersheba: A Gateway Community in Southern Arabian Long-Distance Trade in the Eighth Century B.C.E. *TA* 26 (1): 3–75.
Skinner, Quentin
  1989 The State. Pp. 90–131 in *Political Innovation and Conceptual Change,* ed. Terence Ball, James Farr, and Russell Hanson. Cambridge: Cambridge University Press.
  1999 Hobbes and the Purely Artificial Person of the State. *Journal of Political Philosophy* 7 (1): 1–29.
Smelik, Klaas
  1992 *Converting the Past: Studies in Ancient Israelite and Moabite Historiography.* Leiden: Brill.
Smith, Adam
  2001 The Limitations of Doxa: Agency and Subjectivity from an Archaeological Point of View. *Journal of Social Archaeology* 1 (2): 155–71.
Smith, George
  1901 Notes of a Journey Through Hauran, with Inscriptions Found by the Way. *PEFQS*: 340–61.
Smith, Michael
  1956 On Segmentary Lineage Systems. *JRAI* 86 (2): 39–80.
Smith, Robert Houston
  1973 *Pella of the Decapolis.* Wooster, Ohio: College of Wooster.
Spencer, Charles
  1990 On the Tempo and Mode of State Formation: Neoevolutionism Reconsidered. *JAA* 9 (1): 1–30.
  1993 Human Agency, Biased Transmission, and the Cultural Evolution of Chiefly Authority. *JAA* 12: 41–74.
  1997 Evolutionary Approaches in Archaeology. *Journal of Archaeological Research* 5 (3): 209–64.
Spronk, Klaas
  1986 *Beatific Afterlife in Ancient Israel and in the Ancient Near East.* AOAT 219. Kevelaer: Butzon and Bercker.
Stager, Lawrence
  1985 The Archaeology of the Family in Ancient Israel. *BASOR* 260: 1–35.

1991 *Ashkelon Discovered: From Canaanites and Philistines to Romans and Moslems.* Washington, D.C.: Biblical Archaeology Society.

1995 The Impact of the Sea Peoples in Canaan (1185–1050 B.C.E.). Pp. 332–48 in *ASHL.*

1996 Ashkelon and the Archaeology of Destruction: Kislev 604 B.C.E. *EI* 25: 61*–74*.

1998 Forging an Identity: The Emergence of Ancient Israel. Pp. 123–75 in *The Oxford History of the Biblical World*, ed. Michael D. Cogan. New York: Oxford University Press.

Stallybrass, Peter and Allon White

1986 *The Politics and Poetics of Transgression.* Ithaca, N.Y.: Cornell University Press.

Stanish, Charles

2001 The Origins of State Societies in South America. *ARA* 30: 41–64.

van der Steen, Eveline

1995 Aspects of Nomadism and Settlement in the Central Jordan Valley. *PEQ* 127: 141–58.

1996 The Central East Jordan Valley in the Late Bronze Age and Early Iron Ages. *BASOR* 302: 51–74.

1997 Pots and Potters in the Central Jordan Valley. *ADAJ* 41: 81–93.

1999 Survival and Adaptation: Life East of the Jordan in the Transition from the Late Bronze Age to the Early Iron Age. *PEQ* 131: 176–92.

Stein, Gil

1998 Heterogeneity, Power, and Political Economy: Some Current Research Issues in the Archaeology of Old World Complex Societies. *Journal of Archaeological Research* 6 (1): 1–44.

Steiner, Margreet

2001 Jerusalem in the Tenth and Seventh Centuries BCE: From Administrative Town to Commercial City. Pp.280–88 in *SAIAIJ.*

Steinmetz, George, ed.

1999 *State/Culture.*

Stern, Ephraim

1984 *Excavations at Tel Mevorakh*, vol. 2. *The Bronze Age.* Qedem 18. Jerusalem: Institute of Archaeology, Hebrew University.

1990 Schumacher's Shrine in Building 338 at Megiddo: A Rejoiner. *IEJ* 40 (2–3): 102–7.

Stiebing, William

1989 *Out of the Desert.* Buffalo, N.Y.: Prometheus Books.

Strange, John

1997 Tall al-Fukhär 1990–1991: A Preliminary Report. *SHAJ* 6: 399–406.

2000 The Late Bronze Age in Northern Jordan in the Light of the Finds at Tell el-Fukhar. Pp. 476–81 in *AJB.*

Stroebel, August

1990 Ez-Zara—Mukawer Survey. Pp. 81–86 in *The Near East in Antiquity*, vol. 1, ed. Suzanne Kerner. Amman: Al Kutba.

1997 Ancient Roads in the Roman District of Peraea: Routes of Communication in the Easten Area of the Dead Sea. *SHAJ* 6: 271–80.

Strommenger, Eva

1970 *Die Neuassyrische Rundskulptur.* Berlin: Gebr. Mann Verlag.

Sukenik, Elieazar

1936 Note on a Fragment of an Israelite Stele Found at Samaria. *PEFQS*: 156.

Swiggers, Pierre

1982 The Moabite Inscription of el-Kerak. *Annali Instituto Orientale di Napoli* 42: 521–25.

Tadmor, Hayim
1975 Assyria and the West: The Ninth Century and Its Aftermath. Pp. 36–48 in
*Unity and Diversity: Essays in the History, Literature, and Religion of the Ancient Near
East*, ed. Hans Goedicke and John J. M. Roberts. Baltimore: Johns Hopkins
University Press.
1991 On the Role of Aramaic in the Assyrian Empire. Pp. 419–26 in *Near Eastern
Studies Dedicated to H.I.H. Prince Takahito Mikasa on the Occasion of His Seventy-
Fifth Birthday*, ed. Masao Mori, Hideo Ogawa, and Mamoru Yoshikawa. Wiesbaden: Harrassowitz.
1994 *The Inscriptions of Tiglath-Pileser III King of Assyria.* Jerusalem: Israel Academy
of the Sciences and Humanities.
1997 Propaganda, Literature, Historiography: Cracking the Code of Assyrian
Royal Inscriptions. Pp. 325–38 in *Assyria 1995*.
Tapper, Richard
1997 *Frontier Nomads of Iran: A Political and Social History of the Shahsevan.* Cambridge: Cambridge University Press.
Taylor, Charles
1990 Modes of Civil Society. *Public Culture* 3 (1): 95–118.
Thomas, Nicholas
1989 *Out of Time: History and Evolution in Anthropological Discourse.* Cambridge:
Cambridge University Press.
Thompson, Henry O.
1986 An Iron Age Tomb at Madaba. Pp. 331–63 in *The Archaeology of Jordan and
Other Studies: Presented to Siegfried H. Horn*, ed. Lawrence Geraty and Larry Herr.
Berrien Springs, Mich.: Andrews University Press.
1989 *Archaeology in Jordan.* New York: Peter Lang.
Thompson, Thomas L.
1992 *Early History of the Israelite People: From the Written and Archaeological Sources.*
Leiden: Brill.
Timm, Stefan
1989 *Moab Zwischen dem Machen.* Wiesbaden: Harrassowitz.
1993 Das ikonographische repertoire der moabitischen siegel und seine entwicklung: von maximalismus zum minimalismus. Pp. 161–93 in *Studies in the Iconography of Northwest Semitic Inscribed Seals*, ed. Benjamin Sass and Christoph Uehlinger.
OBO 125. Fribourg/Göttigen: University Press/Vandenhoeck and Ruprecht.
van der Toorn, Karel
1996 *Family Religion in Babylonia, Ugarit and Israel: Continuity and Change in the
Forms of Religious Life.* SHCANE 7. Leiden: Brill.
Tournay, Raymond
1967 Un Cylindre babylonien découvert en Tranjordanie. *RB* 74: 248–54.
Trigger, Bruce
1998 *Sociocultural Evolution.* Oxford: Blackwell.
Tristram, Henry
1873 *The Land of Moab: Travels and Discoveries on the East Side of the Dead Sea and
the Jordan.* New York: Harper and Bros.
Tropper, Josef
1993 *Die Inschriften Von Zincirli.* Münster: Ugarit-Verlag.
Tsukimoto, Akio
1985 *Untersuchungen zur Totenpflege (kispum) im alten Mesopotamien.* Vluyn: Butzon
and Bercker Kevelaer.
Tubb, Jonathan
1988 Tell es-Saʻidiyeh: Preliminary Report on the First Three Seasons of
Renewed Excavations. *Levant* 20: 23–88

1990 Preliminary Report on the Fourth Season of Excavations at Tell es-Sa'idiyeh in the Jordan Valley. *Levant* 22: 21–42.

1995 An Aegean Presence in Egypto-Canaan. Pp. 136–45 in *Egypt, the Aegean and the Levant*, ed. W.Vivian Davies and Louise Schofield. London: British Museum Press.

1997 Tell es-Sa'idiyeh. Pp. 452–55 in *OEANE*. Vol. 4.

Tubb, Johathan and Peter Dorrell

1991 Tell es-Sa'idiyeh: Interim Report on the Fifth (1990) Season of Excavations. *Levant* 23: 67–86.

Tubb, Johnathan, Peter Dorrell and Felicity Cobbing

1996 Interim Report on the Eighth (1995) Season of Excavations at Tell es-Sa'idiyeh. *PEQ* 128: 16–40.

Tufnell, Olga, C. H. Inge, and G. Lancaster Harding

1940 *Lachish (Tell ed Duweir)*. Vol. 2. *The Fosse Temple*. Wellcome Archaeological Research Expedition to the Near East. London: Oxford University Press.

Tully, Dennis, Evan F. Thomson, Ronald Jaubert, and Thomas Nordblom

1985 On-Farm Trials in Northwestern Syria: Testing the Feasibility of Annual Forage Legumes as Grazing and Conserved Feed. Pp. 209–36 in *Research Methodology for Livestock On-Farm, Trials*, ed. Thomas Nordblom, Awad el-Karim, Hamid Ahmed, and Gordon Potts. Ottawa: International Development Research Centre.

Turner, Frederick

1920 *The Frontier in American History*. New York: Holt.

Turner, Geoffrey

1970 The State Apartments of Late Assyrian Palaces. *Iraq* 32: 117–213.

Tushingham, A. Douglas

1972 *The Excavations at Dibon (Dhîbân) in Moab: The Third Campaign, 1952–1953*. AASOR 40. Cambridge, Mass.: ASOR.

1990 Dhiban Reconsidered: King Mesha and his Works. *ADAJ* 34: 183–92.

Tushingham, A. Douglas and Peter Pedrette

1995 Mesha's Citadel Complex (Qarḥoh) at Dhîbān. *SHAJ* 5: 151–59.

Uehlinger, Christoph

1993 Introduction: The Status of Iconography in the Study of Northwest Semitic Inscribed Seals. Pp. xi-xxiii in *Studies in the Iconography of Northwest Semitic Inscribed Seals*, ed. Benjamin Sass and Christoph Uehlinger. OBO 125. Fribourg/Göttigen: University Press/Vandenhoeck and Ruprecht.

Ussishkin, David

1966 King Solomon's Palace and Building 1723 in Megiddo. *IEJ* 16 (3): 174–86.

1973 King Solomon's Palaces. *BA* 36: 78–105.

1978 Excavations of Tel Lachish, 1973–1977: Preliminary Report. *TA* 5: 1–97.

1980 Was the "Solomonic" City-Gate at Megiddo Built by King Solomon? *BASOR* 239: 1–18.

1983 Excavations at Tel Lachish, 1978–1983: Second Preliminary Report. *TA* 10: 97–185.

1989a The Erection of Royal Monuments in City-Gates. Pp. 485–96 in *Anatolia and the Ancient Near East: Studies in Honor of Tshin Özgüç*, ed. Kutlu Emre, Bartel Hrouda, Machteld Mellink, and Nimet Özguc. Anakara: Türk Tarih Kurumu Basimevi.

1989b Schumacher's Shrine in Building 338 at Megiddo. *IEJ* 39 (3–4): 149–72.

Vanderhooft, David

1999 *The Neo-Babylonian Empire and Babylon in the Later Prophets*. HSM 59. Atlanta: Scholars Press.

Van Seters, John

1972 The Conquest of Sihon's Kingdom: A Literary Examination. *JBL* 91: 182–97.

1980 Once Again the Conquest of Sihon's Kingdom. *JBL* 97: 347–51.

Vaughn, Andrew
1999 *Theology, History, and Archaeology in the Chronicler's Account of Hezekiah.* Atlanta: ASOR.

Veblen, Thorstein
1979 (1899) *The Theory of the Leisure Class.* New York: Penguin

Vincent, Andrew
1992 Conceptions of the State. Pp. 43–55 in *Encyclopedia of Government and Politics,* vol. 1, Mary Hawkesworth and Maurice Kogan. New York: Routledge.

Vita-Finzi, Carlo
1969 *The Mediterranean Valleys, Geological Changes in Historical Times.* London: Cambridge University Press.

Wagstaff, J. Malcolm
1981 Buried Assumptions: Some Problems in the Interpretation of the "Younger Fill" Raised by Recent Data from Greece. *Journal of Archaeological Science* 8: 247–64.

Waheeb, Mohammed
1992 A Fortified Agricultural Complex East of Amman (Late Bronze Age-Iron Age): Preliminary Report. *ADAJ* 36: 408–399 (in Arabic).

Walmsley, Alan, Philip G. Macumber, Philip Edwards, Stephen Bourke, and Pamela Watson
1993 Preliminary Report on the University of Sydney's Eleventh and Twelfth Season of Excavation at Pella in Jordan. *ADAJ* 37: 165–240.

Ward, William
1964 Cylinders and Scarabs from a Late Bronze Temple at 'Amman. *ADAJ* 8–9: 47–55.
1972 The Shasu "Bedouin": Notes on a Recent Publication. *JESHO* 15: 35–60.

Ward, William and Martha Joukowsky
1992 *The Crisis Years: The 12th Century B.C. from Beyond the Danube to the Tigris.* Dubuque: Kendall/Hunt.

Ward, William and Malachi Martin
1964 The Balu'a Stele: A New Trancription with Paleographic and Historical Notes.
ADAJ 8–9: 5–35.

Warembol, Eugène
1983 La stèle de Rugm el-'Abd (Louvre AO 5055): une image de divinité moabite du IXème-VIIIème siècle av. N.È. *Levant* 15: 63–75.

Warren, Peter and Vronwy Hankey
1989 *Aegean Bronze Age Chronology.* Bristol: Bristol Classical Press.

Waterman, Leroy
1930 *Royal Correspondence of the Assyrian Empire.* Ann Arbor: University of Michigan Press.

Weber, Max
1978 *Economy and Society.* 2 vols. Ed. Guenther Roth and Claus Wittich. Berkeley: University of California Press.

Weill, Raymond
1938 L'Écriture des tablettes crétoises en Syrie-Palestine, vers le XIIIᵉ siècle. *Revue de Égyptologie* 3: 81–89.

Weiner, Annette
1992 *Inalienable Possessions: The Paradox of Keeping-While-Giving.* Berkeley: University of California Press.

Weinstein, James
1981 The Egyptian Empire in Palestine: A Reassessment. *BASOR* 241: 1–28.

Weippert, Helga
1988 *Palästina in Vorhellenistischer Zeit.* Munich: C. H. Beck.
Weippert, Manfred
1974 Semitsche Nomaden des zweiten Jahrtausends: Über de ŠAsw der ägyptischen Quellen. *Biblica* 55: 265–80, 427–33.
1979 The Israelite "Conquest" and the Evidence from Transjordan. Pp. 15–34 in *Symposia Celebrating the Seventy-fifth Anniversary of the Founding of the American Schools of Oriental Reserach (1900–1975),* ed. Frank Moore Cross. Cambridge, Mass.: ASOR.
1982 Zur Syrienpolitik Tiglathpilesers III. Pp. 395–408 in *Mesoptamien und Seine Nachbarn,* vol. 2, ed. Hans Nissen and Johannes Renger. Berlin: Dietrich Reiner.
1987 Relations of the States East of the Jordan with the Mesopotamian Powers During the First Millennium BC. *SHAJ* 3: 97–105.
1994–1995 Moab. *RLA* 8(3/4–5/6): 318–25.
1995 Rababatora. Pp. 333–38 in *Meilenstein: Festgabe für Herbert Donner zum 16. Februar 1995,* ed. Manfred Weippert and Stefan Timm. ÄAT 30. Wiesbaden: Harrassowitz.
1997 Israélites, Araméens, et Assyriens dans la Transjordanie septentrionale. *ZPDV* 113: 19–38.
Weissert, Elnathan
1997 Royal Hunt and Royal Triumph in a Prism Fragment of Ashurbanipal (85–5–22,2). Pp. 239–258 in *Assyria 1995.*
Wente, Edward
1963 Sheklesh or Shasu? *JNES* 22: 167–72
West, Neil
1991 Nutrient Cycling in Soils of Semiarid and Arid Regions. Pp. 295–332 in *Semiarid Lands and Deserts: Soil Resource and Reclamation,* ed. John J. Skujins. New York: Marcel Dekker.
Wilhelm, Gernot
1989 *The Hurrians.* Trans. Jennifer Barnes. Warminster: Aris and Philips.
Wilkinson, Tony J.
1999 Holocene Valley Fills of Southern Turkey and Northwestern Syria: Recent Geoarchaeological Contributions. *Quaternary Science Review* 18: 555–71.
Williams, Raymond
1977 *Marxism and Literature.* Oxford: Oxford University Press.
Wilson, Robert
1977 *Genealogy and History in the Biblical World.* New Haven, Conn.: Yale University Press.
Wimmer, Stefan
2002 A New Stela of Ramesses II in Jordan, in the Context of Egyptian Royal Stelae in the Levant. Paper read at Third International Congress on the Archaeology of the Ancient Near East, Paris.
Winnett, Fred and William Reed
1964 *The Excavations at Dibon (Dhîbân) in Moab.* AASOR 36–37. New Haven, Conn.: American Schools of Oriental Research.
Wiseman, Donald J.
1951 Two Historical Inscriptions from Nimrud. *Iraq* 13: 21–26.
Wolf, Eric
1982 *Europe and the People Without History.* Berkeley: University of California Press.
Worschech, Udo
1985a *Northwest Arḍ el-Kerak 1983 and 1984.* München: Manfred Görg.
1985b Preliminary Report on the Third Survey Season in the North-West Arḍ el-Kerak, 1985. *ADAJ* 161–73.

1990a *Die Beziehungen Moabs zu Israel und Ägypten in der Eisenzeit.* ÄAT 18. Wiesbaden: Harrassowitz.

1990b Ergebnisse de Grabungen in el-Bālū' 1987 Ein Vorbericht. *ZPDV* 106: 86–113.

1995 City Planning and Architecture at the Iron Age City of al- Bālū' in Central Jordan. *SHAJ* 5: 145–49.

2000 Rectangular Profiled Rims from el- Bālū': Indicators of Moabite Occupation? Pp. 520–24 in *AJB.*

Worschech, Udo and Ernst Axel Knauf

1986 Dimon und Horonaim. *BN* 31: 70–95.

Worschech, Udo and Friedbert Ninow

1999 Preliminary Report on the Excavation at al-Bālū' and a First Sounding at al-Miṣna in 1997. *ADAJ* 43: 169–173.

Worschech, Udo, Uwe Rosenthal, and Fawzi Zayadine

1986 The Fourth Survey Season in the North-West Arḍ el-Kerak and Soundings at Balu' 1986. *ADAJ* 30: 285–310.

Wright, George Ernest

1940 Epic of Conquest. *BA* 3 (3): 25–40.

Wright, G. R. H.

1966 Bronze Age Temple at Amman. *ZAW* 78 (3): 351–59.

Wright, Henry

1977 Recent Research on the Origin of the State. *ARA* 6: 379–97.

1978 Toward an Explanation of the Origin of the State. Pp. 49–68 in *Origins.*

Yadin, Yigael

1970 Megiddo of the Kings of Israel. *BA* 33: 66–96.

Yair, Aaron

1994 The Ambiguous Impact of Climate Change at a Desert Fringe: Northern Negev, Israel. Pp. 199–227 in *Environmental Change in Drylands: Biogeographical and Geomorphological Perspectives,* ed. Andrew Millington and Ken Pye. London: John Wiley.

Yakir, Dan, Arie Issar, Joel Gat, Eilon Adar, Peter Trimborn and Josef Lipp

1994 ^{13}C and [18]O of Wood from the Roman Siege Rampart in Masada, Israel (AD 70–73): Evidence for a Less Arid Climate for the Region. *Geochimica et Cosmochimica Acta* 58: 3535–39.

Yassine, Khair

1984 *Tell El Mazar I: Cemetery A.* Amman: University of Jordan.

1988 *Archaeology of Jordan: Essays and Reports.* Amman: Department of Archaeology, University of Jordan.

Yoffee, Norman

1979 The Decline and Rise of Mesopotamian Civilization: An Ethnoarchaeological Perspective on the Evolution of Social Complexity. *American Antiquity* 44: 5–35.

1993 Too Many Chiefs? (or, Safe Texts for the 90s). Pp. 60–78 in *Archaeological Theory: Who Sets the Agenda?* ed. Stephan Shennan and Norman Yoffee. Cambridge: Cambridge University Press.

Young, John Howard

1956 Studies in South Attica: Country Estates at Sounion. *Hesperia* 25: 122–46.

Younker, Randall

1997a Moabite Social Structure. *BA* 60 (4): 237–48.

1997b The Emergence of the Ammonites: Socio-Cultural Transformation on the Transjordanian Plateau During the Late Bronze/ Iron Age Transition. Ph.D. Dissertation, University of Arizona.

1999 The Emergence of the Ammonites. Pp. 189–218 in *Ammon.*

Zaccagnini, Carlo
1973 *Lo Scambio dei Doni del Vicino Oriente durante i secoli XV–XVIII.* Rome: University of Rome.
1979 *The Rural Landscape of the Land of Arraphe.* Quaderni di Geografia Storica 1. Rome: Università di Roma, Instituto di Studi del Vicino Oriente.
1982 The Enemy in Assyrian Royal Inscriptions: The "Ethnographic" Description. Pp. 409–24 in *Mesopotamien und Seine Nachbarn,* ed. Hans Nissen and Johannes Renger. Berlin: Dietrich Reimer.
1987 Aspects of Ceremonial Exchange in the Near East During the Late Second Millennium BC. Pp. 57–65 in *Centre and Periphery in the Ancient World,* ed. Michael Rowlands, Mogens Larsen and Kristian Kristiansen. Cambridge: Cambridge University Press.
Zayadine, Fawzi
1986 Les Fortifications prè-hellèniques et hellènistique en Transjordanie et en Palestine. Pp. 149–56 in *La Fortification dans l'histoire du monde grec,* ed. Pierre Leriche and Henri Tréziny. Paris: Centre National de Recherche Scientifique.
1991 Sculpture in Ancient Jordan. Pp. 31–61 *in Treasures from an Ancient Land: The Art of Jordan,* ed. Piotr Bienkowski. Phoenix Mill, UK: Alan Sutton/National Museums and Galleries on Merseyside.
Zayadine, Fawzi, Jean-Baptiste Humbert, and Mohammed Najjar
1989 The 1988 Excavations on the Citadel of Amman, Lower Terrace, Area A. *ADAJ* 33: 357–63.
Zertal, Adam
1994 'To the Land of the Perizzites and the Giants": On the Israelite Settlement in the Hill Country of Manasseh." Pp. 47–69 in *FNM.*
2001 The Heart of the Monarchy: Patterns of Settlement and Historical Considerations of the Israelite Kingdom of Samaria. Pp. 38–64 in *SAIAIJ.*
Zevit, Ziony
2001 *The Religions of Ancient Israel: A Synthesis of Parallelactic Approaches.* New York: Continuum.
Zwickel, Wolfgang
1990 *Eisenzeitliche Ortslagen im Ostjordanland.* Wiesbaden: Ludwig Reichert.
van Zyl, A. H.
1960 *The Moabites.* Leiden: Brill.

Index

Acknowledgments

In writing this book, I have benefited from the kindness and wisdom of many people. Such debts can only be paid by acknowledgment, yet sadly, while my creditors are many my allotted pages are few. I would like to thank the series editors, Bob Preucel and Ian Hodder for their encouragement and patience, as well as the editorial and production staff of the University of Pennsylvania Press, who were excellent from start to finish. Among my colleagues, I would single out Ted Banning, Reinhard Bernbeck, Michel Fortin, Steven Grosby, Tim Harrison, Jack Holladay, Øysten LaBianca, David Schloen, Norman Yoffee, and Richard Zettler for their feedback and support. Additionally, Piotr Bienkowski, Carlos Cordova, P. Michèle Daviau, Israel Finkelstein, Avraham Faust, Alex Joffe and Adam Smith sent me unpublished manuscripts or new offprints at key moments. Kevin McGeough read the manuscript and helped prepare the reference list. In addition, the work of Leigh-Ann Bedal, Jonathan Haxell, Matthew Johnson, Justin Lev-Tov, Benjamin Porter, and Ellen Simmons has contributed directly to the formation and completion of this monograph.

In Jordan, I have benefited from the good will, hospitality, and expertise of many individuals and government agencies. In particular, I would single out Dr. Fawwaz al-Khraysheh, Drs. Pierre and Patrica Bikai, Dr. Fawzi Zayadine, Dr. Ghazi Biseh, Dr. Hamsa Mahasneh, and Abouna Bolous Biqa'in, as well as the staff of the American Center for Oriental Research and the British Institute of History and Archaeology in Amman.

The research upon which this book is based has been supported by a variety of agencies in different ways, including most particularly the National Science Foundation (BCS-01661), the University of Pennsylvania Research Foundation, the Social Sciences and Humanities Research Council of Canada, and the American Schools of Oriental Research. I would also like to thank the *Journal of the Economic and Social History of the Orient* for permission to use parts of a previously published article in Chapter 7.

It is traditional, even clichéd, to reserve pride of place in acknowledgments for one's spouse, as a position of honor but also in separation from one's colleagues. Anyone reading this book will know that this is something I cannot do, as I have relied repeatedly and extensively on the work of my wife and colleague, Dr. Carolyn Routledge. Certainly, all the normal platitudes apply (support, sacrifice, love, etc.). Certainly, this book is utterly and completely dependent upon my relationship with her. However, as Carolyn knows all too well, being designated "the loving wife" is often a rather backhanded compliment. One last person deserves special credit, my daughter Isobel, who in the home stretch gave me a much-needed kick in the pants. I was, after all, monopolizing the computer.